The Jury in Lincoln's America

Ohio University Press Series on Law, Society, and Politics in the Midwest

SERIES EDITORS: PAUL FINKELMAN AND L. DIANE BARNES

The History of Ohio Law, edited by Michael Les Benedict and John F. Winkler

Frontiers of Freedom: Cincinnati's Black Community, 1802–1868, by Nikki M. Taylor

A Place of Recourse: A History of the U.S. District Court for the Southern District of Ohio, 1803–2003, by Roberta Sue Alexander

The Black Laws: Race and the Legal Process in Early Ohio, by Stephen Middleton

The History of Indiana Law, edited by David J. Bodenhamer and Hon. Randall T. Shepard

The History of Michigan Law, edited by Paul Finkelman and Martin J. Hershock

The Rescue of Joshua Glover: A Fugitive Slave, the Constitution, and the Coming of the Civil War, by H. Robert Baker

The History of Nebraska Law, edited by Alan G. Gless

American Pogrom: The East St. Louis Race Riot and Black Politics, by Charles L. Lumpkins

No Winners Here Tonight: Race, Politics, and Geography in One of the Country's Busiest Death Penalty States, by Andrew Welsh-Huggins

The Dred Scott *Case: Historical and Contemporary Perspectives on Race and Law,* edited by David Thomas Konig, Paul Finkelman, and Christopher Alan Bracey

The Jury in Lincoln's America, by Stacy Pratt McDermott

STACY PRATT MCDERMOTT

The Jury in Lincoln's America

Ohio University Press ~ Athens

Ohio University Press, Athens, Ohio 45701
www.ohioswallow.com

Printed in the United States of America
Ohio University Press books are printed on acid-free paper ∞ ™

20 19 18 17 16 15 14 13 12 5 4 3 2 1

Library of Congress Cataloging-in-Publication Data

McDermott, Stacy Pratt.
The jury in Lincoln's America / Stacy Pratt McDermott.
p. cm. — (Ohio University Press series on law, society, and politics in the midwest)
Includes bibliographical references and index.
ISBN 978-0-8214-1956-4 (hc : alk. paper)
1. Jury—Illinois—History—19th century. 2. Jury—Illinois—Sangamon County—History—19th century. 3. Jury—Middle West—History—19th century. 4. Justice, Administration of—Illinois—History—19th century. 5. Justice, Administration of—Illinois—Sangamon County—History—19th century. 6. Justice, Administration of—Middle West—History—19th century. I. Title.
KFI1742.M37 2012
347.773'0752—dc23

2011047249

CONTENTS

ILLUSTRATIONS

Plates

Following page 118

Figure

PREFACE

Through an examination of the jury and of the law in the vibrant and dynamic environment of antebellum Illinois and through an analysis of the jury trials of the state's most famous son, this book seeks to demonstrate the importance of the jury and, by extension, the law to nineteenth-century Americans. Abraham Lincoln and his contemporaries exhibited a commitment to the rule of law that not only shaped their understanding of society but also influenced their individual roles within their communities and the world at large. Lincoln stands in history as an iconic figure of the American past, but he was not born ready to lead his nation through a bloody civil war. His development as a man and a national leader took place in the courthouses of antebellum Illinois during a legal career that spanned three decades. The legal environment that shaped Lincoln provides the context of this book, and Lincoln's experiences with the law as an attorney, a litigant, a judge, and a juror provide a fascinating human connection to the history of the law in pre–Civil War Illinois, the Midwest, and America.

Antebellum Springfield and Sangamon County, Illinois, were home to Abraham Lincoln, and therefore, they are the site of this community study of the midwestern legal experience and analysis of local jury composition.[1] But even without the Lincoln connection, this locale is a viable environment in which to study nineteenth-century legal history for several critical reasons. First, Springfield and Sangamon County were settled and culturally diverse. The county represented a cultural blending of the North and the South. Of the states of nativity that Sangamon County residents reported in the 1860 census, Connecticut, New York, and Ohio were as ubiquitous as Kentucky, Tennessee, and Maryland. There was also some ethnic diversity in the region. A relatively large number of Irish and German immigrants lived in Springfield, and a small population of free blacks made their homes there as well.[2]

Second, the county contained elements of both urban and rural mid-nineteenth-century America. Sangamon County was agriculturally based, and farming was central to its economy. Yet Springfield—the county seat, state capital, and home to 29 percent of the county's residents in 1860—was a bustling commercial center with a population of more than nine thousand people. Political, legal, social, and economic systems were in place, and in Springfield and Sangamon, as in many other midwestern towns and counties, churches, civic and literary organizations, professional associations, and schools were numerous. By 1850, Sangamon County had none of the exceptional, frontier-related characteristics (such as absent or makeshift legal institutions or transient populations) that might skew such a study of jury composition. And for its part, Springfield was a typical town in the emerging Midwest.[3]

Finally, the surviving antebellum legal records of the county are abundant. A nearly complete run of the docket books, court records, and fee books of the circuit court during the antebellum period is available to the scholar. As well, county histories and newspapers from that era are plentiful, and manuscript materials compiled by the county's residents are exceedingly rich. From these copious resources, it is possible to reconstruct a demographic picture of jury composition in Sangamon County. Most significant for the current study given its focus on Abraham Lincoln, the county was the home base for this successful midwestern attorney: it provided the social, political, economic, legal, and physical context in which he developed his law practice. In Springfield and in the other county seats of central Illinois, he handled more than fifty-two hundred cases in a legal career that spanned nearly twenty-five years during the most formative era in the history of both American law and the emerging Midwest. This study fully utilizes the records of Lincoln's law practice.[4] Statutes, legal treatises, newspapers, periodicals, manuscript sources, and demographic data collected in the 1850 and 1860 U.S. censuses enhance the richness of the hundreds of trial and appellate case documents examined for this volume. History, environment, people, and power relations that existed within antebellum midwestern communities are never far from the discussion.

This book investigates the status of the jury as a democratic and political institution in antebellum America. Further, it evaluates the characteristics of the jurors, their jury experiences in Sangamon County, and the quality of their verdicts. It is relatively easy to examine the nineteenth-century political and legal rhetoric that antebellum Americans employed to describe the jury, but it is a much more laborious task to analyze the status of the jurors themselves. This book seeks to find out who served as jurors in Illinois and to study their jury box and courtroom experiences. It also explores how the individual status and experiences of jurors informed their service and what juror status meant in terms of jury verdicts for various groups of litigants, especially men without property, women, and African Americans. When we understand the economic, social, political, and professional status of the "gentlemen" who served on grand and petit (or trial) juries, we can begin to see the ways in which jury selection and service played out at the local level. Within the circuit courts, evidence of the law was clear and direct. In the jury box, jurors represented a very human link between legal structures and the community. From that specific convergence of law and society, a vivid picture of the midwestern Illinois legal landscape emerges. Abraham Lincoln's own juror service and the corpus of his jury cases further enhance that landscape.

Community is an integral part of the legal story this book relates. The community in this book is Sangamon County, Illinois, but it is also the broader community of the midwestern region. The analysis of jury composition and of the status of the jury in antebellum Illinois is grounded in a body of literature that defines the Midwest as a valid historical region with distinct geographic, legal, and political boundaries. Historians in recent years have contributed to our understanding of the Midwest's political and social development during the mid-nineteenth century. Their findings have revealed marked geographic and historical differences between the people who settled in the states that developed from the Old Northwest Territory and those who remained in the southern and eastern United States, where far more historical research has been concentrated. However, because there are no similar community studies of juror composition, this book cannot offer an in-depth analysis comparing antebellum midwestern juries and juries in other parts of the country. Instead, it seeks to provide as much detail as possible about the circumstances of the jury and the experiences of jurors in one midwestern locale and to suggest some conclusions about the wider meaning of jury service in the emerging Midwest.[5]

Antebellum midwestern history is an important focus of the book, and midwestern legal history is particularly central. Little scholarship on the history of law in this vibrant region exists, and the legal history of Illinois prior to the Civil War has not yet been told. With the exception of David Bodenhamer's research on the history of the jury in antebellum Indiana, midwestern scholarship has not investigated the jury. This book is intended to provide the antebellum Illinois perspective, adding to Bodenhamer's work, and to fill a significant gap in the scholarship of the history of American law.

The book consists of an introduction and four chapters that combine to show the structures and context of the law, the composition of juries, the experience of jury service, and the power relationships that functioned whenever a grand or petit jury was impaneled. The introduction broadly defines Abraham Lincoln's America and discusses the nineteenth-century political language that Americans used to describe their understanding of juror qualifications, the process of trial by jury, and jury service. The introduction also highlights the antebellum American commitment to the law and, particularly, to the institution of the jury.

Chapter 1, "Jury Law and Tradition in the Antebellum Midwest," examines the statutes and appellate case law pertaining to juries in four midwestern states from the year each attained statehood to 1860: Ohio (which entered the Union in 1803), Indiana (1816), Illinois (1818), and Michigan (1837). In less detail, the chapter looks at the law regarding juries in Iowa (1846) and Wisconsin (1848). Before we can even begin a discussion on the status of jurors and the role of juries, it is imperative to understand the legal structures that state legislatures created to define and maintain jury service in the antebellum Midwest. Consequently, this chapter also compares and contrasts the law from state to state, explores the political and social meaning of trial by jury for midwesterners of the era, and reveals the continuities and discrepancies between law and tradition. It sets the context of the legal foundation of the jury and provides a basis from which an understanding of antebellum midwestern jury politics can emerge.

Chapter 2, "The Composition of Juries in Sangamon County, Illinois, 1830–60," is quantitative in structure and incorporates the research in regard to juror status. It presents raw demographic data on the grand and petit jurors in Sangamon County and offers a community study of the jurors themselves. The data appear in narrative form, and the quantitative analysis is infused with individual stories of jury experiences. The analysis also considers the demographic makeup of Sangamon County beyond the jurors and addresses the meaning of community in terms of the county's legal history. The chapter also provides some complementary statistical analysis regarding jurors who served outside of Sangamon in Lincoln's cases in circuit courts throughout central Illinois. The purpose of this additional evidence is to give broader geographic credence to the Sangamon County context and to make a number of more general claims about midwestern juries as well.

Chapters 1 and 2 draw heavily on the more than ninety-six thousand legal documents from Abraham Lincoln's law practice. Between 1837 and 1861, Lincoln tried cases in the circuit courts across central Illinois, in the federal courts in Springfield and Chicago, and in the Illinois Supreme Court. His caseload was varied and extensive, and his courtroom experiences shed light on the legal systems of Illinois, including key aspects of jury service in the pre–Civil War era.[6] Thus, the documentary evidence from Lincoln's law practice provides a convenient set of primary source materials. But more than research convenience, it offers a legitimate historical narrative regarding the law and community in a vital, developing region during a dynamic period of American history.

Chapter 3, "The Work of Jurors in the Antebellum Illinois Courtroom," presents an in-depth examination of the actual work and experiences of grand and petit jurors. This analysis gives us a sense of how juries functioned and how litigants experienced the law at the local level. The analysis evaluates juror status and what that status meant to the outcome of the legal cases that various panels of jurors interpreted. Four topics—crimes related to drinking and gambling, slander, divorce, and race—are the focus of this examination on jury work, and three groups of defendants and civil litigants—white men without property, women, and African Americans—share the stage with the jurors who heard their cases. The chapter draws meaning from the contrasting status of jurors and litigants, examining different areas of the law to provide some broader understanding and balance.

Chapter 4, "The Struggle for Legal Power in Lincoln's America," considers the push and pull of jury authority, which was one of the central issues of nineteenth-century law. Juror qualifications and service, jury work, and popular discourse regarding the institution of the jury fueled the flames of the power struggle between bench, bar, and jury. As judges sought to redefine the role of the jury in the courtroom and dictate procedure, jurors tried to make sense of the law and a rapidly changing world through their verdicts. And as panels of juries exercised their courtroom authority, the rising professional bar worked to position itself as a broker between judicial dominance and jury independence. Illinois jurors, lawyers, and judges wanted to bring order to the sometimes frightening and chaotic legal, social, economic, and political transformations they were experiencing in the emerging Midwest. The end result was a three-way battle for dominance that became particularly apparent in Illinois courtrooms in the 1840s and 1850s. This chapter analyzes the power struggle in order to better understand the centrality of the jury in the antebellum Midwest, which represented the America of Abraham Lincoln and his courtroom contemporaries.

This study examined the reported summaries and opinions in 175 appellate cases related to the jury in Indiana, Illinois, Iowa, Michigan, and Wisconsin. Although the bulk of the opinions came from the Indiana and Illinois supreme courts, a selective sampling from other midwestern states was instructive. Because of the importance of the appellate cases in the descriptions and analyses presented throughout the book, an annotated list of the 175 cases studied is included in the appendix. Readers will find this a useful reference for each chapter as well as a convenient resource for further inquiry.

Introduction

Abraham Lincoln's America

When the young Abraham Lincoln moved to Indiana with his family in 1816, permanent settlement in the developing states of the Old Northwest Territory was just under way. In 1830, when the Lincoln family crossed the Wabash River to relocate in central Illinois, the states and territories of what was then the emerging Midwest—Ohio, Indiana, Illinois, Michigan, Wisconsin, and Missouri—were still a sparsely populated frontier with a population of just over 1.5 million people, representing only one-eighth of the entire population of the United States. However, after 1830, the region was on a fast track of population growth. Ohio had 1.5 million people by 1840 and nearly 2 million by 1850, and Indiana's population had increased by 300,000 between statehood in 1816 and 1840. In 1830, Michigan's population had been less than 32,000, but over the next ten years, it blossomed to more than 200,000; by 1850, the state population numbered 400,000. Wisconsin's population grew from 30,000 in 1840 to more than 300,000 in 1850. The Lincolns were not the only people who recognized the region's promise and hoped to take advantage of all it had to offer.[1]

By 1840, the population of the emerging Midwest had surpassed 3 million. In the 1840s, there were few large cities in the region, but by 1850, the population of Cincinnati, St. Louis, and Chicago had reached 115,000, 78,000, and 30,000, respectively. In Illinois, the population grew from just over 157,000 in 1830 to nearly 860,000 by 1850. Also by that year, the population of the entire region had exceeded 5 million. An observer of this astonishing population growth shared his views of it in the *Sangamo Journal,* a newspaper in Springfield, Illinois, writing that "the child was then alive who would live to see two million population in Illinois, and that by 2000 A.D. there would be 3,000,000."[2]

Settlers in the region were a "conglomeration of peoples," migrating in homogeneous groups and creating a complex patchwork of ethnic and cultural settlement. They came from the eastern and southern United States and from across the Atlantic Ocean, and some groups predominated in certain areas. Tennesseans and Kentuckians, like the Lincoln family, settled in the southern half of Indiana and in Illinois; New Yorkers settled in Michigan and Wisconsin; and German, Irish, Norwegian, and Scot settlers were also establishing a noticeable presence in the midwestern states. By comparison with other states, few New Englanders and people of foreign nativity settled in Indiana. People from slaveholding states comprised the largest group of setters in that state: in 1850, southern-born settlers made up 44 percent of American-born residents in Indiana. What foreign settlers there were in Indiana tended to be German, whereas Illinois settlement patterns were divided between immigrants from Germany and those from Ireland. In the southern half of Illinois, nearly all of the American-born settlers were from Kentucky and Tennessee. In the northern section, settlers hailed mostly from Ohio. More than 135,000 New Yorkers settled in Michigan by 1850; they also predominated in Wisconsin, but New England provided a significant number of settlers there as well. In Iowa in 1850, southerners and northerners had settled in basically equal proportions.[3]

Although the overwhelming majority of residents of the emerging Midwest were white, the population also included Native Americans, immigrants, and people of color. A New Englander speaking of Wisconsin in the 1840s wrote: "The five races of both continents [are] present . . . the Yankee is in his own latitude, and retains in full his unique identity. Men with European tongues gather in here like the dispersed of the tribes of

Israel. All say welcome to each other. The Frenchman shortens his mustaches, and becomes American . . . Irishman you recognize by his hardy form and native brogue. . . . Jews and Germans are here. . . . I see . . . a respectable representation of the people of color, and one small band of natives—real red men, but wearing paints of different colors on their cheeks." This observer was certainly naive in his harmonious depiction of Wisconsin, but he was accurate in noting that varying groups, both ethnically and racially defined, coexisted in the Midwest.[4]

By 1860, nearly 7 million people, 22 percent of the total population of the United States, resided in the states of Ohio, Indiana, Illinois, Michigan, and Wisconsin. Since the Northwest Ordinance of 1787, which had laid the physical boundaries of the nation's "West," the region was being transformed from the frontier of a young country to a geographic and economic center of a burgeoning nation. With settlement and growth came great environmental change and a landscape that was much altered from the vast prairies and woodlands of the Old Northwest. While the region was undergoing extreme economic depressions in the late 1830s, "people continued to live and to make a living . . . settlements advanced . . . lands were cleared, trade was carried on, small industries were born and grew." One writer marveled that "the growing Midwest was a land of wooden barns and houses, of wooden schools and churches, wooden sidewalks in the towns and plank or wood-block streets in the cities. European travelers, puzzled at the frontier's frame houses, were astonished to see wooden factories, hotels, and even wooden courthouses with oak or ash columns painted like clouded marble." The emerging Midwest was a region of enormous growth and development, and people in other parts of the country and the world took notice.[5]

The vibrant atmosphere of Springfield, Illinois, in 1850 reflected the dynamic nature of the region. The economic, political, and social pulse of the bustling town revealed something of the region's promise. The unpaved streets and boarded sidewalks were full of pedestrian and horse-and-buggy traffic, as business owners, lawyers, litigants, and consumers darted in and out of the numerous shops and offices on and around the state capitol square. The impressive physical landmarks of the town included the Third Presbyterian Church; Ash & Diller's lumberyard; and the large, three-story Tinsley Building, which housed the U.S. Post Office and the U.S. federal court. Standing in front of the Illinois State Capitol, one could see the commanding Greek portico of the Sangamon County courthouse, the handsome American House Hotel, and the Illinois State Bank. It was just a short walk to enter the storefronts of more than a dozen dry goods stores, three drugstores, two bookbinderies, and numerous other businesses, including barbershops, boot and shoe stores, clothiers, gun dealers, and law offices.[6]

Springfield had been the home of the Illinois state government since 1839, when the construction of the capitol building was completed. Set on the public square, the classical and elegant two-story Greek Revival building, constructed of local blond dolomite limestone, featured a dome and substantial Doric columns. Considered one of the most imposing seats of government in the West, the capitol stood as a symbol of the established political and legal institutions of the state. Although Sangamon County and the state of Illinois were predominately rural and agriculturally based, the county and the city of Springfield were not the wild frontier. In 1850, the physical environment was settled, much of the land was developed, and the population and community were booming. Home to nineteen lawyers, sixteen teachers, fourteen members of the clergy, thirteen physicians, four newspaper editors, three dentists, and at least six schools, including the Colored School, Springfield was an established town with a thriving economy; a strong political heartbeat; well-established religious, educational, and social institutions; and entrenched legal structures. Native-born Illinoisans, Kentucky and Tennessee southerners, New York and Connecticut Yankees, and Irish and German immigrants made their homes and earned their livelihoods in Springfield. The rapidly developing transportation networks of the area facilitated settlement and mobility. Springfield and Sangamon County served as transportation crossroads and exemplified "midwestern cultural mixing."[7]

Springfield was Lincoln's town for twenty-five years. It was home to his family and the center of his professional experience; it witnessed his political disappointments and achievements; and perhaps most important, it was where his intellect was honed and where his worldview developed. As he departed from the town in February 1861, he declared, "To this place, and the kindness of these people, I owe every thing."[8] To Lincoln, Springfield and its midwestern context was America. For him and nearly

7 million of his contemporaries throughout the region, the country's midsection was personally and politically vital.

Although the region mirrored some of the legal, social, economic, and political characteristics of other regions and was populated mostly by people from other places, it deserves attention on its own account. The history of the Midwest is an integral part of American history. Indeed, our historical understanding of the growth and development of the United States is impoverished if we overlook the region of the Old Northwest Territory and focus only on the regional histories of New England, the South, and the Wild West.

Moreover, it is time that historians begin to fold midwestern historical experience into the general legal history of the first half of the nineteenth century. It is valuable to gain insights into the ways in which one-fifth of the antebellum American population imitated, revised, developed, and put into practice legal institutions that maintained legal and social order and played a part in the developing history of American law. Until quite recently, the legal history of the nation's middle section either went unnoticed or was lumped in with a less than satisfying history of the frontier. Since the beginning of the twenty-first century, however, legal historians have begun to recognize the distinctiveness and centrality of the region. As a result, a compelling body of scholarship on midwestern legal history, concentrated mostly on the states of Ohio, Indiana, and Illinois, is now developing.[9]

This dynamic and spirited midwestern legal and historical context was the environment that nurtured Abraham Lincoln, whose evolution as a man, a lawyer, and a politician provides a perfect historical example of the significance of region. Of course, Lincoln himself commands much popular interest and scholarly attention, but the significance of his connections to Illinois and to the emerging Midwest have largely gone unnoticed. In many ways, his experiences paralleled the experiences of a large cross section of the midwestern population. Therefore, his story and the story of his legal environment are instructive. Through Lincoln's legal experiences as a lawyer, a juror, and a judge, the vital connection between society and the law in America's heartland is revealed.

Lincoln and his contemporaries in the courtrooms in which he practiced law are the historical actors who breathe life into this study. As the evidence will demonstrate, he and other Illinoisans—like their counterparts throughout the early Midwest and in other areas of the country as well—were committed to the rule of law and supportive of the legal structures that governed them and their communities. For these individuals, law and community were intimately connected, and the law was a central focus of their ideals and of their historical experience. The interwoven stories of the region's legal history and its most famous resident depict the development of law and the legal milieu of Lincoln's America.

The Jury in Law and Society

Many historians have contributed to our understanding of how the rule of law governed the lives and informed the worldviews of nineteenth-century Americans. Most have argued that those who lived during the first half of the 1800s focused on the law more than any other group in U.S. history. Although political persuasion often highlighted differences of opinion on particular political and social points, antebellum Americans were preoccupied with the law, understood its importance, and were engaged in a constant dialogue about it; the law mattered to them. The sophisticated architecture and the quality craftsmanship of state capitol buildings and county courthouses across the nation reflected the importance of established legal institutions and the centrality of law. This veneration of law, embodied within courthouse structures, was a continuation of colonial thought. Yet in Lincoln's America, because of the widespread development of new legal systems and the construction of numerous physical structures to support them, the antebellum generation took this veneration to new heights. The colonial courthouse symbolized "an ideal ordering of society itself," but the antebellum courthouse further democratized this ideal.[10]

Given that the law played such a central role in the nineteenth-century American ethos, it is worthwhile to examine legal institutions, especially those in the Midwest where there is a dearth of scholarship. The development of laws, the administration and practice of law, and the people's interaction with the institutions of the law help explain the character and quality of life in a community. By the same token, the economic, social, and political environment and the demographic makeup of a community shed light on the nature and condition of the law itself. The connection between law and society is clear, and what that connection reveals about the past is both fascinating and instructive.

Because the jury served to link society and the law, that body offers a useful site at which to investigate this connection. When Alexis de Tocqueville published the first volume of *Democracy in America* in 1835, he drew a direct connection between the American institution of the jury and American democracy. What he witnessed in the United States was a profound commitment to law and order, and the jury was a fundamental part of how Americans viewed the law, democracy, and their relationship to both. Of course, the young Frenchman was only observing what Americans already knew. The historical importance of the jury in the United States was already well established.[11]

During the eighteenth century, settlers in the American colonies had used the jury to resist the authority of the British Crown. The case of John Peter Zenger is perhaps the most famous and most evocative example from the colonial era. When Zenger, a printer, went to trial in 1735 for seditious libel, his cause became a rallying cry against British colonial tyranny in America. Although attorney Andrew Hamilton won great fame for defending the embattled printer, it was the jury that ultimately freed him. The verdict represented a major breach between colonists and the distant authority of the Crown, and the institution of the jury at that moment was implanted in the American consciousness, a symbol of the revolution to come. After the American Revolution, the founding fathers codified the jury in the U.S. Constitution and the Bill of Rights, guaranteeing the right of trial by jury in criminal cases and in suits in the common-law division of the courts when the value in controversy exceeded $20. The Northwest Ordinance carried jury guarantees well beyond the boundaries of the original thirteen colonies. As the country stretched westward, the jury went with it.[12]

Throughout the first half of the nineteenth century, Americans connected the institution of the jury to freedom and identified it as a critical element for the well-being of society.[13] They demanded juror competence and expected proper verdicts. Jury law, juror selection, and jury trial procedures worked together to meet this demand by filling jury boxes with older, established, affluent, and respectable men. Only "gentlemen" were deemed competent to guard so sacred a democratic principle. Society expected the law and these gentlemen of the jury to protect the people's rights and liberties. Politicians touted the virtues of the jury; state legislators enacted laws regarding jury service and procedures; and legal scholars devoted much analysis to the jury's history, process, and importance. By 1852, there were at least three major American treatises on trial by jury alone.[14]

The words and imagery that antebellum Americans employed to understand, to describe, to appreciate, and to criticize the institution of the jury were published in newspapers and periodicals of the era. Printed public discourse on the jury was not isolated to a few legal or patriotic journals. From weighty philosophical discussions to simple reporting on local jury trials, articles about the law regularly appeared in the pages of daily newspapers, weekly political organs, and monthly literary magazines and journals. Local, regional, and national publications frequently printed articles, commentary, and literature about the law. These periodicals engaged antebellum Americans in an intellectually stimulating dialogue about developing legal processes that both symbolized and implemented the rule of law. As a result, Americans understood complex legal concepts. The institution of the jury was a central legal topic for discussion in the popular press, and the language of this discourse exemplified the meaning of the jury for antebellum Americans.[15]

The discourse was possible because the early 1800s marked the "golden era of the weekly newspaper." By the1830s, newspapers had become vital in the distribution of knowledge; subscribers anticipated the publication of the latest edition of their local paper, which was full of news about the community, the state, the nation, and the world. One contemporary Indiana newspaper noted that "the newspaper is the great instrument of civilization. All the books ever written are but a feather in the scale compared with newspapers, as a means of affecting the mass. What is the circulation even of a popular novel, to that of a paragraph which runs the round of the press? The one is read by thousands, the other by millions. It is almost entirely to the influence of newspapers that the superior intelligence of the middle classes is to be attributed."[16]

Newspapers and periodicals were readily available throughout the antebellum Midwest. By 1840, there were already forty-five printing offices in Illinois, three daily newspapers, thirty-eight weekly newspapers, and nine periodicals, and the publishing industry employed 175 men and represented more than $70,000 in capital investment. During the 1840s and

1850s, the invention of the telegraph, the development of the railroad, and the organization of political parties had a tremendous impact on the evolution of the press in the Midwest. Technological changes revolutionized the flow of information, and increasing fervor over partisan politics fed popular enthusiasm for political news. Newspapers during this period took advantage of the situation. By 1850, "every important town in Illinois was in telegraphic connection with Chicago and the eastern cities," and by 1860, there were ten daily newspapers in Chicago and thirteen dailies in other cities across the state, not to mention the dozens of weekly and semiweekly papers in dozens of smaller towns. One Illinois newspaper editor claimed in 1835 that "the establishment of newspapers appears to be a leading characteristic of the present age."[17]

Readers read, reread, and shared their newspapers and periodicals, and much of the information they consumed related to the law. As a result, they engaged in philosophical discussions about the institution of the jury, they idealized its importance, and they attached democratic and nationalistic rhetoric to it. Editors and writers scrutinized individual jurors and jury panels, evaluated their capabilities, graded jury outcomes, and shared their own perceptions about the jury. Through the publication of articles about the law, myriad pro and con arguments regarding the process of trial by jury were disseminated, and expert and casual observers alike debated the practicality, efficiency, and competence of the jury system.

The Jury as an Ideal

Nineteenth-century Americans had a plethora of phrases for the institution of the jury: *courthouse democracy, citadel of freedom, voice of the people, consciousness of the community, palladium of liberty,* and *sacred bulwark of a nation,* to name just a few. Words such as *freedom, democracy,* and *liberty* suggested the significance that people ascribed to the jury in the American context. Much of the rhetoric was included in William Blackstone's *Commentaries on the Laws in England,* which largely provided the framework for colonial law in America and continued as a mainstay of American legal scholarship. Blackstone had early on articulated the belief that "trial by jury is a privilege of the highest and most beneficial nature and our most important guardian both of public and private liberty." His writings were standard reading for aspiring attorneys in the new republic and throughout the antebellum period. Like most of his legal contemporaries, Abraham Lincoln read Blackstone's *Commentaries* during his self-training for the law. The legal vocabulary and rhetoric contained therein reinforced connections between law and democracy and helped fashion the ideology of the emerging legal profession.[18]

Law professors, politicians, newspaper editors, and reformers all employed this legal rhetoric for different effects and purposes. For example, Nathaniel Beverly Tucker used it to teach his law students at the College of William and Mary about the importance of the jury. In 1834, he evoked the strong language of Blackstone in his effort to instill vigilance against attack on the jury from any quarter. U.S. senator John P. Hale, an antislavery lecturer from New Hampshire, used similar imagery in an 1856 lecture in Chicago when he charged members of the audience with responsibility for protecting the jury from peril, urgently pressing upon them that, "whatever the consequences were," they had "to stand up for a right which had ever been the bulwark of freedom." A Pennsylvania state senator argued: "Take from him [an American] the right of trial by jury, and you dispossess him of the most valuable of his political privileges. You remove the corner stone of that superstructure which has for its material the institutions of his country, and as a consequence, involve the whole in a common ruin." All of these comments appeared in print form and were distributed, thus carrying well beyond their original audiences.[19]

Such eloquent rhetoric of the jury was part of an even broader rhetoric about the law. Aspiring statesmen such as the young Abraham Lincoln extolled the law's purpose and importance. In an 1838 speech to the Young Men's Lyceum of Springfield, Illinois, Lincoln encouraged "every American" to "pledge his life, his property, and his sacred honor" to the law; further, he declared: "Let reverence for the laws, be breathed by every American mother, to the lisping babe, that prattles on her lap—let it be taught in schools, in seminaries, and [in] colleges;—let it be written in Primmers, spelling books, and in Almanacs;—let it be preached from the pulpit, proclaimed in legislative halls, and enforced in courts of justice. And, in short, let it become the *political religion* of the nation." Other politicians used similar flowery oration on the law and on the jury as part of their own brands of democratic rhetoric, and again, newspapers and periodicals of the era disseminated these ideas to a wider public audience. A Pennsylvania state legislator complained about judges usurping jury rights "with the stealthiness of a midnight assassin," demanding that "no man should be deprived of his life, liberty or property, except by the judgment of his peers and the law of the land." Another state legislator called the jury a "corner stone" of the legal "superstructure." To his constituents, he pitched the idea that trial by jury was one of a number of rights (such as freedom of the press and habeas corpus) that should be "nurtured in the same bosom."[20]

Men were not alone in their admiration of the jury. A "lady of Georgia" wrote: "The right of trial by jury, the freedom of the press, and the other rights which go to make up the sum of that liberty which the English and ourselves alone, of all nations of the earth, enjoy, along with good government, are not the result of sudden changes, but of causes at work through so long a period of years, that their growth in the British Constitution, whence we derived them, can be traced."[21] Women were reading the same newspapers and periodicals as men, and they were willing to join the debate as well: though they could not serve on juries, they *could* voice their opinions about the institution of the jury.

Black Americans could not serve on juries either, nor was the institution of the jury always available for them. The dominant white society did not generally extend such legal guarantees as the jury trial to the country's black population during the antebellum period. White Americans expected the jury to remain in place for them and for the protection of their rights, but black Americans could not be so complacent. One astute writer in the *Philanthropist* observed in 1837 that "men do not always lose a sense of the importance in their own case, of those rights of which they mercilessly deprive others." As the law excluded slaves and free black Americans from basic citizenship rights, it did not always extend to them the basic freedoms that white Americans had come to expect and demand. Thus, jury service was not an option for black men, and with the passage of the Fugitive Slave Act of 1850, captured slaves in the North were not permitted to testify on their own behalf or to enjoy the benefit of a trial by jury. The fugitive slave law stirred up the passions of abolitionists in the North, and with the publication of *Uncle Tom's Cabin* in 1852, public opinion against the law increased.[22]

Discussion of this legal issue appeared in local and national publications, and the debate fueled action. Abolitionists used the federal law to rally support for their cause, and northern state legislatures responded by passing their own laws to guarantee basic rights, such as the right to a trial by jury. Much of the growing opposition to the law in the North was fostered by published arguments contending that the law jeopardized basic legal protections for all people, black and white. The institution of the jury was at the center of the debate. The *Liberator* published a series of articles condemning the law and its blatant disregard for constitutional rights, specifically the right of trial by jury. Other publications, including the *Philanthropist* and the *New York Evangelist,* followed suit. When northern states enacted local laws to defeat the federal act, newspapers and periodicals printed reports of this news and praised the actions of legislators. The *National Era* and the *Circular* applauded efforts in Vermont, New York, and New Jersey to guarantee the "right of trial by jury to *all* people, including fugitive slaves." A letter published in the *Chicago Daily Tribune* in 1854 advocated the repeal of the fugitive slave law, evoking familiar language and imagery: "I regard any law which either directly or indirectly denies any person whatever in times of peace and safety, the benefit of those constitutionally guaranteed safeguards to liberty, the writ of habeas corpus and the right of trial by jury, as dangerous and unjust."[23]

The timely review of lawyer and abolitionist Lysander Spooner's book *Essay on the Trial by Jury,* published in 1852, employed impassioned rhetoric as well. The reviewer, who was a contributor to the *Liberator,* discussed the significance of Spooner's well-written work for the American understanding about the centrality of the jury as well as the dichotomy between the high tenet of the jury trial and the reality that the jury had become something less than Americans might have desired: "The trial by jury has enjoyed and enjoys a most lofty traditional reputation as the 'palladium of English liberty.' Looking at jury trial as it now actually exists . . . the jury seems to have become very much what the late [U.S. Supreme Court] Justice [Joseph] Story was accustomed, in private conversation, to describe it as being—a mere stalking-horse. . . . Such being the practical character of our modern juries, mere cloaks and shields of judicial dictation, it has come, among thinking men, to be a great puzzle how they ever got their immense reputation as a 'palladium of liberty.'" The reviewer went on to say that readers should praise Spooner for calling public attention to the importance of the jury and warning of the dangers if judges were allowed to circumvent it. Most Americans did not purchase or read Spooner's book, but many in the North did learn about it in popular newspapers and periodicals, as reviews and advertisements of the work were widely printed. One well-read correspondent of Abraham Lincoln's in 1860 called Spooner a "Champion of Liberty."[24]

In 1852, legal scholar William Forsyth also published a well-received history of the jury. Other publications respecting the jury appeared in America in the first half of the nineteenth century. One newspaper editor noted: "As trial by jury is esteemed one of the most important privileges which members of Society can enjoy—every man of reflection must be stimulated by the desire of enquiring into its origin and history, as well as to be acquainted with the forms and advantages by which it is accompanied." Another newspaper averred that "it is time for jurymen to understand and to maintain their rights." Antebellum Americans were close observers of the law, and they undoubtedly understood the rhetoric of the jury in the American context. Public discourse on the law and on the jury constantly reinforced an ideal image of the institution.[25]

The Human Element

In 1854 in an early history of Illinois, Thomas Ford wrote: "If the theory of democracy thus demanded that the people, through the jury, should take an active part in the administration of law, American jurors were not slow to put the theory into practice."[26] But though the jury maintained its rhetorical place upon a democratic pedestal, the democratization of jury composition was not assumed. Imbedded within the democratic rhetoric was the idea that the right to a trial by jury was inviolate, yet the right to serve on a jury was not a natural extension of that ideal. It may seem inconsistent that American democracy could have hinged so crucially on the establishment and protection of the jury trial yet have existed in such undemocratic proportions in the nineteenth century. However, much of American history has been marked by such contradictions, and the history of Illinois and the Midwest is no exception. As one astute observer noted, the history of antebellum Illinois "is not a story about the seemingly inevitable triumph of democracy in America. . . . In Illinois, life, liberty and property were conditional rights, held only as long as one incurred the favor of the local majority. They were not inalienable."[27]

Antebellum Americans, including Thomas Ford, understood that juries, much like republican majorities, were "imperfect instruments." In the Midwest, there was no strong legislative effort during the first half of the nineteenth century to expand jury service to include poor men without property, blacks, immigrants, or women. The jury was, after all, a human institution, and the people who made and reinforced the law were not inclined to put such individuals in jury boxes. Legislated juror selection procedures were designed to impanel upstanding citizens who were deemed "competent" for service. Therefore, the selection of established, respected individuals was the norm. The constriction, rather than the expansion, of jury law indicated that lawmakers wanted to ensure that the "good" members of society filled jury panels. Because of the significance of the jury in the legal system, only the most respectable citizens who were "good," "lawful," "discreet," and "moral" were considered qualified to serve.[28]

One observer noted that the most "competent number of sensible and upright jurymen, chosen by lot from among those of the middle rank, will be found the best investigators of truth, and the surest guardians of public justice."[29] An Indiana legislator argued that "as a general practice," jurors were "selected from the best men of the county." The "best" men of "middle rank" were the coveted ideal. There is some evidence that jurors used jury service as an opportunity to assert their respectability, yet their status as jurors did not necessarily make them respectable. An early Indiana jury, made up of settled, well-regarded men in the community, convicted a group of low-class white men of the massacre of nine Native Americans at Deer Lick Creek in Madison County. The jurors utilized their service to assert their respectability in the proceedings and the verdict. Sometimes, jury service made respectable men the target of vicious criticism. However, newspapers and periodicals of the era also provided readers with plenty of articles reporting on the grand achievements of juries, their "good" composition, and their competent verdicts.[30]

Local jury trials were a popular topic in local papers, and newspaper editors printed the names of jurors serving in specific trials, provided details about evidence and procedure, and offered sometimes witty observations and stories related to the courtroom. One humorous report appeared in the *New York Daily Times* in October 1851: "At a recent term of the court, in an eastern county, J—s H—n, or 'Uncle Jimmy,' as he is familiarly called, was a juryman. Several actions of H—, a clock-vender, came on for trial. All the cases, good and bad alike, going against the plaintiff, some one asked 'Uncle Jimmy' how it happened: 'Why,' said he, 'Most all of the jury had some of them clocks!' There was 'retribution, moral and legal!'"[31]

Reports about trials sometimes took a humorous approach as in the preceding story, but they could also be more serious in tone. Frequently, newspaper and magazine articles about the jury took the form of political sermons or lectures on morality and respectability. When the writers of such articles believed that the jury system had failed, they were quick to voice their outrage. Editors and writers alike questioned the intelligence and character of jurors, depicted stories of gross miscarriages of justice at trial, exposed outrageous verdicts, and regaled readers with tales of drunken and corrupt jurors.[32]

The *Chicago Press and Tribune* reported that five jurors hearing a murder case in Cook County Circuit Court in 1859 "had the ill taste to accept an invitation of some or all of the counsel for the prisoner for a junketing and drinking bout at a public saloon last evening, and . . . during the progress of the merriment frequent bumpers were tossed off to the health and prosperity of him (the defendant) upon whom an ineffaceable brand is affixed. . . . Is it not time that a reform in our criminal jurisprudence was attempted?"[33] In another story, a complaint was aimed at the apparent bias of the jurymen in a particular case involving the illegal sale of liquor in Massachusetts. In discussing the case, an attorney noted that he "regretted the difficulties of getting an impartial jury in this country . . . there were influences which seemed to shut up men's minds or wrap their reason in these cases . . . [and] none were so blind, as those who did not want to see."[34]

Published stories like these provided evidence about the defects of the jury system and prompted calls for tough reform measures or for the abolition of the system altogether. Antebellum Americans entertained some creative ideas for reforming the jury system. Some advocated the abolition of the grand jury system, calling it "a bastard child of the common law." Some argued that jury power was out of control and that codification of the limits of jury power was the answer. Some blamed jurors for being too soft. Others blamed newspapers, urging an end to the publication of trial details: some people believed that such printed reports prejudiced the minds of jurors and altered verdicts. Still others called for the usurpation of jury power. The *Democratic Review* suggested that jurors "be made up entirely of the legal profession." In a rebuttal, the *New-Yorker* blasted this idea, arguing that such a notion was ridiculous and "hostile in its aims to the best interests of the Republic."[35]

In one particularly shocking suggestion, the *New York Tribune* advocated the abolition of the entire jury system because "instead of appointing the ablest and most judicious men in the community, it selects its jurors not according to their qualifications of ability and integrity, but by lot, and promiscuously from the community." In response, the *Cincinnati Weekly Herald* argued that such suggestions from a newspaper "will doubtless startle most people, who have been accustomed to regard a jury-trial as the great bulwark of their rights." The Cincinnati article agreed that sometimes "men of the worst qualification" were seated on juries, but it contended that "the jury-trial is a good not to be lightly parted with."[36]

Public debate on the issue of who should serve on juries and how the system should work continued at a fever pitch throughout the period. Antebellum Americans loved jurors, and they hated jurors. They respected the institution of the jury, but sometimes they reviled it. Yet for all the disagreement, these Americans remained, for the most part, committed to the same goal: they wanted competent juries and good verdicts. It was the definitions of the words *competent* and *good* that were at issue. In the end, however, few were willing to abandon the system altogether or make significant changes. As one Indiana legislator articulated, "It is better that ninety-nine guilty persons should go unpunished, than that one innocent man should suffer."[37]

The Search for Competence

In early America, the courtroom was a classroom, as the developing bench and bar, litigants, criminal defendants, and most notably courtroom spectators watched the legal system in action. An article in *DeBow's Review* noted that the trial by jury "has done more to enlighten the people, than all the means of education which have been provided by the munificence of the legislature." The same article also recounted the following story: "Two honest creoles were disputing about a point of law; said one of them, 'How, do you think I don't know, sir? I am a justice of the peace!' 'And I,' said the other, 'I ought to know something about it, I have been twice foreman of the grand jury.'"[38] Such experience cultivated legal knowledge and juror expertise; the courtroom environment was structured not only to operate the community's legal system but also to educate society about the system.

Exposure to the law and experience on a jury vested people in the system, and much of this courtroom education was extended into the arena of the popular press. Heavy newspaper coverage of jury trials, publication of editorials about the jury system in journals and magazines, and legal treatises and other books offered additional educational tools for jurors. In 1831, for example, *The Juryman's Guide* was published in New York. In the opening pages of the book, the author included an early review of the manuscript by a practicing lawyer who noted that it would be "a great benefit to that valuable portion of our fellow-citizens who statedly perform the duties of jurors. To enlighten this branch of the community is an act highly praise-worthy."[39]

That sentiment reflected society's lofty expectations for juror conduct and duty, and those high expectations resulted in much commentary and public dialogue, which in turn exposed problems with the system and suggested ways to improve it. During the 1850s, Americans were increasingly opinionated about the status of the jury system, and many of their frustrations were played out in newspapers and magazines of the era. Both knowledgeable and casual observers held strong opinions on the subject of the jury, from the abolition of the grand jury to less radical changes in the juror selection process. For instance, there was a somewhat widespread effort to reconsider the need for a unanimous verdict. Jury panels that failed to agree unanimously on a decision in a case returned to the court "hung," which meant another trial was needed. Many observers argued that requiring a unanimous verdict led to forced judgments, and some suggested that a majority vote of the impaneled jurors should replace the unanimous verdict. An 1858 article in the *New York Times* urged the adoption of a majority verdict in lieu of a unanimous verdict of twelve men. The article argued that the unanimous verdicts had led to gross miscarriages of justice, citing a murder case in New York. In that particular case, eleven members of the jury wanted to convict the defendant, but the one individual who sought an acquittal forced a mistrial.[40]

Another editorial in the *Boston Cultivator* argued that adherence to the unanimous verdict resulted in tremendous costs in time and money. A trial that ended in a hung jury required a new trial, the impaneling of a new jury, and mounting legal fees. The Boston paper contended that the two-thirds majority practice in Scotland was workable and should be adopted in America. Even social theorist George Fitzhugh agreed, as did the *Knickerbocker,* a New York monthly magazine.[41] That publication suggested that majority verdicts should replace unanimous verdicts because the former aligned more closely with American democracy:

> The requirement of unanimity in making up a verdict, is alike at war with common sense, common justice, and with the well known operations of human nature; involving a profound absurdity upon its very face, and calling upon mankind for the performance of a moral impossibility . . . [because deliberating jurors were denied food, jurors were] urged into unanimity by their appetites, and agree to think alike, lest their dinner should get cold. They coincide rather than go hungry, and under the judicial dread of starvation, sometimes substitute a concurrence of stomach for the identity of opinion required of them in the rendition of a verdict. . . . Eleven jurors may in vain have done their best to reconcile minor discordances of view, if the twelfth man has made up his mind to decide the case according to his own arbitrary (perhaps corrupt) determination. If he chooses to do so, there is no power on earth to prevent him. *He* is the "palladium of liberty," not the jury![42]

As with every other jury reform suggested, there were ample opponents. The *Philanthropist* accepted the unanimity of jury verdicts, declaring, "Give us a jury—and let that jury give a *unanimous* verdict or a mistrial be entered. Much would we prefer 'a little of the law's delay,' to the rank, the foul injustice which must ensue from the abolishing of the trial by jury."[43] The *New York Evangelist* was also supportive of the jury trial and in one issue argued for the abolition of bench trials in favor of *more* jury trials. The paper's editors argued that jurors were less prone to bribery than judges, were less biased, and were more equipped to employ commonsense equity.[44]

One way that antebellum Americans categorized and evaluated their legal and political systems was by comparing them with others. There was a dichotomy in perspectives, as Americans both loved to hate and hated to love the institution of the jury they had built for themselves. Trial by jury was not born in America and in fact enjoyed a much longer life in England as well as incarnation in various forms in other nations, but Americans were proprietary about their own system. They claimed it and took credit for it. They may have complained about juror incompetence and inefficient processes, but when Greece, Russia, Germany, and Switzerland adopted trial by jury in the first half of the nineteenth century, American publications congratulated them and claimed a degree of credit for their actions.[45]

Antebellum Americans were also quick to chastise foreign governments for suspending jury rights or for failing to embrace the value of the jury. *Littell's Living Age* reported that the Irish government, which instituted a state of martial law in response to the Young Irelander Rebellion, had suspended trial by jury, and the publication then editorialized about the reason behind the suspension: "No doubt, Ireland and trial by jury, as they both are at present, are mutually unsuited. Whether mistaught by oppression, or incapacitated by nature, the Irish are so far from perceiving the advantage which the people might gain from trial by jury, that they have destroyed its virtue and compelled its suspension by the government." The article went on to blame the Roman Catholic Church for its effort to convert jurors by intimidation and force the acquittal of criminals. Anti-Irish and Anti-Catholic sentiments played into the journalists' doubts about Irish abilities to adopt such exalted American institutions.[46]

Another article explained how Mexicans were disadvantaged because they had not been "accustomed to" free institutions such as trial by jury and habeas corpus and that these "glorious rights were peculiar to the Colonies of North America, and there were few individuals in them but would have parted with their lives before they would have abandoned one of them."[47] Northerners and southerners alike touted the jury in relation to systems in other parts of the world. In a speech, H. S. Foote of Mississippi opined: "Oh, the institution of jury trial, which our forefathers venerated as one of the greatest bulwarks of human liberty . . . the chief distinguishing feature of civilized freedom . . . shall be kept inviolate."[48] Some observers drew regional comparisons. The *Chicago Press and Tribune* reported its disgust about the way southerners treated visiting northerners, denying them basic constitutional rights. In the South, the paper reported, "the practices of the Inquisition—the scenes of the Reign of Terror,—are daily enacted" and the unwitting traveler "[is] seized by a fanatical, drunken mob . . . his person outraged . . . he has no trial by jury, as guaranteed by the Constitution."[49]

Antebellum Americans saw their own political and legal systems as superior to those in other nations. Despite their complaints about the jury trial and its human components, they remained committed to making the system function. Most admitted that the system "worked admirably in practice."

In 1805, Edmund Butcher, a Unitarian minister and author in England, had published a book in which he told a story about a determined juror he had encountered in Ireland. He recounted the story to celebrate the "inestimable value" and "excellence" of the jury system in his country. In the story, entitled "The Intrepid Juror," a father was on trial for the assault and battery of his landlord, who had allegedly attempted to assault the tenant's beautiful daughter. The defendant, who was poor, could retain no lawyer and thus pleaded his own case. His defense was well argued and appealed to the "judgment and heart" of the jury, which acquitted him.[50]

The judge overseeing the trial was outraged that the jury had returned a verdict so contrary to the facts in the case, and he sent the jurors back to reconsider the matter. After fifteen minutes, the jury returned, and the foreman, "a venerable old man," addressed the bench: "My lord, in compliance with your desire, we went back to our room; but as we found no reason to alter our opinions on our verdict, we return it to you, in the same words as before—not guilty." The fearless juror continued, imparting on behalf of his fellow jurors the panel's respect for the king, the judge, the court, and the jury system. After claiming for himself and for his fellow jurors liberty of speech, he continued, "We sit here my lord, sworn to give a verdict according to our consciences, and the best of our judgments, on the evidence before us. We have in our minds, discharged our duty as honest men." At the end of his speech to the bench, the Irish juror also evoked God, averring to the judge that the jurors were accountable only to a higher authority. With that, Butcher's account of the story concluded with this final observation: "The bench was dumb, the bar silent; astonishment and applause murmured through the crowd, and the poor man was discharged."[51]

Throughout the 1820s, 1830s, and 1840s, this story appeared verbatim in numerous newspapers and journals throughout the United States.[52] Most often, it simply ran as a story in the miscellaneous columns that were popular at the time. Sometimes, Butcher's original publication of the story was mentioned, but rarely was there further comment. The *Boston Morning Post* was an exception. When that newspaper printed Butcher's story in 1835, it first provided a glowing tribute to the jury as a protector of "the rights of individuals," a disseminator of the "principles of civil liberty," and a "bulwark of freedom." It then declared: "It is time for jurymen to understand and to maintain their rights; and, as an encouragement to them, we publish the following relation of the conduct of an intrepid juryman of Ireland."[53] The *Southern Planter* provided an equally impassioned introduction to the story: "In this country, thanks to the free character of our noble institutions, it is not often necessary to vindicate the independence of jurors. But even here, judges have sometimes forgotten the dignity and courtesy due to this humble, but favorite tribunal."[54]

It is interesting that so many newspapers published and republished this little story over the years, and it is equally interesting that the story could stand alone without much comment. Perhaps it was simply an enjoyable and humorous tale appropriate for mass consumption. Maybe the spirited challenge to judicial authority explained the tale's popularity. Or perhaps that intrepid old juror had represented a challenge to judicial authority that early nineteenth-century Americans understood and appreciated. Whatever the reason individual editors had for reprinting the tale, it is clear that for nineteenth-century Americans, the jury was at the forefront of their understanding of democracy. It was a foundational component of the legal and political systems they had built and worked to maintain, and the fact that it was a frequent topic in the popular reading materials of the era is evidence of their attachment to it.

The commitment to an idealized concept of the jury put antebellum Americans on a path, through legislation and courtroom practice and procedure, to create and maintain an efficient, workable, and sound jury system. They may not have always succeeded, but their intent was plain. The drive for competence in an era of developing professionalization and increasing standardization was extended to the institution of the jury. As observers recognized problems in the system, they looked for ways to guarantee the impaneling of competent jurors and to ensure professional jury verdicts. Although sometimes misguided, poorly informed, and blind to their own prejudices, nineteenth-century Americans were pursuing excellence in regard to one of their most cherished institutions.

As evidenced by the reporting and commentary on the jury in the nation's popular press, antebellum Americans cared about the law, and they read a great deal about the jury system. The composition of juries mattered to them because the jury operated as a dynamic, legal instrument of community power that regulated society and fulfilled an important function in American democracy and in the maintenance of law and order. As a citizen, lawyer, and politician, Abraham Lincoln had a lifelong commitment to the rule of law, indicative of the strong connections he and his contemporaries drew between a stable, orderly society and well-maintained legal institutions. The intersection of economic, social, and political influence in a given community was uniquely manifested within courts of law by politicians through legislation outlining juror qualifications and trial-by-jury procedures, by judges and lawyers through legal practice in the courtroom, and by jurors through service on grand and petit juries. Purveyors of the democratic rhetoric of trial by jury were the same individuals who controlled the trial-by-jury process and, most important, worked to impanel "competent" jurors who were capable of rendering respectful jury service in Abraham Lincoln's America.

ONE

Jury Law and Tradition in the Antebellum Midwest

ANTEBELLUM MIDWESTERNERS did not, of course, invent the institution of the jury. Rather, they inherited it from a long-standing Anglo tradition, the common law of England, the Northwest Ordinance, the American Constitution, and the Bill of Rights. From the establishment of the Old Northwest to the entrance into the Union of the states of Ohio (in 1803), Indiana (1816), Illinois (1818), Michigan (1837), Iowa (1846), and Wisconsin (1848), the jury was an honored and steadfast institution. As these new states were settled in the early decades of the nineteenth century, the inherited legal traditions guided the development of state jury law. But the various legal and cultural influences of the places from which the settlers themselves hailed also played a role in the evolution of jury law designed to meet the challenges of the emerging region. As settlers in the Old Northwest cleared land, constructed buildings, and formed economic and physical infrastructures, they were engaged in the development of legal structures as well. And as they carved their homes out of the wilderness, they used their political and legal experiences and knowledge to help shape the states they were creating.[1]

State constitutions of the developing Midwest were not innovative. Instead, political and legal institutions were imitative, reflecting the governmental knowledge of the legislators who came to the region from the eastern and southern United States. The framers of the political and legal institutions of Ohio, Indiana, and Illinois and later those of Michigan, Iowa, and Wisconsin were not blazing trails; they were reproducing systems from other states. One early scholar of the region has argued that the early constitutional history of the Middle West did not support the notion of a democratizing frontier. For example, Indiana's constitution could have been described as consisting of the "outline and details" of the second constitution of the commonwealth of Kentucky (minus slavery), the bill of rights of the Ohio state constitution, and a smattering of the language of the Declaration of Independence.[2] Likewise, the New York state constitution had a huge influence on the constitutions of Michigan and Wisconsin. Michigan was not a "legal satellite" of New York, but settlers in Michigan shared a political and legal culture with those who remained in the East. Since New York's constitution came first, crafters of the Michigan constitution used it as a model. But though midwestern framers of new state constitutions borrowed here and there, no state constitution in the emerging Midwest "swallowed whole" an existing constitution.[3]

With regard to the jury trial, all of the midwestern states protected this fundamental right of democracy in their constitutions, either in the main body of the document or in a separate bill of rights: "the right of the trial by jury shall remain inviolate" was the typical language. But even though legislators included the jury trial in the language of their founding documents, this right was taken as a given. In Ohio, to cite one instance, judges deemed trial by jury a right that existed before the state constitution and a guarantee that had been supported by common law for centuries. Ensuring the right of trial by jury was the primary intent of jury law. However, midwestern constitutions went further. They also provided for related jury rights and dictated some basic procedures. Among other things, these new documents guaranteed "speedy trials" and "impartial" juries, promised panels of jurors who lived within the jurisdictions of the litigants, and bestowed upon juries the right to determine law and fact.[4]

Jury Statutes

During the first half of the nineteenth century, midwesterners were focused on the search for so-called competent jurors. Although the state constitutions of Ohio, Indiana, Illinois, Michigan, Iowa, and Wisconsin protected the right of trial by jury, it was statute law that dictated the terms of service. All of the framers of midwestern constitutions recognized the importance of the jury in crafting the foundational law of the state, but there were slight variations from state to state in the codification of juror qualifications, service exemptions, and jury procedure. It is within the statute law that one can find subtle and not so subtle clues about jury service and legal procedures respecting juries. Early statute laws in all of the states provided the procedural basis for the application of jury law in the developing Midwest. Like midwestern state constitutions, midwestern law borrowed and adapted legislation from older states. Statute laws constructed the "rules" regarding juror qualifications for service, exemption from service, juror oaths, penalties for failing to serve, jury fees, replacement of dismissed jurors, and particulars of the role of jurors and of the jury itself. For the purpose of this discussion of jury law, the focus will largely fall on Indiana and Illinois law, which governed the centralized population of the emerging Midwest prior to 1850. Ohio, Michigan, Wisconsin, and Iowa laws are considered to a much lesser extent, although variations, exceptions, and oddities are noted when applicable.[5]

Early midwestern statutes defined the law respecting grand and petit (trial) jurors, with only a few dramatic changes being made to existing statutes thereafter. With the exception of the prohibition of "professional" jurors in Illinois in 1859, midwestern jury law was basically set by the time Wisconsin was admitted to the Union in 1848. Qualifications for jury service were the primary concern of the early statutes. The laws outlined qualifications pertaining to landownership; age; moral character; and, in some instances, gender, race, and citizenship. In the early nineteenth century, states began moving away from land requirements for service and toward voting requirements. However, this trend was not a given. The laws in the state of Ohio required jurors to be white, male voters over the age of twenty-one who were "good and judicious." Indiana law required jurors to be "taxable householders and freeholders" who were between the ages of twenty-one and sixty. By 1840, Indiana law no longer barred individuals over the age of sixty, and it specified that jurors should be "taxable persons" and "good, reputable freeholders."[6]

Indiana legislators reasoned that jurors should own taxable real estate and be the heads of their households. The latter requirement both restricted from service landowning adult sons who were still living in their fathers' houses and limited service to householders in the jurisdiction of the court. It was not until 1852 that Indiana added "male" to juror qualifications, although there is no evidence to suggest that women had ever served as jurors up to that time. During the antebellum period, race was never clearly defined by Indiana statute, and whereas Ohio statute limited juror service to those "having the qualifications of electors," Indiana law did not directly equate juror service with voting rights.[7]

Iowa and Wisconsin laws in the late 1840s mirrored Ohio's regarding voters. Both states required jurors to be "qualified electors." In Iowa, jurors were to be sixty-five years of age or younger; in Wisconsin, the rule was sixty and younger. Although juror law did not specifically bar minors, the elector qualification implied an age of majority. Of the emerging midwestern states, Iowa offered the most specific law regarding character and physical ability, stipulating that jurors be of "good moral character, sound judgment, and in full possession of the senses of hearing and seeing." Wisconsin joined Illinois as the only midwestern states to directly provide for American citizenship as a legal requirement for juror service by 1850. Next door in Missouri, legislators equated juror service with citizenship as well. A juror in Missouri was required to be "a free white citizen of this State, resident in the county, sober and judicious, of good reputation, over twenty-one years of age, and otherwise qualified." Regarding qualifications, exemptions, selection, and compensation, Missouri jury law was very similar to jury laws throughout the emerging Midwest.[8]

In 1827, Illinois had added a provision for "natural-born or naturalized citizens." Of the midwestern states, Illinois and Wisconsin experienced the heaviest immigration of foreign settlers from Ireland, Germany, Scotland, and the Netherlands, and perhaps that experience played a role in the development of legislation that barred recent immigrants from serving on juries. By contrast, Indiana had little in the way of foreign settlement, and therefore, citizenship requirements for jurors remained unnecessary. In Ohio, where there was substantial foreign settlement, the law specified that parties to criminal and civil suits might challenge the competence of individual jurors on the ground of insufficient knowledge of the English language.[9]

Compared to other midwestern state lawmakers, Illinois legislators did the most tinkering with the law respecting juror qualifications during the first half of the nineteenth century. Illinois also developed a somewhat regular habit of revising the entirety of its code of laws, revisiting its statutes in 1827, 1829, 1833, and 1845.[10] For our purposes of understanding the creation and development of midwestern laws enacted to ensure the service of only "competent" jurors, it will be instructive at this point to trace the law in Illinois, draw some comparisons with other states, and analyze the general character and development of jury law in the antebellum Midwest. This exercise will also illustrate how antebellum midwestern legislators restricted, rather than expanded, access to jury service even as the political rhetoric of the Jacksonian era featured chants of a most democratic and egalitarian nature.

The first jury laws passed in Illinois in 1819 required petit jurors to be "taxable inhabitants" and "good and lawful men." Grand jurors were to be "discreet free holders." At that time, there were no specifications as to race or citizenship and no direct codification of head-of-household or voting status. Gender, landownership, and good character were the only legal qualifications for jurors. These early laws also constructed the basic juror selection procedures. County commissioners were required to create lists of eligible jurors from the tax rolls and select through a blind drawing twenty-four petit and twenty-four grand jurors. The commissioners then delivered the selection lists to the county sheriffs so they could issue summonses. Two petit juries of twelve men and one grand jury of from sixteen to twenty-four men were selected to serve for the upcoming term of court. It is hard to know exactly what Illinois legislators meant by "good," but we can reasonably assume that court officials who compiled juror selection lists in county jurisdictions across the state interpreted the term according to their own perspectives. A growing middle-class ideal of respectability was certainly at play in notions of what kind of person was "good" for juror service.[11]

During the first half of the nineteenth century, jury panels selected for the term heard multiple cases. And though there were provisions for peremptory challenges and challenges for cause, most individual jurors participated in numerous cases during a single term of the court. In the event an insufficient number of potential jurors arrived at court, Illinois law also allowed for the selection of bystanders to serve on jury panels. The law presumed that the selected bystanders would meet Illinois' legal qualifications for service, but tradition—which resulted from the reality of the circumstances—at times dictated otherwise. It was, for instance, quite common for spectators in the courthouses to be placed on juries, and whether they were qualified to serve probably depended upon the circuit clerk's personal knowledge of their individual status and upon the time available for determining such proof. As we will see in chapter 2 in the analysis of jury composition, most jurors, including bystanders, met statute requirements for service. However, in this tradition of impaneling bystanders, there was a chance that some jurors who were not "good" and thus not "competent" might be placed on a jury. This gap in statutory provisions to ensure competence would ultimately be remedied in Illinois with additional restrictive legislation—but not until 1859.[12]

In practice, there was some leeway in the matter of qualifications, but the law took seriously the characteristics of jury service. This commitment was made clear through the words of the oath to be taken by the foreman of the grand jury, as was spelled out in Illinois' first statute respecting juries: "You, as foreman of this inquest, do solemnly swear that you will diligently enquire into, and true presentment make, of all such matters and things as shall be given you in charge or otherwise come to your knowledge touching the present service; you shall present no person through malice, hatred or ill will, nor shall you leave any unpresented through fear, favor or affection, or for any fee or reward, or for any hope or promise thereof; but in all your presentments you shall present the truth, the whole truth, and nothing but the truth, according to the best of your skill and understanding, so help you God."[13]

The foreman was required to recite this oath before each term, and the other grand jurors swore to uphold the oath as well. The words appealed to a juror's diligence and sense of truth. Competence was, again, required: in fact, it was demanded. The law required that grand jurors proceed without malicious intent in their return of indictments in criminal cases. They were to be discreet, above influence and bribery, and willing and able to apply knowledge and skill in their sacred duty as jurors. The swearing in of jurors required an oath to the law and also to God. Most of the midwestern states enacted similar grand jury oaths, reflecting a widespread recognition of the importance of jury service. The oaths in Ohio asked the grand jurors to "diligently inquire," make only "true presentments," "keep secret" their deliberations, and "well and truly observe." In Wisconsin, jurors recited an oath that was practically identical to that of their peers in Illinois and Ohio. Although most states codified the language of oaths, Indiana and Iowa did not.[14]

In Illinois in 1819, there was no statutory bar on jury service for age or profession. However, Illinois law exempted "tavern keepers, constables, overseers of highways, or occupiers of mills or ferries." This provision was largely for the convenience of the citizenry and those individuals whose occupations were vital to the community. If, for example, tavern keepers and millers had to leave their businesses to attend court, the economy of the jurisdiction could suffer, threatening the public interest. By 1827, however, the Illinois General Assembly had enacted a revised code of state laws that included some dramatic amendments to the small existing body of laws respecting juries. Among those revisions was the addition of exemptions and prohibitions on who could serve on petit and grand juries. The 1827 statute governing juror qualifications added a gender, race, and age requirement, confining jury service to white males between the ages of twenty-one and sixty. The new law also required jurors to be natural-born or naturalized citizens, to be of "sound mind and discretion," and to be free from "bodily infirmity, amounting to a disability." The same exemptions as in 1819 remained, but the law added judges, county commissioners, court clerks, sheriffs, postmasters, and licensed attorneys to the list of those exempted or barred from service. Thus, the laws were shrinking the pool of potential jurors, not expanding it.[15]

Most midwestern state statutes barred or exempted ministers, licensed attorneys, and other court officials from jury service. But if the law restricted their service, traditional practice did not. Despite the restrictions, attorneys often sat on juries during the same terms in which they handled litigation. For instance, four attorneys sat on the jury in the Sangamon County Circuit Court case of *H. W. Derby & Co. v. Cary*, and three of them had cases on the same page of the court docket as the *Cary* case. Some court officials served on juries even as they held their court positions, and many served after their tenures in those positions ended. Josiah Francis was one such official: he served as a juror in a trespass case during the fall 1850 term of the Sangamon County Circuit Court, and as sheriff, he served writs of execution in at least four of the cases that ended in the same term.[16]

In just eight years since the first state statutes were enacted in 1819, Illinois legislators had moved from a legally expansive view of juror qualification—namely, male landowners—to a far more constricted view of what constituted a competent juror. By 1827, the law confined juror service to white, male, landholding citizens between the ages of twenty-one and sixty.[17] Although Ohio and Illinois were the only states to specify whiteness as a juror qualification, black service on juries in Indiana, Michigan, Iowa, and Wisconsin was nonexistent. What is instructive here is that Illinois legislators were constricting service, not expanding it. They were also engaged in the process of defining and formalizing the law. As the state struggled to clarify its connection to slavery (Illinois had flirted in 1823 and 1824 with the prospect of becoming a slave state), as foreign immigrants flooded across the state's borders, and as vast economic and demographic changes occurred, lawmakers sought to take control of these rapid and frightening circumstances. In the eyes of the legislators in the Illinois General Assembly, confining jury service to a "good," select, and elite few protected the legal system from the chaos of rapid change and, perhaps more directly, sheltered the social and legal status quo from the infiltration of "others."[18]

During the first half of the nineteenth century, most of the other midwestern states also enacted additional legal exemptions and prohibitions to jury service. Beyond the exemptions and exclusions outlined previously, various states at various times excused or banned from service the aged and infirmed, individuals with ill family members, convicts, holders of public offices, physicians, clergymen, professors, teachers, disabled persons, and land office agents. From 1819 to 1859, a number of amendments and changes to the statutes altered Illinois law respecting jurors to varying degrees. For example, there was a steady increase in fees paid to jurors for their service. In 1835, juror fees increased from $.25 per day, as established in the statute of 1819, to $.75 per day. In 1853, fees increased again: jurors began earning $1.50 in addition to $.05 per mile for travel between their homes and the courthouse. The fee increases in Illinois were typical for the midwestern states. Indiana was paying jurors $.75 per day in 1831. In 1852, the state allowed jurors serving in the circuit courts $1.50 per day and all others $1.25 per day. At that time, Indiana was also paying jurors $.04 cents per mile for travel to and from court. Iowa was only slightly behind Illinois and Indiana, paying $1 per day and $.05 per mile.[19]

Fines levied on jurors for failure to serve also increased gradually. In Illinois, they moved from a $5 limit in 1819 to $20 in 1827. In Indiana, the fine was a maximum of $3 in 1824. Failure to appear in court could cost Iowa jurors up to $10 in 1851 and Wisconsin jurors up to $40 in 1858. Juror fees and failure-to-serve fines increased with the changing economy, and the number of individuals summoned to serve as trial jurors grew as well with the expanding court dockets of larger, busier counties.[20]

In Illinois, the state legislature raised the number of individuals called for service from twenty-four to forty-eight in counties where the court term had expanded from one to two weeks. A similar increase also happened in Indiana in 1831. In Indiana and Illinois, jurors were summoned before each term of court, but in Ohio, 108 potential jurors were summoned annually to be selected to serve as grand and petit jurors, except in Hamilton County (Cincinnati), which called eighty-four on its own. Iowa and Wisconsin also summoned jurors annually, with 150 being called for grand and petit jury service in Iowa and 75 tapped as petit jurors and 140 as grand jurors in Wisconsin.[21]

Over the years, state legislators in Illinois continued to renew their commitment to the institution of the jury. In 1853, the Illinois General Assembly enacted a law prohibiting embracery—the attempt to corrupt or influence a jury or to influence individual jurors to favor one side by offering money, making promises, or issuing threats. The Illinois statute subjected all embracers to a fine of up to $500 and imprisonment in the state penitentiary for up to but not exceeding one year. A juror who was convicted of taking "money, gain, or profit, or corruptly being influenced" by an embracer was subject to the same punishment and "forever disqualified to act as a juror." The law applied to both petit and grand jurors. Iowa had enacted a similar measure in 1851. The penalty there for embracers was a fine of up to $1,000 and as much as five years in the state penitentiary. For jurors accepting bribes, the fine was the same, but the sentence could go as high as ten years.[22]

Antebellum midwesterners expected their grand and petit jurors to be upstanding individuals dedicated to preserving the right of trial by jury and respectful of the institution. Jury service was regarded as a privilege, and the law demanded that it be treated as an honor. In Illinois, grand jurors were also responsible for inspecting and reporting on the condition of prisons and jails. Their role in the system mattered on a number of levels. In return, Illinois law shielded grand jurors from arrest, except for treason and felonies, during their time of service. All jurors were paid for their services and reimbursed for their travel to court. All states compensated jurors. However, Illinois was the only midwestern state to extend the privilege from arrest: in that respect, Illinois law was unique. What is key here is that this section of Illinois jury law reflected the serious business of the grand jury. It was considered vital that grand jurors in session be free from distractions while in pursuit of "truth" and "true bills of indictment."[23]

During the antebellum period, midwestern jury laws tended to ignore any semblance of what might be called a rotational theory of juror service, which was common in the eastern United States. (In Massachusetts, for example, jurors could only serve once every three years.) It is unclear why this was not a priority restriction in the Midwest, but perhaps the focus on competence trumped a democratic, rotational philosophy. For legislators and court officials, seating competent jurors was the goal, and if that intent resulted in the repeat service of "good" men, it was an appropriate and successful result. In most state law and tradition, pools of potential jurors were not exhausted before individuals served a second or third time. In practice, many jurors served in consecutive terms; conversely, many legally qualified jurors were never called to serve. In the Midwest, only Illinois crafted legislation to demand rotational service—but not until the state's population was dense enough to warrant the change. With the Illinois revised statutes of 1845, jury law provided that "it shall be the duty of the county commissioners' court to arrange and select grand and petit jurors . . . so that no one person shall serve on the jury a second time, before all fit persons of the county shall have respectively served in rotation."[24]

Two important and related nineteenth-century midwestern circumstances impinged upon rotational jury service, and together, they explain why most states did not bother to enact legislation to enforce rotational service. First, many qualified individuals lived in remote areas, far from the county seats where courthouses were located. If those individuals did not possess adequate transportation, attending court might well have been impossible. Furthermore, the list of remotely located potential jurors on whom a sheriff or his deputy might serve venire (the writ to summon jurors) was only as long as the officer's ambition or tenacity. Traveling to the farthest locations in the county was not always feasible for the sheriff, nor was it a task he enjoyed. Finding a qualified potential juror plowing a field in a remote rural area with poor roads could be difficult, and some sheriffs and deputies lacked the ambition to seek out such a person when there was a plethora of qualified jurors in town. As a result, many qualified jurors who lived far away were never summoned and thus never served.

Second, there was often a shortage of potential jurors to fill panels, especially in smaller jurisdictions. And typically, there was little time for the sheriff or any other officer of the court to calculate who had already served. Court was proceeding, with the judge and lawyers working to maintain the circuit schedule: the judge, prosecutor, and defense attorney had to finish up in time to travel to the next court. The court officer was therefore pressed to round up jurors to satisfy the legal requirements for petit and grand juries—normally, twelve individuals for the petit and sixteen to twenty-four for the grand. As a result of the shortages and the time constraints, the use of bystanders became necessary. Bystanders were most often people who resided within the county seat or near the courthouse, and they tended to be repeat jurors who may well have served recently. The supreme courts of Ohio, Indiana, Iowa, and finally Illinois upheld the use of bystander jurors, noting that the tradition of seating such individuals was frequently both convenient and cost-effective. In Indiana, the use of bystander jurors was the norm, especially in the metropolitan county of Marion, home to Indianapolis. Generally, bystander jurors there were younger and less affluent than regular jurors, but they met the statutory requirements for service.[25]

The use of bystanders was an accepted and common practice throughout most of the antebellum period. Statute laws in Ohio, Indiana, Illinois, Iowa, Michigan, and Wisconsin provided for the use of bystanders, and tradition followed. In the four midwestern states in which bystander juries were at issue in appellate cases—Ohio, Indiana, Illinois, and Iowa—supreme court opinions upheld their use. One justice in Ohio wrote: "It is often times convenient, and a saving of expense that this authority [to use bystander juries] should exist in the court, and we think it is expressly conferred. It has been so held on the circuit." Two other appellate cases in Ohio during the antebellum period upheld the seating of bystander jurors. The 1847 opinion in one of these cases was clear in its approval of the practice, citing the statute and arguing the necessity for it: "This point is settled by section 12 of the act directing the mode of trial in criminal cases, which provides that the jurors summoned, or such of them as are not set aside on challenge, together with so many of the bystanders having the necessary qualifications . . . shall be a lawful jury for the trial of the prisoner. Under this section we think the court was not required to delay proceedings till the sheriff had named the bystander whom he should first call when the entire array should be exhausted."[26]

The opinion reveals the practicality of placing bystanders on juries to maintain court schedules; it also indicates that the use of bystander jurors did not violate a defendant's right to a trial by jury. It should be noted, too, that the law assumed bystanders who were impaneled were qualified and would be competent jurors. The law did not ignore qualifications on this issue: courts could use bystanders for the sake of convenience, but they had to be legally qualified for service.

In Illinois, the use of bystander juries was standard in the circuit courts. Each jury statute enacted from 1819 to 1860 included a provision for the practice, and no appellate cases in the state turned on the matter of bystander jurors. It was not until 1862 that the Illinois Supreme Court addressed the issue, and in that case, the court upheld the practice. The opinion argued that it was "regular" for sheriffs to summon jurors from bystanders at court and that no error could result when bystanders were impaneled. Bystander juries were the norm in Iowa, Michigan, and Wisconsin as well, and only one appellate case in those three states took up the issue during the first half of the nineteenth century. In an 1855 Iowa case, the court upheld the seating of bystanders on a jury in a debt action.[27]

Despite the fact that the use of bystander jurors was common in that period, not all observers accepted the practice. For instance, Allen G. Thurman, chief justice of the Ohio Supreme Court, expressed his distaste for bystander juries in an 1855 appeal, writing: "With the policy of this law we, as a court, have nothing to do; but speaking for myself alone, I cannot help remarking, that it seems strange to me, that, in this humane and civilized age, our statutes create a direct pecuniary interest in the clerks and sheriffs who draw our juries, and by the latter of whom vacancies are filled with bystanders." Hostility to the practice of using bystander juries was greater still in Indiana. Though some people there accepted and supported the use of bystanders based on the "need for economy and efficiency of government," many others characterized bystanders at court as part of the class of "idle and dissolute persons" and "loafers and drunkards." Opponents of the practice also asserted that the placement of bystander jurors gave defendants an opportunity to pack the court with friends and family on the day of their trials. There was great concern that bystanders were not true representatives of the community and therefore that their use threatened to erode public confidence in the institution of the jury. One legislator argued that jury panels composed of bystanders "would destroy the good effects of jury trials, as well as impair public confidence and acquiescence in their decisions." In contrast, a smaller number of supporters of bystander jurors suggested that panels so made were actually better than regularly impaneled juries because they "guaranteed a higher quality of justice." Others vehemently argued that "there were not drunk and idle individuals within their communities," contending that Hoosiers were "honest" and that "upright juries could always be selected from among the bye-standers." It is uncertain why Indiana was somewhat unique in its concern for the use of bystander jurors.[28]

What the debate might have meant to Hoosier opinions regarding the legal institution of the jury is unclear. What is clear, however, is that Indiana circuit and lesser courts (such as justice of the peace courts and municipal courts) continued to seat bystanders as jurors, and the Indiana Supreme Court did not overturn cases decided by bystander juries. Two Indiana appellate cases during the pre–Civil War period affirmed the tradition not only for trial juries but for grand juries as well. Litigants filed no other appeals respecting these panels. Therefore, at the end of the day, most midwesterners accepted the practice. The bystander debate in Indiana reveals the importance that was attached to the status of the jury. The integrity of the system was at stake, and like their counterparts throughout the region, Hoosiers cared about juror competence. Though there was disagreement about how best to seat competent jurors, antebellum midwesterners were dedicated to that goal. Crafting specific juror qualifications and juror selection procedures was of paramount concern to them.[29]

Appellate Case Law and the Jury

Appellate case law in all of the developing midwestern states was thriving, as high courts protected rights, tested new statutes, debated technical procedures, weighed legal precedents, and often established precedents of their own. The supreme courts of Ohio, Indiana, and Illinois were in full swing by 1840, and even though they were citing case law from New York, Massachusetts, Kentucky, and other older states, they were actively engaged in the creation of case law that would have an enormous impact on the history of their region and of the United States as well. Midwestern appellate courts delivered opinions regarding railroads, corporations, finance, personal injury, and eminent domain, to name only a few of the legal issues they faced. The opinions in these cases were positioning the region to be a legal force in the industrial, economic, and social revolutions of the second half of the nineteenth century.[30]

All aspects of the institution of the jury came up in appellate court opinions across the region. Issues involving the selection of jurors, the availability of juror challenge for cause as well as the peremptory challenge, courtroom procedures respecting panels of juries, and the duty incumbent upon the jurors themselves were addressed in dozens of cases that state supreme court justices heard during this formative period. In supreme courtrooms, the tradition of law was tested against the construction of the law itself. Therefore, appellate case law is a revealing site at which to examine the convergence and divergence of law and tradition. This section of the chapter will look at appellate case law in five midwestern states pertaining to five specific but overlapping themes: the right to trial by jury, juror qualifications, juror conduct, juror selection, and jury trial procedures. Each theme relates directly to the search for competent panels of jurors and the sometimes shifting definitions of *competence* itself. The large number of appeals involving issues of the jury and the language justices utilized in their opinions indicate just how key the institution of the jury was to antebellum Americans. The jury was central for lawyers and jurists as well as they worked to establish the legal parameters of the institution and obtain a workable legal system maintained by competent jury service.[31]

In the Midwest, surprisingly few appellate cases dealt specifically with the constitutional right to a jury trial. Indeed, state supreme courts in Illinois,

Wisconsin, and Indiana rarely grappled with the issue in the antebellum period. Perhaps the institution of the jury was so entrenched in the legal system that people were not compelled to test it in the appellate courts. Inferior courts may have respected it so completely that appeals were simply unnecessary. Regardless of the reason, there were no appellate cases in the antebellum Midwest resulting from the denial of a jury trial in a criminal matter. When the right *was* tested, the challenge tended along two specific lines: the number of men on the panel or the question of whether a jury or a court-appointed commissioner would assess damages for the taking of property involving eminent domain. Both of these issues were tied to the question of what constituted a complete and competent panel of jurors.[32]

Although the U.S. Supreme Court did not address jury size until 1898, decisions rendered in Indiana and Wisconsin appellate cases in the 1840s and 1850s were emphatic on the issue of what constituted a legal panel of jurors. After a Dearborn County Circuit Court jury of eleven men convicted a person on an indictment for riot, the opinion of the Supreme Court of Judicature of Indiana reversed the guilty verdict because the eleven-man jury represented an incompetent panel and was thus a "fatal defect." In the Wisconsin case of *Norval v. Rice et ux.*, Justice Samuel Crawford wrote: "The trial *per pais,* or by a jury of one's country, is justly esteemed one of the principal excellencies of our Constitution; for what greater security can any person have in his life, liberty or estate, than to be sure of not being divested of, or injured in any of these, without the sense and verdict of *twelve* honest and impartial men of his neighborhood."[33]

The 1853 opinion imparted the democratic rhetoric of the institution of the jury and clearly asserted that only twelve men could guard the individual's sacred right to a trial by jury. Ohioans agreed that twelve-man panels were fundamental in criminal prosecutions. The *Norval* decision set a precedent in Wisconsin law, which prohibited what had become in many midwestern states a traditional use of six-member juries in justice of the peace, municipal, and county courts. The 1854 case of *May v. Milwaukee & Mississippi Railway Company* reiterated the *Norval* decision: the practice of using six-man juries was unconstitutional. An 1852 Iowa case found the same for grand juries, arguing that Iowa law required a minimum of fifteen-member grand juries and that a panel of fewer than fifteen was legally unable to return an indictment.[34]

The use of six-man juries in some courts in Illinois was widely established both in law and in practice. In 1819, Illinois' first statute concerning juries permitted six-man jury panels in justice of the peace courts, although the law also allowed for the use of twelve men if the parties agreed. The 1827 statute that replaced the early law permitted justice of the peace courts to impanel from six to eight jurors, and it was not at all uncommon for county courts and even circuit courts to impanel fewer than twelve men to hear a case. But common though the practice was at the circuit court level, the consent of the parties was required. If parties to a suit or criminal defendants demanded, they were entitled to a twelve-member panel. In the law practice of Abraham Lincoln, from 1836 to 1861, there were dozens of jury trials in which fewer than twelve men served. For instance, there were eleven jurors in *Alexander v. Brown* (assumpsit, 1847) and *Casey v. Bowles* (debt, 1849), ten in *Baker v. VanBergen* (assumpsit, 1841), eight in *Haines v. Jones & Gaither* (trespass vi et armis, 1852), and only six in *People v. Alsop* (forgery, 1861). In two of these cases, the clerk noted in the court record that the parties had agreed to a reduced number of jurors.[35]

The way the issue evolved in Indiana and Illinois is instructive, as both states handled the matter differently. Indiana settled the issue very early in a case that involved the appointment of commissioners to assess damages to an individual who had made improvements to land. The 1825 opinion turned on an Indiana relief statute that featured an article providing for the court appointment of three commissioners, in lieu of a jury, to assess the award. The court argued that the section of the Indiana law allowing commissioners to decide the issue "cannot be reconciled to that clause in the fifth section of the first article of the constitution that secures the right of trial by jury, where the value in controversy exceeds twenty dollars." The Indiana Supreme Court found commissioners incompetent as jurors in such cases and overturned the circuit court's decision. It also invalidated the Indiana statute, which was later repealed.[36]

Indiana jurists had been adamant on the issue, and the U.S. Supreme Court agreed. The practice of using court-appointed commissioners had become the norm in Ohio when a case involving a Cincinnati man who had been ejected from his property reached the nation's highest court in 1829. In his opinion for the Court, John Marshall argued that "the seventh amendment to the United States Constitution declares that 'in suits at common law, where the value in controversy shall exceed twenty dollars, the right of trial by jury shall be preserved.' This is a suit at common law, and the value in controversy exceeds twenty dollars . . . it must be submitted to a jury." In this case and in others, the U.S. Supreme Court supported the Seventh Amendment, regardless of the specific legal context. If the value in controversy exceeded $20, trial by jury was *always* required. Commissioners were not deemed competent in these situations.[37]

The U.S. Supreme Court decision notwithstanding, Illinois statute, legal practice in the state's county and circuit courts, and Illinois appellate case law maintained a commitment to the use of court-appointed commissioners. Illinoisans found commissioners competent in this regard. One of the volatile issues facing antebellum midwesterners was the taking of private lands for the development of railroads and other public works projects. Thus, when a railroad company took private property for building its road, it entered into negotiations with the owner. In Illinois, the landowner was entitled to a court proceeding to assess damages and thereby determine just compensation. In some states, a jury assessed damages, and in others, the court appointed commissioners to do so. In Illinois, it became the job of court-appointed commissioners. So when a landowner and a railroad could not agree on compensation for the land to be taken for the railroad's right-of-way, either party could file an assessment of damages claim in a county court. There, the commissioners would assess the value of the landowner's property and set a dollar amount that the railroad would have to pay in compensation. In most circumstances, the value of the land at issue far exceeded $20. Many displeased landowners in Illinois filed circuit court appeals in these cases and were granted juries to assess their cases. However, the norm was that court-appointed commissioners had the power to make assessments for the payment of private property taken for the "public good."[38]

Illinois law and practice made a distinction between the right to trial by jury in typical lawsuits, on the one hand, and in suits focused on the assessment of damages, on the other. The level of competence here was distinct in the two circumstances. Two Illinois appellate cases in the early 1850s supported the state legislature's provision for court-appointed commissioners in lieu of trial by jury. In the opinion in the first case, heard in 1851, the Illinois Supreme Court ruled that "it was competent for the legislature to provide" that cases in which the issue was the awarding of damages "should be ascertained without the intervention of the jury." The second case, in 1852, involved the court appointment of seven commissioners to assess the value of improvements in two ejectment cases, appealed from Pike County, Illinois. The appeal related to Illinois' occupant law and was similar in legal circumstances to the Ohio case previously discussed. The case tested article 8, section 8 of the Illinois constitution, which averred that "no freeman shall be disseized of his freehold, or in any manner deprived of his property, but by the judgment of his peers." The purpose of the appeal was to determine if the mode of estimating the damages or improvements with the "intervention of the jury" was constitutional.[39] The opinion argued:

> What, under such circumstances, must have been the understanding of the framers of the constitution of 1818, as to the validity of assessments made without the intervention of a jury? . . . The framers of our State government were practical men, and adopted a constitution with reference to the state of things as they were then understood to exist . . . there is [now] another view in which a jury is not required, under the constitution, to carry into effect the provisions of the law. Trial by jury is only required on issues of fact in civil and criminal cases in courts of justice, which is not understood to embrace the case of a mere assessment of damages, or value, made out of court.[40]

Assessment of land value and of damages in Illinois remained within the purview of court-appointed commissioners throughout the antebellum period. To maintain the efficiency of the legal process, Illinoisans submitted to a tightly constructed view of what issues invoked the right to trial by jury.

Practice in Iowa and Wisconsin was similar to that in Illinois. By contrast, Ohio and Indiana used juries to assess damages in disputes between private landowners and public companies before appeals became necessary. Case law in those states supported the idea that the assessment of damages was "peculiarly adapted to a jury" and that landowners were "entitled to a jury to assess damages sustained by the establishment of a county road."[41] The constitutional provisions, statutes, and case law precedents in other states did not always reflect the practice in the antebellum Midwest.

The use of court-appointed commissioners to determine damages in certain midwestern states no doubt violated the Seventh Amendment rights of some landowners who lost their property to advancing economic development. It is clear that at particular times in particular midwestern states, the commitment to trial by jury was subject to the pressures of economic pursuits, and the definitions of *competence* could shift to reflect those goals.

As we have seen, midwestern laws respecting juries were specific about just what constituted qualified or competent jurors. Antebellum appellate cases entailed issues relating to specific state requirements. It is important to note here that appellate cases in state supreme courts were typically less about issues of law and more about the appellants' tenacity in obtaining agreeable verdicts. Generally, cases won appeal because of errors involving legal technicalities. Many appellants filing appeals in midwestern supreme courts assigned for error various violations of statutory juror requirements. Such proceedings might expose jurors for failing to be householders,[42] or they might challenge the age of jurors. In an 1857 Illinois case, a defendant assigned for error the fact that one of the jurors who delivered the verdict in his case was over the age of sixty. The Illinois Supreme Court held that although the statute required jurors to be sixty or younger, the defendant should have entered a challenge to the seating of that individual: "That a juror is over sixty years of age, is not a disqualification, and if he is accepted, with a knowledge of that fact, by the accused, it is not ground for a new trial." In other words, the defendant would have had a ground for challenge, but his failure to assert that challenge cost him cause for his error in the appeal.[43]

In an Indiana case, a defendant charged that one of the grand jurors who returned his indictment was over the age of sixty. The court interpreted the state statute, which at that time required jurors to be younger than sixty, as an exemption from service, not as a bar to service: if a juror over the age of sixty chose to serve, he could claim the privilege. In Iowa and Wisconsin, where voting status was required for juror service, litigants filed appeals when jurors in their cases lacked the qualifications of electors. In a Wisconsin case, the court argued that "any person not having all the qualifications of an elector [was] disqualified." In an appeal filed in Indiana, individual jurors were challenged for having served both on the grand jury that had indicted the defendant and on the petit jury that had convicted him.[44]

In Iowa in 1860, an appellant charged that one of the jurors in his criminal seduction case had not been a resident of the state. As previously noted, Iowa law contained an elector-status requirement for jurors, and there was a question regarding the juror's status as an elector based on the location of his residence at the time he served on the trial (electors, of course, were required to live within the state where they cast their ballots). Evidence clarified the matter, placing the juror's residence in Kansas when the trial was held. In its opinion, the Supreme Court of Iowa declared: "It is claimed by the State that the defendant can not take advantage of this objection to the juror by a motion for a new trial, that he passed his time by not challenging the juror before the trial, for cause. We think it is the duty of the State to place twelve legal jurors in the box, and that it is not the duty of the defendant to inquire whether jurors are qualified or not. It is presumed that the officer whose duty it is to select the jurors will select those who are competent and legal."[45]

Most midwestern states, regardless of their particular juror requirements, put the burden of challenge in the hands of the litigants, especially criminal defendants. Rarely did supreme court justices order new trials when appellants allowed allegedly unqualified jurors to hear their cases and then appealed after obtaining an unsatisfactory verdict. The opinion in a case in Michigan in 1844 succinctly summed up this tradition: "The want of qualifications in the talesmen [jurors], if there had been any in fact . . . were waived by the party's going to trial on the merits."[46]

Not all appellate cases related directly to the statutory requirements for juror service. Some dealt instead with the competence of jurors. Finding competent jurors was the primary philosophy behind the crafting of legislation that defined and regulated juror selection. But to be competent, jurors not only had to meet residence, age, and other standards, they also had to be unbiased. Put another way, biased jurors were not competent to serve. Some biased jurors were incompetent because they had formed and expressed an opinion in a case prior to the introduction of evidence. To cite one example from 1849, a circuit court judge in Iowa had denied a murder defendant's challenge to a juror on the grounds that the juror had "formed and expressed an opinion from the rumor or report he had heard in his neighborhood" immediately following the murder. On appeal, the Supreme Court of Iowa deemed the juror incompetent and overturned the manslaughter conviction.[47]

In another early Iowa case, the litigants in a trespass suit in civil court appealed the jury verdict because six of the jurors had also served on the jury that convicted the defendants in a related criminal case. In its opinion, the higher court ruled: "Six of the jurors who had tried and convicted the defendants upon an indictment involving the same questions and facts, were permitted to sit as jurors, and as we think it was impossible for them not to have formed an opinion upon the same matter involved in the issue at law (although they may innocently have thought differently) yet we are fully satisfied that they were incompetent jurors, and that it should have been so ruled by the court." This issue turned on the competence of the jurors and not specifically on the fact that they had served on the previous jury. Rather, since they had reached an opinion about the litigants in the criminal case, they were no longer competent on the issue in the civil case. Contrary to traditional jury selection procedures, the court in this instance did not place the burden of juror challenge on the defendants but instead clearly defined the circumstances as unconstitutional and awarded the defendants a new trial. At least thirty-eight appellate decisions in Indiana, Illinois, Michigan, Iowa, and Wisconsin hinged to some degree on juror bias or established opinions prior to the submission of evidence at trial. Although juror bias was a common assignment of error in the supreme courts of the antebellum Midwest, it was primarily a legal technicality, and most of the opinions that were delivered were not earth-shattering to the development of jury law.[48]

Juror bias went hand in hand with juror character when it came to the construction of nineteenth-century jury law to impanel "good" jurors. The law defined the legal characteristics of jurors (such as age and citizenship), but it also attempted to limit service based on character as well. Statutes required jurors to be "good and judicious," "reputable," "lawful," and "of good moral character."[49] Antebellum midwesterners expected jurors to conduct themselves in a respectful manner and in such a way as to bring honor and integrity to their duties. Chapters 2 and 3 provide thorough discussions regarding the status of the people who actually served as jurors, but it is useful to note here that, generally speaking, jurors hailed from the leading economic, social, and professional classes. Therefore, as far as most antebellum legislators believed, individuals from elite groups would be competent jurors and serve with respect and dignity.

Most jurors in courthouses across the antebellum Midwest conducted themselves competently and represented themselves with middle-class respectability. However, evidence from some appellate opinions reveals that jurors did not always behave. And when there was juror misbehavior, the litigants' attorneys let their state supreme courts hear about it, filing appeals on the grounds of juror incompetence. In all of the following cases,the appeals pertained to juror misconduct. One drunken juror in Indiana was intoxicated during trial proceedings, and another engaged in a conversation with a bystander without the consent of the court. During deliberations in a case in Illinois, a juror introduced to the other jurors his own evidence, which had not been submitted to the jury during the trial. And in Iowa, a panel of jurors could not agree on a verdict and thus drew lots to determine their decision in the case.[50]

Some jurors who served on grand and petit juries in the nineteenth century were not legally qualified to serve, and not all qualified jurors who served were competent. However, these were isolated incidents and did not pose a serious threat to antebellum midwestern efforts to seat competent jurors and to maintain a working jury trial system. As has been shown, the variety of appellate cases involving the qualifications and competence of jurors was vast. All of these cases exposed the growing pains of legal institutions in the Midwest during the early 1800s, illustrating the many ways in which rapid population growth, economic development, the construction of infrastructure, and industrial expansion impinged upon the legal system.

Another impact on the law was the influx into the midwestern states, especially Ohio and Illinois, of large numbers of mostly German and Irish immigrants. Regarding juror qualifications, one of the most interesting issues (although not the most common) was the question of alienage. In 1827, Illinois statute required that jurors be natural-born or naturalized citizens, and defendants had just cause to challenge the seating of "alien" jurors in the jury box. The first of two prominent Illinois cases involving the citizenship qualification for jury service began in 1838. In June of that year, a jury convicted Antoini Guykowski of the murder of Nelson Ryall in Clinton County Circuit Court. After the conviction and sentence of death, the defendant and his attorney learned that one of the jurors was not an American citizen. John Burnside, who had immigrated from Ireland, had resided in the United States for at least thirty years at the time of his jury service, but apparently, he had never become a naturalized citizen.[51]

Guykowski, himself an immigrant from Poland with limited English-language skills, appealed his case on the error that Burnside was an alien and therefore not qualified to serve. His attorney, Gustav Koerner, later recalled making the appeal based on that one juror's national heritage: "The fact was true. The man, an Irishman, had been living in the county for some twenty years, but had never been naturalized." In the supreme court opinion, written by Theophilus Smith, the justices argued that "there can be no doubt whatever, that an alien is not qualified to serve as a juror in any case . . . an alien is not capable in law to discharge the functions of a juror." The Illinois Supreme Court overturned Guykowski's conviction and sent the case back to the circuit for another trial.[52]

The *Guykowski* case was the first to test alienage, and the decision stood until 1846 when the Illinois Supreme Court heard *Greenup v. Stoker.* That case, which originated in St. Clair County Circuit Court and involved a breach of promise to marry, took the teeth out of the *Guykowski* decision. In *Greenup,* a jury found in favor of the plaintiff, and the defendant assigned for error the point that two of the jurors were aliens. In an opinion written by Norman Purple, the supreme court argued that the *Guykowski* decision was correct in overturning the defendant's conviction but it went too far in declaring that all aliens were unqualified for jury service. The *Greenup* opinion stated: "By this statute, as well as by the common law, unnaturalized aliens are disqualified to serve on juries. Although we are aware that it has been stated in the opinion of the court, delivered in the case of *Guykowski v. The People,* that 'an alien is not capable in law to discharge the functions of a juror' . . . [we] feel called upon . . . by a sense of justice and propriety to limit the rule to capital cases." The opinion went on to discuss the reality of jury composition given the influx of immigrants into the state. It also made the all-important assertion that alienage of a juror should be limited to the independent challenge of an individual juror by a party to the suit. Such a charge of alienage after the rendering of a verdict was not, in this revision, a valid error for appeal. Justice Purple concluded:

> It is well known, and part of the general history of the country, that our population is composed, to a considerable extent, of

> emigrants from almost all portions of the world. From the peculiar character of our institutions they become entitled, almost upon their arrival here, to many of the privileges of natural born and naturalized citizens; they readily accommodate themselves to our habits, laws and customs, and often with the knowledge and tacit assent of the parties are permitted to serve on juries, and thus to determine conflicting claims between citizen and citizen. . . . I propose now, to show upon authority, that in misdemeanors and in civil cases at least, alienage and other disqualifications are grounds of challenge only, and can not be assigned as reasons for new trials or to reverse a cause on error.[53]

The opinion in *Greenup v. Stoker* not only overturned the broad interpretation in *Guykowski* but also cut deeply into the muscle of the Illinois jury statute that required all grand and petit jurors to be natural-born or naturalized citizens.[54] The case is the ultimate example of the collision of law and tradition. Established in 1827, the qualification of American citizenship stood firm in Illinois jury law. In practice, however, it became unworkable. As more and more immigrants settled in the state and as the court dockets grew clogged with cases, it proved impractical to reject all aliens from civil cases and misdemeanor criminal cases. In addition, as immigrants increasingly became established and respectable residents of the state, opinions as to their competence for jury service undoubtedly changed, at least to a small extent. Although cases such as the two cited here were relatively isolated proceedings, they do provide evidence that, in some ways, jury law might have been expanding instead of shrinking.

The Illinois Supreme Court was, of course, too busy to hear every cry of error from a dissatisfied party when a panel of jurors with an alien returned an unfavorable judgment. The court recognized the importance of strict construction in capital cases, in which a defendant's life and civil liberties were at stake, but in lesser cases, the justices were willing to leave the matter to the circuit courts. And it was not as if the state's high court was abolishing the citizenship requirement. Rather, it was placing the power to overrule the seating of an alien juror in the hands of the parties at suit. If individuals objected to alien jurors hearing their cases, they were entitled to challenge for cause.

Greenup v. Stoker set the precedent for alienage in the antebellum Midwest, but the issue of a juror's skills with the English language was another matter altogether. An 1859 appellate case in Indiana involved the seating of a juror who was a German immigrant with a limited ability to understand English. The supreme court in that state argued that Samuel Wehr was incompetent, quoting state statute in its opinion: "A competent juror must be a man of sound mind, of ordinary intelligence, and having a sufficient acquaintance with the English language . . . unless a man understands the language sufficiency to appreciate the testimony so as to form some intelligent judgment of what it proves, and be able to apply the instructions of the court to it, he ought not, in justice to the parties, be permitted to sit upon a jury. Wehr could do neither, and was, therefore, incompetent." The court affirmed the lower court's decision, which had granted a new trial by reason of Wehr's incompetence to serve.[55]

As previously mentioned, appellate cases mostly hinged on legal technicalities. Appellants, appellant attorneys, and state supreme court justices sought to protect constitutional rights and provide a system of checks and balances for juror competence and competent jury trials. The overall body of appellate case law in the antebellum Midwest reflects a legal system engaged in the process of building the law, redefining the law, negotiating the terms of the law, and reconceptualizing competence and the jury. Of the 175 midwestern appellate opinions systematically examined for this study, themes discussed in the previous section—the constitutional right to trial by jury, juror qualifications, and juror misconduct—were at issue in 57 (33 percent) of the cases, and of those cases, 22 related directly to questions of juror qualifications. Since most appellate cases revolved around a technical issue, juror selection processes and jury trial procedures were the most common errors assigned on appeal. Juror selection processes were assigned for error in 35 appellate cases examined, and jury trial procedures were assigned in 47, the largest percentage of the entire group of cases studied.[56]

Another significant category was jury instructions. The role of jury instructions in the power relationships that existed between the jury, the bench, and the bar is the topic of discussion in chapter 4, but it is worth noting here that jury instructions were among the more legally technical issues examined in antebellum midwestern appellate cases. The instructions given by attorneys and judges (as well as attorney-prepared instructions that judges refused to relay to juries) were a frequent bone of contention in appellate cases. As a result, it was not uncommon for state supreme court justices to use their written opinions to proselytize about the power struggle—namely, about which segment of the legal system had the power to decide issues of law and fact.[57]

Procedure-based cases involved such issues as the recording of names in official court records, the accuracy of information entered into the record and properly prepared legal paperwork, the validity of juror affidavits attesting to jury verdicts, the separation of the jurors and outside interaction with jurors during deliberations, the evidence permitted in the jury room, grand jury sessions during special terms of the court, and the polling of jurors after the rendering of verdicts. Because of the technical nature of these cases and their less-than-exciting characteristics, they will only be discussed briefly here. However, they are important because they offer additional evidence about the significance that antebellum midwesterners attached to the institution of the jury. In working through the legal minutiae of jury law, these individuals exhibited their commitment to promoting and maintaining a workable, competent system.[58]

Twenty-eight of the cases in this category were in the Supreme Court of Iowa, which is not surprising in that jury procedural laws were most specifically defined in that state. Dozens of details in the Iowa statutes related to how jurors were selected and summoned and how grand and petit juries functioned within their carefully constructed roles. There were scores of rules for courts to sort out and keep straight, and when county commissioners, sheriffs, clerks, judges, or jurors slipped up, attorneys were ready to assign errors and appeal their cases on these legal technicalities.[59]

Jury selection involved the creation of lists of potential jurors for service by county commissioners (who held this responsibility in most of the midwestern states), the service of venire by county sheriffs, and the seating of jurors on grand and petit panels. Out of necessity, it was very common in the first half of the nineteenth century for individual jurors, especially those living at or near county seats, to serve in back-to-back terms of the court. However, most states had particular procedures for officers of the court to follow, and appellants did not shy away from assigning for error deliberate and inadvertent mistakes in the selection process. One common error assigned in appellate cases was the violation of the requirement for "blind" selection, or drawing, of potential juror names. Another error related to repeat service of individual jurors. As mentioned earlier, sheriffs often played a role in limiting the number of potential jurors summoned, which in some states was a violation of statutes calling for rotational service. In jurisdictions where rotational service of jurors was valued, jurors who served in violation of the standard rotation were deemed incompetent; appeals to state supreme courts reflected this situation.[60]

The Winnowing Process in Search of "Competence"

Lawmakers in the new "western" states maintained their faith in the institution of the jury, and they exhibited a staunch determination to protect this democratic ideal. By developing legal descriptions of competent jurors, they defined the caliber of persons they deemed capable and worthy of serving on their juries. As a result of their own high expectations, only those whom the state legislatures deemed uniquely qualified could fulfill this sacred responsibility of citizenship. Consequently, jury panels were not always representative of "the people," and most criminal defendants and many litigants in civil cases were not judged by their real peers. The wealthiest and most socially, professionally, and politically influential members of the community determined who was indicted to stand trial in criminal cases, and jurors in criminal trials rarely judged members of their own economic and social groups. State statutes and legal processes provided that only those "gentlemen" who were "good and lawful," "discrete," "reputable," and "judicious" men of "good moral character" could serve. Certainly, those were subjective characteristics. Objectivity in this regard was not the goal; impaneling presumably competent jurors was.[61]

Let us take Illinois as an example. In 1818, the Illinois constitution protected the right to trial by jury as "inviolate." The First Illinois General Assembly passed a jury law that restricted jurors to "taxable inhabitants" and "good and lawful men." In 1827, the state legislature became more serious about juror qualifications. The law now provided that both grand and petit jurors be "free white male taxable inhabitants" who were natural-born or naturalized citizens between the ages of twenty-one and sixty years and who were of "sound mind and discretion and not subject to any bodily infirmity." These qualifications remained in force for the entirety of the antebellum period.[62]

Basically, only male, white property owners could serve as jurors. Obviously, this fundamental requirement disqualified women, who accounted for 403,000 (47 percent) of Illinois' 851,000 inhabitants in 1850. The law also disqualified 5,000 black Illinoisans from jury service. Therefore, nearly half of the total population was, according to law, "unfit" to serve. In addition to eliminating women and blacks, the law also disqualified males under the age of twenty-one, men over the age of sixty, and men subject to bodily infirmity. Further, the law required all jurors to be natural-born or naturalized citizens of the United States. With the exclusion of women, blacks, children, the elderly, the sick, and unnaturalized immigrants, the pool of qualified jurors was no more than one-quarter of the total population of Illinois in 1850. On top of all that, many of the remaining potential jurors did not own property. Although the exact number is not known, it is reasonable to suspect that as many as one-quarter or more of the remaining 25 percent may not have owned taxable property. Thus, people who were qualified to serve on juries—regardless, at this point, of their economic, social, and political status—were already members of an elite group of citizens.[63]

While the legislators outlined juror qualifications that reduced the pool of those qualified to less than perhaps 20 percent of the state's entire population, the court officials and attorneys who worked within the legal system performed yet another sifting process. County commissioners hand-selected potential grand jurors and determined which individuals the sheriffs would summon as potential petit jurors. Rural residents who lived farthest from county seats were often difficult for sheriffs to contact, and many county residents could not afford the trip to court or the time away from their small farms. This simple fact eliminated even more people from service. Court officials had a direct hand in who would show up at court for possible selection as grand and petit jurors. The law required only that potential jurors meet the basic qualifications previously outlined.[64]

Perhaps county commissioners filtered their choices by selecting friends, political allies, or prominent community residents. Maybe they chose people they honestly believed were best suited to the legal and moral requirements of exalted jury service. Whatever their reasoning, their role in the process meant that an elite group of potential jurors arrived at court. But arriving at court did not necessarily guarantee that a potential juror would serve on a jury. Attorneys exercised challenges that the law allowed them in jury selection, which further decreased the number of people within any given community who actually participated in the process.[65]

The sifting process of juror selection in Illinois

This chart shows how the Illinois court system seated grand and petit panels from the eligible pool of jurors.

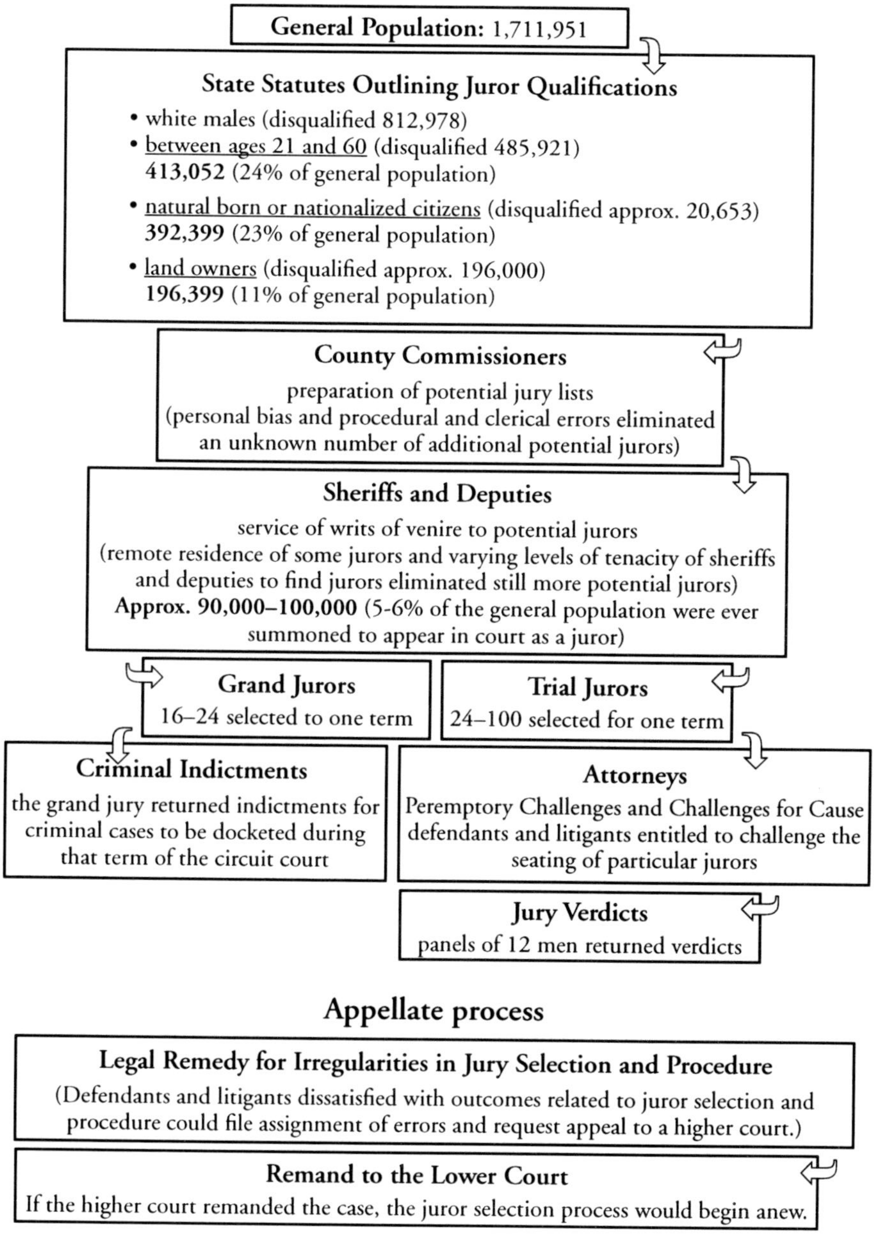

The law, the procedure of summoning jurors, the nature of the lawyers' role in selecting jurors, and the reality of life on the prairie precluded as much as 90 percent (and perhaps more) of the population from jury service. It is safe to assume that the legislators, county commissioners, sheriffs, and attorneys who had a direct impact upon the trial-by-jury system in Illinois worked, either consciously or unconsciously, to impanel competent men in the jury boxes across the state. Court officials and members of the bar identified with people they believed harbored the same level of commitment to the trial-by-jury process. And who better to protect that essential American right than members of their own social, economic, and political circles?

The county commissioners selected twenty-three grand jurors possessing the qualifications outlined in the statute, tapping at least sixteen from that pool to serve, and they appointed a foreman to speak for the group. The law placed the power of indictment in the hands of the grand jury, and grand jurors were responsible for seeing that the judicial branch enforced the state's criminal code. The law gave the grand jury the ability to regulate the community's notion of what crimes the state's attorney should and would prosecute and what cases juries would hear. One scholar has noted that frontier grand juries were "effective sounding boards in making known the desires of the people and served as a curb upon the activities of public officials."[66] However, given that grand juries in Illinois were selected from probably only 10 percent of the total population, those grand jurors who handed down indictments spoke from their own economic, social, and political perspectives and did not necessarily represent all residents of their counties and communities.

Settlers in Illinois and in other states in the antebellum Midwest carried with them an inherent reverence for the institution of the jury. Upon establishing their nascent legal institutions and traditions, they codified the democratic institution of the jury in their new state constitutions and developing body of statute and appellate case law. Adopting jury law from older states and often adapting it to fit their particular circumstances, they constructed a legal system for themselves in their emerging states. Filling jury boxes with competent men and maintaining a workable jury system were the goals. In each jury law enacted and within dozens of state appellate opinions published, legislators and judges defined and redefined the ideal characteristics of jurors and honed jury trial practice and procedures. In the coming chapters, we will see how midwestern jury law and the pursuit of competence constrained the composition of jury panels; affected jury work and experience; played into the political rhetoric of the jury; and impinged upon the courtroom relationships between judges, lawyers, and the jurors themselves.

TWO

The Composition of Juries in Sangamon County, Illinois, 1830–60

IN THE spring of 1833, when he was an unaccomplished but ambitious young man living in the tiny village of New Salem, Illinois, Abraham Lincoln served as a juror in the Sangamon County Circuit Court. Just months earlier, he had briefly served in the Black Hawk War and had lost election to the Illinois General Assembly. In another month, Lincoln would become the postmaster for New Salem, and in less than a year, he would win election to the Illinois House of Representatives. In April 1833, though, he was just a poor man with little more than hopes for a bright future. Lincoln's juror service marked not only his initial foray into the legal world that would become his chosen professional arena for twenty-five years but also his emergence as an active, committed citizen.[1]

In antebellum America, jury service was a responsibility of citizenship, and legislators of the era crafted laws that they believed would guarantee the impaneling of competent grand and trial jurors. Jury service, in turn, provided a type of educational reinforcement of community values. In 1833, Lincoln was a twenty-four-year-old man seeking acceptance among his peers within the county of his residence, and he was looking for an initiation into a national community of republican citizenship. His jury service validated his ambitions. Lincoln's fellow jurors that spring were a combination of established elites and young newcomers like himself. They included a wealthy physician, a successful wool carder, an established farmer who had settled in the county in 1818, a man who would later serve as a county sheriff, and two men who, like Lincoln, had unsuccessfully run for the Illinois General Assembly.[2]

Of course, juror service did not ensure continued elite status, nor did it guarantee the attainment of elite status for jurors who had not already succeeded in professional, political, economic, or social circles. In Lincoln's case specifically, early jury service did not provide the sole means of his rise to middle-class respectability. However, juror affiliation did foster shared ideals of citizenship and strengthen community values among the established and aspiring elites who served together. The jury box was a schoolroom and the courthouse was a schoolhouse for the teaching of democratic ideology and the reinforcing of notions about what constituted proper social relationships and engagements. The legal experiences attendant on jury service connected jurors to a central component of American democracy; they also played a vital role in the jurors' understanding of themselves as citizens and of their place within their immediate locales and the nation. And as the experiences taught and reaffirmed those connections, the meting out of justice from the jury box validated and empowered them.

Illinois judge Richard Yates noted in 1839 that jury panels consisted of the "best citizens of the county."[3] The research presented here will test the validity of his observation. The composition of jury panels in one location is the focus of this chapter. As a case study, the narrative analyzes juror demographics in the antebellum midwestern county of Sangamon, Illinois, presenting demographic data, biographical stories, and jury trial vignettes. The chapter begins with a brief description of Sangamon County and of the county seat of Springfield; it then turns to an analysis of the pool of potential jurors from which grand and trial juries were created. An explanation of the categories of demographic analysis employed in the research follows. The chapter presents the demographic data in two sections, looking specifically at the Sangamon County jurors who served in 1850 and then at those who served a decade later. The chapter concludes with a composite portrait of antebellum jurors and offers some conclusions about the status of those who served on midwestern grand and petit jury panels.

Springfield, Illinois

In 1828, Springfield, Illinois, consisted of only 300 to 400 residents and a small clustering of log buildings. By 1840, the population had reached 2,600, the city was incorporated, and the community was continuing to develop and grow. In 1856, Springfield merchants reported $3 million in sales, an increase of $750,000 from 1854. The city was the bustling seat of Sangamon County government: it had a developing economic infrastructure and a busy state capitol building, which served as the anchor of a vibrant commercial town square. Springfield was maturing, covering more than a square mile, and much of the city's growth was due to the town's role as the county seat. In the antebellum Midwest, the county courthouse and, by extension, the county seat hosted society's legal system. The courthouse served as the focal point of the legal, economic, and social structures of the county, and the county seat offered a blend of governmental, legal, and economic services and opportunities for the county's population. It is not surprising that midwestern towns competed to become the county seat because the economic benefits such a designation brought were innumerable.[4]

Picket fences and shade trees around the Springfield public square, as well as the numerous shingles hanging above the doors and windows of the businesses surrounding the state capitol and the county courthouse, announced the economic prosperity and stability of the city. In downtown Springfield, residents of and visitors to the county seat could purchase "Real Havana Cigars" from Corneau & Diller's store, fancy and well-made hats from John H. Adams, gold rings at Chatterton Jewelers, books from Johnson & Bradford Booksellers, and parasols and Queensware dishes from Grover Ayers's Cheap Cash Store. They could also solicit the services of at least nineteen lawyers, seek medical attention from the city's two dozen doctors, or have their portraits painted.[5]

Springfield and Sangamon County were thriving and expanding.[6] Sangamon was one of the most influential counties in the state, enjoying strong political representation in the Illinois General Assembly. In 1844, it sent one senator and four representatives to the Fourteenth Illinois General Assembly. Political power, combined with general economic prosperity, created a dynamic environment for the community's residents. In 1860, the county boasted a population of 32,274 people, 68 percent of whom were under the age of thirty. Of the inhabitants, 15,183 (47 percent) were female, 5,331 (16 percent) were foreign born, and 311 (1 percent) were African American. Nearly 40 percent of the heads of households in Illinois in 1860 made their living as farmers, and the state's agricultural proclivity was reflected in Sangamon County. No other occupation came close in terms of representing the economic livelihood of such a large percentage of the county's residents. Although dependent to some degree on developing state and regional markets, most of the county's residents lived in rural areas surrounding Springfield and on the outskirts of the small towns that had popped up throughout the county. Only 9,320 (30 percent) of Sangamon's population resided in the county seat of Springfield, but the city was the area's legal and economic epicenter.[7]

Springfield's civic life and cultural spirit also thrived. In 1850, there were at least six schools, including the Springfield Young Ladies Institute and the Colored School. Both the Democratic and Whig political parties were well represented in the city, where local, state, and national politics was a popular spectator sport for both men and women. At any given time, there were at least two newspapers in publication, enabling residents to keep up with the political issues of the day and read news from across the country and around the world. The *Illinois Journal,* the *Illinois Register,* the *Illinois Organ,* and the *Liberia Advocate* were all in circulation in 1850. Later, there was also a German-language newspaper and the *Capital Enterprise.* The *Journal,* the newspaper of the Whig Party, and the *Register,* the newspaper of the Democratic Party, operated in Springfield throughout the entire period of this study. By 1860, both papers were still in business, and Springfield residents had access to the *Illinois Farmer,* the *Illinois State Democrat,* the *Illinois Staats Anzeiger,* the *Lincoln Clarion,* and the fraternal magazine *Mememto,* all published in their city.[8]

Springfield hosted two state fairs in the 1850s, sponsored numerous theater troops and theatrical productions, and had a local chapter of the American Colonization Society; it also had several temperance organizations, including the Sons of Temperance and the Maine Law Alliance. In addition, the city boasted the Sangamon County Horticultural Society, a lyceum, a library association, and a public library as of 1856.[9] Springfield was, moreover, a stop on the lecture circuits of prominent speakers such as the writer Ralph Waldo Emerson, the newspaper editor Horace Greeley, the minister Henry Ward Beecher, the transcendentalist Theodore Parker, and the internationally known Hungarian revolutionary Louis Kossuth.[10]

Springfield was a culturally sophisticated city and a hotbed of county and state politics, and it enjoyed a generally prosperous economy and solid commercial structures. Residents of the town and the surrounding county had access to education as well. Of the 2,045 Springfield children between the ages of five and fifteen in 1859, 75 percent were enrolled in public or private schools. Given the dominance of agriculture as the occupation that supported most families and often required the labor of farm children, this was an impressive figure.[11] Community residents also had exposure to the arts, access to a variety of reading materials, contact with German and Irish immigrants, varying degrees of interaction with the legal system (either as participants or spectators and observers), and the market advantages of living in a commercial center. It was from this flourishing community that individuals were drawn for service on Sangamon County's grand and petit juries.

The Jury Pool

Given the economic, political, and social circumstances of life in Springfield and Sangamon County, it is clear that county court officials had access to a potentially sophisticated pool of jurors. But like the shallow waters of the unnavigable Sangamon River, the jury pool in the antebellum period lacked depth. As we will see, midwestern jury law and process restricted and controlled access to the jury boxes in Illinois courts. To illustrate the sifting process of jury selection, the next several paragraphs will paint a picture of the jury pool by using data from the 1860 census, which by and large provided complete and detailed demographic information.[12]

As discussed in chapter 1, the nineteenth-century Illinois legislature made jury service the domain of white, male property owners. The basic requirements regarding gender and skin color barred from jury service all females, who totaled 805,350 (47 percent) of Illinois' 1,711,951 inhabitants in 1860, as well as 7,628 black Illinoisans. Therefore, nearly half of the total population was considered incompetent by law to serve. The law also disqualified males under the age of twenty-one and over the age of sixty, thereby reducing the potential juror pool by an additional 485,921 people. Consequently, before landownership requirements were applied at the local level, only 413,052 (24 percent) of Illinois' residents met the statute's gender, race, and age requirements for jury service.[13]

Illinois law also required all jurors to be natural-born or naturalized citizens of the United States. In 1860, there were 324,643 foreign-born residents, only 181,529 of whom were white males. And fewer than 84,000 of those were of legal age for jury service. This decreased the pool of potential jurors by an additional 5 percent. So after the law eliminated women, African Americans, elderly men, and unnaturalized immigrants from service, the pool of qualified jurors was at best one-fifth (19 percent) of the total population of Illinois in 1860. Furthermore, many of the remaining individuals did not own property, which disqualified them from service.[14] The real number is not known, but we can surmise that as many as half of those who remained likely did not own real property or else lived in remote areas far from the county seats in which they would have served. Conservatively, then, perhaps no more than 10 percent of the inhabitants of the state of Illinois in 1860 were legally qualified and available to serve on a jury—comprising a small and elite group regardless of their particular economic, professional, social, or political status.

It is possible to extrapolate the number of qualified jurors in Sangamon County in 1860. Of the total population of 32,274 people that year, the following were automatically disqualified by statute: 15,007 females, 8,237 underaged males, 513 overaged males, and 311 free blacks. Thus, the law eliminated 24,068 Sangamon County residents, or 75 percent of the total population. Additionally, jury law disqualified approximately 1,000 of the 3,044 unnaturalized, white, male immigrants in the county. But that is not all. In the 1860 census, at least 2,000 heads of households in the county reported no real property, and the law also disqualified them from jury service, bringing the countywide pool of potential jurors down to, at most, 5,200, or just 16 percent of the total population.[15]

State legislators thus established qualifications that dramatically cut the number of legally sanctioned potential jurors, and a further sifting process was undertaken by officials in the legal system. From the list of qualified citizens, county commissioners individually selected potential jurors, typically perusing tax lists or voting rolls to do so. Bias in constructing the list, clerical errors, misinformation, and failure to acknowledge or ensure rotational service of potential jurors certainly resulted in the inadvertent disqualification of some individuals. County commissioners may also have deliberately chosen their friends and political allies or community leaders as they developed the list that was ultimately given to the county sheriff. In turn, the sheriff and his deputies eliminated more potential jurors through their failure to deliver writs of venire to every individual on the list that commissioners provided. This failure may have been the result of bias, laziness, or the physical difficulty of serving writs in remote locations of the county.[16]

The geographic distance that separated some qualified jurors from the county seat at Springfield and the limited transportation routes and poor roads in the region also decreased the depth of the juror pool. Many small farmers in rural areas were simply unable to attend court, and even among those who could, the lack of ambition on the part of some sheriffs eliminated still more individuals. As a result, most of the jurors who were finally impaneled resided in Springfield and communities in the immediate vicinity of town. Realistically, then, Sangamon County court officials assembled panels of jurors, especially for petit juries, from the 4,551 male inhabitants of Springfield. It was easier for these officials to locate potential jurors living in town, and it was easier for townspeople to attend court. Without disqualifying men in Springfield who did not own real property, the actual pool of potential jurors who were most likely to serve represented only 14 percent—and probably far less—of the entire population of Sangamon County. Wealthier citizens lived near and around the town center; and as jurors tended to live in proximity to the courthouse (at the town center), courts tended to draw jurors from among the affluent, centrally located citizenry.[17]

Consequently, only a small number of individuals were summoned for jury duty, and even fewer were ultimately selected to serve. The winnowing process continued within the court, for the pool dwindled further when attorneys challenged certain potential jurors as the law permitted. In the end, given the legal stipulations, the procedures used to summon jurors, the attorneys' invocation of juror challenges, and the difficulties encountered in pulling jurors from remote corners of the county, 90 to 95 percent, if not more, of the population was excluded from jury service.[18]

Now let us turn to the individuals who actually survived the winnowing process. The research conducted to this end resulted in the creation of a database incorporating demographic details about all the grand and petit jurors who served in 1850 and 1860 in Sangamon County Circuit Court and all the petit jurors who served in the 1,075 jury cases in the law practice of Abraham Lincoln. Those latter jurors served from the 1830s to 1860 and in numerous counties throughout Illinois, with a concentration of numbers in central Illinois counties. The data collected included personal, economic, professional, political, and social information on 1,410 jurors in Sangamon County. More specifically, these data consisted of marital status, real property wealth, personal property wealth, age, nativity, occupation, political activity, and social standing. In addition to the information on these Sangamon County jurors, there is further (albeit less complete) information on the 2,680 jurors who appeared in all of Lincoln's jury cases. The 1850 and 1860 federal census reports provided the bulk of the information employed in this analysis, but county tax records, county histories, newspapers, manuscript sources, biographies, and secondary sources filled in numerous gaps. The resulting 18 MB database forms the strong foundation of this book and is the most important research component of the entire work.[19]

Categories of Demographic Analysis

During the initial analysis of the demographic data on jurors in antebellum Sangamon County, it became evident that a large percentage of individuals who served as grand and trial jurors had substantial wealth, made their living in agriculture or a professional occupation, were involved in party politics, and were members of the county's prominent families. However, drawing quantitative meaning out of all the data was proving difficult. To make sense of the overwhelming demographic information, categorization of the jurors was necessary. Therefore, the data presented here categorize jurors in four demographic groups based on their economic, professional, social, and political status.

To that end, the status of individual jurors has been evaluated based on whether or not they were economic, professional, social, and/or political elites. There is considerable overlap among the four categories, and in order to analyze the jurors in a uniform manner, each category must be defined separately. Definitions in this regard are crucial.

Some scholars have used the term *elite* to describe individuals "who exercise authority, accumulate wealth, and command respect" and the phrase *elite groups* for those who "wield power or possess high status and large fortune." One scholar has defined *elites* as "those enclaves whose influence is primarily local and regional, whose functions are specialized, or that occupy auxiliary positions in the leadership hierarchy."[20] This book takes to heart much of this scholarship, but at the same time it employs unique definitional tools in approach and organization. Because categorizing individuals based on their status is fraught with pitfalls, it is necessary at this point to provide workable definitions in the context of this particular research project.

First among the elite groups in this study are the economic elites. These are the individuals who had influence within the community due to their real estate holdings and personal wealth. Generally, an economic elite is classified here as any head of household who reported to census takers more than $5,000 in real and personal wealth. Christopher Elliott Wallace, a scholar who examined elites and family persistence in Springfield, Illinois, qualified as wealthy all individuals who reported $2,500 in real property in the 1850 census, which constituted only 10.7 percent of the town's total population. Drawing from that figure, the present study has factored in the reality that many farmers, members of the dominant profession of the era, reported wealth well in excess of the median figure of $1,300 in this locale. Because their wealth was tied up in the land, farmers who were worth $2,500 or less were not necessarily wealthy. What separated most economic elites from ordinary citizens was the possession of personal wealth. A farmer with $2,500 was probably doing well financially, but his economic circumstances were quite different from the farmer who owned twice as much real and personal property. The farmer with $5,000 or more tended to have substantially greater personal wealth—exhibited in larger, more elaborately furnished homes; more livestock; and more personal items from the marketplace, such as manufactured furniture, clocks, and china and glassware. Consequently, this farmer closely approximated antebellum notions of economic elite status.[21]

The choice of a specific dollar figure to designate an economic elite is arguably somewhat arbitrary. However, the need for a benchmark requires a hard decision. Based on an examination of Wallace's research and an analysis of the 1850 census, it is fairly clear that an individual with $1,300 in wealth was an average citizen in a community; an individual with $2,000 to $4,000 was somewhat above average but not uncommonly wealthy; and an individual with $5,000 or more was truly elite in terms of economic status. Antebellum midwesterners in this economic category were not numerous.[22]

The second category encompasses professional elites. This category primarily includes individuals whose occupations, regardless of their wealth, elevated them to elite status. For example, the professions of law, medicine, business, highly skilled trades, and the ministry earned the individuals who chose them the respect of the community and afforded them elite status within it. This was true even though many of them never acquired a great deal of personal wealth. The elite status of merchants, bankers, and other businessmen was more overt. They had influence within the community based on wealth *and* occupation. As one scholar has written, "Antebellum Americans expected merchants, particularly wealthy and well-bred entrepreneurs, to be active in the community. In western cities, as in eastern urban centers, businessmen played important roles in municipal politics, voluntary associations, and civil affairs."[23] These individuals were direct participants in the marketplace, manufactured consumable products, and provided financial structures and webs of credit. Many local merchants also functioned as banking and lending institutions. The emerging professional classes were building and participating in professional organizations, which were wielding more and more community influence. Many of these professional elites were amassing personal fortunes as well as positions of power within the community based on their professional associations and status. Even in the pioneering West, community elites held tremendous sway in the cultural and social structures of their developing towns.[24]

Social elites make up the third category. This category is the most difficult to define but is in some ways the most significant. It appears that family relationships, persistence within the community of residence, and age were keys to determining social elite status. Economic elites and professional elites were typically social elites as well. For this study, though, it made sense to isolate social elites as those individuals who gained leadership positions directly through their familial connections to prominent people, through their residence in the community for twenty or more years, through their involvement in civic organizations and societies, or simply by the virtue of their age, with older men commanding more social respect than younger ones. Sons of economic, professional, and political elites were often—regardless of their own personal wealth, occupation, or political activity—elevated to elite status. The public meetings that honored Old Settlers, for instance, illustrated the authority and respect that individuals with deep roots in the community enjoyed. These individuals were also involved in civil voluntary organizations. For the purpose of the study, individuals who had social elite status were defined as those who belonged to prominent families, especially those that were original settlers in the community.[25]

Within the growing body of literature on the Midwest, population mobility is a recurrent theme, and some scholars have argued that with the high turnover in community populations, certain elite groups became more entrenched. "People most interested in maintaining the stability necessary to ensure their continued security or success," one historian has written, "were the people most likely to stay around long enough to achieve and maintain community control." From their situations as persistent residents, community leaders were the engineers of legal conduits of community power in the emerging Midwest. During the early to mid-nineteenth century, when social, economic, political, and legal systems were in development, "elite families and individuals were a stabilizing force in mobile and rapidly changing communities."[26] Persistence in the community equated directly with positions of leadership; in spite of the mobility of populations in the antebellum Midwest, a stable core of individuals and families survived over time. These "stakeholders" were the older, wealthier, professional members of the community, and their influence extended to the legal structures that governed the communities in which they lived.[27]

The fourth and final category is made up of political elites, defined, simply, as people who ran for political office, who held a public office, or who participated in local party politics. Political elites occupied two positions of power regarding jury selection and service. First, they wrote and enacted legislation that established juror qualifications and jury selection procedures. As politicians, they were engaged in the enduring rhetoric that connected the jury to American democracy. Second, as community elites, they served on grand and petit juries. They determined law and fact, returned criminal indictments, and handed down verdicts in criminal and civil cases.[28]

Political elites—who were sometimes economic, social, and professional elites as well—dominated the state constitutional conventions in Ohio, Indiana, Illinois, Michigan, Wisconsin, and Iowa. When they constructed their state constitutions in the first half of the nineteenth century, they reiterated the importance of the jury trial. Even though the U.S. Constitution and the Bill of Rights guaranteed trial by jury, legislators in all the emerging midwestern states enacted numerous statutes to regulate jury selection, juror qualifications, and trial-by-jury processes. From their elite perspective, they directed the law of their states in regard to who was qualified for exalted jury service.[29]

As noted, this analysis of juror status focuses on economic, professional, social, and political elites. In the antebellum Midwest, cash money was scarce, and complex webs of credit were vital to the economy of the region, the state, and the individual communities. Thus, vast personal wealth practically guaranteed at least some economic influence and probably brought strong social and political influence as well. Merchants, bankers, large landowners, and some lawyers who had accumulated real and personal wealth earned the respect of the community because of their economic status, and their opinions held tremendous sway. Yet in the context of the era, the degree of community respect and authority that individuals commanded was not always based on their wealth, as many well-respected, established families did not have vast personal fortunes. Original settlers of the area garnered respect but did not necessarily own large tracts of land. Political party participation and candidacy for public office did not necessarily require or depend upon wealth, and individuals who held local and state offices, as well as others who participated in party organization and political campaigns, were influential members of the community regardless of their economic status. There were also people involved in their churches and engaged in civic leadership roles who did not own a great deal of land or possess great personal wealth but who were influential members of the community nonetheless.[30]

In short, although wealth was a visible characteristic of many midwestern elites and although wealthy farmers and businessmen had tremendous economic, social, and political influence in the community, the ruling elite class was not composed solely of wealthy individuals. Politicians and people engaged in party politics, court and public safety officials, family members of pioneer settlers, and other prominent citizens were also influential and were part of the persistent ruling elite in antebellum towns. Some had leadership roles in the economic structure of society because their businesses were central to the local economy. Others led through their past and present political service as mayors, legislators, and local party organizers. Antebellum midwestern elites were generally heads of households and members of families that had been settled in the community for twenty or more years. Typically, they were not recent immigrants—although some German and, to a lesser extent, Irish individuals fared well in business and functioned within the upper echelons of society. Most important, elites in midwestern towns were leaders because they could afford to be. Unlike many nonelite residents, who were concerned with day-to-day survival for themselves and their families, elites enjoyed the privileges of economic comfort and had the time necessary to build and maintain conduits of community power. One of the ways that they fulfilled this role was through their service on grand and petit juries.

The Composition of Antebellum Juries in Sangamon County

For this study, in addition to organizing the data into four demographic groupings, it was also useful to zero in on a particular time frame. Therefore, all 57 grand and 121 petit jurors who served in the Sangamon County Circuit Court throughout 1850 were analyzed as a group; then, the 64 grand and 97 petit jurors who were impaneled throughout 1860 were analyzed. The focus on 1850 and 1860 proved particularly workable because those samples coincided with the two federal censuses. Following the analysis of the complete demographic picture of jurors in 1850 and 1860, three samples of Sangamon County petit jurors were studied: one group from the 1830s, a second group from the 1840s, and a third from the 1850s. The jurors in these groups comprised all of the jurors who served in Abraham Lincoln's legal cases in the Sangamon County Circuit Court, the federal court in Springfield, and other local courts. Lincoln's entire law practice yielded a large enough sample for analysis, with the added benefit of being appropriately spread across the period being examined. It also provided a useful counterpoint to the complete picture of juror service in 1850 and 1860.[31]

The two groups of jurors from 1850 and 1860, combined with the three samplings of jurors from the 1830s, 1840s, and 1850s, offer an evenhanded account of juror demographics in Illinois during the antebellum period. Infused with a few of the interesting legal stories of the jurors themselves and of the cases in which they played such a pivotal role, the statistical analysis of the economic, social, professional, and political backgrounds of Sangamon County jurors illustrates their status as a group and contributes a key component to the larger arguments of this book. By the end of the chapter, an overall portrait of grand and petit juror demographics will emerge.

Grand and Petit Jurors in 1850

During the March, August, and November terms of the 1850 Sangamon County Circuit Court, the three grand juries handed down forty-seven indictments against forty-nine people, two of whom were women. The indictments involved fifteen different crimes, including murder, larceny, obstructing roads, and adultery. Twenty-three (49 percent) of the indictments related to issues of morality, including selling liquor or keeping a common gaming house. Eleven cases (23 percent) entailed crimes against property, such as larceny, and nine cases (19 percent) concerned obstruction of roads. The grand jurors in 1850 also indicted three people for assault and one for murder. Thirteen cases (28 percent) resulting from the forty-seven indictments were tried in 1850, which was a relatively fast turnaround for criminal indictments: it typically took more than one term of the circuit court for a judgment to be reached in a criminal trial. In six of those thirteen trials, juries found seven defendants guilty; in the remaining seven cases, another seven defendants were found not guilty.[32]

In 1850, some 63 percent of the fifty-seven grand jurors made their living as farmers, 12 percent were businessmen or professionals, and 12 percent worked in the skilled trades. The professionals included lawyers, doctors, and engineers. Individuals in the skilled trades were identified for this study as producers of items for the consumer market whose occupations required a high level of specific training and skills as well as the use of specialized tools. Carpenters, tailors, shoemakers, bookbinders, and harness makers, among others, made up this group. Labor classifications are certainly more complex than stated here, but for the purposes of this study, the categorization was sufficient.[33]

Two of the grand jurors in this sample were physicians, one was a printer, and another made wagons. The median age of this group was forty-nine. Fifty-four percent of the grand jurors were in their forties and fifties, but only 16 percent were in their twenties and thirties; grand jurors tended to be significantly older than their counterparts serving on trial juries. Even though state law barred men over sixty from jury service, ten (18 percent) of the grand jurors in 1850 were in fact in their sixties. Thirty-one (26 percent) of the grand jurors who served in 1850 were southerners by birth, eighteen (15 percent) were born in northern states, one was English, and another was Irish. Of the thirty-one southerners, eighteen—or 35 percent of those whose nativity is known—hailed from Kentucky. In 1850, eighteen (35 percent) of the grand jurors were living within Springfield, and the rest resided elsewhere in Sangamon County.[34]

The total real property holdings of the fifty-one grand jurors whose wealth is known was $208,650, for an average of over $4,000 per person and a median wealth of $3,000. Obviously, grand jurors were by and large older men who were well-established members of the community and affluent. The wealth of six grand jurors is not known, but it is interesting that only twelve (21 percent) of the jurors for whom wealth is known owned less than $1,000. Twenty-three (40 percent) held real property worth between $1,000 and $4,999. Six jurors reported no real property holdings to the 1850 census taker, but it is unlikely that they owned nothing, as the tax roles provided the county commissioners with the names of qualified jurors. Fifteen (12 percent) of the grand jurors held $5,000 or more in real property, making them some of the wealthiest residents of Sangamon County. The most affluent grand jurors in 1850 were A. Bowen Cass and John Penn. Both men operated large farms, each owning more than $16,000 in real property. Cass had been an early settler in the area, arriving in 1826 from Kentucky.[35]

Like the grand jurors, more than half of the one hundred and thirty petit jurors who served in 1850 were farmers. However, the petit juries had more men from the skilled trades and the laboring classes than did the grand juries. Eleven jurors were carpenters; five were shoemakers; and there was a bricklayer, a miller, a silversmith, and two laborers. Included among those who served in 1850 were a school commissioner, a butcher, and a stonecutter. Petit jurors were generally younger than grand jurors, averaging forty-four years of age. Only 55 percent of them were in their forties and fifties, and only 8 percent (about half that of the grand jurors) were in their sixties. Some 26 percent were in their twenties and thirties. Petit jurors who served in Sangamon County in 1850 had a combined wealth of $165,440, for an average of $1,993 per juror, roughly half as much as the average grand juror.[36]

Despite the fact that Illinois law disallowed (or exempted) licensed attorneys from serving on grand or petit juries, they *did* serve in Sangamon County. Eight licensed attorneys-at-law served on three different panels of jurors, and in two of those instances, lawyers made up more than half of the panel. Necessity probably dictated the use of attorneys, who were, of course, already present in the courtroom. If the judge wanted to dispense with a case at the end of the term, for example, he might suggest that a jury of bystanders be seated. With the agreement of the lawyers representing both sides in the case at hand, other lawyers in the court were called for this temporary jury service. Since lawyers attending court were known to the judge and to the attending court officials, there could be little doubt that they met the key qualifications for jury service, namely, county residence, age, citizenship, and moral character. Abraham Lincoln served on six juries during his career at the bar, and in two separate cases in 1850, attorneys comprised more than half of each jury. The service of lawyers may not have been legal, but it apparently was accepted practice among judges, lawyers, and litigants, as there were no appeals of judgments to the Illinois Supreme Court based on the participation of attorneys on trial juries.[37]

Antebellum Illinoisans likely relegated grand jury service to the community elites on purpose. Since grand jurors were the direct link between the community and the law and since they held the personal freedom of individuals in their hands, it was vital to seat responsible and competent individuals on these panels. Court officials in charge of developing lists of potential grand jurors, as well as the physical selection of jurors, might have believed that older, wealthier stakeholders in the community were better suited to the task of determining which alleged criminals would suffer indictments and with what crimes the court docket would be filled. The most mature, affluent, and well-respected members of the community—individuals with the biggest stake in its peace and prosperity—were therefore seen as the most qualified and most competent for service.[38]

Grand jurors may generally have been more affluent and prominent than their trial jury counterparts, but some of the most influential people in Sangamon County served at both levels. Those men included: James Bradford, a wealthy farmer; James Conkling, an attorney, Illinois state legislator, and member of the socially prominent Conkling clan; Sangamon County sheriff Josiah Francis; William Carpenter, a miller who was worth more than $20,000; Lucian B. Adams, deputy clerk of the Sangamon County Circuit Court; Antrim Campbell, an attorney and master in chancery; John Todd Stuart, an Illinois Whig who served in the state legislature and in the U.S. Congress; and another Whig party leader and lawyer named Abraham Lincoln. Sangamon County and especially Springfield boasted many prominent and wealthy residents, so the density of politically and economically powerful people in the county may have contributed to the high percentage of well-regarded jurors. However, Sangamon was also a populous county with a mix of residents—rich and poor, native-born and immigrant, prominent and ordinary—and as a result, a good number of nonelite individuals were considered qualified, competent, and available for service.[39]

More than one-quarter of the jurors who served in Sangamon County in 1850 were members of families who had been original settlers in the area. Given the mobility of the population of Sangamon and Springfield, that number seems fairly substantial. Granted, there were several jurors who were members of the laboring class, some who made their living as small farmers, and some who had only recently moved into the county. But the overwhelming majority of both grand and petit jurors were wealthy, were socially prominent, were members of powerful political and legal circles, or were closely related to the founding families of the communities in which they lived. The composition of Sangamon County jury panels defies the conclusion that antebellum frontier juries were egalitarian institutions because a very large percentage of the jurors were affluent community stakeholders. And there is little doubt that their influence and power within the community spilled into the jury box and the deliberation room as well.[40]

The notion of the right to be judged by one's peers was a fundamental political principle in antebellum America. As farming was the primary occupation in Sangamon at that time, grand and petit jurors mirrored the community in terms of their dominant means of economic survival. Many litigants and jurors shared farming as a common denominator. However, grand and petit jurors were more economically successful in that endeavor and owned more productive real property than did the typical Sangamon farmer who did not serve as a juror. On average, grand jurors were nearly twice as wealthy as petit jurors, but petit jurors were wealthier than Sangamon County men who were qualified but did not serve on juries. The average white, male, taxable citizens in the county owned $1,298 in real property, $695 less than the average petit juror. Jurors were men of property, not average residents.[41]

Following is a discussion of one case that illustrates the status difference between jurors and criminal defendants, highlighting the fact that a jury of peers was not the norm for criminal trials in antebellum Illinois. In August 1850, the grand jury indicted Eli Judd and Perlina Field for adultery. Judd was a forty-two-year-old, unlanded laborer who had moved to Illinois from Canada. There is no surviving record of the female defendant, but since she left no visible trace except for her name as a defendant in this case, it is probably safe to assume that she was not a wealthy, high-ranking member of the community. The grand jurors who indicted Judd and Field had combined real estate holdings of more than $50,000. For the most part, they were wealthy farmers, but one owned a lucrative Springfield boardinghouse; one was a physician; one was a moderately successful wagon maker; and another was Simeon Francis, publisher of the *Illinois Journal.* Eight were members of families who were original settlers to the county, and only one was an immigrant who became a naturalized U.S. citizen. Just days after the indictment, a jury of twelve men who owned a total of approximately $15,500 in real property (an average of $1,292 each) found Judd and Field guilty of adultery. Their sentence, unfortunately, is not known, but a typical fine in an antebellum adultery case was $50, which was likely more than the value of any personal property the defendants owned.[42]

Judd and Field were not members of the economic, social, and political elite. They were not influential. They were not affluent. They were, though, typical of many Sangamon County residents who experienced the judicial system in antebellum Illinois. The grand jurors who indicted them and the petit jurors who convicted them were far removed from the defendants' economic experiences. A large economic, social, and political divide existed between criminal defendants, on one hand, and the grand jurors who indicted them and the trial jurors who convicted them, on the other. Could the grand and trial jurors have empathized with the circumstances of the criminalized couple? Did the jurors employ their middle-class moral perceptions when they deliberated in the jury room? Would the jurors have indicted or convicted Judd and Field had the defendants been members of their own social and economic circle?

The answers to these questions are not known, of course, but the characteristics of Judd and Field as litigants and the contrasting characteristics of the grand and petit jurors who judged them aptly illustrate the differences between litigants and jurors in Sangamon County and, by extension, across the state and the region. Antebellum jurors in Sangamon were not egalitarian. They were not representative of the average inhabitant in the state. They were white, male property owners whose status as affluent, prominent, and influential residents of their counties set them far apart from the vast majority of those they judged. Grand and petit jurors, along with their associates at the bar and in the courthouses across the state, wielded tremendous power and had a marked impact on the legal system. And as a result of their involvement, the social, economic, political, and legal elites tightly controlled the trial-by-jury process in antebellum Illinois.

Grand and Petit Jurors in 1860

The status disparity between jurors and criminal defendants in 1860 was no different than it had been in 1850. In October 1860 in the Sangamon County Circuit Court in Springfield, the grand jury indicted Eliza Lucas, Margaret Lucas, and Robert Jones, three free blacks. The defendants stood charged with poisoning, with the intent to murder, two white men—William C. Huey and R. P. Officer—and their families. Authorities charged Eliza and Margaret, aged fourteen and fifteen, respectively, with the crime and indicted Robert Jones as the instigator of the "diabolical deed." At the time of the alleged incident, Eliza was living as a servant in the household of R. P. Officer, a twenty-eight-year-old lumber dealer in Springfield. Her sister, Margaret, was also living in Springfield but in the household of William Huey, a clerk. Authorities charged Robert Jones, a minor, with hatching the plot to poison the employers of the young girls and charged the girls with attempting to carry out the plan.[43]

The foreman of the grand jury at the time of the indictment was William Hickman, a wealthy landowner with $21,000 worth of real property. Hickman had served as a representative in the Illinois General Assembly and as a Sangamon County justice of the peace.[44] Other members of the panel included a Springfield doctor, a constable, the superintendent of the Sangamon County Almshouse, and five farmers. Five of the grand jurors possessed personal wealth of more than $15,000 each, the wealthiest being one of the farmers, Preston Gibson, who had combined real and personal holdings totaling $23,000. The median wealth of the sixteen jurors about whom wealth is known was $2,500. Thirteen of the grand jurors were residents of Springfield. The median age of the panel was forty-five. Nearly half of the twenty-three grand jurors who signed the indictment against the three defendants were politically active, eight had been candidates for public office, and six had won an election. The members impaneled in this term of the court were not recently arrived immigrant laborers who held little or no property or other wealth, and none of them was a servant like Eliza and Margaret. Rather, the jurors enjoyed wealth and came from established families with considerable real property and social and political influence.[45]

On October 31, Eliza and Margaret Lucas pleaded guilty to the charges, and the court sentenced them to one year in the county jail at hard labor. Robert Jones pleaded not guilty, so the court impaneled a jury to hear his case. William Herndon, Abraham Lincoln's law partner, defended Jones, appealing to the jurors to consider the boy's tender age in their deliberations. Although the trial jurors were less affluent and less socially prominent than the grand jurors who indicted in this case, the trial panel still consisted of one elected official, a former Sangamon County treasurer, one individual who held real and personal property totaling $26,000, and another with $14,780. Despite Herndon's pleas regarding his client's status as a minor, the jury found Jones guilty on November 8 and sentenced him to one year in the state penitentiary. The guilty pleas of the two girls had spared them from a jury trial and resulted in confinement in the county jail, a less harsh sentence than that handed down in Jones's case.[46]

The indictment against the three minors in the poisoning case was one of a handful of indictments of minor defendants submitted to the Sangamon County state's attorney during the antebellum period. Children were rarely indicted for offenses other than murder. It is important to note here that neither Huey nor Officer nor their families had experienced direct physical harm from the crime. In fact, there is no evidence that the defendants even carried out the plot to poison the alleged victims. Had the defendants been white, there is little doubt that the grand jury would not have handed down indictments. In the context of Illinois' stringent Black Laws—which restricted African American settlement and movement within the state—the crime itself, however unsuccessful, most likely furthered racial stereotypes and heightened racist feelings and beliefs. The race of the defendants may well have guaranteed the indictments against them.[47]

As for the trial jury's conviction of the black male defendant in the case, assumptions about race, gender, and class also likely played a role. In sentencing Robert Jones to a harsher penalty than the one handed down to the two girls, who had confessed, the trial jury was essentially placing more responsibility for the crime on the boy. Antebellum Illinois courts were less severe in their punishment of girls and women than of men and boys. But trial juries were hesitant to send male and female minors convicted of offenses other than murder to the penitentiary. It was much more common for them to confine convicted minors to brief stints in the county jail—unless, of course, they were African American. Certainly, Robert Jones's status as a black male trumped his status as a minor. This case highlights an obvious legal distinction between those situated in positions of power to enforce the law and the community will and those for whom positions of power were inconceivable. In Illinois, a free northern state, women and African Americans had a tenuous legal standing, and it was white men with property who controlled the legal system that governed the economic, social, and political structures of each community. The courtroom was a site at which community elites reinforced those boundaries. Within the legal system, there was no room for mitigating circumstances in criminal cases involving blacks, even when their status as minors was evident. White, elite control of the jury reflected the racism of the community's ruling elites and of society at large.[48]

By 1860, Sangamon County had grown to more than thirty thousand residents. Women, children, and free blacks made up 73 percent of the youthful and vibrant population of the still expanding, agriculturally based home county of the bustling urban center of Springfield, the state capital. And though the composition of jury panels did not reflect the general population, it did reflect the general characteristics of Sangamon

County's ruling elites. Of the men who served on grand and petit juries during that year, 83 percent possessed real property worth at least $1,000, and 38 percent were worth more than $5,000. By contrast, most individuals residing in the county did not own any real property at all. Granted, nearly one-fifth of all jurors who served had economic circumstances that were more like those of the community as a whole—yet they were overwhelmed numerically by jurors who possessed substantially more wealth than men who did not serve on juries. The median wealth of grand jurors was $5,000 (with a high of $61,000 and a low of $300), and for petit jurors it was $3,225 (high of $26,000, low of $50). The median wealth of the county residents who did not serve as jurors was $1,300.

Joseph Inslee, Horace Hickox, and Gershom Keyes were like many of the jurors who served in 1860. Keyes was a farmer from Virginia who possessed $17,000 in real and personal property. Inslee was a sixty-three-year-old farmer from New York who owned more than $14,000 in real property. He was an active Whig and was a delegate to the 1847 Illinois State Constitutional Convention. Hickox was a prosperous miller from Connecticut worth $4,000. He and his wife, Sarah, housed several boarders and were engaged in many civic activities. Keyes had been a Sangamon resident for more than twenty years and was a former mayor of Springfield. He was an active member of the county Whig Party and was engaged in civic and political events in Springfield. During the 1840s and 1850s, Keyes served on at least half a dozen trial juries in the Sangamon County Circuit Court, and both Inslee and Hickox had a history of prior service as well.[49]

As previously stated, farming was the most common occupation of heads of households in Illinois. However, it is striking that farmers who served on juries had more real wealth than those who did not serve. Forty-three percent of grand and petit jurors who served in the Sangamon circuit court in 1860 were farmers, but the median real wealth of those farmers who served was $4,600 and their median real and personal combined wealth $5,600, much more than the holdings of the average Sangamon County farmer. Evidently, farmers who served as jurors were prominent landowners with considerable wealth.[50]

Twenty-five percent of the jurors were skilled craftsmen or laborers, and 16 percent were businessmen. Of the 127 jurors whose occupations are known, ten were carpenters, seven were merchants, six were court or public officials, three were doctors, and one was a law student. Individuals classified as businessmen in this study were proprietors of retail and wholesale establishments and either service providers or middlemen in the market exchange between producers (skilled craftsmen and farmers) and consumers. This group consisted of dry goods merchants, distributors of agricultural machinery, bankers, and hotelkeepers, among others. Public officials were constables, clerks, and justices of the peace. Also included among the jurors who served in 1860 were a laborer, a railroad engineer, a bridge builder, and a "gentleman."

Generally speaking, grand and petit jurors were either prosperous farmers, independent professionals, or public servants. Slightly more petit jurors were farmers, but in 1860, there were fewer occupational differences between grand and petit jurors than there had been in 1850. This observation suggests a growing degree of wealth and influence among the men who were chosen to fill trial jury panels and a lessening of distinctions between the status of grand and petit jurors over time. Interestingly, twenty of the men who served as jurors in Sangamon County in 1860 reported no real property in the federal census, even though Illinois statute barred individuals without real property from serving. Perhaps the census taker neglected to record the information or the head of the household intentionally declined to report landownership. Contrary to statute, however, some unlanded individuals did serve. Illinois law also prohibited court officials from jury service, but court clerks, sheriffs, deputy sheriffs, constables, and even justices of the peace nonetheless served on juries during the mid-nineteenth century. For example, William Hickman, the grand jury foreman in October 1860, was a sitting justice of the peace. As with lawyers who served on juries, the service of other such exempted individuals probably was dictated by convenience and was generally accepted and unchallenged.[51]

Such oddities of jury composition were the exception, however, and not the rule. There was a close correlation between wealth and community leadership and between professional occupation and community leadership in antebellum America. Given those relationships, it is safe to assume that wealthy professional men who served on juries were, in fact, community leaders. And community leaders enjoyed economic, political, and social power. Obviously, there was some overlap among economic and social elites. Wealth certainly played a role in elevating individuals socially, and various occupations brought many individuals both wealth and social standing. Generally speaking, male social elites possessed considerable real property and were members of the landed gentry or engaged in professional, self-supporting occupations. They were not, say, farm laborers. More than 75 percent of the jurors who served in 1860 were heads of households with wives and children. Few unmarried men served as jurors, since single men typically were less established and more transient.[52]

The demographic data regarding jurors in Sangamon County reveal a good deal about community stability and persistence. An impressive number of grand and petit jurors who served in 1850 and 1860 were either community residents for twenty or more years or close family members of original settlers in the county or both. Some 82 percent of the jurors who served (and for whom settlement in the community is known) had resided in the county for at least ten years, and 60 percent had settled in the area at least twenty years prior to their service. Members of long-established Sangamon County families sat on juries in the antebellum period and served far more frequently than did more recent arrivals. In this group were the sons of some of Sangamon's earliest settlers and the most prominent men in the community. They included James Y. Alkire, whose father, Harmonious Alkire, was among the county's first settlers; Elijah F. Iles, whose uncle, Elijah Iles, was the founder of Springfield; and Madison Cartwright, a son of Peter Cartwright, a well-known and long-standing Methodist Episcopal reverend. One scholar has found that a large proportion of residents in Springfield during the antebellum period had higher persistence rates than contemporaries in other parts of the country. Springfield was a relatively stable community, and that persistence was reflected in the jury box as well.[53]

Typically, older men in the community held more leadership roles and commanded more authority. Although men in their twenties and thirties did serve on antebellum Illinois juries, the median age was forty-eight (the oldest was seventy, the youngest nineteen) for grand jurors and forty-two (oldest seventy-two, youngest twenty-two) for petit jurors. Only three grand jurors (7 percent) were under thirty years of age, and only 15 of the petit jurors (18 percent) were in their twenties. In this regard, jury composition in Sangamon County violated the statutory age requirement at both ends of the range of twenty-one to sixty, further indicating that the community elites who controlled the jury process made exceptions to the rules to permit younger and older members of elite society to serve in spite of the legal stipulation. Except for the involvement of licensed attorneys and court officials on juries, there is no evidence to suggest that Sangamon County jury composition regularly violated other statutory requirements pertaining to juror service. However, it is likely that a handful of jurors owned no property at the time of their service and that one or two individuals who served were not naturalized citizens.[54]

Many Sangamon County jurors also belonged to the community's political elite. Nearly a third of all who served in 1860 ran for or won public office, secured a political appointment, or participated in local party politics such as party organization or campaign meetings for other candidates. A larger number of grand jurors were so engaged. Among the elected public offices Sangamon jurors had held were Illinois state representative, city alderman, mayor, justice of the peace, city treasurer, constable, sheriff, and county judge. In addition, many jurors had held politically appointed positions such as city wood inspector, land office receiver, bridge commissioner, and city jailor.

A Brief Comparison of Service in 1850 and 1860

Grand and petit jurors who served in 1860 differed little from those who served a decade earlier. Grand jurors were slightly older than petit jurors in both years. The median age of each group decreased slightly from 1850 to 1860—grand jurors from 49 years to 45 years and petit jurors from 44 years to 41.5 years. Most jurors who served either on grand or petit juries were in their thirties and forties. The occupations of the jurors were also similar, with the overwhelming majority earning their livelihoods from farming. Still, there was a slight increase over time in the number of businessmen and professionals and of those in the skilled trades who were seated in the jury box at Sangamon County Circuit Court. By 1860, there was a 6 percent increase in the number of businessmen and professionals who served and a 2 percent increase in the number of those engaged in a skilled trade.

Grand jurors in 1860, like their counterparts ten years before, were wealthier than those who served as petit jurors during the same time. What is interesting, however, is that jurors overall were becoming more wealthy. Even with the more frequent use of bystander jurors—whom some antebellum observers accused of being young, unemployed men—the wealth of jurors as a whole was climbing.[55] In 1850, some 56 percent of Sangamon County jurors owned $1,000 or more in real property and 20 percent owned $5,000 or more. In 1860, those percentages rose, with 61 percent owning $1,000 or more and 30 percent owning $5,000 or more. This change may have reflected an overall increase of the wealth of all Sangamon County residents, but it is also possible that elites were gaining more control over grand and trial juries.

Jurors in the county were more likely to have been born in the southern United States, especially in Kentucky, than anywhere else. Only thirteen jurors in the sample from 1850 and 1860 were foreign born—three jurors each hailed from Germany, Ireland, and Scotland; two jurors were English; and one each came from Canada and France. Jurors impaneled in trials in the Sangamon County Circuit Court were also most likely to be residents of Springfield or outlying towns. Far fewer were from rural, more remote areas of the county. In 1850, some 61 percent of the trial jurors resided within the Springfield city limits, compared with 65 percent ten years later. Only 41 percent of all the grand jurors who served during both years lived in Springfield. Perhaps in the seating of grand jurors, the court officials were more careful to pull from all areas of the county in an effort to be more representative. Perhaps grand jurors, especially those who were wealthier and more established than petit jurors, had more free time to spend at court. Whatever the reason, it is clear that grand juries represented more communities outside of Springfield than did trial juries.

In sum, the data show that throughout the antebellum period, elites dominated grand jury rooms and petit jury boxes in Sangamon County Circuit Court. Affluent professionals with social status and active engagement in party politics served with great frequency. Except for the fact that elites more fully dominated grand juries in 1860, the elite composition of grand and petit juries in Illinois was relatively steady over the years. Older, wealthy, socially connected citizens were active participants in the legal system in antebellum Illinois as both grand and trial jurors.

A Composite Portrait of Antebellum Jurors in Sangamon County

Crunching the numbers of juror demographics reveals the various characteristics of a representative juror. Combining that demographic makeup with some biographical information gives us a sharper portrait of typical jurors who served in antebellum Illinois. Zachariah Peter and William C. Foley are two such jurors, and the case of *Luckett v. Garvey* illustrates the nature of most trial-by-jury cases that jurors such as Peter and Foley heard. Although not as sensational as the poisoning case presented earlier, the *Luckett* case was far more characteristic of the cases for which most antebellum Illinois jurors returned verdicts.

Zachariah Peter was like most petit jurors who served in Sangamon County in that period. He was a native-born southerner, made his living as a farmer, and was in his thirties when he sat as a juror. In 1850, he owned $1,700 worth of real property, just $100 more than the median wealth of jurors who served during the 1850s. Peter was born in Virginia in 1781 and moved in 1818 to Sangamon County in the newly formed state of Illinois. He married six years later. In 1826 and 1827, he purchased 236 acres of public land in the county, and he continued to accumulate real estate throughout the 1830s and 1840s. He ran (unsuccessfully) for the state legislature as an independent Whig in 1820, 1826, and 1832. In 1846, he was again a candidate for public office, this time as a delegate to the Illinois Constitutional Convention of 1847. Although he never won election to office, he remained active in Whig politics.[56]

Like most antebellum Americans, Zachariah Peter paid debts with promissory notes and received payments for debts with such negotiable instruments. It was common at the time for debtors and creditors to end up in court over the trading of notes, and Peter periodically sued debtors who failed to satisfy their notes. In fact, between 1838 and 1844, he retained the legal services of Abraham Lincoln and filed ten different lawsuits to collect various debts. In those ten cases, Lincoln was successful in obtaining judgments in favor of his client. In another case, Peter was a defendant in criminal court, accused of assault, and Lincoln succeeded in quashing the indictment against his client. Most jurors were not defendants in criminal cases, but like Peter, they *were* familiar with the legal system. It was quite common for them to have served on previous jury panels or to have been involved with litigation in civil actions.[57]

Peter served as a petit juror in at least twenty cases in Sangamon County between 1838 and 1859. Interestingly, in fourteen of those cases, the attorney of the winning litigant was a client of Abraham Lincoln's. In one case, the jury returned a $2,300 judgment for Lincoln's client. We can only speculate as to how Zachariah Peter's connection to an attorney in the cases in which he served as a juror might have affected his service. There are no clues from the deliberations in the jury room, nor is other source material available that might shed any light on his personal experiences as a juror. But it is difficult indeed to ignore the connection. The salient point is that such connections were not uncommon. Because of their status within the community, jurors often were well acquainted with the attorneys, judges, court officials, and sometimes even the litigants in the cases they were judging.[58]

Although wealthier than Peter, William Foley was another typical Sangamon County juror. Foley made his living as a carpenter and held $6,200 in real and personal wealth. He made Springfield his home when he arrived from Virginia in 1838. Foley married Elizabeth Hutchinson two years later, and like most jurors of the period, he was the head of his household. He had campaigned for a constable position at one time, and he served on at least twenty-four jury panels between 1844 and 1860. His business success within the community, his persistence as a resident in the county seat, and his involvement with politics and the legal system made him a perfect candidate for jury service.[59]

Both Zachariah Peter and William Foley compiled impressive records of jury service, reaping the benefits of the small fees paid to jurors. And given their repeat service, they presumably enjoyed and appreciated the experience as well. Some of the individuals whose cases the two men heard from their vantage point in the jury box were Archer G. Herndon, a onetime member of the Illinois General Assembly and a receiver of public moneys in the land office at Springfield; John Taylor, a member of the Springfield Board of Trustees and commissioner of the state bank; William Duff, a small farmer; and the Sangamon County commissioners. The cases they heard as jurors involved, among other matters, trespass, divorce, replevin, forgery, and larceny. The majority of their cases, however, were suits related to various debts or disputes between neighbors, such as the one between Harriett Luckett and Samuel Garvey.[60]

In early 1850, Samuel Garvey trespassed on the land of Harriet Luckett in Sangamon County and damaged some of her property. The details of the damage are unknown, but a portion of the legal records of Luckett's case against Garvey survives. In March, Luckett hired the Springfield law firm of Abraham Lincoln and William H. Herndon and sued Garvey in the August term of the Sangamon County Circuit Court for trespass, asking for damages. On August 29, a jury of twelve men heard the evidence, found Garvey guilty of trespassing, awarded Luckett $38.97 in damages, and ordered Garvey to pay the court costs. Both Garvey, age twenty-five, and Luckett, age fifty, made their living as farmers, although Luckett held $3,500 in real property to Garvey's $800. Native-born Springfield landholders held real property averaging just $1,573, so Luckett appears to have been doing quite well; for his part, Garvey, who was newly married, was making a good start in life.[61]

The plaintiff in this case enjoyed the status of an established landholder who had lived in the county since at least 1840. She possessed the means to hire legal counsel and cover the court fees entailed in a lawsuit. The defendant was younger, but he too had roots in the community, having settled as a boy in Sangamon County with his parents in 1830. Although he was less affluent than Luckett, he was able to pay $60 of the $64.15 in court fees associated with the lawsuit against him. Whether he was able to pay the legal fees of the two prominent attorneys handling his case or the jury-awarded damages to Luckett is unknown. Of the panel of petit jurors who served in the case of *Luckett v. Garvey,* more than half were farmers, half resided in Springfield, and over half were members of established and prominent Springfield or Sangamon County families. The median wealth of this panel was $1,150; the median age was 46.5 years. Two of the jurors had served in the Illinois General Assembly, one was elected to the Springfield City Council two years after serving on this jury, and another was a successful carpenter from one of the county's founding families.[62]

The gulf between jurors and litigants in civil cases was less obvious than the differences between jurors and defendants in criminal cases. Unlike Perlina Field and the black servant girls described earlier in the chapter, most civil litigants were not especially vulnerable. Samuel Garvey risked losing money in the civil suit that his neighbor had filed against him, but his personal liberties were not at stake. Jurors in civil suits had less physical power over litigants, but they still influenced the parties' lives via the rendering of verdicts with potentially serious financial consequences. In common-law courts, jurors delivered verdicts in various types of civil disputes between residents of the communities in which they lived. They understood how valuable it was to settle disputes peacefully, and they played a vital role in their communities as a result. Jurors weighed evidence and determined judgments through the lens of their personal experiences, and there is little doubt that their economic, professional, social, and political status in the community affected their responsibilities as jurors. Their life circumstances also filtered into the meaning and perceptions they brought to the jury box and into the deliberation rooms of circuit courts across Illinois and the emerging Midwest.

The personal experiences and worldviews of antebellum jurors in Sangamon County derived from the elite, white, male perspective of a developing middle-class ethos. Chosen from a high-ranking group of only the most legally "competent," those who served were more representative of the controlling community elites than of the general populace. Jurors in Sangamon County Circuit Court from 1830 to 1860 were for the most part affluent, middle-aged farmers with families; they had considerable real estate holdings and were members of prominent, persistent families within the community and not recent immigrants. They were community leaders who were engaged in local, state, and national party politics, some even holding elective office. In addition, they were connected to the economic and political establishments by way of their social status, professional affiliations, or business-related economic activities. Grand jurors were wealthier than those who served on petit juries, and petit jurors were wealthier than members of the community who did not serve on juries at all. Sangamon County jurors were the ruling professional, economic, social, and political elites of their community. Given that juries operated as conduits of community power, it would be naive to argue that juror status was irrelevant in courthouses throughout Illinois and the emerging Midwest.

THREE

The Work of Jurors in the Antebellum Illinois Courtroom

WHAT WAS it like to serve on a jury in antebellum Illinois? What did jurors do? What cases did they hear? What types of verdicts did they render? And what did jury verdicts mean for defendants and civil litigants who were subject to them? This chapter seeks to address such questions and to provide some answers about the service of jurors and the meaning of their power to deliver legal decisions that directly affected those who entered the courthouse as parties in civil and criminal cases. The chapter describes jury trials and demonstrates the function of the institution of the jury and of individual jurors within the legal structure. The trial cases of Abraham Lincoln provide the legal evidence, and the litigants, lawyers, judges, and jurors give a human connection to the midwestern legal past. The stories of courtroom trials and jury box experiences show how the jury was a vital link between society and the law. Jury trials in the mid-nineteenth century were central to the development of legal processes, and the jurors were witnesses to and historical actors in this evolution during a formative era of American law.

The discussion of jury experience begins with the legal story of one ordinary American family and proceeds with a brief examination of the work performed by the grand jury. Grand jurors were the community's most important and direct connection to the legal structure, and their work within the criminal justice system is instructive. The discussion then turns to trial jury panels in criminal cases. After some analysis of criminal cases and verdicts, the chapter investigates the role of jury service in civil cases, particularly those involving the ever-present creditor-debtor relationships that preoccupied both society and the courts in this time period. Throughout the discussion, the focus is on the experience of jury service, the competence of jury panels, and the meaning of jury verdicts. Although some quantitative data from Lincoln's law practice ground the analysis, much of the narrative presents specific anecdotal evidence in order to paint a vivid image of the working jury system in antebellum Illinois and of broader midwestern legal experiences as well.

The Crow Family and the Jury System in Illinois

On March 26, 1851, Charles Gardner left his home on the northeast corner of Sixth and Market streets near downtown Springfield and traveled to the Sangamon County courthouse. Gardner, a trader by profession, owned real property valued at $10,000, making him one of Springfield's wealthiest men. The neighborhood in which his house stood was also home to banker John Irwin and merchant Virgil Hickox, two of the city's most prominent residents. Given the chilly March weather and his economic and social status, Gardner probably took a horse-drawn carriage down the three blocks on Sixth Street that morning, on his way to take his seat in the jury box in Sangamon County Circuit Court.[1]

Gardner was no stranger to the courtroom, having served as a juror in at least five other cases in three previous terms of the circuit court.[2] During the 1840s, he had also been a plaintiff in five cases and a defendant in another.[3] In the antebellum Midwest, jurors were often familiar with the courtroom and legal proceedings because a large number of them had been litigants in civil trials. In fact, many jurors were merchants and businessmen who exhibited a penchant for civil litigation. Given the economic difficulties midwesterners faced in that era, debt suits were common, with businesses frequently suing debtors to collect payments owed on various products and services that had been purchased on credit. As the law and the economy converged in this context, creditors were often plaintiffs in local debt litigation.[4]

When Gardner arrived at the courthouse that morning, he took his seat in the jury box with eleven other men: Abraham Lincoln; Stephen T. Logan, an attorney and former judge; Silas W. Robbins, another Springfield attorney; Erastus Wright, a wealthy land agent and former school commissioner; Elliot B. Herndon, attorney and brother of William H. Herndon, Lincoln's law partner; Thomas Moffett, an attorney and sitting Sangamon County judge; William Thomas Gibbon, a Springfield shoemaker; A. B. McMurray, a prosperous Sangamon farmer; J. B. West; G. A. West; and William Foster.[5] At least nine of these jurors, including Gardner, were community elites. Although Illinois state law barred licensed attorneys from serving as jurors, there were actually five lawyers on Gardner's panel. As previously noted, this situation was not uncommon. While he was a practicing attorney, Lincoln, for example, served as a trial juror in three other cases and as a juror in at least five writs of inquiry proceedings between 1837 and 1861.[6]

When attorneys did serve as jurors, it was often on a panel that was assembled by the court to assess damages in a case already decided by default. Thus, in 1852, Lincoln served as foreman of a jury assessing damages for an unpaid debt. Although the defendant had retained counsel, he ultimately defaulted, and Judge David Davis created an ad hoc jury from bystanders to determine what the plaintiff was due. Lincoln was one of three attorneys who served on that panel. Interestingly, his law partner William Herndon was the attorney for the defendant in the case. Few of our modern notions about conflicts of interest were part of legal practice and procedure in nineteenth-century courtrooms.[7]

Charles Gardner was acquainted with most, if not all, of his fellow jurors. As law partners, Stephen Logan and Lincoln had represented him in four lawsuits in the 1840s, and Gardner had sued Thomas Moffett for a debt in 1842. He also sued Erastus Wright for a debt a year later, and Wright subsequently testified against Gardner in yet another debt case. In 1844, Gardner was a juror in a case in which Silas Robbins and Elliot Herndon were defendant attorneys. Obviously, then, Gardner was acquainted with all these individuals from his contact with the legal system, but it is also probable that he knew them and the other members of the jury through his business dealings or social interactions.[8]

On that court day in March 1851, Charles Gardner sat in his straight, wooden seat in the jury box and heard the petition of William Crow. There is little doubt that Gardner knew the petitioner, who was a member of a prominent family that owned a Sangamon County mill. In antebellum courtrooms, even in larger counties such as Sangamon, court officers, lawyers, civil litigants, and jurors were normally acquainted with each other, and more often than not, they were friends, neighbors, business associates, or political allies or enemies. The Crows and their mill business were well known, and the members of the jury likely knew the thirty-eight-year-old William Crow and his brother David, who was the focus of their attention that day. David Crow, age forty-three, had become so debilitated by mental illness that he could no longer care for himself. Many people in the community must have been aware of this heartbreaking family problem, and it was probably no secret to most that William was in court to seek the appointment of a conservator to act as a legal guardian for his brother and manage his affairs.[9]

According to Illinois law, family members and creditors of "idiots, lunatics, and persons distracted" could petition the circuit court for the appointment of a conservator, and a jury had the right to determine the mental health of the allegedly insane person. On that March morning, it was the duty of Gardner and his fellow jurors to assess the mental status of David Crow and to appoint a conservator on his behalf if they found, based on the evidence presented, that he was indeed incompetent. Consequently, the jury heard the evidence, declared David Crow insane, and ordered his other brother, Edward Crow, to act as his conservator.[10]

Rendering judgment in this type of case was one of the major functions of juries in the nineteenth century. The legal status of the allegedly incompetent person was thus in the hands of a panel of citizens who had the power to take away that individual's right to manage his or her own personal and economic affairs. The mentally disabled person had no right to an attorney and was at the mercy of the evidence presented—evidence submitted, at times, by a creditor—and the jury's decision. In this case, the petitioner was a member of a leading family with wealth in a lucrative mill and the mentally incompetent individual was his brother. There is no historical evidence to explain David Crow's illness, so we can only speculate about his condition. We do know, however, that at the time of the petition, he was living in the household of his sixty-nine-year-old widowed mother, who was probably his primary caregiver.

In the Crows' case, it is likely that the disabled person had a family who loved him and acted responsibly on his behalf. But this type of jury proceeding could potentially be used by an unscrupulous person to advance a fraudulent or vindictive petition. Although this role of the trial-by-jury system may have been set up to protect the rights of insane or otherwise disabled individuals, the circumstances of a particular case could have put the supposedly incompetent person in a serious legal predicament. The power of the jury in this regard was profound.[11]

The Crow family's case was only one of the more than one thousand jury trials in Abraham Lincoln's twenty-five-year law practice, each of which offers a window into the experience of juror service across central Illinois. Individual legal documents, crafted in dry, formulaic language, might not on the surface appear to provide much information about courtroom experiences, but taken together, they do in fact convey a wealth of detail about the cases jurors heard and the various legal problems and situations that faced different kinds of criminal defendants and civil litigants. Through those documents, we see that women, poor laborers, slaves, free blacks, children, and immigrants were parties in numerous cases heard in antebellum midwestern courtrooms, and the jury decisions that were pronounced there had direct and sometimes profound impacts on their lives. Jury trials occurred in justice of the peace courts, circuit courts, and federal courts throughout Illinois, from as far north as Galena in Jo Daviess County to as far south as Shawneetown in Gallatin County.[12]

The jurors in these trials returned verdicts in cases involving, among other issues, debt, trespass, slander, replevin, appeals of railroad rights-of-way, seduction, divorce, mechanics' liens, and crimes ranging from larceny to murder. Some of the most common legal actions in jury trials from Lincoln's practice related to assumpsit (237 cases), trespass (164), slander (51), replevin (41), appeals of railroad rights-of-way (14), seduction (3), divorce (16), and mechanics' liens (15). There were also 147 criminal jury trials, including 25 murder cases and 23 larceny cases.

The outcomes of trials—from simple debt cases to murder prosecutions—were frequently crucial to the litigants. Verdicts could, after all, affect an individual's physical freedom or economic circumstances. And though judges, lawyers, and witnesses could certainly influence trial outcomes, the ultimate power rested with the jurors.[13]

The Work of the Grand Jury

It makes sense to focus first on the experience of grand jurors because they were responsible for determining which crimes the state's attorney would prosecute in a given term and because they had the most direct power over local residents. The circuit court grand jury was charged with applying the muscle of the legal system to the eradication of certain criminal behaviors within the community. Grand jury indictments for crimes such as the illegal sale of alcohol would often appear in clusters at a particular term of a circuit court, revealing the social concerns of genteel society at that moment in the community's history. But even if grand jurors were in a position of great influence, law and tradition regulated their jury work and experience. Once chosen for a panel, the jurors swore an oath to uphold the law pertaining to their service. The foreman of the grand jury solemnly pledged to "diligently enquire into, and true presentment make, of all such matters and things as [were given him without]" without "fear, favor or affection, or for any fee or reward." The court also swore in the other members of the typically twenty-four-man panel. State laws required grand jurors to be above bribery and undue influence and to uphold the sacred ideal that they were protectors of individual freedom and liberty as well as American democracy.[14]

Service on a grand jury was a prime way for residents of a community to participate in law enforcement. Since frontier grand juries had the ability to regulate the community's notion of what crimes would be prosecuted and what trials would be heard, they were, as one scholar has noted, "effective sounding boards in making known the desires of the people and served as a curb upon the activities of public officials."[15] Grand jurors were particularly involved because they had administrative duties as well. For instance, they inspected the jails and made reports about conditions there. "In democratic theory and in law, grand jury duty imposed an obligation on all white adult males to take part in governing their community."[16]

After a grand jury was seated, the judge normally offered a charge to the jurors, defining their responsibilities. Such charges were infused with democratic rhetoric about the sacred task that the jurors had before them. These speeches from the bench, which sometimes sounded remarkably like political stumping, were filled with cautions and reminders. Grand jurors were lectured about the significance of the institution of the jury and about the trust that society vested in them and their fellow panelists. In the 1850s, David Davis, a circuit judge in Illinois, delivered just such a charge:

> Let me urge you to inquire whether there are any gambling houses, or quart doggeries in the County. I presume that in Springfield whoever retails liquor has a legal license to keep a grocery. There may be places, however, in the Co. where the law is evaded by pretending to sell a quart when a less quantity is really sold. Such pretences will not avail; & such conduct should not be tolerated. There can be no greater nuisance than a quart doggery. It leads to idleness, vice, gambling & drunkenness & immorality of every kind. The youth of the Country should not be subject to the temptations afforded by such places; & you, as conservators of the morals of the county should see that the sin of their continuance [is] not at your door.[17]

Impassioned charges to grand juries revealed the worldviews of the judges who delivered them. They also reflected the social concerns of the middle-class community at large. After hearing a sermon on the evils of liquor and the duties of grand jurors to protect the morality of the county, the jurors were given license to seek out and return indictments against gross violators of the law. One grand juror wrote about a panel on which he served, noting that there was "a strict search being made to find out the offenders who kept gameing houses [because] there was considerable excitement about the dram shops [and] constant gambling."[18] As a result, grand jurors and then trial jurors became conduits of community power and policing by doing what white, middle-class citizens perceived as necessary for the maintenance of public safety and social decency. By returning true bills to the criminal court, grand jurors had the power to focus the legal energy of their community on individuals who allegedly jeopardized the local quality of life. After members of a grand jury took their oaths, they listened as the state's attorney presented his cases and then determined whether to indict individuals on criminal charges.

The grand jury of each circuit court met during the court term to hear presentments regarding various crimes committed within the community. For example, during the March 1850 term of the Sangamon County Circuit Court, the grand jury returned fifteen true bills, all signed by the foreman, A. G. Henry, a prominent Springfield physician. Periodically throughout the term, the grand jury would return indictments, and the circuit clerk would place the cases on the criminal docket. Most of the cases would begin during the same term, and a small percentage of these would also conclude in that term. The grand jury indicted sixteen people for crimes ranging from larceny to murder in the March 1850 term.[19]

The nature of a grand juror's work placed him in a position to determine the legal future of an alleged criminal. When an indictment was returned, the defendant faced fines, jail time, or both. Therefore, the jurors had enormous power over the economic future and personal freedom of an individual who came before them. In rare circumstances, defendants were established residents in a community: Delos W. Brown, to cite one instance, was a successful farmer with real property valued at $3,600 when the Sangamon County grand jury indicted him in 1850 for the illegal sale of liquor. However, most criminal defendants had limited economic and social ties to the community. As demonstrated in chapter 2, grand jurors were drawn from the county's most wealthy and socially well-connected families. Henry's grand jury was no exception, for the average and median age of these jurors was fifty-one, their average wealth was $2,600, and their median wealth was $2,100.[20]

By contrast, individuals who faced criminal indictment were generally younger and far less affluent than the grand jurors who indicted them; in fact, the social and economic gap between these groups was vast. In one term of the Sangamon circuit court, the defendants' average age was thirty and their median wealth only $450; four of the people indicted in March 1850 reported no wealth at all. Only nine of the sixteen individuals indicted that term appeared in the 1850 census. Therefore, most or all of the nine were not likely long-established residents. Legal records regarding grand jury presentments that did not result in criminal indictments have not survived, so we cannot know anything about those the grand jurors failed to indict. All we can conclude from the surviving evidence is that criminal defendants tended to be young, unestablished people who had few, if any, ties to the communities in which they were indicted.[21]

The Criminal Defendant and the Jury

After grand juries returned indictments, trial jurors had the power to determine the legal remedies and impose the legal and economic penalties on those found guilty of threatening the peace and tranquility of the community. In many cases, criminal defendants were immigrants from Ireland or Germany or were of Irish or German descent. Illinois residents Peter Gutzweller of Alton, Frederick Grosberrit of Mount Pulaski, Morris Kane of Decatur, Thomas Maloney of Clinton, David Salzenstein of Pleasant Plains, and Patrick Sullivan of Macon County were just a few of the immigrants who found themselves in the criminal courts.[22]

Alcohol consumption was one of the top social issues of the nineteenth century, and the antebellum preoccupation with the issue demonstrated the ideals of the developing white middle class. The temperance movement epitomized the growing social chasm between the emerging professional, middle-class person and the poor, laboring immigrant. It also fed into American politics, culminating with the birth of the Know-Nothing Party in the 1850s. The rhetoric of temperance and Know-Nothing politics emphasized the degraded status of alcoholic immigrants—staggering Irish and German laborers who beat their wives, failed to provide for their families, and contributed to the ever-expanding criminal element in society. Stereotypes about hard-drinking, low-class immigrants infused the legal as well as the social and political systems. During the 1840s and 1850s, alcohol-related cases were frequently listed on midwestern circuit court dockets. The criminal defendants faced charges of public drunkenness and selling liquor in illegal quantities, on the Sabbath, or without a license.[23] Alcohol consumption also played a role in family law and vigilante justice. Midwestern petitioners of the era often filed for divorce on the grounds of habitual drunkenness, and radical temperance advocates were sued in civil court for the destruction of distilleries and of liquor supplies kept in local groceries. These vigilantes also landed in criminal courts as defendants in riot cases. In some locales, grand juries targeted criminal liquor cases as part of an effort to eradicate particular social and economic problems they connected to "demon rum."[24]

A majority of the criminal cases involving the illegal sale of liquor did not go to a jury, since many defendants pleaded guilty and accepted their fines. But in the liquor cases that did reach a jury, the jurors tended to return guilty verdicts. If an individual faced such an indictment, he or she was virtually guaranteed to pay a fine, ranging from $10 to $75. In Lincoln's law practice, there were twelve jury trials regarding the illegal sale of alcohol, and all but three of the defendants (one of whom was a woman) were convicted and subjected to fines and, in some cases, jail time.[25] One of those convicted was Irish immigrant Patrick Sullivan. He was charged with selling liquor in illegal quantities, and a jury convicted him under the Illinois criminal code and fined him $10. Although Sullivan appealed his conviction to the Illinois Supreme Court, his conviction was upheld.[26]

To the developing middle class, social "problems" such as gambling and alcohol consumption endangered the fabric of a community. Gambling and liquor were often linked together in tippling houses, which some residents perceived as detrimental to morality and social decency. A tippling house—known today as a saloon, tavern, or bar—was often the scene of the illegal sale of alcohol, cardplaying, gambling, prostitution, brawling, rioting, and other activities that many citizens considered loud, obnoxious, and corrupting influences on community values. Residents often deemed these businesses public nuisances and took the law into their own hands to shut them down. The public outcry applied pressure on community leaders to enforce laws and to enact new ones to curtail such unseemly behaviors.[27]

Some communities, among them Petersburg, Illinois, were zealous in their efforts to eradicate gambling and other vices. A cluster of criminal indictments, followed by a series of jury trials in that community, provides an interesting example of how jurors exerted community power over unsavory elements in their midst. On May 22, 1844, the president and trustees of Petersburg passed an ordinance banning unlawful gaming and riotous conduct in groceries; the measure also prohibited such businesses from opening on Sundays. Thereafter, when the town issued licenses to local grocers, the merchants were required to sign over a $500 bond to the city to guarantee that their establishments would adhere to the ordinance. For example, George S. Pillsbury and Richard W. Goldsby, who operated a grocery known as the Red Church on the south side of the public square in Petersburg, presented a bond to the city promising to "keep an orderly house" and prevent "any unlawful gaming or riotous conduct therein." Basically, the law declared all groceries a "nuisance" and subjected all of them to security bonds, which gave the city the right to fine them and sue them in civil courts. The bonds acted as de facto licenses, and establishments that operated without them could be subject to civil and criminal action.[28]

An early test of the law came in October 1844 when town officials cited Chester Moon for violating the law and fined him $10 and, subsequently, $80 more for eight additional violations. When Moon failed to pay the fines, the city sued him in a local justice of the peace court, where a jury found in favor of the defendant. The city appealed, and a Menard County Circuit Court jury overturned the lower court judgment, ordering Moon to pay the fine. Later, the city agreed to collect $50 of the $90 that Moon owed. What can we derive from these diverse outcomes?[29]

A six-man jury that included only one prominent citizen, a wealthy farmer named Edward Potter, had found Moon innocent of the charges in the justice of the peace court, whereas a twelve-man circuit court jury that was packed with affluent community residents had found him guilty. Both panels consisted of jurors who lived within the town of Petersburg, and both were mostly made up of farmers. But there were significant differences between the two sets of jurors in terms of their status and experiences. There is limited documentary evidence from the case argued before the justice of the peace. Justices of the peace controlled their own legal records, their courts being less formalized, so the survival of their records is spotty. John C. Ley, the justice of the peace in the Moon case, does not appear in the 1840 or 1850 Menard County censuses, nor is he listed in county histories, all of which suggests he was not a long-term resident of the community (though since he served as a justice of the peace, he must have enjoyed some prominence). Furthermore, there is no record regarding the appearance of licensed attorneys for either side in the case Ley heard, and it is possible that there were none. The justice of the peace, the jurors, and the justice of the peace court were less directly connected to the community's legal structures, and perhaps this lower court was not a strong conduit of community power.[30]

By contrast, the second jury panel in Menard County Circuit Court was closely connected to the formalized legal system and to the forces of community elites. The circuit court jury was more representative of Menard County's prominent citizens. The average wealth of the panel was over $1,100, and two of the jurors reported wealth of $2,000 or more. The average age of the jurors was thirty-five, the oldest being forty-nine and the youngest twenty-two. At least six of the jurors were from long-established Menard County families, possessed some wealth in real estate, or were skilled tradesmen in Petersburg. In the circuit court case, both parties were represented by able attorneys, Abraham Lincoln for the city and Silas W. Robbins and Thomas L. Harris for Moon.[31]

Based on Chester Moon's case, it might appear that the justice of the peace jury, which was less connected to community elites and less restricted by formalized legal systems and proceedings, would side with the defendant in a matter involving the authority of municipal power. Similarly, this case might seem to show that the circuit court jury, which was more representative of elite authority and formal legal structures, would side with the municipality at the expense of the nonelite defendant. However, the marked differences between jurors and procedures in justice of the peace courts, on the one hand, and circuit courts, on the other, did not necessarily result in verdicts as obvious as those handed down in the two trials involving Chester Moon.

In an 1848 case against John Wright, the outcomes were reversed. Wright allegedly violated the same city ordinance that Moon had violated, and the city of Petersburg fined him $50, which he failed to pay. When the city took the issue to a local justice of the peace, William Truth, a jury in his court found for the city. That court then ordered Wright to pay $5 of the fine. When the man appealed his case to the circuit court, the jury there reversed the lower court's decision. No extant legal record lists the jurors who appeared in the justice of the peace court, but the jury in the circuit court appeal mirrored the jury that heard Moon's circuit court case. The average wealth of this panel, which mostly consisted of affluent farmers, was just over $1,400. The average age was thirty-five, the oldest juror being fifty-five and the youngest twenty-eight. So despite the similar composition of the two circuit juries in the Moon and Wright cases, there were dramatically different outcomes.[32]

In 1850 and 1852, the city of Petersburg was involved in two additional cases respecting an 1844 ordinance enacted to curtail unlawful gaming and the riotous activities associated with it. Juries in both of those cases sided with the municipality.[33] Lawyers in the cases instructed jurors that the owners of establishments indicted for unlawful gaming and riotous conduct must have permitted such activities on their premises. Jurors heard arguments against business owners, claiming gross violation of the city's ordinance. They also heard arguments from defendants, claiming that the city had no legal standing to sue in these cases. Ultimately, the Illinois Supreme Court decided that the city had authority to pass the ordinance, require the bond, sue to collect fines, and make settlements with violators of the law. The point of the matter in all these cases was that the city used the court system to reinforce laws enacted by the citizens of the community and, further, that juries played a key role in that process. In the Petersburg cases, the majority of jurors were supportive of the city's efforts. Yet elite jury composition did not necessarily mean unconditional support, as was seen in the outcome in one of the cases against Moon.[34]

By way of some extended legal context, it is interesting to note that only eight criminal gambling cases in Abraham Lincoln's law practice went to a jury. Those cases involved individual gambling or the illegal operation of a gaming house. Grand juries returned indictments for individual gambling—such as playing for money the card game called seven-up—and for the operation of gambling establishments.[35] Juries in these cases were more likely to find operators of gaming houses guilty as opposed to individuals who were caught playing cards or placing bets at the local dry goods store, tavern, or boardinghouse. For instance, in 1837 and 1838, Sangamon County Circuit Court juries found the owner of a gaming house guilty whereas a defendant charged with playing a card game known as faro was acquitted.[36]

In Lincoln's practice, too, the not guilty verdicts tended to be meted out to individual gamblers and the guilty verdicts to proprietors of gaming establishments. In 1850, four men appeared in criminal court in Eureka, Illinois, charged with playing games for money and valuable objects. In the spring of 1852, a jury found just one of the four defendants guilty, perhaps the man who had hosted the gaming, and fined him $10. Four years earlier, in Christian County Circuit Court in Taylorville, Illinois, a grand jury had indicted Charles Clark and Henry Dixon for playing cards, but the trial jury acquitted them. And in two cases involving individuals charged with running gaming houses—John Capps in Sangamon County and Francis Miller in Woodford County—juries returned guilty verdicts. In Miller's case, the court ordered him to jail until he paid his $15 fine. Jurors might have been more willing to overlook individual instances of gambling, but they were less forgiving when individuals set up businesses to encourage it.[37]

The Work of the Petit Jury

Grand jurors selected the crimes that the community wished to prosecute, but they had no interaction with the individuals over whom they passed judgment. By contrast, the legal experience of petit jurors was far more interactive. These jurors also had more direct interaction with court officers, lawyers, and judges. They were privy, for example, to the sometimes "comical remark, or clever joke" delivered by an able litigator such as Abraham Lincoln. Even though some might have thought these humorous distractions "upset the dignity of the Court," most jurors appreciated the attempts to keep the courtroom in "good humor." The trial jury experience took place within the busy courtroom, and the individuals who sat in jury boxes were exposed to all the proceedings of the court as well as all the potential distractions.[38]

The trial jurors' overall experience with the legal system was quite different from that of the grand jurors. To begin with, unlike the seating of grand jurors, the court's summoning of potential petit jurors did not guarantee service. When potential jurors arrived at court, it was not a foregone conclusion that they would serve, as statues allowed attorneys on both sides of the dispute to use peremptory challenges as well as challenges for cause. Typically, midwestern attorneys were entitled to ten peremptory challenges in criminal cases, up to twenty in criminal capital cases, and three to five in civil cases. Attorneys could also request challenges for cause, which were granted or denied at the discretion of the judge.[39] To seat an impartial jury, lawyers subjected jurors to a litany of questions about their opinions and biases regarding issues pertinent to the case. A proper question that attorneys might ask a potential juror in a criminal case was "Have you made up and delivered an opinion, that the prisoner is guilty or innocent of the charge lain in the indictment."[40] In one Sangamon County murder trial, the court summoned 240 persons before finally seating a full jury panel to hear the case. In another instance, 70 people were summoned and examined. In that case, the defendant's counsel issued seventeen peremptory challenges, and the state's attorney issued eight. The court dismissed the remainder for cause.[41]

An attorney might also ask a potential juror if he had heard other opinions or information about the guilt or innocence of a defendant or if he believed in God or the death penalty.[42] The question of juror bias was an important one in the antebellum Midwest. In fact, at least forty-three appeals in state supreme courts in Indiana, Illinois, Michigan, Iowa, and Wisconsin from 1822 to 1860 addressed this issue. Generally, individuals who had a financial stake in the outcome of the case, who were related to a party in the suit, or who had already formed an opinion in the dispute were undesirable jurors. Challenges to jurors, in addition to the legal requirements pertaining to jury service, drastically reduced the number of individuals who ultimately served.[43]

Once a panel of trial jurors was seated at the beginning of a circuit court term, the jurors were required to take an oath similar to the oath taken by grand jurors. The law and the court officers took the duties of the jury seriously, and both demanded a solemn demeanor on the part of the jurors as well. After the court administered the oaths, the petit jurors were seated on hard wooden chairs in a jury box situated in the courtroom, in contrast to the "secret" and private circumstances of grand juror service. The trial jury box was inside the bar, facing the judge's bench and near the table where the attorneys sat. The jury's placement within the bar—separated from the gallery of spectators—was a physical reminder of its close connection to the legal proceedings. The jury was of the community, but it was also a part of the law and of the court. The austere physical environment reflected the weightiness of court proceedings and the somber intentions of the court officers to ensure respect for the legal institutions that the courtroom represented. The judge's gavel and the presence of the clerk and bailiff were additional signs of rigid procedures and of the ever-present demand for attention and respect. Visiting easterners may well have dismissed the emerging Midwest as a wild frontier, but with regard to legal proceedings, structure and decorum were very much in place.[44]

The physical environment of the courthouse reflected the physical conditions of the natural midwestern surroundings. In the first half of the nineteenth century, courtrooms were crowded. They were filled with local attorneys and court officials; dusty-from-the-road, circuit-riding lawyers with court documents carried in their hats; litigants anxiously awaiting the call of their cases from the docket; chattering townspeople taking their seats as they streamed in to hear the arguments of the attorneys; and young, wide-eyed law students. In the courthouse, jurors were subject to extreme temperatures—unbearable heat in muggy midwestern summers and bone-chilling cold as prairie winds blew in with the late arrivals to court in winter sessions. Various pests took up residence in courthouses, and other unpleasant sights and smells were the norm. Fly- and rattraps were ubiquitous fixtures, as were spittoons for those who chewed tobacco. The floors were dusty in summer and muddy in winter. Moreover, these public buildings were subject to almost constant use. In addition to court proceedings, the buildings were often sites of political rallies, lyceums, and public lectures and amusements. Janitorial services were apparently not a priority or a justifiable expense to the governments that maintained the facilities. Candles dripped wax on the tabletops and floors, toppled inkwells stained the green baize covering the lawyers' tables, wood-burning fireplaces and stoves often filled the courtroom with black smoke, and oil lamps smoldered. And to contribute to these unpleasant circumstances, the livestock wandering on the courthouse yard and nearby streets lofted their odors through open courthouse doors and windows.[45]

In smaller, one-room courthouses, jurors often went outside to deliberate, or they might utilize a nearby outbuilding for that purpose. Some midwestern state laws barred the officers of the court from providing food and drink (other than water) to deliberating jurors, but in other instances, court officers offered meals to jurors before they retired to deliberate—perhaps featuring wild turkey or fried chicken as well as buckwheat cakes, baked squash, sweet potatoes, egg bread, peach cobbler, sweet cider, and coffee or tea. There were also times when court officials provided food by stealth to the deliberating jurors. Some trials took only an hour, and some lasted many days; one federal case in Chicago ran for fourteen days. It was not uncommon for jurors to listen to a case all day and not be dismissed to deliberate until "the late hour of the evening." Circuit courts sat from Monday through Saturday, so jurors often found themselves at court or in jury deliberations late on a Saturday night.[46]

In certain instances, the court allowed a jury to disperse and go home for the evening, returning to court the next day. Once dismissed for deliberations, a jury could spend an hour or two or much longer to reach a verdict. In a sensational Sangamon County murder case, the jury deliberated only two hours before issuing a not guilty verdict. A jury in federal circuit court in Chicago spent five hours deliberating before returning its verdict. By contrast, a jury in one medical malpractice case filed in Logan County Circuit Court deliberated for eighteen hours but ultimately failed to reach a verdict.

Jurors had to endure unpleasant courtroom conditions, drawn-out testimony and legal arguments, and lengthy deliberations after traveling to court, often in poor weather, on foot, on horseback, or in open wagons or buggies. For their trouble, they were typically paid from $.25 to $.75 per day in the 1830s, 1840s, and 1850s, up to around $1.50 by 1860. Courts also reimbursed jurors for mileage.[47] Although not the norm, the situation for some antebellum midwestern jurors may not have been all that much different from the experiences of southern jurors at the end of the eighteenth century. One judge in South Carolina remarked that "some of those poor men [jurors] come to Court and return on foot from ten to fifty miles often without a shilling in their pockets . . . their sallow sickly and dejected countenances, their apparel wet or frozen or soiled, speak of what sort of night they had of it."[48]

Legal records provide evidence about the payment of jury fees and about the sheriff's duties and costs for providing for the jurors' needs. However, they do not tell us how jurors felt about the physical conditions of their jury service.[49] What we do know is that even if some jurors complained about the uncomfortable seating, the extreme temperatures, or the lack of food during deliberations, the adverse conditions did not deter most of them from serving. Some potential jurors may have found ways to avoid jury service, but a large number of antebellum midwestern jurors served during multiple terms of the court and over many years. Among them was William Carpenter, a wealthy miller and prominent landowner in Springfield who served as a juror in at least sixteen cases in seven terms of the Sangamon County Circuit Court and two terms of the federal circuit court in Springfield between 1841 and 1857. Repeat juror service illustrates the commitment that many community elites made to their civic responsibilities. Perhaps it also suggests that those who served saw their contribution as jurors as central to maintaining their community's quality of life.[50]

The twelve-man panel that included Charles Gardner, the man mentioned at the beginning of this chapter who helped decide David Crow's legal fate, was in most respects a typical jury in Sangamon County, in the state of Illinois, and in the emerging Midwest as a whole. Twelve jurors were legally required for circuit court trials, although it was not uncommon for juries to sit with fewer members. Parties could consent to go with fewer jurors to make up a panel. Sometimes, this reduced number resulted from agreement of the parties; at other times, it was an unfortunate outcome of a court's failure to seat enough jurors.[51]

For instance, the parties in an 1839 covenant case in Sangamon County agreed to submit their suit to a panel of eight jurors. Abraham Lincoln and his law partner John T. Stuart, who had twelve years of experience as an attorney, represented Albert G. Williams in his suit against John and George Cabiness, entailing a $100 debt. The impaneling of small juries was a traditional practice, so it is not surprising that Judge William Thomas accepted the agreement for an eight-man panel, even in a county that had no shortage of available qualified jurors. The $100 debt at issue was a significant amount of money for the parties involved. Therefore, the fact that they all agreed to the small jury indicates they probably believed a reduced number of jurors would be competent to render a fair verdict in the case.[52]

As previously discussed, potential jurors were selected at the county level (normally by county commissioners), and then county sheriffs served notice on those whose names were selected from a blind drawing. After notification, jurors arrived at court at the beginning of the court term to be seated. The selected grand jurors generally sat for a full year, handing down indictments prior to the opening of the circuit court. Typically, a panel of jurors was selected at the beginning of the court term to hear all of the cases requiring a jury at that particular term. Unlike today's jury system, where jurors are selected for a specific trial, antebellum midwestern jurors were selected to serve throughout the entire court term. Attorneys and litigants could challenge jurors for cause and exercise their right of peremptory challenge, resulting in the calling up of more jurors from the selection list. Nonetheless, individual jurors in a given court term often heard all or most of the jury trials that took place during that time. This was especially true in smaller jurisdictions.[53]

Regardless of the size of the county seat, circuit court officers took care to provide comfort to jurors who were sequestered in lengthy trials. In Illinois at least, jurors were not permitted to dine at the public tables of hotels during their service in criminal trials of capital cases. Despite sometimes uncomfortable physical conditions, they appreciated whatever comforts the court could arrange for them. Thus, a group of jurors in Sangamon County in the 1850s was pleased about the accommodations the court secured for them during a long murder trial: the jurors were guests at Springfield's American House Hotel, just down the street from the courthouse.[54] They were so pleased, in fact, that they placed the following notice in the *Daily Illinois State Journal:* "We the Jurors impaneled and sworn to try the issue joined—wherein the people complain of Theodore and Jane Anderson—present our thanks and kind acknowledgements to our host Isaac H. Gray, of the American House, for the kind and gentlemanly manner in which we have been treated while guests at said house during the trial; also to Hon. Judge D. Davis for the kind feelings which he expressed for our comfort; to sheriff Cook, and officers having us in charge, we also give our grateful thanks for the kind treatment which we received from them." The notice concluded with the names of the twelve jurors, who represented some of Springfield's elite.[55] Among them were Philemon Stout, a wealthy landowner; Moses B. Horn, the superintendent of the local almshouse; and John B. Beard, a prominent farmer. Given that leading residents tended to dominate jury service in the antebellum Midwest, it is not surprising that court officers would concern themselves with the comfort of the men sitting on jury panels.[56]

Though the court could work to make the job of jury service less unpleasant, it could not and would not alter legal process or procedure in the courtroom in order to curry favor. In all likelihood, there was some degree of what we might today call jury tampering, but there is no historical evidence to suggest it was widespread or even common. In midwestern appellate cases that related to jury procedure at trial, the issue generally revolved around unintentional interaction between jurors and nonjurors. These unauthorized written or verbal interactions occurred in the absence of the bailiff and may or may not have influenced the jury verdict. In the first half of the nineteenth century, there was only one case in the states of Indiana, Illinois, Iowa, and Wisconsin in which lawyers or other officers of the court were charged with intentionally interfering with jury deliberations or procedure. In that case, the bailiff informed the jurors that they would be kept from Saturday evening until Monday morning without food unless they agreed upon a verdict before Monday. Subsequently, the jurors were quick to reach a verdict, although it is not certain if they did so because they grew hungry. Nothing in the case suggested that the bailiff was lobbying for a particular outcome, but the Supreme Court of Iowa considered such deprivation an undue influence on the verdict.[57]

The small number of appellate cases for such offenses may indicate that there were few jury procedural violations in antebellum Midwest circuit courts. Or perhaps litigants and lawyers were by and large not concerned about whatever violations did occur. Though jury service was serious business, court officials and individuals who were involved with the law at the local level were at least somewhat flexible in terms of what constituted competent jury panels. State laws did indeed constrict jury service, but particular circumstances in county courtrooms doubtless helped shape the trial experiences of individual jurors and jury panels.

Verdicts in Criminal Cases

Although less common on circuit court dockets than civil cases were, criminal cases had a more substantial impact on the personal freedom of defendants. These cases comprised under 10 percent of the caseload of circuit courts in certain antebellum Illinois counties: for example, only 6 percent of the cases that Abraham Lincoln and his partners handled from 1837 to 1860 were in the criminal division of the court.[58] Criminal cases covered four basic areas: crimes against person (murder, manslaughter, rape, assault), crimes against property (larceny, arson, and stealing from the mail), crimes against morality (illegal sale of alcohol, gambling, and adultery), and crimes against the public welfare (obstructing roads and waterways, disturbing the peace, rioting, and delaying or opening the mail). As to the variety and distribution of criminal cases, Lincoln's practice was much like that of other attorneys in the antebellum Midwest. Of the 150 criminal cases Lincoln took to trial in which the action is known, 48 (32 percent) involved crimes against person, 32 (21 percent) involved crimes against property, 34 (23 percent) involved crimes against morality, and 36 (24 percent) involved crimes against the public welfare.[59]

In all of these cases, defendants faced fines, jail time or confinement in the state penitentiary, or a combination of both. The jurors had the power to inflict harsh punishments upon defendants they found guilty. Interestingly, however, they were not heavy-handed in their rendering of verdicts, and they appear to have acted based on the evidence presented and not wholly out of fear or prejudice against defendants who were potentially dangerous to the public welfare. Of the 147 jury trials in criminal cases from Lincoln's law practice in which a judgment is known, juries returned convictions in 69 cases (47 percent) and acquittals in 52 (35 percent). In 16 additional cases, the state's attorney suspended prosecution or the court dismissed the case, resulting in a de facto acquittal. In effect, 68 cases (48 percent) resulted in the freedom of the defendant. Despite economic and social chasms that separated jurors from criminal defendants, jury panels were not overzealous in their conviction rates.[60]

Jurors often demonstrated a capacity for rendering merciful verdicts. Of 22 murder cases in Lincoln's practice, the jury convicted in only 10 of them. In 7 of those cases, the jury downgraded the conviction from murder, which was a capital crime, to manslaughter, which carried the lighter sentence of up to eight years in the state penitentiary.[61] The jury found the murder defendant guilty in only 2 of the cases. One of the defendants was executed; the other escaped his death sentence by fleeing the jurisdiction. In another murder case, the jury found that the defendant acted in self-defense and sentenced him to seven years in the state penitentiary instead of applying the death penalty required for a murder conviction. Some scholarship has suggested that juries were skeptical of expert medical testimony and were hesitant to let such testimony affect their approach to criminal defendants. Yet in two of Lincoln's murder cases, the jury found the defendants not guilty by reason of insanity; and in both cases, the jurors heavily relied on the testimony of several doctors who attested to the mental incompetence of the defendants.[62]

Jurors demonstrated compassion for individuals convicted of other crimes as well. It was not uncommon for jurors involved in convicting a criminal defendant to later sign petitions for his or her early release from jail. That was the case with Henry Heath, who was convicted of larceny in Pekin, Illinois, in 1850. The jury sentenced him to one year in the penitentiary, but then each juror signed a petition calling for his early release. The petition for clemency submitted to Illinois governor Augustus C. French argued: "From the facts developed on the trial, as well as from our personal knowledge we are satisfied that this is his first criminal offence that he is quite young and has hitherto sustained a fair and unblemished character and that even in the opinion of the jury who tried him there is doubt whether he intended to commit a larceny." The petitioners added: "We therefore earnestly recommend him as a fit subject for executive clemency believing that the exercise of the pardoning power vested in you will in this case prove acceptable to the people as it will be most judicious and deserving."[63] Jurors also showed concern about the financial situations of convicted men's families. Because families required the economic support of husbands and fathers, the early release of a convict—even one who was guilty of murder—might be a desired outcome. Nineteenth-century midwestern juries demonstrated compassion in numerous instances, which may well have contradicted mainstream society's sometimes harsh approach to criminal elements within their communities.[64]

Illinois jurors may well have been less compassionate, however, with regard to the personal freedoms of people of color. In the case against Robert Jones—the free black minor mentioned earlier who was convicted with two black servant girls of attempting to poison a couple of white men—the jury refused to consider the boy's youth as a mitigating factor. Despite the impassioned plea of his attorney, the jury convicted the boy and sentenced him to one year in the state penitentiary. There was no attempt on the part of the jurors or others in the community to seek a pardon for him.[65] Jones and the two girls were the only African American criminal defendants in Lincoln's law practice, and no defendants on the Sangamon County Circuit Court criminal docket in that period were identified as "negro" or "mulatto." Therefore, we cannot know whether juries in that locale would have shown compassion for them in murder cases. Yet in the context of harsh midwestern Black Laws and other restrictive measures respecting people of color, blacks were the most vulnerable of litigants.[66] The racial and social perspectives of white jurors trumped any paternal feelings they may have held. Thus, when James Hayes, a black man in Indiana, was beaten by a group of whites in 1859, no criminal indictment was issued against the attackers. Hayes was also unsuccessful in a civil suit against the man who had organized the attack. The attorneys working against Hayes cited the *Dred Scott* case, arguing that as a black man he had no legal standing.[67]

One Illinois case against a Native American is revealing, showing how white juries may have introduced their prejudices into deliberations. The case of Nomaque, a Pottawatomie Indian, illustrates the potentially precarious legal situation of individuals who were discounted and separated from mainstream white society. In November 1825, a Peoria County Circuit Court jury in Peoria, Illinois, found Nomaque guilty of the murder of Pierre Londri, a white man. The case was fraught with legal problems from the start. First, the grand jury had not endorsed the indictment and returned a true bill; consequently, the panel had not properly indicted Nomaque. Second, at the end of the first day of jury selection, the court had allowed nine selected jurors to disperse until the following day, when the panel was completed—a move that was contrary to legal jury proceedings. Third, the court allowed the jurors to deliver their guilty verdict to the clerk without reading the decision in open court in the presence of the defendant. Fourth, the court denied the motion of Nomaque's attorney for a new trial. This motion was based upon the evidence, provided by two witnesses, that prior to being seated on the panel, a juror had openly declared Nomaque was a "damned rascal" and had then offered to give $5 to a witness to testify against the defendant.[68]

Public sentiment was probably against Nomaque from the beginning, for he was an Indian who stood accused of killing a white man. The community feared Indians, and when it had an allegedly murderous one in its midst, it did what it could to ensure the safety of white residents. In their zealous attempt to have justice, it appears the grand jury, the circuit court judge, the state's attorney, and at least some of the jurors were willing to abandon their commitment to the sanctity of the institution of the jury. For them, the right to a legal trial-by-jury process did not extend to a Native American. The law protected only white defendants. Fortunately for Nomaque and the institution of the jury in antebellum Illinois, his attorney was not so eager to concede his client's rights. He filed an appeal to the Illinois Supreme Court.[69]

In the high court's opinion, Justice Theophilus W. Smith expressed his disgust with the lower court's sloppy procedures in Nomaque's case. Smith chastised the court for the errors already discussed, especially for the failure of the judge to grant a new trial based on the evidence of so biased an impaneled jury. The opinion concluded with a diatribe against the court for allowing a verdict to be rendered to the clerk and not to the open court in the presence of the defendant. In so doing, the lower court had denied the defendant his right to poll the jury after the verdict was read. On this point, the Illinois Supreme Court was especially direct:

> In the present case, the verdict was not even sealed; it was liable to alteration, and besides, the court had no legal evidence that it was the verdict of the jury. While on this part of the case the court feel it their indispensable duty to reprobate the tolerance of a practice which might lead to the most dangerous consequences, in that case affecting the life of an individual, and to express their disapprobation of it, in the present instance. The judgment of the circuit court of Peoria must be reversed, and a *supersedeas* awarded;[70] and as a flagrant crime has no doubt been committed, and possibly by the prisoner, and in order that public justice may not be evaded, the court make this additional order, that the prisoner remain in custody for thirty days from this day in order to enable the local authorities to take measures to bring him again to trial.[71]

The appellate court had overturned Nomaque's conviction, but it had not done so in an effort to protect the rights of a Native American. It had done so only to prevent the potential harm such a blatant disregard for the trial-by-jury process might do to future white defendants in a similar situation. Although the opinion reiterated the centrality of the jury system in protecting the rights of antebellum Americans, it also reinforced the nineteenth-century practice of denying people of color the full protection of the law. As further evidence of this practice, Smith's opinion did not hide the court's assumption of Nomaque's guilt in the murder. As well, the court made the unusual decision to order the lower court authorities to hold the defendant in custody until he could be tried and convicted without the illegal conduct and process that had tarnished his first trial.

Jury Deliberations and Competence

Because few legal records provide clues about the jury deliberation process for antebellum midwestern trial panels, like that in Nomaque's case, we can only speculate about the jurors' legal knowledge and intellect or about the human dynamics that were at work in jury rooms of the period. Certainly, jurors brought their personal beliefs, religion, social status, professional affiliation, and politics to the deliberation process. Yet a few appellate and circuit court cases in Illinois, Indiana, Iowa, and Wisconsin do offer insights about how some juries arrived at verdicts and how some jurors conducted themselves.[72] Perhaps not surprisingly, jurors did not always pay attention during trials; some read newspapers during witness testimony and lawyers' arguments. In isolated incidents, jurors showed up intoxicated and were dismissed by the court. In other instances, their drinking was tolerated. In a time when the average adult man consumed a half-pint of liquor each day, alcohol was often for sale near the courthouse. Judges and officers of the court tried to keep liquor from entering deliberation rooms, but they could not always control drinking that might be done before court opened. There were also cases in which jurors were deemed mentally incompetent. Some jurors did not take their role seriously, and others were overeager, taking documents such as depositions with them into the jury room for use in their deliberations. If jurors used documents that the court had not sanctioned, they were in violation of the law. This violation was a valid legal error and could become grounds for an appeal, but this did not deter every jury panel.[73]

Reaching a verdict could be a daunting process, and outside influences could play a role. For example, a new trial was ordered in an Ohio case when jurors were found to have had conversations with people on the street: as the jurors were deliberating in the jury room, they leaned out windows and conversed with pedestrians on the sidewalk below. Also, complicated laws, confusing and contradictory testimony, and convoluted evidence could pose problems for jurors. Perhaps at a loss to determine how twelve men might agree on a damage award in a civil suit, it was not unheard of for a jury to skip the deliberation process altogether. In at least four cases, a jury panel decided to have each juror provide what he thought was a reasonable damage award, find the sum of all of the proposed awards, and divide that by the number of jurors. Thus, in assessing the damages in an 1856 libel suit in Davis County District Court in Iowa, all the jurors agreed to "make up their verdict by marking each a certain sum and dividing the aggregate by twelve" to determine the award. When an attorney asked the judge to compel the jurors to provide affidavits attesting to their method of deliberation, the judge refused. In the appeal of the case on that ground, the Supreme Court of Iowa argued that only voluntary affidavits of jurors were admissible and that to compel affidavits from jurors was "to invade and interfere with the rights of jurors and the discharge of their duties in the jury-room." The opinion admitted that even if the jurors had engaged in "fraud or unfair dealing on their part," it was not for the court to compel them to disclose how they had reached their verdict. In order for the court to take action, misconduct of the jury would have had to result in a bad verdict. If the verdict was, in the court's opinion, proper, it was no concern to the court if the jurors had arrived at their decision "improperly." Jury deliberations were closed by law, and the law of the general verdict protected the jury in this regard.[74]

Despite the unseemliness of such deliberation methods, the practice of balloting by jurors was welcomed by some. After the publication of a notice about a murder trial in Sacramento, California, the *State Journal* in Springfield, Illinois, commented on the practice. In that case, the jurors could not agree on a decision, and "on being sent back to the jury-room, they put twenty-four tickets into a hat, on twelve of which was written 'guilty,' and on the other twelve, 'not guilty,' and drew for a verdict," pulling a majority of "not guilty" tickets. The Springfield newspaper reported that it favored the idea "because the matter is settled at once." The paper also suggested that "the drawing take place hereafter before the trial to save expense and trouble."[75]

In an attachment suit in Woodford County, Illinois, a jury reached a verdict by playing a game of chance in the jury room. Learning of this through one of the jurors, an attorney in the case filed an affidavit attesting to this fact and requested the court to set the verdict aside. The judge refused the motion to set aside the verdict, thereby allowing the rendering of the jury's judgment.[76] In another Iowa case, the jurors agreed to draw lots to determine the verdict, and all agreed to support the outcome. Some of the jurors signed affidavits attesting to the "balloting" system they had employed in the jury room. The affidavits were used to appeal the verdict. In this case, the misconduct of the jury was a viable issue because some of the jurors had voluntarily provided their affidavits, which proved the jury's misconduct and resulted in a bad decision. It may have seemed improper for jurors to find damages in that fashion, but courts were not comfortable invading the jury room, especially when the verdicts appeared just and correct. This hesitation spoke volumes about the ultimate power that antebellum Americans ceded to juries.[77]

The jury deliberation room was off-limits to judges, attorneys, and others, but the opinions and possible biases of jurors before they were seated were not. Ideally, jurors were not permitted to have formed or expressed opinions about a case. Lawyers worked hard to eliminate those who were biased, and to this end, the law gave them peremptory challenges and challenges for cause.[78] Jurors were obligated to state under oath that they had not previously formed opinions. Nonetheless, biased jurors were sometimes seated in the jury box. Alfred Howlett, a juror in a murder case in Shelby County, Illinois, was one such juror. Prior to being seated in 1842, Howlett publicly stated that the defendant "would be hung; that he ought to be hung; that nothing could save him; that salt could not save him; and that there was no law to clear him."[79] Shortly thereafter, he visited the defendant in jail, telling him that he should not be hung and that if Howlett were on the jury he would clear him. Yet when questioned as a potential juror, Howlett declared that he had not formed or expressed any opinion regarding the murder case. In the end, he was seated on the jury, and the jury convicted the defendant. Obviously, Howlett was not without bias, and the Illinois Supreme Court overturned the conviction on that ground. Juror bias was a serious legal issue and resulted in least thirty-eight appellate cases in Indiana, Illinois, Iowa, Michigan, and Wisconsin from 1822 to 1860.[80]

Once the ranks of potential jurors were scrutinized and presumably undesirable jurors were weeded out for bias and other reasons, the jury panel that was seated was of course expected to return a verdict. But a small percentage of them failed to do so. Of Abraham Lincoln's 1,075 trial-by-jury cases, 48 (5 percent) resulted in hung juries. In most of those cases, the court seated a second jury that did render a verdict. Usually, when a court seated a trial jury, the panel returned a verdict relatively quickly, and most circuit court judgments were never appealed to midwestern supreme courts.[81]

By far the largest percentage of civil cases on antebellum midwestern dockets related to debtor-creditor relationships, and in these cases, the jury system appears to have functioned competently within the economic context of the era. Local banks at that time issued notes in differing amounts, resulting in fluctuating and questionable value in circulation. As a result, consumers and users of credit were often confused and made mistakes in purchasing and accepting notes. This confusion and the complex creditor-debtor relationships led to numerous lawsuits. In fact, more than 60 percent of the cases in Lincoln's nearly twenty-five-year law practice involved debt, including the actions of debt, assumpsit, petition and summons, foreclosure of mortgage, and mechanics' liens. And of the 1,075 jury trials in his practice, 461 cases (43 percent) involved debtors and creditors. This legal situation stemmed from a widespread economic environment in which specie was scarce, bankable paper values were unstable and confusing, and the economy functioned via extensive and complex webs of credit.[82]

Antebellum Americans could purchase anything on credit. They bought land and livestock with promissory notes. They used promissory notes received from others to buy dry goods or pay for the services of blacksmiths, carpenters, and the like.[83] It was extremely common for people to purchase goods such as flour and cloth, which were necessary for basic survival, on credit. And it was common for merchants to extend credit and accept promissory notes as payment. If customers failed to pay, merchants often filed lawsuits against these debtors.[84] Many debt cases involved merchants who were suing their customers, some of whom were in particularly dire economic circumstances. In Lincoln's practice, over 700 cases involved actions of debt in which some of the litigants were businesses. Although debt cases involved both elite and nonelite litigants, they hit the latter especially hard. In these numerous debt cases, jurors were called upon to validate or invalidate the claims of creditors against debtors, enforce monetary contracts, and assess damages and determine monetary awards. Because debt was such a common condition in the nineteenth century, most, if not all, jurors had personal experience with it. Consequently, the personal financial experiences of jurors undoubtedly informed their deliberations and the resulting verdicts is such cases. In 353 (or 76 percent) of the 465 debt-related jury trials in Lincoln's practice, jurors found for the plaintiff, or creditor.[85]

Creditors such as merchants and manufacturers were vitally important because their economic success was a huge factor in the overall economic well-being of the communities in which they operated. As a result, antebellum midwestern jurors showed limited mercy toward defendants who owed money to these critical local businesses. The case of James Gambrel is illustrative. After Gambrel failed to pay on a promissory note he had signed for the purchase of land, the owners of the note sued him in Sangamon County Circuit Court. Gambrel argued that the contract was void because the land purchased was conducive to milk sickness and therefore worthless. The jury was unmoved by Gambrel's unfortunate circumstances and ordered him to pay $207.65—the $200 purchase price plus interest.[86] In another instance, John W. Priest and Orson N. Stafford did some carpentry work for David Spear and Jonathan Hoyt, two wealthy landholders in Springfield. Spear and Hoyt failed to pay for the work, and Priest and Stafford sued them in Sangamon County Circuit Court. A jury found the defendants liable for the debt and ordered them to pay the plaintiffs $169.46. In yet another example in 1854, George W. Myers sued Joseph J. Brown in Champaign County Circuit Court for the debt on a $380 promissory note used to purchase livestock. The jury found for Myers and awarded him $386.20 for the debt plus interest owed.[87]

Regardless of the economic circumstances of the defendants in debt cases, jurors were generally not sympathetic on the subject of unpaid obligations. Whether debtors were wealthy or poor made little difference to panels of jurors who tended to validate creditors' claims. When juries delivered verdicts against debtors, ordering them to pay the moneys owed and sometimes interest and damages as well, the court had the power to sell the debtors' real and personal property in order to compensate the creditors. When Springfield businessman Virgil Hickox failed to pay a debt to Nathaniel Hay, Hay sued. The jury awarded him $105.11, and the court then sold a city lot that Hickox owned for $133.34, which easily covered the debt. Hickox was a successful merchant with substantial real property, so he probably could have paid the debt prior to the suit against him. For some reason, however, he refused. The weight of the legal system was necessary to ensure Hay's rightful claim to the money Hickox owed him.[88]

Not all debtors were as well off as Hickox, and a debt action and verdict against such individuals often had dire consequences. In 1857 when a creditor filed a suit on a failed promissory note against Eli Strode, a struggling farmer with no real estate or personal wealth, the jury found for the creditor and awarded $1,000. The sheriff found no property to satisfy the judgment when he served the writ of execution on Strode in November 1857. But years later, in October 1864, when the sheriff called on Strode again, he found some property on which to levy the judgment. At that time, the sheriff sold five head of cattle and one-third of Strode's twenty acres of corn. The proceeds covered a portion of the debt, and Strode finally paid the remainder in November 1865. For Strode, payment of the debt was far more difficult than it had been for Hickox, for the sale of his cattle and a good chunk of his crop represented a real hardship. Apparently, he was able to recover, but the legal and financial setback posed potential financial ruin for him and his young family.[89]

Though juries more often than not ruled in favor of creditors and ordered the payment of debts and interest on those debts, winning creditors were sometimes denied payment because the debtors simply had no ability to pay. If a losing defendant had no cash, no land on which to levy the judgment, no personal property to cover the debt, and no wages to garnish, the creditor was probably out his debt and his legal fees. The legal system and juries demanded much of those who accumulated debts, but neither could squeeze money out of truly impoverished individuals. Repeated suits for debt might discredit a person and mark him as an unworthy credit risk, but there was little else the system could do to him. Therefore, even though jurors had considerable power to apply the law in support of the creditor who was suing to recover a debt, that power was significantly trimmed when a debtor held no assets or when he could not be found because he had fled the jurisdiction for brighter economic pastures in another state.

In contrast, juries had much more direct power to affect the lives of women in divorce, child custody, and slander cases. More than other types of proceedings (with the possible exception of estate settlement cases, which usually did not involve jury trials), divorce and slander suits could hold serious consequences for female litigants who entered antebellum midwestern courtrooms. Many divorce cases were uncontested—because one person in the relationship had deserted the other and left the jurisdiction—and thus required no jury. But when divorce suits went to a jury, the jurors had considerable power to define the parameters of a woman's future. They could grant a divorce decree, which gave a woman the legal right to remarry; award custody of children; order the payment of alimony and child maintenance; and determine the division of family assets. For women in the antebellum Midwest, unlike many of their counterparts on the eastern seaboard and in the South, the legal access to divorce with the right to remarry could be a source of empowerment, and juries could play a role in this sometimes liberating process.[90]

Consider the case of Mary Blue of Bloomington, Illinois. When she married Martin Beard in October 1850, she probably had no idea that she would be seeking a divorce from her young husband two years later. But she was abused by her husband leading up to after the birth of her son and therefore filed for divorce in McLean County Circuit Court on the grounds of repeated cruelty. Martin Beard filed his answer, denying the charges.[91] After a change of venue to Champaign County and after the testimony of twelve witnesses was presented, the chancery court jury found Martin guilty of cruelty, and the court granted custody of the couple's infant son to Mary. Without the jury verdict and the resulting divorce decree and order of custody, Martin Beard may have continued the abuse and threatened the safety of the infant. The jury verdict also granted Mary Beard the legal privilege to remarry, which she did in January 1853.[92]

Sarah Ogden's experience with a jury verdict was much more distressing than was Mary Beard's. When Sarah filed for divorce from her husband, Jonathan, in Macon County Circuit Court in Decatur, Illinois, the jury granted the divorce but awarded custody of the couple's children to their father. Despite Sarah Ogden's charges that her husband was abusive and hiding family assets, the jury had denied her custody of the children and awarded her only $400 in lieu of alimony.[93] Such verdicts obviously had emotional and economic costs, and the panels of jurors who delivered them certainly understood the sometimes serious ramifications of the decisions they rendered.

Like verdicts in divorce cases, verdicts in slander cases had the power to affect the social and sexual reputation of women. Charges of sexual impropriety could jeopardize social status in a community or deter potential marriage proposals, both of which might have economic repercussions. As a result, sexual mudslinging could have real (and imagined) social *and* economic impacts on the life of a slandered woman. Verbal assaults of this type often compelled women to file slander suits. In these suits, as in divorce proceedings, jurors became involved in the most intimate details of the litigants' lives.

Jurors in slander cases could also play a powerful part in shaping the lives of ordinary antebellum Americans. In 1852, Missouri Mitchell and her husband, Elijah, sued James Mitchell after he called Missouri a "base whore" and a "nasty, stinking strumpet." James was a close neighbor in the small town of Wakefield, Illinois, and the two men may have been related. Both were farmers, each having a comfortable share of real property.[94] Missouri and Elijah had married three years earlier, and the trouble between the couple and James seems to have stemmed from a rumor that Missouri was having sex with other men in the community. In her declaration filed in the slander suit in Shelby County Circuit Court, Missouri alleged that the "false" statements "greatly injured . . . her good name, favor & credit, & brought into public scandal and disgrace with & among all her neighbors & other good & worthy citizens of their state."[95]

Missouri and her husband requested $500 in damages in their suit, but they were really seeking a public affirmation of Missouri's good reputation. They were desperate to clear her of these scandalous charges. The legal case was thus a public vehicle for restoring her reputation and the good name and credit of her family, and a jury verdict in her favor, more than the damages the jurors might award her, could accomplish just that. On May 24, 1852, after hearing the evidence presented and the testimony of seven witnesses from the community—all testifying on Missouri's behalf—the jury found James Mitchell guilty of spreading the ugly rumors and awarded Missouri $500 plus court costs.[96] Immediately following the verdict, she and her husband remitted $400 of the award but accepted $100, which covered their attorney's fees in the case. It was typical in slander suits for a winning plaintiff to remit a large portion of the judgment because the suit was, after all, about restoring that person's reputation in the community and not about obtaining a substantial jury award, which the defendant was most likely incapable of paying anyway.[97]

Whether in slander suits, divorce cases, or other legal actions, female litigants in the pre–Civil War Midwest had limited legal standing. Missouri Mitchell was the injured party in her slander suit, but she could not sue without her husband, and it was her husband's credit that was jeopardized. Jurors in her case held the power to validate her claims or to reinforce the slanderer's accusations about her sexual reputation. It seems that jurors cared about the reputation of women. When they found the evidence compelling, they had the ability to restore a woman's good name—and they did so by awarding some slandered women as much as $1,600 in damages.[98]

On Competence and in Conclusion

Missouri Mitchell, Chester Moon, Virgil Hickox, Nomaque, and Mary Beard were just a few of the thousands of litigants in jury trials held in courtrooms across the antebellum Midwest. The jurors who heard their cases were a mere handful of the many men who sat on countless juries in countless courts across the region. Each of the litigant and juror narratives presented in this chapter reflects the wide-ranging dynamics of historical experience through the connections between society and the law. Every jury trial was unique, but some general characteristics are apparent. Jurors in Illinois approached their work on grand and trial juries with a degree of compassion and viewed their service as a serious business. Despite their mostly elite composition, juries were willing to empathize with less affluent litigants and to reach verdicts that reflected the evidence heard at trial. *Individual* jurors may well have viewed their jury service as a way to exercise community authority in the courtroom, but *panels* of jurors were capable of setting aside prejudices, were willing to understand mitigating circumstances, and were reluctant to apply the full force of their power in rendering verdicts, especially in capital cases. In the majority of cases they heard, elite jurors were by and large "good" and "competent" men.

Much scholarship on the history of American law has argued that judges, lawyers, and jurors worked cooperatively to maintain the status quo at the expense of individuals on the bottom rungs of society. Had this scholarship investigated midwestern source materials, much evidence to the contrary would have been found.[99] Most jurors in Illinois and the emerging Midwest demonstrated paternalism, not patriarchy, in their deliberations and through their verdicts. Jurors were not perfect, and their behavior could be less than impeccable. At times, their deliberations were irregular and their verdicts flawed. On occasion, they failed to check their prejudices and assumptions at the courthouse door. However, through their general behavior and through the quality of their verdicts, midwestern jurors evinced an independent and fair-minded approach to their jury work and to the law.[100]

In the end, the human element inherent in the jury system was the system's most striking attribute. It was also the human element that best characterized the impact jury verdicts made in the lives of individuals who came in contact with the law in antebellum midwestern courtrooms. Despite the institutionalized inequality of nineteenth-century America and despite the imperfect nature of all humans, jurors were typically solemn and respectful. In answering the call to jury service that was fashioned in midwestern jury law and legal practice, most jurors were competent and delivered competent verdicts. They displayed empathy and concern for criminal defendants, especially those under indictment for murder. They respected the sexual reputation of women in divorce and slander suits. And even though juries overwhelmingly favored the rights of creditors over debtors, they returned verdicts that they believed were both legally correct and socially responsible. We might stand in harsh judgment of them from our more egalitarian, modern perspective, but we would be wrong to accuse them of deliberately sabotaging the jury system they so honored and, with competence, attempted to protect and to maintain.

PLATE 1. Sangamon County Courthouse, Springfield, Illinois, c. 1846. Image taken from a painting of the Springfield public square, hanging in the Old State Capitol in Springfield. *(Image courtesy of the Abraham Lincoln Presidential Library, Springfield, Ill.)*

PLATE 2. Abraham Lincoln, February 1857. Lincoln sat for this photo in Chicago. *(Image courtesy of the Abraham Lincoln Presidential Library, Springfield, Ill.)*

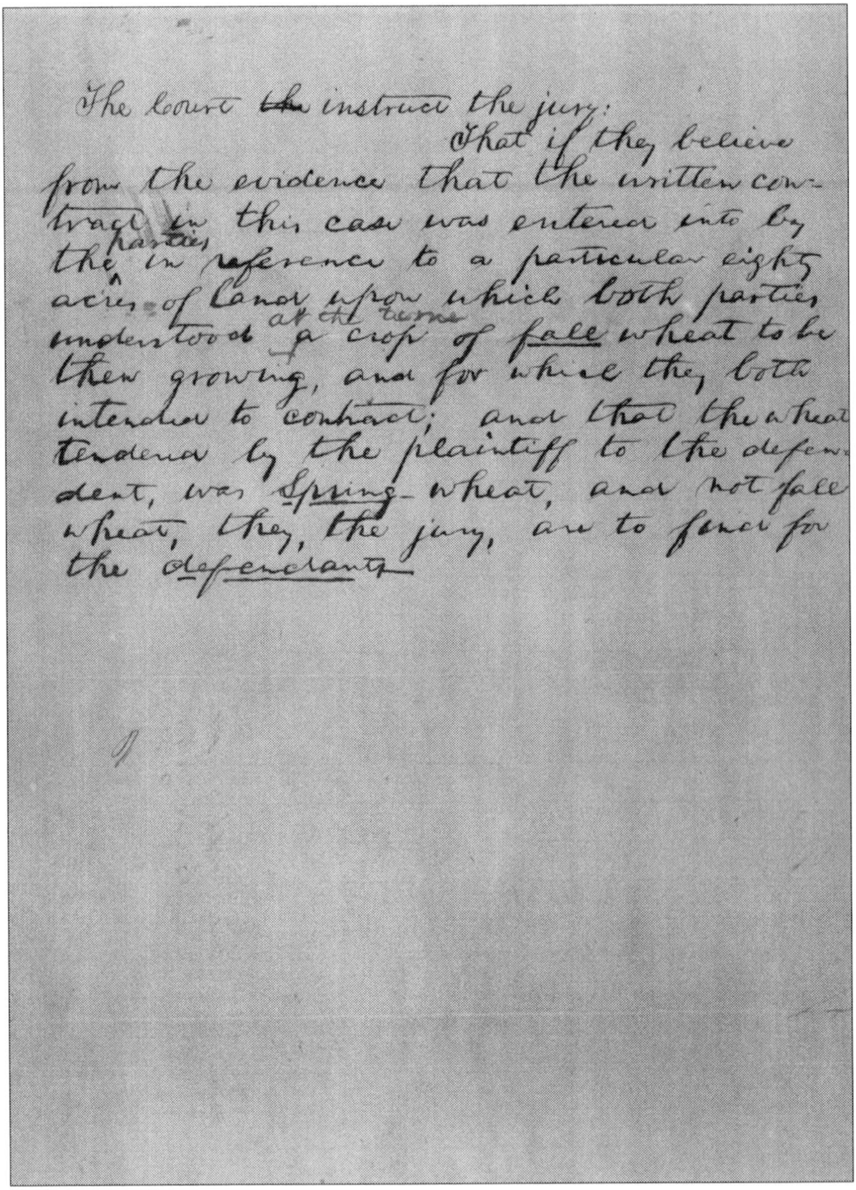
The Court ~~the~~ instruct the jury:

That if they believe from the evidence that the written contract in this case was entered into by the parties in reference to a particular eighty acres of land upon which both parties understood at the time a crop of fall wheat to be then growing, and for which they both intended to contract; and that the wheat tendered by the plaintiff to the defendant, was Spring-wheat, and not fall wheat, they, the jury, are to find for the defendants

PLATE 3. *(above and opposite)* Jury instruction in *Fairchild v. Capps and St. Clair,* September 1859. Abraham Lincoln wrote this jury instruction in a case involving a disagreement over the sale of five hundred bushels of wheat. The jury returned a verdict in favor of the defendants. *(Image courtesy of the Library of Congress, Rare Book and Special Collections Division, Alfred Whital Stern Collection of Lincolniana, Washington, D.C.)*

[Apr 1859]

People }
vs }
Patterson }

The court instructs, the jury:

1 If they believe from the evidence that when Patterson threw the weight, he had a reasonable and well grounded fear that he was in immediate danger of his life, or of great bodily harm, from Dehaven, with the spade, they are to find Patterson "Not guilty"—

2 That if they have any reasonable doubt whether Patterson then was in such reasonable and well grounded fear, they are to find him "Not guilty"—

3 That if, upon the whole case, they have any reasonable doubt of Patterson's guilt, as charged in the indictment, they are to acquit him—

David Davis's Hand

The Jury are not to decide the ~~cause~~ the question of the Defendants guilt, or innocence by a preponderance of testimony, or by the probabilities of the defendants guilt or innocence

In a criminal case, the Jury will not convict, if they entertain a reasonable doubt of the defendants guilt

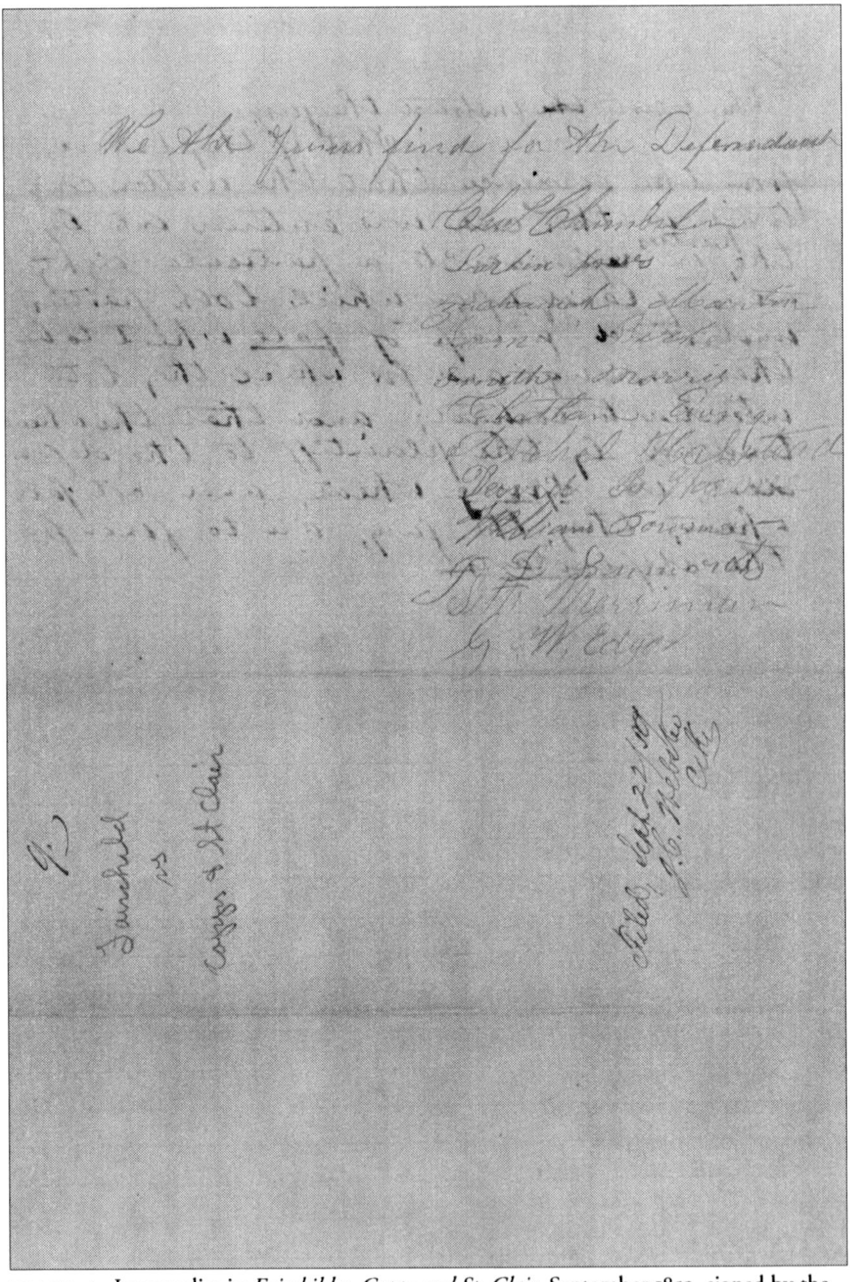

PLATE 4. Jury verdict in *Fairchild v. Capps and St. Clair,* September 1859, signed by the twelve jurors in the case. Few of these jury verdicts survive. *(Image courtesy of the Library of Congress, Rare Book and Special Collections Division, Alfred Whital Stern Collection of Lincolniana, Washington, D.C.)*

PLATE 5. Jury room, federal court, Springfield, Illinois, 1841–55. The federal court in Springfield rented space in the Tinsley Building on the public square. This restored jury room is now part of the Lincoln-Herndon Law Office State Historic Site in Springfield and shows the somewhat makeshift accommodations provided for jurors deliberating cases in federal court. *(Image courtesy of the Papers of Abraham Lincoln, Springfield, Ill.)*

FOUR

The Struggle for Legal Power in Lincoln's America

AS ANTEBELLUM Americans witnessed the rise of the professional classes and the development of professional expertise, they came to expect a greater level of competence from those in positions of authority. The advent of lawsuits for medical malpractice, personal injury, and negligence on the part of corporations and businesses during this period was an overt indication of the rising expectations regarding professional expertise and responsibility. Criticism of those in power was a by-product of such rising expectations. Developing professionals, including those in the law, medicine, science, and education, responded to that pressure and worked to combat negative images of their respective fields. To that end, they tried to standardize professional qualifications and ethics, to differentiate their expertise from that of other professional groups, to justify their elite status as members of those professions, and to set themselves apart from society at large.[1] This process was tied to the evolution of a middle-class ethos that was gaining strength and status during this era of vast legal and social change. The emerging middle-class worldview was framed in the context of politics, economics, consumer culture, and changing social experiences.

Within that context, the legal profession, composed of both the bench and the bar, sought to distinguish itself from the broader society and to define the legal profession within local communities. At the same time, judges and lawyers also worked to delineate and shape their separate spheres.[2]

Within antebellum society, judges and lawyers enjoyed elite economic and social status in their communities. Moreover, they dominated local party politics and wielded considerable power in their state legislatures. Throngs of young, ambitious men flocked to the law for their chance at upward mobility and middle-class status. Expanding court dockets opened up opportunities for judges and lawyers to develop more professional expertise, accumulate more wealth, and enjoy more power. The growth of the legal profession in terms of sheer numbers, the increasing participation of legal professionals in the political system, and the amassing of great wealth by many of these men invigorated and reinforced the profession's formidable presence in nineteenth-century American society.[3]

As discussed in the previous chapters, the law was a central component of the way in which antebellum Americans viewed the world around them, and they were astute observers of the rise of the legal profession. As the profession, particularly the bar, gained more and more prominence within society, antebellum Americans paid a great deal of attention to various aspects of it. Writers explored the character of lawyers in short stories and in novels. Newspaper editors and magazine writers exposed voracious readers to legal issues and debates. Papers and periodicals published numerous articles and opinion pieces examining and questioning the character, quality, and competence of judges, of lawyers, and of the legal system. In the public's intellectual engagement with the law, judges, attorneys, and the institution of the jury all had their detractors. Judges raged against lawyers. Lawyers ranted about judges. Observers cursed jurors and the jury system. And newspapers railed against them all. For nineteenth-century Americans, the law was a spectator amusement. It engaged them in the same way that intercollegiate and professional sports engage us today.[4]

The increased public interest in and scrutiny of the legal profession created a sense of urgency among judges, lawyers, and their colleagues impaneled in jury boxes. Actors in each part of the legal system—bench, bar, and jury—recognized the need to demonstrate competence in their respective roles, and they all worked to achieve specific expertise that would justify their place within that system. In the process, the jury box became the site for an intriguing and revealing power struggle, and the institution of the jury became the rope in a legal tug-of-war in which the victor was still undetermined by the time of the Civil War. Some historians have equated the professional rise of the bar during the first half of the nineteenth century as a significant aspect of industrial and corporate America's dominance in the antebellum legal system. They argue that the era's capitalists in business and industry teamed up with members of the bench and bar to enforce their own collective will on the law and on society at large at the expense of juries and nonelites. Charles Sellers's now famous accusation against lawyers that they were, by midcentury, the "shock troops of capitalism" epitomizes the belief that the American bar was, indeed, a powerful force. Given the rise of the bar and given the already established power of judges within and outside the courtroom, it might be easy to assume that the power of lawyers and judges came at the expense of juries. But on the contrary—and as revealed in the previous chapters—jurors were themselves members of elite circles in antebellum society, and they exhibited their own power within the courtroom as well.[5]

Much scholarship in legal history has sought to determine which groups dominated American law in the first half of the nineteenth century, yet no scholarship has directly engaged the ongoing power struggle inside the courtroom. Scholars have generally been too quick to assume that juries had complete power, too willing to blame lawyers for attempting to usurp the authority of the jury, or too eager to cast judges as purveyors of evil capitalistic intentions. No scholarship has tried to challenge these absolute interpretations or to address the interrelationships among judges, lawyers, and jurors. The evidence in the midwestern context suggests that during the first half of the 1800s, no single group dominated. Juries were not all-powerful. Not all lawyers were trying to diminish jury power. And not all judges were sleeping with the capitalistic enemy. In fact, there was constant negotiation and renegotiation, and as we will see, the outcome of an enduring power struggle between the three groups—the bench, the bar, and the jury—was not inevitable.[6]

This struggle for power was waged in the courthouses of the antebellum Midwest, an environment that underwent vast change in the first half of the nineteenth century. The earliest courthouses were primitive places, often makeshift buildings used for other purposes. Courts were frequently held in local taverns or houses, and it was not uncommon for them to be held outdoors. The first official courthouse for the Sangamon County Circuit Court in Springfield, Illinois, commissioned in 1822, was "built of logs, twenty feet in length, one story high, with plank floor, a good cabin roof, a door and window cut out."[7] It was a simple structure, but it was an important one. The courthouse also served as a meeting place where "most of early western society evolved," and court days were "gala affairs": in county seats across the Midwest, court days were "almost as exciting as a county fair." Indeed, court week in the Midwest was vital to the socialization process for men, women, and children who attended the legal proceedings. When court was in session, people in the community came together, "visited with their neighbors, traded horses, shot craps, drank liquor, flirted with the gals, ran horse races, [and] listened to fiddlers." In between all that celebration, they conducted some legal business too.[8]

Courthouses, however humble, stood as temples of justice. They symbolized the society's "veneration for ordered liberty and the rule of law." Over time and with the developing affluence of the community, they became more and more stately in structure and in design. By 1825, the Sangamon County Circuit Court had built a second courthouse; in 1831, a third was erected. "[A] square building, two stories in height, with a hip-roof and a cupola rising on the center," this more extravagant building was located in the center of the public square. It was a focal point not only of the community's legal life but also of its economic life. Businesses popped up around the courthouse, and the courthouse yard was a bustling, noisy hub for the developing town. By 1846, the Sangamon County Circuit Court was operating out of yet another new courthouse, this one across the street from the new state capitol on the square. This structure was a grand, two-story, Greek Revival edifice with a portico, flanked by six Doric columns and pilasters. As the county grew, so did its courthouse. Other midwestern towns and cities experienced similar development and, like Springfield, witnessed the increasing opulence of court buildings. As communities became more affluent, the buildings that contained and symbolized their legal institutions reflected that prosperity.[9]

The opulence of a community's courthouse also reflected the enhanced stature of the legal profession. As judges and lawyers assumed more prominent roles in social, economic, and political affairs, symbols of their profession made indelible marks on their communities. The law was central to American society's vision of itself, and symbols of the law instilled in citizens a deep pride, a sense of purpose, and a personal attachment to legal institutions. Members of the bench and the bar understood the meanings inherent in those symbols, and they seized the moment on behalf of their own power and self-interests. Inside the walls of the ever more majestic houses of "legal worship," a power struggle was under way throughout the antebellum Midwest as the bench and the bar fought for dominance while the institution of the jury struggled to maintain its position in American jurisprudence.

The following three sections will provide brief "biographical" snapshots of each of the three players in the struggle for dominance in the courtroom—the bench, the bar, and the jury—detailing their status, reputations, and positions of power. The section on the bench analyzes the efforts of judges to take control of their courtrooms and restrict the influence of the jury. The bar section discusses the rise of the professional bar, the greater formalization of pleading and legal practice, and the arrival of lawyers among the ranks of leading citizens; it also traces the emergence of the bar as a recognizable force both in the community and in the courtroom. The jury section examines the dichotomy between the jury's status as a democratic ideal and its growing reputation as a fallible institution. Each of the sections will address the interaction between the players in the power struggle and how their relationships both contributed to and distracted from the developing expertise of all individuals involved. The chapter will conclude with a case study that looks at the interrelationships among judges, lawyers, and jurors through the lens of one murder trial. The criminal case illuminates the professional expertise of these groups and reveals how each negotiated the power relationships present in antebellum midwestern courtrooms.

The Bench

> One of the chief village functionaries was the squire, or justice of the peace, and his office was not infrequently the arena where the neighborhood pettifoggers fought their wordy battles.
>
> —*Charles Beneulyn Johnson*[10]

American justices of the peace, county judges, circuit-riding judges, and state supreme court justices all served as symbolic directors of the legal system and as functional arbiters of the legal process. In jury trials, the judge acted as a presiding officer of the court. In chancery courts and in bench trials in the criminal- and common-law courts, when there was no panel of jurors hearing a case the judge made law, determined facts, and had much more latitude to exercise community authority. Since the colonial period, judges enjoyed positions of extreme power, and in the early years of the nineteenth century, they often possessed more legal knowledge and training than their contemporaries at the bar. Given their power in the courtroom and their dominance in their communities, they also inspired fear and loathing from their constituents—lawyers practicing in their courts, newspaper editors, and casual observers alike. Despite negative attention and public distrust, the bench endured as a powerful profession, and judges maintained their individual legal, social, and political power throughout the first half of the 1800s.[11]

In Illinois and other states of the emerging Midwest, juries were the finders of law and fact—at least in criminal trials—but judges lorded over procedure and practice in the courtroom, served in state legislatures, and engaged in professional activities of the bench, which further enhanced their elite position within society. Part of the power position of the bench was related to the development of the judges' legal knowledge and professional expertise. Through the printing of judicial opinions, the authoritative power of the bench was enhanced. Judges reinforced their status as legal elites and professionals through the official publication of the state appellate opinions they were writing as well as through the popular dissemination of instructional compendiums of state precedents. These published materials connected the bench and the bar, as lawyers increasingly relied upon these volumes to prepare their cases for trial. During this period, lawyers looked to judges to develop their own legal expertise. In Illinois, for example, the *Illinois Reports* were published at the end of each session of the Illinois Supreme Court. Every volume contained summaries of the appellate cases, together with the judgments and the written opinions of each case. Over time, lawyers came to depend heavily on these volumes to support their own cases. Abraham Lincoln, who handled more than four hundred appellate cases at the Illinois Supreme Court, frequently cited Illinois cases; his partner William Herndon kept a book of legal authorities from Illinois and other states arranged by legal topic for use in the cases that their law firm handled over the years. Other attorneys engaged in the same practice.[12]

As the bench gained authority within the legal profession, it also maintained authority in the courthouse. The first opportunity that nineteenth-century judges had to exhibit their authority was in their charges to grand juries at the beginning of each circuit court term. At such times, judges frequently delivered speeches to the incoming grand jurors, espousing their own political views from this legal platform. In the process, they could persuade grand jurors to focus on a particular criminal activity with which to crowd the court docket—and antebellum midwestern judges did not shy away from utilizing their influence.[13]

In 1839, Judge Richard Yates delivered a twenty-two-page speech to the Scott County grand jury in Winchester, Illinois. This lengthy oration probably took in excess of an hour to deliver, and the length and breadth of the document reveal the degree of judicial authority that judges such as Yates possessed. In the charge, he waxed philosophical about the duties of the men impaneled on the jury, asking them to "at once comprehend the magnitude and the importance" of their responsibilities. He also took the opportunity to preach about the evils of gambling and alcohol in the community, asking the grand jury to look hard for this category of criminal activity, which "most tarnish[es] the face of human society."[14] In two different charges to juries in the late 1840s, Judge David Davis also noted the significance of the grand juror's position. He, too, asked the grand jury to "inquire whether there are any gambling houses or quaint doggeries in the County," adding that there was "no greater nuisance to a Country" than liquor.[15] These sometimes indulgent grand jury charges (or sermons, as they might otherwise be known) gave judges a chance to direct the criminal docket. Considering how influential judges were in their communities, it is no great leap to assume that they held tremendous sway with the captive audience of an impaneled grand jury.

At trial, judges continued to assert their judicial authority. Antebellum midwestern judges enjoyed myriad powers in the courtroom. For instance, as bench trials—cases in which litigants waived their rights to a trial by jury—gained acceptance and became more common, judicial power expanded: in these cases, the bench assumed the role of the jury. Judges also had authority to allow or exclude testimony. They could entertain the motions and instructions of attorneys, or they could refuse them. In addition, they had the power to offer their own instructions to clarify, refute, or provide supplementary charges to jurors. Sometimes, appellate decisions displaced the power of jury verdicts, as state supreme court justices could overturn jury decisions and sentences meted out at the lower level. Despite the fact that state law made jurors the arbiters of questions of law, supreme courts required lower court judges to instruct juries based on the law found in the developing body of legal literature—specifically, in published appellate reports. This requirement potentially impinged upon the power of trial juries as well.[16]

Trial judges were also responsible for ensuring proper procedure. Among other things, they could order that verdicts be rendered in a particular form, or they could suggest sentencing.[17] Further, judges could directly influence jury deliberations and verdicts by giving or refusing to give attorneys' jury instructions, as happened in an 1846 case involving a breach of promise to marry. The defense attorney in the case asked the judge to instruct the jurors to decide the issue and award damages based *only* on the defendant's failure to complete the contract. The judge agreed to submit the instruction—but with a significant rewording. In the revised instruction he delivered, he asked the jurors to consider not only the failure to complete the contract but also "the injury inflicted to the feelings of the plaintiff, and to her standing in society," which he believed was a consequences arising out of the breach of contract. The defense attorney would have had the jury decide on one specific issue, but the judge was able to expand the scope of the case. His rewording of the instruction gave the jury greater leeway in determining the damages, to the detriment of the defendant. In the appeal, the supreme court upheld the trial judge's right to do so.[18] One early historian of Illinois observed that some judges, "through fear of doing wrong, or feeling a timid anxiety to avoid censure if they were compelled to give instructions which might decide the verdict on one side, were careful to accompany them with such exceptions and explanations as served to mystify what they had previously said, and destroy its force with the jury."[19]

The power of midwestern judges was exhibited in other ways as well. In Illinois, it was customary for elected circuit court judges to appoint temporary judges to serve during their absences from the bench. This custom was contrary to state law, which required that the court adjourn to the next scheduled term if the seated judge failed to convene the current term. Among the judges who disregarded this law was David Davis of the

Eighth Judicial Circuit in central Illinois, who appointed Abraham Lincoln to replace him on several occasions. When Davis was ill or had to be away for personal or business reasons, he sought the approval of the other attorneys at court and seated Lincoln in his stead. Lincoln had no judicial expertise, but his stature as an attorney on the circuit likely made this an agreeable arrangement for all parties. Though Lincoln was never officially appointed or elected to the bench, he presided over at least 321 cases from 1850 to 1859 in six central Illinois counties. And apparently, Davis's power to appoint him was never questioned. Waiting for the absent elected judge to return or for the next term to begin was probably not a desirable option, for litigants and attorneys were anxious to move forward with their cases. For practical reasons, the attorneys and litigants willingly invested this appointment power with the circuit judge so as not to suffer continuances of their pending cases, which would entail additional expense.[20]

For Lincoln, acting as a judge must have been a natural experience. He was always an arbiter at heart, his judicious spirit stretching back as far as his days in New Salem where he frequently presided over cockfights and horse races conducted by his friends. Lincoln often served as a mediator in the disputes of his clients as well, urging them to settle their differences out of court. In preparing notes for a law lecture, he suggested that attorneys should "discourage litigation," persuade their neighbors to compromise, and "point out to them how the nominal winner is often the real loser, in fees, expenses, and a waste of time." Judge Davis no doubt appreciated these judicious qualities in Lincoln, and when Lincoln took the bench in the judge's absence, those same qualities may well have kept other members of the bar from complaining; the attorneys and others in the courtroom apparently were quite comfortable with Lincoln's temporary judgeship. Yet the key point here is that it was the power of the bench (in this case, Judge David Davis) and not the law that allowed for such a breach of legal decorum.[21]

Judicial authority extended to the community as well, as legal power was often negotiated within the political arena during the antebellum period. Whether appointed by state legislators or popularly elected, judges of that era were engaged in partisan politics. Illinois judges were selected by the General Assembly until 1849, when the state law was changed to call for the election of judges. Ohio and Indiana soon followed suit, moving to an elective system in 1851. The election of judges for lifetime terms represented a democratization of the bench, making these individuals accountable to the public and, some might argue, less powerful.[22] Meanwhile, in addition to being candidates themselves, judges also participated in party politics, campaigning for other candidates and facilitating local and state political activities. Many were members of Congress, state legislatures, and state constitutional conventions; some served as judge and legislator simultaneously. Consequently, a sizable number of judges enjoyed the especially powerful position of making laws in their legislative capacity and then enforcing them in their courtrooms.[23]

In the antebellum Midwest, the law and politics were intricately connected, and the courtroom was the scene of legal business by day and politicking by night. The judge ruled the courtroom and often presided over political activity within it. The courthouse served both a legal and a political function, and sometimes there was considerable overlap between the two. As stated earlier, judges used the bench to espouse their political viewpoints via the charges they issued to grand juries. Gustav Koerner, an Illinois attorney who later was a justice on the state supreme court, offered some insights about the connectedness of law and politics. Relating his experiences as a young lawyer in Edwardsville, Illinois, in the 1830s, he reported in his memoir that the "weather was very hot; lawyers, jurors and witnesses were mostly in their shirt-sleeves. But Judge Smith kept the house in most perfect order. The first day the court adjourned at noon, giving way to political speech-making."[24]

The judge in Koerner's reminiscence was Theophilus W. Smith, whose own experiences offer further insights about the overlap of law and politics. Smith was an ardent Democrat who became embroiled in a court-packing controversy a few years after his tenure as a circuit-riding justice. The controversy stemmed from two appellate decisions rendered by a Whig-dominated Illinois Supreme Court, both of which angered Illinois Democrats. The 1839 case of *People ex rel. McClernand v. Field* involved the attempt by a Democratic governor to remove from office Illinois secretary of state Alexander P. Field, a Whig. The legal action led to a Whig-controlled supreme court decision that favored Field and supported his right to retain his office. The second case, *Spragins v. Houghton,* involved the issue of voting requirements and the legality of votes cast by unnaturalized citizens.

In this case, the Illinois Supreme Court rejected the right of an alien to vote, arguing that Thomas Spragins, a Jo Daviess County election judge, allowed the vote of an unnaturalized Irish immigrant; a Whig judge, Dan Stone, had ruled that Spragins was wrong to do so. Democrats were so incensed by these court decisions that the democratically controlled Illinois General Assembly enacted legislation to change the political makeup of the state's highest court. Nine judicial districts were created, thereby adding five justices to the court for a panel of nine. The legislature appointed five Democrats (including Theophilus Smith) to the new positions, giving the Democrats a six-to-three majority in the court. These developments vividly illustrate the intimate connection between law and politics in that period, as well as the significant role of party politics in the power relations in the courtroom.[25]

Some antebellum observers were beginning to express concern about the extent of judicial power. A nineteenth-century historian, to cite one example, warned that judges were becoming "legislators" as they devised their own interpretations of the law. The concern was not unfounded. As noted, judges had the power to instruct juries, and it was here that their influence was particularly impressive. The bench's potential power over juries extended from the Illinois General Assembly down to the courtroom. But not all judges were interested in defeating jury power. Justice John D. Caton of the Illinois Supreme Court cautioned that "courts cannot be too careful, in so framing their instructions, as to not have the least appearance of an attempt to influence the jury in their determination of facts, especially in criminal cases."[26] Apparently, maintaining at least some semblance of judicial propriety was important to Caton, and perhaps it was to other judges as well. Caton never held elective office, nor had he served as a delegate at a state constitutional convention, but he was active in party politics. Judges who did not serve in a legislative office were rare (in Illinois at least), but they did exist. Justice Theophilus Lyle Dickey of the Illinois Supreme Court was involved in party politics, but he never ran for public office. Another justice, Norman H. Purple, was a presidential elector in 1844, but he was never a candidate himself.[27]

Candidacy for office and engagement in party politics may or may not have influenced the judicial views and practices of judges. We know at least that Caton was capable of separating law and politics. But not all judges were as cautious as he was, and some were not afraid to push the envelope. The previously mentioned David Davis is a case in point. In an 1850 debt case in the Sangamon County Circuit Court in Springfield, the jury returned a verdict against the defendant. Judge Davis, who believed that the jury had erred in weighing the testimony, overturned the verdict and found for the plaintiff. In the appeal that followed, the Illinois Supreme Court upheld Davis's action because it was deemed good law. So it is clear that judges had some authority to overturn jury verdicts, and they could enforce their own sometimes discretionary power as well. A number of American judges enjoyed an informal relationship with jurors, commenting casually on evidence; others preferred a more formal approach. Either way, there was no question that the relationship between the professional bench and the increasingly competent jury was an evolving and frequently contested association.[28]

If the courtroom relationship between judges and jurors was marked by colliding power at worst and cool distance at best, the relationship between members of the bench and the bar, although at times adversarial, was much more collegial. A circuit-riding judge traveled from circuit court to circuit court accompanied by a cadre of circuit-riding attorneys. They rode in the same carriages, slept in the same beds, took meals as a group, and practiced politics together. Their shared travel experiences and hardships helped them form lifelong personal and professional bonds. The fraternity of the bench and bar was the result of such close interactions and contributed much to the development of the legal profession. When Abraham Lincoln traveled the Eighth Judicial Circuit during the 1840s and 1850s, it was with the circuit judge, the prosecuting attorney, and a number of other circuit attorneys. He and his colleagues talked about their cases, held mock trials, practiced political speeches on each other, and shared personal stories. Lincoln was a well-known beneficiary of this powerful fraternity. His relationship with Judge Davis, who ultimately became his presidential campaign manager, illustrates the power politics in which the bench engaged. Over time, the relationship between the two men would play a significant role in Lincoln's election to the presidency and Davis's ascendancy to the U.S. Supreme Court.[29]

Midwestern judges enjoyed rising, middle- to upper-class elite status. Given their overlapping positions of power in politics, in legislation, in their profession, and in their courtrooms, they may have experienced a golden age of judicial control during the antebellum era.[30] The judicial authority they exercised was the product of several factors—the development of legal and professional expertise, participation in party politics and legislative activities, a deliberate exertion of power within the courtroom, and a maintenance of collegial interactions with the bar.

The Bar

> [Lawyers are the] highest political class and the most cultivated circle of society.
>
> —*Alexis de Tocqueville, 1835*[31]

By the time de Tocqueville published that praise of lawyers in *Democracy in America* in the 1830s, the legal profession was still gaining in status. For the most part, attorneys had overcome the widespread negative opinions associated with their field in the colonial era; they had emerged from the American Revolution with a new professional purpose. However, they were still evolving, comprising only one of many professional classes that were acquiring greater social, political, and economic prominence.[32]

Ambitious young men in the first half of the nineteenth century saw a career in the law as a vehicle for self-advancement and upward mobility. Because the profession was in its infancy and without particularly strict educational and admission requirements, it offered opportunity to men without great financial means. In an effort to democratize the bar, many state legislatures "redefined professional standards, scaling down educational requirements for lawyers or eliminating them altogether in such states as New Hampshire, Wisconsin, and Indiana." Suddenly, every citizen of "good moral character" was entitled by statute to engage in legal practice, and many lawyers who gained prominence at the bar during this time were men of very modest economic backgrounds. Abraham Lincoln was a quintessential example. Born into a farming family of limited means, Lincoln, with practically no formal education, used the law to achieve middle-class status. Through a career at the bar, he earned a middle-class income, married a wealthy and socially prominent woman, developed personal ties with elite members of society, and established and maintained a career in politics: as a lawyer, he became a member of the professional, economic, and social elite. The money he earned and the contacts he developed at the bar were absolutely critical to his achievements in politics as well as in society.[33]

The upward mobility of lawyers such as Lincoln and the enhanced status of the bar directly corresponded with the rise of the middle class. But the growing prominence of the field also stemmed from a conscious effort on the part of the legal profession broadly and lawyers more specifically to distance themselves from the general population. Legal scholar Roscoe Pound viewed this period as a time of decline in the bar, which he blamed on the democratization of the profession: the infusion of "illiterates," he believed, contributed to the falling status of lawyers in society. Conversely, other research has argued that lawyers in this era were committed to competence and expertise. Members of the bar were trying to justify their status and preserve the power they were gaining by developing professional expertise, and their eloquence brought spectators to court to hear their well-crafted arguments. Though most lawyers during this era did not attend colleges or law schools (of which there were very few), an examination system was taking shape at the local level. The profession attempted to grant law licenses to individuals who had at least a rudimentary understanding of law and legal pleading and practice. Practicing lawyers tutored aspiring young lawyers, and local bar associations took ownership of this educational process, examining "students" and recommending to the circuit courts their competence to begin practice on their own.[34]

In the context of the occupational and social mobility of the nineteenth century, American lawyers were certainly making a name for themselves, gaining wealth and political status as well. They were becoming more and more affluent, as the ever-expanding court dockets and the expertise required to navigate the complex legal system provided opportunities for earning income. In one Kentucky county in 1850, some 38 percent of the lawyers practicing there owned $5,000 or more in real property. Four attorneys living and practicing law in Springfield, Illinois, in 1860 owned $110,000, $82,500, $30,000, and $15,000, respectively, in real and personal property. No doubt, lawyers were cashing in on their professional opportunities.[35]

Based on their professional expertise and wealth, lawyers were also becoming influential in their local communities as social and political elites. Moreover, the bar emerged by 1850 as a dominant force in local, state, and national politics. In mounting numbers, lawyers served in state legislatures, won election as mayors, participated in state constitutional conventions, and engaged in party politics on a variety of levels. Lawyer-legislators were not uncommon on the East Coast either. Twenty-five percent of the councilmen in Philadelphia were lawyers, as were 20 percent in New York City and 15 percent in Boston. By 1813, lawyers also represented the largest majority in Congress. The high percentage of attorneys who gained elective office clearly spoke to their growing reputation and influence. One study of lawyer-politicians found that in 1850, lawyers made up 34 percent of the Kentucky House of Representatives and 42 percent of the Kentucky Senate. Of the twenty-two men elected as senators in the Illinois General Assembly in 1848, eight (36 percent) were lawyers.[36] When Andrew Jackson won election as the seventh president of the United States in 1828, he became the fifth lawyer-president. When Lincoln won the presidency, all but four of the men who had served before him were attorneys.[37]

Many individual lawyers enjoyed considerable respect from the public at large, despite the fact that the bar, as a profession, was still in its infancy. The bar was stretching and growing. Bar associations were working to control admission to the profession, and legal periodicals were springing up as well. Prior to 1830, there were only twelve law journals, but by the 1850s, thirty-seven new legal periodicals had come into existence. Publications such as the *Monthly Law Reporter,* the *New York Legal Observer,* and the *Western Law Journal* disseminated legal knowledge to both aspiring and practicing attorneys. John Livingston, a New York attorney and publisher, was one of a number of lawyers who put out journals and various publications that spread legal knowledge and promoted the growth and development of their profession. State supreme courts published their opinions, and various legal scholars created compendiums of laws for mass distribution. Despite the dearth of formal law schools during this period, the legal profession was evolving and becoming unified as a result of bar association activities; the standardization of licensing practices; and the publication of legal treatises, laws, and periodicals. While they amassed fortunes and social status, lawyers were working together to establish themselves as intellectual elites as well.[38]

The burgeoning influence of lawyers and the bar escaped the notice of very few nineteenth-century Americans. As the profession grew, public interest in it and in the lives of its members increased dramatically with the publication of novels and stories in which lawyers were central characters—novels such as *Drayton: A Story of an American Life* or *The People's Lawyer* and short stories such as "Bartleby the Scrivener," to mention just a few. In one popular story, the central character was an uneducated, lazy, and undisciplined man whose shortcomings did not hinder his ability to become a successful lawyer. Whether as heroes or villains, lawyers emerged as popular characters in American fiction.[39]

Novelists and storytellers were not the only people to spread negative opinions of lawyers. Judge John Dudley of the New Hampshire Supreme Court once said, "You've heered what has been said by the lawyers, the rascals!"[40] A newspaper reporter in Chicago criticized the greed of lawyers in a case involving land along Lake Michigan, writing that members of the Chicago bar viewed the lakefront property as their own El Dorado. The article went on to say that the lawsuit had become "a mint of coined gold" for the lawyers, who were purposely taking their time resolving it at an outrageous expense to the actual parties in the legal dispute. In 1851, an article in the *Illinois Daily Journal* in Springfield accused lawyers of being "God's forsaken beings, who prowled around the purlieus of the jail, stirring up . . . litigation" between the state and "the poor prisoners."[41] Late in his career, Abraham Lincoln addressed the negative stereotype of lawyers and encouraged young attorneys to make it a cause to change such damaging images of their profession. He wrote: "There is a vague popular belief that lawyers are necessarily dishonest . . . the expression is common—almost universal. Let no young man, choosing the law for a calling, for a moment yield to this popular belief. Resolve to be honest at all events; and if, in your own judgment, you can not be an honest-lawyer, resolve to be honest without being a lawyer. Choose some other occupation, rather than one in the choosing of which you do, in advance, consent to be a knave." In that same missive, Lincoln also cautioned young attorneys against stirring up litigation: "A worse man can scarcely be found than one who does this. Who can be more nearly a fiend that he who habitually overhauls the Register of deeds, in search of defects in titles, whereon to stir up strife, and put money in his pocket. A moral tone ought to be infused into the profession, which should drive such men out of it."[42]

There might have been quite animated disagreements regarding the respectability of individual lawyers and of the profession at large, but few, if any, would have denied that lawyers were becoming a dominant force in American society, law, politics, economics, and literature. As they gained status in society, nineteenth-century lawyers battled for dominance inside the courtroom as well. One scholar has noted that southern and western attorneys were particularly "aggressive and jealous of courtroom control" and that they were "entrepreneurial and independent of court control in the matter of fees. They commanded good fees for their legal expertise, and they demanded full reign to sway juries in the representation of their clients."[43] Their power in state legislatures assisted them in this regard. Attorneys participated in the codification of rules of practice, pleading, and evidence through their service in state legislatures. In the courtroom, they continued to provide more and more instruction to jurors, directly competing with the authority of judges at trial.[44]

A number of historians have argued that judges and lawyers were in cahoots to conquer American society, but in fact, they often struggled against each other. Over time, lawyers submitted more extensive instructions, demanded greater control over pleading and practice, and grew ever more skillful in manipulating juries. Abraham Lincoln, for one, became famous for his use of humor, emotion, and storytelling in swaying juries to his clients' sides. Such tactics diminished the influence of the judge in favor of the solicitor. Lincoln also refused to presume that the presiding judges had an all-knowing expertise in the courtrooms in which he practiced. Indeed, he once stated, "I argued the case on the presumption that the court did not know any thing."[45] In this instance, he had given the jury a lengthy history of the law at issue in his case. The history lesson he delivered then as well as the humorous stories he employed in other cases were all part of his effort to exercise his legal power as an attorney and to win the day for his clients. And Lincoln was not the only midwestern attorney to display powerful expertise in the courtroom.[46]

Judges responded to these efforts and to the growing expertise of lawyers by exerting their own influence. Most notably, a judge could refuse to deliver a lawyer's jury instructions; he could issue only an edited version of them; or he could deliver his own instructions, countering those of the attorney. The issue of jury instructions illustrated the head-to-head courtroom struggle that pitted lawyers and judges against each other. Judges were responsible for maintaining procedure and process. Lawyers were charged with convincing judges to make rulings, accept pleas, and deliver instructions that would result in desirable outcomes for their clients. All the parties were playing to the jury. So, as a matter of course, a lawyer proposed instructions to the judge, but the judge could determine whether the jury heard those instructions; additionally, the judge could reword the instructions. The lawyer could object to the judge's ruling and could assign errors for appeal, but at trial, the judge had ultimate power in this regard.[47]

Dialogue with the jurors was at the heart of this power struggle, and thus, the giving or denying of jury instructions was critical: judges and lawyers battled primarily over attorneys' attempts to instruct juries and judges' ability to give or refuse the desired instructions. One early historian of Illinois recounted: "I knew one judge who when asked for instructions would rub his head and the side of his face with his hand as if perplexed and say to lawyers, 'Why, gentleman, the jury understand the case; they need no instructions; no doubt they will do justice between the parties.'"[48] In a case in Illinois in the 1840s, the judge refused an attorney's jury instruction because he found it unintelligible. In the appeal that followed, the Illinois Supreme Court upheld the lower court judge's refusal, arguing that "the object of instructions is to convey to the minds of the jury correct principles of law . . . instructions ought not to be given unless they may be fairly understood and easily comprehended by the jury." The judge was the final arbiter of what was comprehensible and what was not. In another case, the Illinois Supreme Court upheld a trial judge's ruling that a prosecuting attorney was not adequately acquainted with the law related to the issues of the suit. Therefore, the judge had instructed the jury to the detriment of the attorney's arguments.[49]

The substance of jury instructions and oral arguments was also a bone of contention. Thus, in Indiana, the question of whether lawyers had the power or right to argue law before juries was in constant flux during the antebellum period. The Indiana legislature denied lawyers this right in 1828, gave it in 1830, and denied it again in 1851. A state constitutional revision in 1858 again returned this power to the lawyers.[50] Given that the state legislature was filled with attorneys, it appears that either the bar frequently changed its mind on this question or individual lawyers themselves did not agree on what was appropriate dialogue with jurors. The underlying question was far from settled. The interrelationships among bench, bar, and jury were not written in stone, nor were they guaranteed by statute or by legal practice and proceeding.

At least twenty appellate cases in the antebellum Midwest hinged on the issue of jury instructions. An opinion in one case argued that a circuit court judge had the right to refuse an attorney's jury instructions if, in the opinion of the judge, those instructions were "drawn, either from carelessness or design," to "mislead" rather than instruct jurors. The opinion went on to say that it was the judge's duty to see that instructions conveyed to the jurors "correct principles of law, as applicable to the evidence which has been laid before them." The opinion also chastised lawyers for giving incomprehensible instructions.[51] The circumstances of jury instructions in an Iowa case incurred the wrath of that state's supreme court. In reversing the lower court opinion in a simple replevin case, Justice George Greene complained of an attorney's power to instruct jurors, arguing that instructions should exert no "undue influence on a jury." In this case, the defendant's attorney, who had won the case for his client at the circuit court, had "very adroitly managed to decide [the] facts for the jury" by crafting his "gilded and embellished" instructions so as to sway jurors to his client's side. Greene wrote: "Most jurors are glad to escape the trouble of an investigation, and the perplexity of deciding; and are more than inclined to adopt any judicial decision, or intimation, that may be submitted to them. Hence great caution should be exercised, and jurors should often be admonished by the courts that they alone are to investigate and decide the facts in the case submitted to them."[52]

Greene overruled the lower court judge's allowance of such "repugnant" instructions, was horrified at the misuse of instructions by the attorney in the case, and showed scant faith in the competence of the jurors themselves. Obviously, the struggle over jury instructions involved the rights and expertise of lawyers and of judges within the confines of the courtroom. But they were also closely related to the constriction of jury power and the production of competent verdicts. As the bench and bar flexed their authoritative muscles, the institution of the jury was at stake. And as we will see, instructions could prove to be very dangerous weapons: when instructions were misused, the competence of jurors and their verdicts were compromised.

The Jury

> The jury serves to give to the minds of all citizens a part of the habits of mind of the judge; and these habits are precisely those that best prepare the people to be free.
>
> —*Alexis de Tocqueville, 1835*[53]

The democratic institution of the jury enjoyed an honored reputation in the antebellum American context. There was a general consensus, exhibited in the law and through the political rhetoric of the early nineteenth century, that the right of trial by jury was intrinsic to the freedom of the American people. State legislators in the emerging Midwest codified their faith in the jury, entrusting to jurors the power to decide law. This power, combined with the general verdict—guilty or not guilty returns, without details as to the finding of such verdicts—instilled in jurors an understanding of and appreciation for the power they could wield in the courtroom. Thus, American laws gave jurors power, most Americans accepted the power that juries held, and jurors employed that power in courtrooms across the Midwest. One obvious historical example of jury power was the debate about jury guarantees in fugitive slave cases. Proslavery forces opposed the use of juries in such cases, whereas fervent abolitionists favored them. Supporters of slavery understood that jurors had the power to influence policy with their verdicts and ignore at the local level federal laws that protected the slaveholder's interests.[54]

As we have seen, most jurors in the antebellum Midwest were from the same economic, social, and political circles as members of the bench and bar. When Abraham Lincoln sat on his first jury in 1833, he was a popular young man on the path to middle-class status and respectability. By the time he sat on his last jury nineteen years later, he had become a well-known politician, an accomplished lawyer, a practiced "judge," and an expert juror (and onetime foreman). His experiences as judge, lawyer, and juror reveal the interconnectedness of the three groups of players involved in the power struggle waged in courtrooms across the country. Like Lincoln, many jurors held the same middle-class values and beliefs as the judges and attorneys who sought to control their verdicts. The power struggle was not, as some historians have suggested, an attempt by the elite bench and the elite bar to dominate juries composed of nonelites.

Morton Horwitz has argued that legislatures were taking power away from juries, as indicated by legislation enacted in the 1830s requiring the use of commissioners' assessments, rather than jury verdicts as in the past, to determine damages in right-of-way cases. But in the midwestern context, such legislation was more about efficiency and less about any effort to dominate juries. The fact was that members of all three groups in the legal setting—judges, attorneys, and jurors alike—enjoyed affluence and influence in their communities. Perhaps because jurors had elite status, contemporary observers generally found them competent and their verdicts mostly reasonable. Evidence suggests that when the public railed against jury verdicts, they charged the jurors involved with lacking intelligence, class, and honor—characteristics ascribed to elites.[55] Therefore, it stands to reason that perceptions of what constituted expertise and which individuals were competent were closely tied to emerging middle-class values. As long as jurors looked like white, middle- or upper-class elites, they could competently serve. Since antebellum jurors did, indeed, look like those elites, there was general public acceptance of the jury system and the verdicts it delivered in that era.

Nonetheless, grand and trial juries had their critics. Judges sometimes threw out verdicts, claiming that a jury had failed to provide a judgment consistent with the law.[56] State supreme court justices were also known to criticize the personal character of jurors, charging them with misconduct during trials and disregard of their responsibilities. In an 1856 opinion of the Supreme Court of Iowa, a justice complained that "some of the jurors paid no attention whatever to the law or evidence, and were reading newspapers during the progress of the trial, and while defendants' counsel were making their speeches."[57] Another judge, in Illinois, complained that the jurors were drinking "spirituous liquors in company with persons not belonging to the jury . . . after they had been sworn."[58]

Some state legislators were disgruntled with the grand jury system and proposed to strike it down because they believed grand juries were incompetent and were frequently responsible for the miscarriage of justice. In Indiana, the controversy broke out along political lines. Arguing for individual rights, Democrats attempted to abolish or restructure the grand jury system. They contended that a more public, open examination of grand jury presentments would protect personal rights. Whigs worked to maintain the system as it existed, arguing that the secret grand jury sessions that produced indictments contributed to the public good.[59] A member of the Indiana House of Representatives offered a proposal to eliminate the grand jury in his state, proclaiming in 1850 that he was "in favor of the entire abolition of the Grand Jury system; for I consider that it has been an instrument in the hands of bad and designing men to set aside the claims of justice." One of his colleagues took an opposing stance, pointing out that grand jurors were, according to general practice, selected from the "best men of the county" and were "generally men of some standing . . . who are supposed to combine among themselves both education and intelligence."[60]

There were claims throughout the 1800s that jury panels were elitist, but these claims were far less prevalent than charges of outright juror incompetence. Americans wanted their judges and lawyers to be capable and responsible, and they expected no less from impaneled jurors. Therefore, when jurors slipped up or when juries returned "bad" verdicts, critics abounded. Newspapers and periodicals joined judges and legislators in ranting against jurors and juries. A critique published in a Kentucky newspaper in 1858 screamed that jurors were "miserable wretches." In the late 1850s, *Harper's Weekly* published a number of articles probing the competence of jurors, spoofing the conduct of jury panels in specific cases, revealing the corruption of jurors, and complaining about the "absurdity of the jury system in criminal cases" and the "defects" of the institution and its "maladministration of justice."[61] One 1857 editorial was prompted by the dismissal of a panel of jurors who could not agree on a verdict in a case involving an Italian immigrant who allegedly murdered a police officer. The language employed by the writer of the critique was particularly scathing:

> It has long been the opinion of the soundest minds on the Bench and the Bar that the jury system, as we have it, is an actual hindrance to justice. Rogues and criminals justly regard our jury law as their best friend. Experience indeed, teaches that so long as we are compelled to select twelve jurymen who have formed no opinion on the guilt or innocence of a culprit, and to secure unanimity among these twelve either to acquit or convict, failure of justice will be the rule, and vindication of law the exception . . . without a reform . . . it were far better for the interests of justice to dispense with juries altogether, and leave the facts as well as the law to the decision of the judge.[62]

All types of publications carried editorial opinions and news articles related to the jury, and practically every newspaper and periodical covered jury trials with some regularity. The jury system, with its human quality and direct contact with the citizenry, was a constant fascination for readers. Questions regarding juror competence, the moral character of jurors, jury verdicts, and the quality of the jury system were constantly in the public literature.[63]

These questions occupied some of the country's best legal minds as well. A large percentage of the case law that state supreme courts established in the first decades of the nineteenth century centered on the power of the jury, the role of the judge, and the position of lawyers to influence jurors. In the Midwest, Illinois led the charge in this regard: the Illinois Supreme Court heard at least a dozen cases relating to judicial, jury, or attorney power.[64] A series of legal incidents in the famed Massachusetts Supreme Court of Lemuel Shaw demonstrated the struggle, which spilled out of the East and soon sparked the interest of midwesterners. In the 1845 case of *Commonwealth v. Porter,* Shaw's court ruled that in criminal cases only judges had the right to decide questions of law and that juries were obligated to apply the law they received from the trial judges. There was much public hostility toward the ruling, and in 1853, the state constitutional convention decided to put forth an amendment to give juries the right to decide law.[65] The amendment failed, but the state legislature passed a law in 1855 declaring that "in all trials for criminal offences, it shall be the duty of the jury to try . . . both the fact and law involved in the issue."[66]

Commonwealth v. Antes tested the statute and gave Lemuel Shaw his platform to confirm, reiterate, and demand his solution to the power struggle. The judge's role—and his power—was "to adjudicate the law, as it is conceded to be that of the jury to judge of the fact." In the opinion, Shaw argued that the power of the judge to determine law was "not controverted, but confirmed as the ancient and fundamental rule of the common law."[67] For Shaw, there was no question; and for the legislature that passed the statute, there was no question. There was, however, a huge question: did judges have ultimate power in the courtroom, or did juries enjoy that position?

The issue remained unsettled in Massachusetts. And it was no different in the western states, where appellate courts constantly engaged with the power struggle. Granted, not all state supreme court decisions packed the punch of one written by the powerful Lemuel Shaw, but supreme court justices in the emerging Midwest were no less committed to settling the question. Increasingly instrumental jury law in the first half of the nineteenth century may have begun to shift power away from juries.[68] The desire for competent juries and competent verdicts led Americans to want predictable outcomes, and this trend perhaps resulted in a tightening of the reins of jury power. Certainly, by the end of the nineteenth century, jury power would be nearly chiseled away. But statute law and case law in the antebellum Midwest illustrate that the total usurpation of jury power was far from complete at midcentury. Midwestern legislators and appellate judges generally remained committed to the ideal of the jury and the importance of the institution, at least in theory. The final outcome of the power struggle in midwestern courtrooms was not inevitable, and debate over the question was definitely in full bloom.

Many judges were exercising judicial power by tightly controlling procedure in the courtroom. Lawyer-legislators worked to constrain jury power. Public opinion ebbed and flowed between reform-mindedness and support of the status quo. However, "jury power was enormous, and subject to few controls" during the era, according to one scholar. This scholar has also argued that the jury system was not infallible and that jury outcomes were sometimes "unprofessional and unpredictable." Jurors were never "totally circumscribed by legal rules," and their deliberations remained quite separate from the power of the bench. In the Midwest, juries still held the power to make law in criminal cases. Jurors were at liberty to consider or ignore instructions from judges and lawyers (as per the general verdict), and their verdicts were generally accepted unless based on erroneous error worthy of appeal. All through the nineteenth century, state legislatures (made up of lawyers) were writing more and more rules of evidence to control the jury, yet the nineteenth-century jury remained, in practice, relatively independent, with the judge "little more than an umpire." In the deliberation room, jurors could put their personal views and the ethical and moral standards of their communities on the table. Unlike lawmakers, they did not face consequences for their verdicts. All jurors had an equal right to be heard in that context, and the ways in which they deliberated did not generally impinge upon their power to deliver general verdicts.[69]

A humorous story from Illinois provides some insights about this power struggle. In his 1854 history of the state of Illinois, Thomas Ford recounted an anecdote from a circuit court trial regarding the question of law and fact and who—the judge or the jury—was to decide:

> If some judges were unwilling to risk censure by giving instructions to juries, there was at least one who was very positive in his mode of instructing them. This one, being more ambitious to show his learning and ability, gave very pointed instructions on one occasion; but the jury could not agree on a verdict. The judge asked to know the cause of their difference, whereupon the foreman answered with great apparent honesty and simplicity, "Why, judge, this *'ere* is the difficulty. The jury want to know whether that *ar* what you told us when we first went out was *raly* the law, or whether it was *ony jist* your notion." The judge of course informed them that it was really the law, and they found a verdict accordingly.[70]

The story reveals Ford's bias as a former judge, in his assertion that judges were, "of course," the true judges of law and that juries were subordinate to them. Although the law presumed jurors were intelligent, many lawyers and judges thought otherwise. Ford's characterization of one juror's intelligence—by quoting the man's uneducated dialect—exposed that predilection.[71]

To investigate the power of the jury and detail the power struggle at play in midwestern courtrooms in the early 1800s, it is useful to consider the question of law and fact in jury trials. Juries had the most power in criminal cases, as they were granted the right to find law and fact. Midwestern state constitutions and statutes authorized and protected this power. Defendants in criminal cases had the protection of the constitutional right to trial by jury, and trial judges and appellate justices were more careful in protecting their rights than they were in guarding the rights of litigants in, say, debt actions in civil court.[72] In the antebellum Midwest, state appellate courts routinely upheld the criminal jury's power to find law. Civil juries were also granted considerable power. In one case, the Illinois Supreme Court ruled against a justice of the peace who had refused to properly instruct jurors as to their power in the case. The high court's opinion argued that the jury, not the judge, was the appropriate determiner of the definition of "reasonable time" in a particular contract dispute.[73] By the end of the nineteenth century, as competence and expertise were demanded from the legal system, jurors would be stripped of that power after the prevailing attitude toward them changed from general enthusiasm and support to distrust and suspicion of incompetence. That change would not come until jurors began to look less and less like ruling white elites. But in 1860, bench, bar, and jury were still on even footing in terms of economic, social, and political status. This fact both simplified and complicated the power struggle.[74]

The Complexity of Power

The case of Wesley B. Fisher, a twenty-five-year-old boatman, illustrates the power struggle between the bar and the bench and between jury and judge.[75] The La Salle County grand jury, sitting in Ottawa, Illinois, indicted Fisher for murder in the death of his wife, Clarissa Randull Fisher, in 1859. The defendant's sanity at the time of the murder was central to the trial and the outcome of the case. The trial and subsequent Illinois Supreme Court appeal raised a series of legal questions surrounding the limitations of an attorney's instructions to a jury, a judge's power to give or deny instructions and to direct a jury, a jury's right to determine law in criminal cases, and the legality of communications between judge and jurors during jury deliberations. As we will see, the outcome of the power struggle was far from decided in 1859, as each legal group was still negotiating its position within the developing legal system.[76]

During Fisher's murder trial in the circuit court, the jury became engaged in a legal dialogue of sorts with Judge M. E. Hollister regarding jury instructions, questions of law, and legal distinctions between murder and manslaughter and sanity and insanity. It all began after the presentation of evidence and witness testimony at the trial, when the prosecution and the defense submitted jury instructions to the court. The judge agreed to give all of the instructions written by the prosecutor but only part of the instructions written by the defendant's attorneys, and not surprisingly, the defense objected to the court's ruling. The prosecution's ninth instruction would become a major issue for the jury. It read: "The prosecution are not bound to prove that the defendant was sane at the time of the act complained of, and if the whole evidence in the case should leave it doubtful in the minds of the jury whether the prisoner was sane or insane at the time, they should not in that case excuse the prisoner on the ground of insanity."[77]

After the judge gave the instructions, jurors retired to consider the evidence and find a verdict. The following day, they sent a written question to the judge: "Does a deliberate intention to kill, as found in the ninth instruction of The People v. W. B. Fisher, mean, or intend to mean, a full consciousness on the part of the prisoner of the enormity of the crime, or merely a calculation or contrivance of means to kill, without such consciousness?"[78] Judge Hollister responded to the jury with two very specific instructions:

> The law of provocation, when applied to sane persons so as to reduce the killing from murder to manslaughter, is the unlawful killing of a human being without malice express or implied, and without any mixture of deliberation whatever. If from motives of hatred, revenge, jealousy, or any wrong or injury, real or imaginary, one person kill another, the killing shall be referred to malice, and must be considered murder. If, however, the killing is the result of a sudden, violent impulse of passion, caused by a serious and highly provoking injury inflicted upon the person killing, which is sufficient, in the minds of the jury, to excite an irresistible passion in a reasonable person . . . then it is manslaughter and not murder.
>
> The law makes the killing of a human being murder when there is an intention deliberately formed to take the life of another, and another is killed. In determining the question of intention, it is competent for the jury to take into consideration any facts in proof, which show that the mind of the person killing was affected with insanity at the time of killing. If they believe that at such time the mind was so far and so much affected with insanity as to satisfy them that he had not, prior to the killing, deliberately formed an intention to kill, or that at the time of the killing he had so far lost the control of his reason, by reason of his insanity, as to be incapable of acting upon such intention . . . the killing is manslaughter and not murder.[79]

The judge emphasized the distinction in the law between murder and manslaughter and thus defined (or found) the law for the jury. The instructions asked the jury to take the judge's depiction of the law and apply the facts presented at trial to that law, noting specifically that the question pertained to malice. Based on the judge's clarifications, if the jury found that Fisher acted with malice, then a murder conviction should result. If Fisher expressed no malice, then the jury should return a verdict of manslaughter. The judge also urged the jurors to consider the sanity of the defendant. If Fisher was insane at the time of the killing, then a manslaughter (not murder) conviction should result. The right of juries to find law in addition to facts was not a guarantee of the U.S. Constitution, but by 1800, it had become customary in most states, and midwestern state constitutions allowed juries to determine both law and fact.[80] Thus, not only was Judge Hollister going against this tradition in the murder case against Wesley Fisher, he was also directly violating Illinois criminal code, which provided that "juries, in all cases, shall be judges of the law and the fact."[81]

The defendant objected to the judge's second set of instructions to the jury, and the jurors again retired for deliberation. That evening, they returned and submitted two statements to the court:

> The jury maintains that whatever evidence was produced on the trial in regard to any supposed provocation or provocations, or in regard to any state of mind indicating insanity, may have any weight, or such weight, in the mind of the juror, as in his judgment it may demand, either in excusing or mitigating the crime of murder.
>
> The jury maintains that he is competent to judge of the correctness of any or all of the instructions of the judge, as his, the juror's own opinion of the law may dictate.[82]

In these statements, the jury was asserting itself and declaring its right to take or leave the judge's instructions. The jurors were obviously aware both of the power they could wield and of the limitations of judicial power. In response to this rather forceful declaration, the judge reiterated his distinctions between manslaughter and murder and reasserted his previous instructions regarding the issue of sanity versus insanity in the case. In his final instruction, Judge Hollister, perhaps frustrated with the jury's questioning of his power to instruct, chastised the jury for challenging him:

> The jury must take the law as given to them by the court as the law which is to govern them in this case. It is for the jury to determine whether the law, thus laid down by the court, is

> applicable to the proofs in the case. If the jury find the facts to be such as to make the law applicable, either to a case of murder, manslaughter, or to a case of insanity, or to a state of innocence, the law as laid down to them must be made to apply. It is not for the jury to say that the instructions given are not the law by which they are to determine the guilt or innocence of the prisoner.[83]

The next day, one of the jurors presented in writing yet more questions for the judge. The jury asked if it was "lawful for a juryman to go behind our statue law and search the Bible to see whether our statute laws are not void in consequence of their disagreement with a higher law." The panel of jurors also asked if they could consult medical books to assess the testimony of a doctor and search law books to "see whether the judge did not exclude some testimony that ought to have been admitted." These questions were yet another direct challenge to the judge and his procedure and authority. They were also a challenge to the attorneys who had conducted the trial.[84]

A day later, the judge informed the jury that they could not "lawfully disregard the statute of the State" by taking "the Bible for the law." He also cautioned the jurors to govern their decision by the sworn testimony and forbade them from consulting medical works or law books. He argued that it was, in fact, illegal for the jury to go "outside of the case as given them by the testimony and the instruction of the court." The jury retired yet again for deliberation and finally returned a guilty verdict against the defendant.[85]

The extent of the jury instructions from the bar and the bench and the back-and-forth interaction between the panel of jurors and the presiding judge in this seemingly routine murder case were somewhat unusual. The situation was not, however, uncommon, and it reveals an interesting struggle at play in the midwestern courtroom. On one hand, it illustrates the role of the judge as the ultimate arbiter of courtroom procedure. On the other hand, it demonstrates how the power of the judge was negotiated by attorneys from both sides of the case and by the jurors, whose responsibility it was to return a verdict. The negotiation of those power positions and relationships in the context of the law and the courtroom shows that the roles of the bench, the bar, and the jury were not set by the time of the Civil War. Rather, they were very much in flux.

As judges and jurors were asserting themselves in trial courts throughout the Midwest, jurists were also debating the issues exhibited in the Fisher case. The courtroom struggle in that case did not end in the La Salle County Circuit Court. After Fisher's request for a new trial was denied, the defense attorneys filed an appeal to the Illinois Supreme Court. In a divided decision, the high court reversed the lower court conviction. The high court found no fault with the instructions given to the jury prior to deliberations, nor did it object to the judge's refusal to give certain other instructions. But the appeal court did find fault with the judge for usurping the jury's right to decide law and fact. Citing a previous Illinois case, Justice Sidney Breese wrote that jurors were deemed by Illinois statute to be judges of law and fact; they were not "bound by the law, as given to them by the court," but "could assume the responsibility of deciding, each juror for himself, what the law is."[86] In his concise written opinion for the majority of the court, Breese reiterated the point:

> If they can say, upon their oaths, that they know the law better than the court, they have the power so to do. If they are prepared to say the law is different from what it is declared to be by the court, they have a perfect legal right to say so, and find the verdict according to their own notions of the law. It is a matter between their consciences and their God, with which no power can interfere. There can be no apprehension of oppression to the citizen in so looping this power, for erroneous decision of the jury against a prisoner can be corrected by the power remaining in the court to award a new trial. The jury were not bound to take the law as "laid down" to them by the court, but had the undoubted right to decide it for themselves, and in refusing so to declare, the court erred.[87]

In summary, Breese was arguing that Illinois law gave juries the right to determine law and that no judicial power allowed interference by the judge at trial. Breese also asserted that no excuse—not even a bad verdict—could justify an infringement of this right of jurors, for if there was an erroneous verdict, the appeal process could remedy it.

The opinion in *Fisher v. People* settled the issue: Illinois law gave juries the power to decide law and fact in criminal cases. The circuit court judge in Fisher's case had taken away the jury's right by dictating the law that the jury was to apply in this instance. The Illinois Supreme Court, albeit in a divided judgment, chastised the trial judge's overbearing control of the jury, upheld the applicable statute, and reversed Fisher's murder conviction. But of course, others on the court saw things differently. In a dissenting opinion, Justice Pinckney H. Walker provided another perspective. Though he agreed with the court that the criminal code gave jurors the right to decide law and fact, he did not read the law as literally as did his colleague Sidney Breese. Walker asked: "Can it be possible that the legislature ever intended to confide to twelve men, who have never perhaps even read the criminal code of our State, unacquainted with the law of evidence and the rules of construction, and uninformed as to the whole theory of criminal jurisprudence, such absolute power over the life and liberty of the citizen?"[88]

Although Walker believed in the sanctity of the institution of the jury and expressed faith in jurors to make good verdicts, he argued that without the learned guidance of judges, jurors were incapable of rendering good decisions. He did not believe that Breese's reading of the law was close to what the legislature had intended. For Walker, the judge's role was to ensure that juries understood the law before them. He had specific questions and concerns, which he fully expressed in his dissenting opinion:

> If the jurors are the uncontrolled judges of what it is, and their finding in a particular case settles the law of that crime, is a jury in a subsequent case to be governed by it, or may they disregard it, or if bound by it, who can know and conform his actions to it? Or if, on the contrary, every jury may settle the law for themselves, give a construction to the statute, and either acquit or convict upon the construction thus given, in defiance of the decision of the highest judicial tribunal known to the law and the instructions of the circuit judge, or even in the teeth of the statute itself, no one can, by any possibility, know what the law is until the jury have announced it by the decision of the case. And while I may concede all that is claimed for the trial by jury, I am irresistibly impelled to conclude that such an uncontrolled power, placed in the hands of twelve men, uninformed even in the elementary principles of the law, is fraught with dangers, and

> is liable to abuse, however honest their purpose, to an extent equal to all its benefits.

Walker was convinced that the "true construction" of the statute required the jury to "receive and act upon the law as announced to them by the court." The judge was to determine the law that should be applied to a particular issue and guide the application of evidence with his legal knowledge. The jury would then "judge" the facts upon that law and determine if the evidence applied to the issue at hand. Walker's dissenting opinion was not just a challenge to Breese (and the majority of the Illinois Supreme Court), nor was it simply a different reading of Illinois law and the events specific to Fisher's murder trial. More important, it was a frontal assault on an entrenched antebellum midwestern legal tradition that gave ultimate power to the jury. Walker was frustrated that jurors, unknowledgeable in law and legal procedure, were put in positions of power over judges, who possessed legal knowledge and were experienced in legal processes. He wanted judges to gain strength in that legal tug-of-war and to assert their professional expertise in the courtroom.

Perhaps Walker's dissenting opinion in this 1859 Illinois Supreme Court appeal was the beginning of the end for the power of the jury in the state. Though Breese's opinion stood as the case law in Illinois, Walker's dissent offered a challenge and perhaps laid the foundation of the struggle that would eventually culminate, at the end of the century, with the curtailment of jury power. The *Fisher* case illustrates the ways in which the bar, the bench, and the institution of the jury negotiated the distribution of legal power within the courtroom. The case also demonstrates three points about the character of the power struggle that was in progress in antebellum midwestern courts. First, lawyers, by way of jury instructions, advocated for their clients at the same time that they promoted the interests of the bar itself. But the judge's power could mitigate the bar's power, and the jury's right to find law and render general verdicts could restrict that power as well. Second, judges had considerable control over trials at the local level. They had wide discretion to give or refuse the jury instructions of the lawyers, and they reigned over courtroom procedure. However, attorneys were in constant negotiation with them, and jurors were not content to be passive when judges asserted authority over the their right to find verdicts. Third, as of the late 1850s, jurors still had a voice in the courtroom. The institution of the jury had considerable clout in trial courts, and appellate courts were unwilling to support blatant challenges to jury power.

The midwestern courthouse was thus the scene of a lively negotiation among the three power brokers in the American legal system. By the Civil War, there was no clear victor in this contest, and it was not a foregone conclusion that the institution of the jury would be the ultimate loser. The elite members of the bench and of the bar sought to control juries, but the jurors stood as the equals of their would-be conquerors. They were no less affluent and no less influential. They had also developed expertise in their legal roles; the jurors in the Fisher case, for instance, were not an ignorant, uninformed panel. Judges, lawyers, and jurors alike developed expertise and competence, and they were most unwilling to relinquish power they had already enjoyed or newly gained. They were in a battle with each other to reaffirm their status and seize all of the control they could within the context of a growing and changing legal system and burgeoning middle-class society.

Conclusion: On Jury Competence and Power

Antebellum midwestern jurors had status and influence, and their position in the courtrooms in which they served as well as in the communities in which they lived rivaled the status and influence of judges and lawyers. As the legal system became more professionalized, jurors developed competence in their responsibilities much like that of the bench and bar members with whom they competed for power. In that power struggle, the jury maintained a strong position of authority during the first half of the nineteenth century. Widespread American support bolstered the jury's exalted position as a legal institution, and a vociferous democratic rhetoric placed the jury upon a virtually unbreakable pedestal. The jury was of central importance to antebellum Americans, whose commitment to the rule of law shaped their perceptions and worldviews. No American institution more clearly demonstrated the nation's ideals and democratic tenets—the concepts that grounded the developing legal systems of the midwestern states—than did the jury.

When settlers established the states of Ohio, Indiana, Illinois, Iowa, Michigan, and Wisconsin, they brought to their constitutional conventions and general assemblies an inherent reverence for the institution of the jury. Imitating and adopting jury law from older states and then adapting it to fit their particular circumstances, they constructed a jury system for themselves in their emerging states. Laws respecting juror service outlined qualifications of landownership; age; moral character; and in some instances gender, race, American citizenship, and voter status. Juror laws required jurors to be "good," "judicious," and "reputable." Interpretation of those subjective qualifications was left to the court officials who compiled juror lists and issued writs of venire for service, calling prospective jurors to court.

Through an investigation of the status of the jury and an analysis of the status of jurors, this book has demonstrated how antebellum Americans revered the jury and how they developed and maintained jury service to impanel competent jurors who delivered competent verdicts. Filling jury boxes with "gentlemen" capable of respectful service was of paramount importance to them. Society's elites defined the character of these gentlemanly jurors and, as a result, tightly controlled the parameters of service. Only 5 to 6 percent of the entire population of antebellum Illinois ever received a summons for jury duty, and Illinois was not the only midwestern state in which this was the norm. The demand for competent jurors led to the seating in midwestern jury boxes of men who mirrored the legislators in status, attitudes, and ideals.

The quantitative portrait of jury composition in Sangamon County, Illinois, has offered a local study to depict juror demographics in the Midwest from 1830 to 1860. Midwestern legal history has yet to emerge as a field of study, and the research herein takes one small step toward integrating the midwestern legal experience in a wider understanding of American legal history. As seen in this investigation, jurors were, generally speaking, affluent, middle-aged men who were prominent residents and members of persistent families with strong stakes in their communities. They were not recent immigrants but were long-established individuals who were engaged in local, state, and national party politics. They were people connected to the economic, social, and political establishments by way of their social status, professional affiliations, or business-related economic activities. Sangamon County jurors were representative of the ruling professional, economic, social, and political elites of the community, and individuals like them filled jury boxes throughout the emerging Midwest.

Despite their elite status and perceived good character, jurors were not perfect, and their imperfections and misbehaviors highlighted the very human quality of the jury system. They sometimes failed to be diligent and respectful of their duties, and certainly their personal biases affected their deliberations and interpretations of legal evidence. When jurors erred, defendants, civil litigants, judges, lawyers, and observers showed no hesitation in chastising them. Antebellum Americans were engaged in a loud and often hostile dialogue with the legal system. They were quick to point to its flaws, comment on its shortcomings, and suggest reforms. When jurors acted disrespectfully or when juries delivered allegedly bad or unpopular verdicts, the American public delivered swift and eloquent rebuke. Newspapers and periodicals of the day provided a conduit for such verbal assaults.

In spite of the occasional failings of jurors and the rendering of flawed verdicts by some jury panels, jurors were generally competent and by and large delivered competent verdicts. Overall, they demonstrated the ability to sort out complicated evidence and sophisticated legal arguments; they exerted their authority when judges attempted to control them; and they showed mercy on criminal defendants, especially those under indictment for murder. From our modern, egalitarian perspective, we might be as quick as the nineteenth-century media were to criticize them, yet most antebellum midwestern jurors lived up to the challenge. They did not sabotage the system through blind allegiance to their ruling, elite class. Instead, they honored the system and served with the intelligence and the competence that their fellow Americans demanded. Antebellum midwestern jurors achieved that competence partly by virtue of their elite social, economic, political, and professional backgrounds and partly through repeat service on grand and trial jury panels. Jurors developed expertise through accumulated experience, enhanced knowledge, and increased ability over time. The ultimate result was a "professional" jury with expertise that rivaled that of the bench and the bar. By the end of the period covered in this study, the competent jury was on a collision course with the established power of the bench and the developing power of the bar.

Impaneling competent men on grand and petit jury panels and adapting a workable jury system to midwestern conditions had been a key goal for new state legislatures during the opening decades of the nineteenth century.

Through the passage of their state constitutions, the enactment of statutes, and the accumulation of appellate case law, each midwestern state had put juror competence at the forefront. Developing jury law in the Midwest and the pursuit of competence constricted, rather than expanded, jury composition; it also affected jury work and experience and impinged upon the courtroom relationships between judges, lawyers, and the jurors themselves. Due to circumstances such as the distribution of qualified jurors across the rural landscape, poor roads and transportation, the degree of tenacity of a sheriff's search for such jurors, and the increasing heft of court dockets, ideal rotational juror service was not the norm. Instead, repeat juror service, especially of town elites living near their county courthouses, was typical. Though these repeat jurors met legal qualifications for service and performed their duties with competence, it was their emergence as so-called professionals that ultimately signaled what would become their fall from grace in the second half of the nineteenth century. During the antebellum period, however, jurors maintained their position even as legal structures constricted and as the bench and the bar rivaled them for dominance.

As midwestern legal systems outgrew their modest beginnings in single-story log buildings and came to occupy massive and elegant structures such as the limestone Greek Revival courthouse in Sangamon County, the jury thrived. The physical construction of the courtroom reflected a hierarchal arrangement of the court—with the judge elevated to preside over the bar, the jury box, and the witness stand—and the jury's place inside the bar demonstrated the institution's inclusion in the legal process and its distinct separation from the wider community, which was represented by the gallery of spectators. Although respectful of the somber environment of the courtroom and of legal processes and proceedings, jurors seated within jury boxes did not bow to judges' authority. Instead, they conducted themselves as a separate but equal part of the judicial process.

Jurors such as Zachariah Peter, William Foley, Charles Gardner, and Abraham Lincoln determined for themselves what they heard and understood from evidence in the courtroom and decided for themselves how they would process meanings in the jury deliberation room. Attorneys could influence jurors through skillful arguments and with humorous anecdotes. Judges could instruct jurors in an attempt to lead them to one verdict or another. However, closed deliberation rooms, the general verdict, and widespread support for jury independence—especially in the form of appellate case law—gave juries considerable power to return the verdicts that they believed were supported by the evidence, the circumstances, and society at large. State supreme courts could overturn jury verdicts, but as most jury trials did not go up on appeal, it was, by and large, the local jury panel that controlled trial outcomes. This study has revealed that juries were, despite their elite composition, generally independent of elite control and competent to render sound judgments, and they tended toward a paternalism that most legal historians have either failed to recognize or chosen to downplay in favor of a patriarchal interpretation.[89]

Since the local trial court determined the final disposition of most criminal and civil jury trials, it was the institution of the jury that stood front and center in the legal process. Verdicts at the local level touched the lives of the defendants and civil litigants who were subject to them. Chester Moon, Nomaque, and Mary Beard had certainly recognized the authority that jurors in their cases commanded: their economic well-being, personal freedom, and individual safety, respectively, had rested in the hands of the elite jurors who heard their cases. The jury was the ultimate thread that connected these private individuals to the legal system. It was the juror, not the attorney or the judge, who wielded the most power over the lives of the people who entered the courtroom. In the end, the jury was a human system, with human failings and human triumphs. And assuring the general competence of jurors and of the system may well have been the best Americans could have hoped for in regard to the institution of the jury in Abraham Lincoln's America.

APPENDIX

Annotated Appellate Case List

(Case Name, Legal Citation, State, Year, Grounds of Appeal)

Abel et al. v. Kennedy et al., 3 Greene 47 (Iowa, 1851), appeal of civil case from District Court of Lee County—juror misconduct

Adams v. State, 11 Ind. 249 (Indiana, 1858), appeal of larceny case from Sullivan County Circuit Court—jury trial procedures

Alexander and another v. Dunn, 5 Ind. 139 (Indiana, 1854), appeal of assumpsit case from Owen County Circuit Court—juror bias, juror misconduct, jury instructions, challenges to jurors

Archer v. Spillman and Reed, 2 Ill. 552 (Illinois, 1839), appeal of debt case from Edgar County Circuit Court—right of trial by jury, questions of law and fact

Armstrong v. Jackson, on demise of Elliott, 1 Blackf. 374 (Indiana, 1825), appeal of ejectment case from Dearborn County Circuit Court—right of trial by jury

Barger et al. v. State, 6 Blackf. 188 (Indiana, 1842), appeal of trespass case from Decatur County Circuit Court—juror qualifications

Barlow v. State, 2 Blackf. 114 (Indiana, 1827), appeal of manslaughter case from Hendricks County Circuit Court—juror qualifications, juror misconduct

Baxter v. People, 8 Ill. 368 (Illinois, 1846), appeal of murder case from Warren County Circuit Court—juror qualifications, juror bias, jury instructions

Beauchamp v. State, 6 Blackf. 299 (Indiana, 1842), appeal of murder case from Parke County Circuit Court—challenges to jurors

Bell v. People, 2 Ill. 397 (Illinois, 1837), appeal of larceny case from Municipal Court of Chicago—juror qualifications

Benaway v. Conyne et ux., 3 Pin. 196 (Wisconsin, 1851), appeal of slander case from Rock County Circuit Court—juror selection procedures

Birchard v. Booth, 4 Wis. 85 (Wisconsin, 1855), appeal of civil assault and battery case from Rock County Circuit Court—juror selection procedures, juror misconduct, jury trial procedures

Bissell v. Ryan, 23 Ill. 517 (Illinois, 1860), appeal of debt case from Sangamon County Circuit Court—juror qualifications, juror selection procedures, jury trial procedures

Bradford v. State, 15 Ind. 347 (Indiana, 1860), appeal of murder case from Vigo County Circuit Court—juror qualifications, juror bias, challenge of jurors

Bradshaw v. Hubbard et al., 6 Ill. 390 (Illinois, 1844), appeal of assumpsit case from Lee County Circuit Court—juror bias

Browder v. Johnson, 1 Ill. 96 (Illinois, 1825), appeal of covenant case from Washington County Circuit Court—juror misconduct

Burgwin et al. v. Babcock et al., 11 Ill. 28 (Illinois, 1849), appeal of debt case from Hamilton County Circuit Court—jury trial procedures

Burnham v. Hatfield, 5 Blackf. 21 (Indiana, 1838), appeal of trespass-on-the-case case from Huntington County Circuit Court—jury trial procedures

Butt v. Tuthill, 10 Iowa 585 (Iowa, 1859), appeal of contract dispute from unknown district court—jury trial procedures

Byrne and Kinney v. State, 12 Wis. 519 (Wisconsin, 1860), appeal of criminal sanction of illegal voting from Dane County Circuit Court—juror qualifications, alienage

Cable v. State, 8 Blackf. 531 (Indiana, 1847), appeal of keeping a tippling house case from Decatur County Circuit Court—challenges to jurors

Campbell v. Head, 13 Ill. 122 (Illinois, 1851), appeal of replevin case from McDonough County Circuit Court—right of trial by jury

Claussen, guardian v. La Franz, 1 Iowa 227 (Iowa, 1855), appeal of civil case from Scott District Court—juror selection procedures, jury instructions

Cole v. Swan, 4 Greene 32 (Iowa, 1853), appeal of debt-on-judgment case from Polk District Court—jury trial procedures

Conkey v. Northern Bank, 6 Wis. 447 (Wisconsin, 1857), appeal of civil case from Outagamie County Circuit Court—challenges to jurors

Cook v. Scott, 6 Ill. 333 (Illinois, 1844), appeal of trespass case from Knox County Circuit Court—questions of law and fact

Cook & Owsley v. Watters, 4 Iowa 72 (Iowa, 1856), appeal of contract dispute case from Marion District Court—jury trial procedures

Cook, Sargent & Cook v. Sypher, 3 Iowa 484 (Iowa, 1856), appeal of civil case from Polk District Court—jury trial procedures, poll of jurors

Cowen and Cowen v. People, 14 Ill. 348 (Illinois, 1853), appeal of fraud case from Recorder's Court of Chicago—jury instructions

Cowgill v. Wooden, sheriff, 2 Blackf. 332 (Indiana, 1830), appeal of replevin case from Owen County Circuit Court—right of trial by jury

Crippen v. People, 8 Mich. 117 (Michigan, 1860), appeal of public nuisance (mill dam) case from Branch County Circuit Court—juror bias, challenges to jurors

Crocker v. Goodsell and Keyes, 2 Ill. 107 (Illinois, 1833), appeal of assumpsit case from Adams County Circuit Court—jury instructions, questions of law and fact

Davis v. People, 19 Ill. 73 (Illinois, 1857), appeal of murder case from Hardin County Circuit Court—juror qualifications, juror bias, juror misconduct, jury instructions

Driskill v. State, 7 Ind. 338 (Indiana, 1855), appeal of murder case from Tippecanoe County Circuit Court—juror bias

Drummond v. Leslie, 5 Blackf. 453 (Indiana, 1840), appeal of slander case from Clark County Circuit Court—juror misconduct

Durham, administrator v. Hudgson, administrator, 4 Ind. 501 (Indiana, 1853), appeal of assumpsit case from Vigo County Probate Court—juror selection procedures

Dutell v. State, 4 Greene 125 (Iowa, 1853), appeal of larceny case from Mahaska District Court—jury trial procedures

Fisher v. People, 23 Ill. 218 (Illinois, 1859), appeal of murder case from La Salle County Circuit Court—juror misconduct, jury instructions, questions of law and fact

Fleming v. State, 11 Ind. 193 (Indiana, 1858), appeal of arson case from La Grange County Circuit Court—juror bias, jury trial procedures

Foreman and Foreman v. Baldwin, 24 Ill. 299 (Illinois, 1860), appeal of civil fraud case from Superior Court of Chicago—jury instructions

Forester and Funkhouser v. Guard, Siddell & Company, 1 Ill. 74 (Illinois, 1823), appeal of civil case from Gallatin County Circuit Court—juror misconduct

Forshee v. Abrams et al., 2 Iowa 571 (Iowa, 1856), appeal of libel case from Davis District Court—juror misconduct, questions of law and fact

French v. State, 12 Ind. 564 (Indiana, 1859), appeal of murder case from Carroll County Circuit Court—juror qualifications

Fuller v. State, 1 Blackf. 63 (Indiana, 1820), appeal of murder case from Dearborn County Circuit Court—juror selection procedures

Gardner v. People, 4 Ill. 83 (Illinois, 1841), appeal of murder case from Moran County Circuit Court—juror bias, jury trial procedures

Gates v. People, 14 Ill. 433 (Illinois, 1853), appeal of murder case from La Salle County Circuit Court—juror bias

Gilmore v. Ballard, 2 Ill. 251 (Illinois, 1836), appeal of trover case from Clay County Circuit Court—right of trial by jury

Goodwin v. Blachley et al., 4 Ind. 438 (Indiana, 1853), appeal of debt case from Henry County Circuit Court—juror bias

Grable v. State, 2 Greene 559 (Iowa, 1850), appeal of manslaughter case from Clinton District Court—jury trial procedures

Granger v. Warrington, 8 Ill. 299 (Illinois, 1846), appeal of malicious prosecution case from Du Page County Circuit Court—juror misconduct

Greenup v. Stoker, 8 Ill. 202 (Illinois, 1846), appeal of assumpsit case from St. Clair County Circuit Court—juror qualifications, alienage, jury instructions

Guykowski v. People, 2 Ill. 476 (Illinois, 1838), appeal of murder case from Clinton County Circuit Court—juror qualifications, alienage, juror misconduct

Hall v. State, 4 Greene 73 (Iowa, 1853), appeal of assault with intent to commit bodily injury case from Jefferson District Court—jury trial procedures

Hall v. State, 8 Ind. 399 (Indiana, 1857), appeal of larceny case from Decatur County Circuit Court—jury instructions

Harless and Adams v. United States, 1 Morris 169 (Iowa, 1843), appeal of gambling case from Johnson County Circuit Court—juror qualifications

Harrison v. Singleton, administrator of Jewett, 3 Ill. 21 (Illinois, 1839), appeal of right to property case from Monroe County Circuit Court—jury trial procedures

Harter v. Seamon, 3 Blackf. 27 (Indiana, 1832), appeal of trespass-on-the-case case from Tippecanoe County Circuit Court—jury trial procedures

Heaton v. Kemper, 3 Ill. 367 (Illinois, 1840), appeal of covenant case from Edgar County Circuit Court—jury instructions

Hoard v. Bulkley, 8 Ill. 154 (Illinois, 1846), appeal of assumpsit case from Cook County Circuit Court—jury fees

Holliday v. People, 9 Ill. 110 (Illinois, 1847), appeal of abortion case from St. Clair County Circuit Court—jury trial procedures

Holmes et al. v. People, 10 Ill. 478 (Illinois, 1849), appeal of larceny case from Kane County Circuit Court—jury trial procedures

Hudson and Indian v. State, 1 Blackf. 317 (Indiana, 1824), appeal of murder case from Madison County Circuit Court—juror selection procedures, juror bias

In re Detroit & Pontiac Railroad Company, 2 Doug. 367 (Michigan, 1846), appeal of inquest from unknown court—juror selection procedures, challenges to jurors

Jackson and another v. Pittsford, 8 Blackf. 194 (Indiana, 1846), appeal of assumpsit case from Madison County Circuit Court—challenges to jurors

Jackson et al. v. State, 6 Blackf. 461 (Indiana, 1843), appeal of riot case from Dearborn County Circuit Court—right of trial by jury

Johnson v. Howe et al., 7 Ill. 342 (Illinois, 1845), appeal of replevin case from Jo Daviess County Circuit Court—poll of jurors

Jones v. State, 2 Blackf. 475 (Indiana, 1831), appeal of murder case from Bartholomew County Circuit Court—juror selection procedures, juror bias, jury trial procedures, challenges to jurors

Jones v. State, 3 Blackf. 37 (Indiana, 1832), appeal of murder case from Bartholomew County Circuit Court—juror selection procedures

Joy v. State, 14 Ind. 113 (Indiana, 1860), appeal of murder case from Wabash County Circuit Court—juror bias, jury trial procedures, poll of jurors

Judah v. M'Namee, 3 Blackf. 269 (Indiana, 1833), appeal of assumpsit case from Knox County Circuit Court—jury trial procedures

Keenan v. Wisconsin, 8 Wis. 132 (Wisconsin, 1858), appeal of murder case from Iowa County Circuit Court—juror qualifications, alienage, jury trial procedures, jury instructions

Kimball et al. v. Cook, 6 Ill. 423 (Illinois, 1844), appeal of mechanics' lien case from Kendall County Circuit Court—jury instructions, jury trial procedures

King v. Dale, 2 Ill. 512 (Illinois, 1838), appeal of criminal conversation case from Hamilton County Circuit Court—juror bias

Lafayette Plankroad Company v. New Albany & Salem Railroad Company, 13 Ind. 81 (Indiana, 1859), appeal of civil case from Clinton County Circuit Court—juror qualifications

Langworthy v. Myers et al., 4 Iowa 18 (Iowa, 1856), appeal of forcible entry and detainer case from Dubuque District Court—juror misconduct, jury instructions

Latimer v. Woodward, 2 Doug. 368 (Michigan, 1846), appeal of forcible entry and detainer case from Lenawee County Justice of the Peace Court—juror selection procedures

Lindley and Stallcup v. Kindall, 4 Blackf. 189 (Indiana, 1836), appeal of assault and battery and false imprisonment case from Crawford County Circuit Court—juror qualifications, juror selection procedures

Lloyd v. McClure, 2 Greene 139 (Iowa, 1849), appeal of account case from Des Moines District Court—jury trial procedures

Luman v. Kerr's administrator, 4 Greene 159 (Iowa, 1853), appeal of replevin case from Lee District Court—jury instructions

Lumsden v. City of Milwaukee, 8 Wis. 485 (Wisconsin, 1857), appeal of bill in equity case from Milwaukee County Circuit Court—jury trial procedures

Magee v. Carmack, 13 Ill. 289 (Illinois, 1851), appeal of civil case from McDonough County Circuit Court—jury instructions

Maize v. Sewell, 4 Blackf. 447 (Indiana, 1837), appeal of breach of promise to marry case from Fayette County Circuit Court—juror bias

Manix v. Malony, 7 Iowa 81 (Iowa, 1858), appeal of debt for damages case from Dubuque District Court—juror misconduct

Maton et al. v. People, 15 Ill. 536 (Illinois, 1854), appeal of robbery case from Recorder's Court of Chicago—jury trial procedures

May v. Milwaukee & Mississippi Railway Company, 3 Wis. 218 (Wisconsin, 1854), appeal of assumpsit case from Rock County Court—right of trial by jury

McClintock v. Crick, 4 Iowa 453 (Iowa, 1857), appeal of slander case from Jefferson District Court—jury trial procedures

McKinney v. People, 7 Ill. 540 (Illinois, 1845), appeal of murder case from Rock Island County Circuit Court—jury trial procedures, juror misconduct

M'Gregg v. State, 4 Blackf. 101 (Indiana, 1835), appeal of robbery case from Montgomery County Circuit Court—juror bias, jury trial procedures

Minter et ux. v. Hite et ux., 4 Iowa 583 (Iowa, 1857), appeal of debt case from Jefferson District Court—jury trial procedures

Mississippi & Missouri Railroad Company v. Rousseau, 8 Iowa 373 (Iowa, 1859), appeal of assessment of damages case from Washington District Court—juror selection procedures, juror bias

Mitchell v. Likens, 3 Blackf. 258 (Indiana, 1833), appeal of civil case from Harrison County Circuit Court—juror selection procedures

Mitchell et al. v. Denbo, 3 Blackf. 259 (Indiana, 1833), appeal of debt case from Harrison County Circuit Court—juror selection procedures

Morgan and Morgan v. Stevenson and Hobbs, 6 Ind. 136 (Indiana, 1855), appeal of covenant case from Dearborn County Circuit Court—juror bias

Morris v. State, 7 Blackf. 607 (Indiana, 1846), appeal of voting fraud case from Marion County Circuit Court—challenges to jurors

Munly v. State, 7 Blackf. 593 (Indiana, 1845), appeal of unknown criminal case from unknown county—challenges to jurors

Neely v. People, 13 Ill. 685 (Illinois, 1852), appeal of rape case from Stephenson County Circuit Court—juror bias

Noble v. People, 1 Ill. 54 (Illinois, 1822), appeal of forgery case from St. Clair County Circuit Court—juror bias

Nomaque, an Indian v. People, 1 Ill. 145 (Illinois, 1825), appeal of murder case from Peoria County Circuit Court—jury trial procedures

Norris' House v. State, 3 Greene 513 (Iowa, 1852), appeal of illegal dram shop case from Davis District Court—juror selection procedures

Norval v. Rice et ux., 2 Wis. 22 (Wisconsin, 1853), appeal of assumpsit case from Rock County Court—right of trial by jury

Oshoga v. State, 3 Pin. 56 (Wisconsin, 1850), appeal of murder case from St. Croix County Circuit Court—jury trial procedures

Owners of the Ship "Milwaukie" v. Hale et al., 1 Doug. 306 (Michigan, 1844), appeal of contract case from Wayne County Circuit Court—jury trial procedures

Pate v. People, 8 Ill. 644 (Illinois, 1846), appeal of forgery case from Adams County Circuit Court—juror trial procedures, jury instructions, questions of law and fact, juror misconduct

Perry v. State, 9 Wis. 19 (Wisconsin, 1859), appeal of murder case from Jefferson County Circuit Court—juror selection procedures

Pierson v. State, 11 Ind. 277 (Indiana, 1858), appeal of receiving stolen goods case from La Grange County Circuit Court—juror bias

Rainey v. People, 8 Ill. 71 (Illinois, 1846), appeal of murder case from Clinton County Circuit Court—jury trial procedures

Rector v. Smith, 11 Iowa 302 (Iowa, 1860), appeal of libel case from Fremont District Court—jury trial procedures

Rice v. State, 7 Ind. 264 (Indiana, 1855), appeal of murder case from Tippecanoe County Circuit Court—juror bias, jury trial procedures

Rigg v. Cook, by his next friend Edwards, 9 Ill. 336 (Illinois, 1847), appeal of ejectment case from St. Clair County Circuit Court—jury trial procedures, jury instructions, poll of jurors, juror misconduct

Rock Island & Alton Railroad Company v. Lynch et al., 23 Ill. 597 (Illinois, 1860), appeal of assessment of damages case from Scott County Circuit Court—juror bias

Rogers v. Lamb, 3 Blackf. 155 (Indiana, 1832), appeal of malicious prosecution case from Madison County Circuit Court—challenges to jurors

Romaine v. State, 7 Ind. 51 (Indiana, 1855), appeal of murder case from Allen County Circuit Court—juror bias

Ross v. Irving; Pryor v. Irving (appealed together), 14 Ill. 170 (Illinois, 1852), appeals of ejectment cases from Pike County Circuit Court—right of trial by jury

Ross v. State, 1 Blackf. 390 (Indiana, 1825), appeal of larceny case from Marion County Circuit Court—challenges to jurors

Rowland v. State, 14 Ind. 478 (Indiana, 1860), appeal of assault and battery case from Vanderburgh County Circuit Court—juror misconduct

Ruble v. McDonald, 7 Iowa 90 (Iowa, 1858), appeal of trespass case from Clinton District Court—juror misconduct

Russell and Peyton v. Hamilton, 3 Ill. 56 (Illinois, 1839), appeal of debt case from Municipal Court of Chicago—juror bias

Sawyer v. Stephenson, 1 Ill. 24 (Illinois, 1820), appeal of civil case from Madison County Circuit Court—juror misconduct

Schanler v. Porter et al., 7 Iowa 482 (Iowa, 1859), appeal of action to recover damages case from Dubuque District Court—juror misconduct

Schnier v. People, 23 Ill. 17 (Illinois, 1859), appeal of murder case from Clinton County Circuit Court—questions of law and fact

Schoeffler v. State, 3 Wis. 823 (Wisconsin, 1854), appeal of murder case from Outagamie County Circuit Court—juror bias, challenges to jurors

Schumacker v. State, 5 Wis. 324 (Wisconsin, 1856), appeal of murder case from Milwaukee County Circuit Court—juror qualifications, alienage, challenges to jurors

Sellers v. People, 4 Ill. 412 (Illinois, 1842), appeal of murder case from Shelby County Circuit Court—juror bias, juror misconduct

Settle v. Batie, 1 Iowa 141 (Iowa, 1855), appeal of account case from Lucas District Court—juror selection procedures, challenges to jurors

Sharp v. State, 2 Iowa 454 (Iowa, 1856), appeal of murder case from Dubuque County Circuit Court—challenges to jurors, juror selection procedures

Shattuck v. State, 11 Ind. 383 (Indiana, 1859), appeal of forgery case from Noble County Circuit Court—jury trial procedures

Shaw and another v. Wood and another, 8 Ind. 467 (Indiana, 1857), appeal of debt case from Randolph County Circuit Court—juror selection procedures

Smith v. Eames, 4 Ill. 76 (Illinois, 1841), appeal of assumpsit case from Morgan County Circuit Court—juror bias

Smith v. State, 4 Greene 189 (Iowa, 1853), appeal of disturbing a worshipping congregation case from Appanoose District Court—challenges to jurors

Snodgrass et al. v. Hunt, 15 Ind. 274 (Indiana, 1860), appeal of civil assault and battery case from Henry County Circuit Court—challenges to jurors

Spear et al. v. Spencer, 1 Greene 534 (Iowa, 1848), appeal of trespass case from Jones District Court—juror qualifications

Spencer v. De France, 3 Greene 216 (Iowa, 1851), appeal of civil case from Jefferson District Court—challenges to jurors

State v. Cain, 6 Blackf. 422 (Indiana, 1843), appeal of misfeasance case from La Grange County Circuit Court—juror selection procedures

State v. Cameron, 2 Wis. 490 (Wisconsin, 1850), appeal of murder case from Crawford County Circuit Court—juror selection procedures, challenges to jurors

State v. Conner et al., 5 Blackf. 325 (Indiana, 1840), appeal of extortion case from Floyd County Circuit Court—juror selection procedures

State v. Dixon, 3 Iowa 416 (Iowa, 1856), appeal of assault with intent to commit murder case from Lucas District Court—challenges to jurors

State v. Gillick, 7 Iowa 287 (Iowa, 1858), appeal of murder case from Dubuque District Court—juror bias

State v. Gillick, 10 Iowa 98 (Iowa, 1859), appeal of murder case from Dubuque District Court—juror bias, jury trial procedures, challenges to jurors

State v. Grady, 4 Iowa 461 (Iowa, 1857), appeal of criminal misdemeanor case from Davis District Court—jury trial procedures

State v. Groome, 10 Iowa 308 (Iowa, 1860), appeal of seduction case from Marion District Court—juror qualifications, challenges to jurors

State v. Herndon, 5 Blackf. 75 (Indiana, 1839), appeal of assault and battery case from Montgomery County Circuit Court—juror qualifications

State v. Howard and Cress, 10 Iowa 101 (Iowa, 1859), appeal of larceny case from Muscatine District Court—juror selection procedures

State v. Miller, 2 Blackf. 35 (Indiana, 1826), appeal of assault case from Floyd County Circuit Court—juror qualifications

State v. Nash, 10 Iowa 81 (Iowa, 1859), appeal of murder case from Lee District Court—juror misconduct, jury trial procedures

State v. Newer, 7 Blackf. 307 (Indiana, 1844), appeal of illegal sale of alcohol case from Fountain County Circuit Court—juror selection procedures

State v. Pierce, 8 Iowa 231 (Iowa, 1859), appeal of forgery case from Linn District Court—juror selection procedures

State v. Pitts, 11 Iowa 343 (Iowa, 1860), appeal of criminal case from Clinton District Court—jury trial procedures, jury instructions

State v. Sater, 8 Iowa 420 (Iowa, 1859), appeal of larceny case from Des Moines District Court—juror bias

State v. Shelledy, 8 Iowa 477 (Iowa, 1859), appeal of murder case from Johnson District Court—juror bias

State v. Taylor, 8 Blackf. 178 (Indiana, 1846), appeal of unknown criminal case from unknown court—juror qualifications, alienage

State v. Thompson, 9 Iowa 188 (Iowa, 1859), appeal of manslaughter case from Van Buren District Court—juror bias

State v. Wilson, 8 Iowa 407 (Iowa, 1859), appeal of larceny case from Des Moines District Court—juror bias

Stewart v. Burlington & Missouri River Railroad Company, 11 Iowa 62 (Iowa, 1860), appeal of debt case from Des Moines District Court—jury trial procedures, juror misconduct

Stewart v. Ewbank, 3 Iowa 191 (Iowa, 1856), appeal of debt case from Pottawattamie District Court—juror bias

Stone v. People, 3 Ill. 326 (Illinois, 1840), appeal of murder case from Cook County Circuit Court—juror selection procedures

Territory of Wisconsin v. Doty et al., 1 Pin. 396 (Wisconsin, 1844), appeal of civil case from Walworth District Court—juror selection procedures, jury trial procedures

Thayer v. People, 2 Doug. 417 (Michigan, 1847), appeal of burglary case from Calhoun County Circuit Court—juror selection procedures, challenges to jurors

Thomas v. Leonard, 5 Ill. 556 (Illinois, 1843), appeal of assumpsit case from St. Clair County Circuit Court—juror bias, jury trial procedures

Thompson v. People, 24 Ill. 61 (Illinois, 1860), appeal of fraud case from Stephenson County Circuit Court—juror bias

Tifield v. Adams, 3 Iowa 487 (Iowa, 1856), appeal of contract dispute case from Dubuque District Court—jury trial procedures, jury instructions

Trimble v. State, 2 Greene 404 (Iowa, 1850), appeal of murder case from Lee District Court—juror qualifications, juror bias

United States v. Cropper, 1 Morris 190 (Iowa, 1843), appeal of larceny case from Johnson County Circuit Court—juror selection procedures

Van Blaricum v. People, 16 Ill. 364 (Illinois, 1855), appeal of larceny case from Recorder's Court of Chicago—juror bias

Van Vacter v. M'Killip, 7 Blackf. 578 (Indiana, 1845), appeal of criminal conversation case from Union County Circuit Court—juror bias

Vattier v. State, 4 Blackf. 73 (Indiana, 1835), appeal of assault and battery with intent to murder case from Dearborn County Circuit Court—juror selection procedures

Vennum v. Harwood, 6 Ill. 659 (Illinois, 1844), appeal of slander case from Iroquois County Circuit Court—juror bias

Wau-kon-chaw-neek-kaw et al. v. United States, 1 Morris 332 (Iowa, 1844), appeal of murder case from Dubuque County Circuit Court—juror bias, jury trial procedures

Webster v. McKinster, 1 Pin. 644 (Wisconsin, 1846), appeal of civil case from Racine County District Court—poll of jurors

Weinzorpflin v. State, 7 Blackf. 186 (Indiana, 1844), appeal of assault and battery case from Gibson County Circuit Court—jury trial procedures

White and White v. Martin, 3 Ill. 69 (Illinois, 1839), appeal of assumpsit case from Hancock County Circuit Court—juror misconduct

Wickersham v. People, 2 Ill. 127 (Illinois, 1834), appeal of malfeasance from Clay County Circuit Court—questions of law and fact

Wiley v. State, 4 Blackf. 458 (Indiana, 1838), appeal of murder case from Hendricks County Circuit Court—challenges to jurors

Woods v. Commissioners of Van Buren County, 1 Morris 441 (Iowa, 1845), appeal of civil case from Van Buren County Circuit Court—jury trial procedures

Wyatt v. Noble, 8 Blackf. 507 (Indiana, 1847), appeal of unknown civil case from unknown court—challenges to jurors

NOTES

Preface

1. Two important and well-received community studies attest to the viability of Illinois as a focus of historical inquiry and to the wealth of sources available: John Mack Faragher, *Sugar Creek: Life on the Illinois Prairie* (New Haven, Conn.: Yale University Press, 1986); Don Harrison Doyle, *The Social Order of a Frontier Community: Jacksonville, Illinois, 1825–70* (Urbana: University of Illinois Press, 1978). Illinois has been hailed as the "miniature cross section of the Union" and "representative of the nation." Cullom Davis, "Illinois: Crossroads and Cross Section," in *Heartland: Comparative Histories of the Midwestern States,* ed. James H. Madison (Bloomington: Indiana University Press, 1988), 127–57; Daniel J. Elazar, *Cities of the Prairie: The Metropolitan Frontier and American Politics* (New York: Basic Books, 1970), 282.

2. Douglas K. Meyer, *Making the Heartland Quilt: A Geographical History of Settlement and Migration in Early-Nineteenth-Century Illinois* (Carbondale: Southern Illinois University Press, 2000), 7, 125, 237; Christopher Wallace, "The Opportunity to Grow: Springfield, Illinois, during the 1850s" (Ph.D. diss., Purdue University, 1983), 43, 147–60.

3. Robert P. Howard, *Illinois: A History of the Prairie State* (Grand Rapids, Mich.: William B. Eardman's Publishing, 1972), 145; Joseph C. G. Kennedy, comp., *Population of the United States in 1860* (Washington, D.C.: Government Printing Office, 1864), 87; Rebecca Looney, "Migration and Separation: Divorce in Kane County, 1837–1869," *Illinois Historical Journal* 89 (Summer 1996): 70–84; Terry Wilson, "The Business of a Midwestern Trial Court: Knox County, Illinois, 1841–1850," *Illinois Historical Journal* 84 (Winter 1991): 249–67; Stacy Pratt McDermott, "Dissolving the Bonds of Matrimony: Women and Divorce in Sangamon County, Illinois, 1837–1860," in *In Tender Consideration: Women, Families and the Law in Abraham Lincoln's Illinois,* ed. Daniel W. Stowell (Urbana: University of Illinois Press, 2002), 71–103. Theodore Calvin Pease has argued that the frontier in Illinois ended in 1848. James Davis has contended that by 1861, frontier Illinois "changed, faded, and largely disappeared." Pease, *The Centennial History of Illinois,* vol. 2, *The Frontier State: 1818–1848* (Springfield: Illinois Centennial Commission, 1918; repr., Urbana: University of Illinois Press, 1987), 410; Davis, *Frontier Illinois* (Bloomington: Indiana University Press, 1998), 355.

4. Martha L. Benner and Cullom Davis, eds., *The Law Practice of Abraham Lincoln: Complete Documentary Edition,* 2d ed. (Springfield: Illinois Historic

Preservation Agency, 2009), available at www.lawpracticeofabrahamlincoln.org (hereafter cited as *LPAL*). This fifteen-year project created a derivative archive of more than ninety-five thousand Lincoln documents held in county courthouses, libraries, museums, and private collections across the county. The collection provides scores of legal documents and correspondence that would otherwise be difficult to obtain.

5. Prominent community studies on the antebellum Midwest that have contributed to my understanding of community include Jeffrey F. Adler, *Yankee Merchants and the Making of the Urban West: The Rise and Fall of Antebellum St. Louis* (New York: Cambridge University Press, 1991); Richard S. Alcorn, "Leadership and Stability in Mid-Nineteenth-Century America: A Case Study of an Illinois Town," *Journal of American History* 61 (December 1974): 685–702; Paul M. Angle, *"Here I Have Lived": A History of Lincoln's Springfield, 1821–1865* (New Brunswick, N.J.: Rutgers University Press, 1935); Douglas E. Booth, "Transportation, City Building, and Financial Crisis: Milwaukee, 1852–1868," *Journal of Urban History* 9 (May 1983): 335–63; Jeffrey P. Brown, "Chillicothe's Elite: Leadership in a Frontier Community," *Ohio History* 96 (Summer–Autumn 1987): 140–56; Kathleen Neils Conzen, *Immigrant Milwaukee, 1836–1860: Accommodation and Community in a Frontier City* (Cambridge, Mass.: Harvard University Press, 1976); Doyle, *Social Order of a Frontier Community*; Perry R. Duis, *Challenging Chicago: Coping with Everyday Life, 1837–1920* (Urbana: University of Illinois Press, 1998); Faragher, *Sugar Creek*; Wallace, "Opportunity to Grow." Early works that attempted to categorize and develop theories of midwestern culture and experience include Dixon Ryan Fox, ed., *Sources of Culture in the Middle West: Backgrounds versus Frontier* (New York: D. Appleton–Century, 1934); Henry Clyde Hubbart, *The Older Middle West, 1840–1880: Its Social, Economic, and Political Life and Sectional Tendencies before, during, and after the Civil War* (1936; repr., New York: Russell and Russell, 1963); Thomas D. Clark, *The Rampaging Frontier: Manners and Humors of Pioneer Days in the South and Middle West* (New York: Bobbs-Merrill, 1939); Carlyle R. Buley, *The Old Northwest: Pioneer Period, 1815–1840*, 2 vols. (Bloomington: Indiana University Press, 1951); Walter Havighurst, *The Heartland: Ohio, Indiana, Illinois* (New York: Harper and Row, 1956); John J. Murray, ed., *The Heritage of the Middle West* (Norman: University of Oklahoma Press, 1958); James R. Shortridge, *The Middle West: Its Meaning in American Culture* (Lawrence: University of Kansas Press, 1989); Thomas D. Clark, *Frontier America: The Story of Westward Movement*, 2d ed. (New York: Charles Scribner and Son, 1969). Topical scholarship on the Midwest includes Richard Wade, *The Urban Frontier: The Rise of Western Cities, 1790–1830* (Cambridge, Mass.: Harvard University Press, 1959; repr., Cambridge, Mass.: Harvard University Press, 1967); Paul Kleppner, *The Cross of Culture: A Social Analysis of Midwestern Politics, 1850–1900* (New York: Free Press, 1970); Adler, *Yankee Merchants*; Timothy R. Mahoney, *River Towns in the Great West: The Structure of Provincial Urbanization in the American Midwest, 1820–1870*

(New York: Cambridge University Press, 1990). Studies that examine ideas of regionalism and explore the conception of the Midwest as a distinct region include William N. Parker, "From Northwest to Midwest: Social Bases of a Regional History," in *Essays in Nineteenth Century Economic History: The Old Northwest*, ed. David C. Klingaman and Richard K. Vedder (Athens: Ohio University Press, 1975), 3–34; Shortridge, *Middle West*; James H. Madison, ed., *Heartland: Comparative Histories of the Midwestern States* (Bloomington: Indiana University Press, 1988); Andrew R. L. Cayton and Peter S. Onuf, *The Midwest and the Nation: Rethinking the History of an American Region* (Bloomington: Indiana University Press, 1990). Recent works on midwestern history that combine quality historical analysis with strong, interpretive frameworks include Timothy R. Mahoney, *Provincial Lives: Middle-Class Experience in the Antebellum Midwest* (Cambridge: Cambridge University Press, 1999); Nicole Etcheson, *The Emerging Midwest: Upland Southerners and the Political Culture of the Old Northwest, 1787–1861* (Bloomington: Indiana University Press, 1996); Lucy Eldersveld Murphy and Wendy Hamand Venet, eds., *Midwestern Women: Work, Community, and Leadership at the Crossroads* (Bloomington: Indiana University Press, 1997).

6. *LPAL*.

Introduction

1. David Herbert Donald, *Lincoln* (New York: Simon and Schuster, 1995), 23–26, 36; Richard K. Vedder and Lowell E. Gallaway, "Migration and the Old Northwest," in *Essays in Nineteenth Century Economic History: The Old Northwest*, ed. David C. Klingaman and Richard K. Vedder (Athens: Ohio University Press, 1975), 159; Frederick Jackson Turner, *The United States, 1830–1850: The Nation and Its Sections* (New York: Henry Holt, 1935; repr., Gloucester, Mass.: Peter Smith, 1958), 4, 258, 269–72; R. Carlyle Buley, *The Old Northwest: Pioneer Period, 1815–1840*, 2 vols. (Bloomington: Indiana University Press, 1951), 2:141; James E. Davis, *Frontier Illinois* (Bloomington: Indiana University Press, 1998), 204, 306; Robert P. Howard, *Illinois: A History of the Prairie State* (Grand Rapids, Mich.: William B. Eardman's Publishing, 1972), 145, 255; Douglas K. Meyer, *Making the Heartland Quilt: A Geographical History of Settlement and Migration in Early-Nineteenth-Century Illinois* (Carbondale: Southern Illinois University Press, 2000), 39. For the purpose of defining the midwestern region *demographically* and because of the vital economic connections of St. Louis (where much of the population of Missouri resided), Missouri is considered here as part of the Midwest. However, because of its southern connections and its status as a slave state, Missouri is less relevant from a *legal* history perspective. Missouri thus plays a very limited role in this analysis of antebellum midwestern jury law. Yet it is worth noting that there were shared legal experiences between Missouri and Illinois. Lawrence O. Christensen, "Missouri: The Heart of the Nation," in *Heart Land: Comparative*

Histories of the Midwestern States, ed. James H. Madison (Bloomington: Indiana University Press, 1988), 86–106.

2. Turner, *United States,* 258, 260, 271–72; Buley, *Old Northwest,* 2:99; *Green River Advocate* (Hopkinsville, Ky.), cited in *Chicago American,* November 26, 1833; *Chicago Democrat,* July 2, 1834; *Chicago Democrat,* April 13, 1833.

3. Andrew R. L. Cayton and Peter S. Onuf, *The Midwest and the Nation: Rethinking the History of an American Region* (Bloomington: Indiana University Press, 1990), 27; Meyer, *Making the Heartland Quilt,* 2; Buley, *Old Northwest,* 2:108; Turner, *United States,* 269–74; Martha Mitchell Bigelow, "Michigan: A State in the Vanguard," in *Heart Land: Comparative Histories of the Midwestern States,* ed. James H. Madison (Bloomington: Indiana University Press, 1988), 40; Peter T. Harstad, "Indiana and the Art of Adjustment," in *Heart Land: Comparative Histories of the Midwestern States,* ed. James H. Madison (Bloomington: Indiana University Press, 1988), 167. Although Iowa, like Missouri, lay west of the Mississippi, the state took on many of the early characteristics of the antebellum Midwest, and ultimately, its identity would be linked with that of the greater Midwest. James H. Madison, ed., *Heart Land: Comparative Histories of the Midwestern States* (Bloomington: Indiana University Press, 1988), 167.

4. Buley, *Old Northwest,* 1:102–3; Josiah B. Grinnell, *Sketches of the West, or the Home of the Badgers,* 2d ed. (Milwaukee, Wis., 1847), 17.

5. Vedder and Gallaway, "Migration and the Old Northwest," 159; David K. Klingaman and Richard C. Vedder, eds., *Essays on the Economy of the Old Northwest* (Athens: Ohio University Press, 1987), vii, ix; Buley, *Old Northwest,* 2:319; Walter Havighorst, *The Heartland: Ohio, Indiana, Illinois* (New York: Harper and Row, 1956), 122.

6. Earl Shenck Miers, ed., *Lincoln Day by Day: A Chronology, 1809–1865,* 3 vols. (Washington, D.C.: Lincoln Sesquicentennial Commission, 1960), 2:39; Joanne Towers Wheeler, "Springfield, 1850: The City, Its Places, Its People," manuscript, 1978, Abraham Lincoln Presidential Library, Springfield, Ill., pullout map, 12, 34–37; Susan Krause, *From Log Cabins to Temples of Justice: Courthouses in Lincoln's Illinois* (Springfield: Illinois Historic Preservation Agency, 2000), 68.

7. Howard, *Illinois,* 210; Krause, *From Log Cabins to Temples of Justice,* 39; Christopher Elliott Wallace, "The Opportunity to Grow: Springfield, Illinois, during the 1850s" (Ph.D. diss., Purdue University, 1983), 35, 38–40; Office of the U.S. Census, Seventh Census of the United States (1850), Sangamon County, Ill., 69–126; *Sangamon County Illinois 1850 Census and Mortality Schedule* (Springfield, Ill.: Sangamon County Genealogical Society, 1976), 154–200; Wheeler, "Springfield," 33, 40, 51; Meyer, *Making the Heartland Quilt,* 66, 167, 184, 237; Theodore Calvin Pease, *The Centennial History of Illinois,* vol. 2, *The Frontier State: 1818–1848* (Springfield: Illinois Centennial Commission, 1918; repr., Urbana: University of Illinois Press, 1987), 410; Davis, *Frontier Illinois,* 355.

8. Abraham Lincoln, "Farewell Address at Springfield," February 11, 1861, Abraham Lincoln Papers, Library of Congress, Washington, D.C.

9. Renee Lettow Lerner, "The Transformation of the American Civil Trial: The Silent Judge," *William and Mary Law Review* 42 (October 2000): 199; Daniel W. Stowell, ed., *In Tender Consideration: Women, Families, and the Law in Abraham Lincoln's Illinois* (Urbana: University of Illinois Press, 2002); Michael Les Benedict and John F. Winkler, eds., *The History of Ohio Law,* 2 vols. (Athens: Ohio University Press, 2004); David J. Bodenhamer and Randall T. Shepard, *The History of Indiana Law* (Athens: Ohio University Press, 2006). Good scholarship in western legal history includes Charles Cook, *The American Codification Movement: A Study of Antebellum Legal Reform* (Westport, Conn.: Greenwood Press, 1981); John McLaren, Hamar Foster, and Chet Orloff, eds., *Law for the Elephant, Law for the Beaver: Essays in the Legal History of the North American West* (Pasadena, Calif.: Ninth Judicial Circuit Historical Society, 1992). Good scholarship in southern legal history includes David J. Bodenhamer and James W. Ely Jr., eds., *Ambivalent Legacy: A Legal History of the South* (Jackson: University of Mississippi Press, 1984); James W. Ely and David J. Bodenhamer, "Regionalism and American Legal History: The Southern Experience," *Vanderbilt Law Review* 39 (April 1986): 539–67; Paul Finkelman, "Exploring Southern Legal History," *North Carolina Law Review* 64 (November 1985): 77–116.

10. John Philip Reid, *Law for the Elephant: Property and Social Behavior on the Overland Trail* (San Marino, Calif.: Huntington Library, 1997); James W. Gordon, *Lawyers in Politics: Mid-Nineteenth Century Kentucky as a Case Study* (New York: Garland Publishing, 1990); Morton Horwitz, *The Transformation of American Law, 1790–1860* (New York: Oxford University Press, 1992); Jamil Zainaldin, *Law in Antebellum Society: Legal Change and Economic Expansion* (New York: Alfred A. Knopf, 1983); Cook, *American Codification Movement*; Phillip S. Paludan, "Lincoln, the Rule of Law, and the American Revolution," *Journal of the Illinois State Historical Society* 70 (February 1977): 10–17; James Willard Hurst, *Law and Social Order in the United States* (Ithaca, N.Y.: Cornell University Press, 1977); Paludan, "The American Civil War Considered as a Crisis in Law and Order," *American Historical Review* 77 (October 1972): 1013–34; James Willard Hurst, *Law and the Conditions of Freedom in the Nineteenth Century United States* (Madison: University of Wisconsin Press, 1956); James Willard Hurst, *The Growth of American Law: The Law Makers* (Boston: Little, Brown, 1950); Daniel D. Blinka, "Trial by Jury on the Eve of the Revolution: The Virginia Experience," *University of Missouri Kansas City Review* 71 (Spring 2003): 533; Rhys Isaac, *The Transformation of Virginia, 1740–1790* (Chapel Hill: University of North Carolina Press, 1982), 88; Krause, *From Log Cabins to Temples of Justice,* 5–7.

11. Alexis de Tocqueville, *Democracy in America,* trans. Harvey C. Mansfield and Delba Winthrop (Chicago: University of Chicago Press, 2000); Jacqueline Edelberg, "Justice Here? Alexis de Tocqueville and the Role of the Jury in the American Judicial Process and Republican Democracy," *Tocqueville Review* 17, no. 2 (1996): 67–97; Lynn L. Marshall and Seymour Prescher, "American Historians

and Tocqueville's Democracy," *Journal of American History* 55 (December 1968): 512–32; Lee C. Soltow, "Tocqueville's View of the Northwest in 1835: Ohio a Generation after Settlement," in *Essays on the Economy of the Old Northwest,* ed. David C. Klingaman and Richard K. Vedder (Athens: Ohio University Press, 1987), 131–55; Kirk W. Wood, "Alexis de Tocqueville and the Myth of Democracy in America," *Southern Studies* 5 (1994): 1–17; Albert W. Alschuler and Andrew G. Deiss, "A Brief History of the Criminal Jury in the United States," *University of Chicago Law Review* 61 (Summer 1994): 870–71.

12. Robert von Moschzisker, *Trial by Jury: A Brief Review of Its Origin, Development and Merits and Practical Discussions on Actual Conduct of Jury Trials, Together with a Consideration of Constitutional Provisions and Other Cognate Subjects of Importance* (Philadelphia: George T. Bisel, 1922), 266; Jeffrey Abramson, *We, the Jury: The Jury System and the Ideal of Democracy* (New York: Basic Books, 1994), 73–75; Leonard W. Levy, *The Palladium of Justice: Origins of Trial by Jury* (Chicago: Ivan R. Dee, 1999), 79–81; Stanley N. Katz, ed., *A Brief Narrative of the Case and Trial of John Peter Zenger by James Alexander* (Cambridge, Mass.: Harvard University Press, 1963); Alschuler and Deiss, "Brief History of the Criminal Jury," 871–75; Stephen Botein, *Early American Law and Society* (New York: Alfred A. Knopf, 1982), 63. See also Shannon C. Stimson, *The American Revolution in the Law: Anglo-American Jurisprudence before John Marshall* (Princeton, N.J.: Princeton University Press, 1990); Blinka, "Trial by Jury on the Eve of Revolution"; The Northwest Ordinance, enacted July 13, 1787, art. III; Ohio const. of 1802, art. VIII, § 8; Theodore Calvin Pease, "The Ordinance of 1787," *Mississippi Valley Historical Review* 25 (September 1938): 167–80; Indiana const. of 1816, art. I, § 20; Illinois const. of 1818, art. VIII, § 6; Buley, *Old Northwest,* 2:191; Cayton and Onuf, *Midwest and the Nation,* xviii. The following essays in one issue of the *William and Mary Quarterly* discuss the law and the American Revolution and shed light on the status of the jury as a democratic institution: J. R. Pole, "Reflections on American Law and the Revolution," *William and Mary Quarterly* 50 (January 1993): 123–59; Peter Charles Hoffer, "Custom as Law: A Comment on J. R. Pole's 'Reflections,'" *William and Mary Quarterly* 50 (January 1993): 160–67; Bruce H. Mann, "The Evolutionary Revolution in American Law: A Comment on J. R. Pole's 'Reflections,'" *William and Mary Quarterly* 50 (January 1993): 168–75.

13. Abramson, *We, the Jury*; James J. Gobert, *Justice, Democracy, and the Jury* (Brookfield, UK: Alderson, 1997); Godfrey D. Lehman, *We, the Jury: The Impact of Jurors on Our Basic Freedoms* (Amherst, N.Y.: Prometheus Books, 1997); Levy, *Palladium of Justice*; Maximus A. Lesser, *The Historical Development of the Jury System* (Rochester, N.Y.: Lawyers' Co-operative Publishing, 1894; repr., Buffalo, N.Y.: W. S. Hein, 1992); Lloyd E. Moore, *The Jury: Tool of Kings, Palladium of Liberty* (Cincinnati: W. H. Anderson, 1973); Richard D. Younger, *The People's Panel: The Grand Jury in the United States, 1634–1941* (Providence, R.I.: Brown University Press, 1963).

14. An Act Relating to Juries (February 9, 1831), *Statutes of the State of Ohio* (1831), 489–96; An Act to Regulate the Mode of Summoning and Empannelling Grand and Petit Jurors (January 29, 1831), *Revised Laws of Indiana* (1831), 291–92; An Act Prescribing the Manner of Impanneling Petit Jurors, the Number and Compensation Thereof (May 20, 1852), *Revised Statutes of the State of Indiana* (1852), 2:24–25; "Jurors," *An Act for Revising and Consolidating the General Statutes of the State of Iowa* (1851), 241; "Of Grand and Petit Jurors," January 13, 1858, *Revised Statutes of the State of Wisconsin* (1858), 655; "Jurors," 1851, 241; "Jurors," December 5, 1855, *Revised Statutes of the State of Missouri* (1856), 2:910; George Worthington, *An Inquiry into the Power of Juries to Decide Incidentally on Questions of Law* (London: S. Sweet, 1825; repr., Littleton, Colo.: F. B. Rothman, 1997); William Forsyth, *History of Trial by Jury* (1852; repr., New York: James Crockcroft, 1875); Lysander Spooner, *An Essay on the Trial by Jury* (Boston: John P. Jewett, 1852; repr., New York: Da Capo Press, 1971). Unlike the right to trial by jury, jury service was deemed a political right, not a constitutional right. Vikram David Amar, "Jury Service as Political Participation Akin to Voting," *Cornell Law Review* 80 (January 1995): 203–59.

15. Reid, *Law for the Elephant,* 202–14.

16. Charles Beneulyn Johnson, *Illinois in the Fifties or a Decade of Development: 1851–1860* (Champaign, Ill.: Flanigan-Pearson, 1918); Collin McCoy, "Democracy in Print: The Literature of Persuasion in Jacksonian America, 1815–1840" (Ph.D. diss., University of Illinois, 2001); *Logansport (Ind.) Canal Telegraph*, June 25, 1836, quoted in Buley, *Old Northwest,* 2:523.

17. Michael H. Harris, "Books for Sale on the Illinois Frontier: De Kalb County, 1855–1865," *American Book Collector* 2 (January 1971): 15–17; Edward W. Stevens Jr., "Structural and Ideological Dimensions of Literacy and Education in the Old Northwest," in *Essays on the Economy of the Old Northwest,* ed. David C. Klingaman and Richard K. Vedder (Athens: Ohio University Press, 1987), 180; Isabelle Lehuu, *Carnival on the Page: Popular Print Media in Antebellum America* (Chapel Hill: University of North Carolina Press, 2000); Franklin William Scott, *Newspapers and Periodicals of Illinois, 1814–1879* (Springfield: Illinois State Historical Library, 1910), liv–lxxi; *Illinois State Gazette and Jacksonville News,* May 9, 1835. This review of newspapers and periodicals is not based on a systematic survey of nineteenth-century publications; rather, it describes some popular notions about the jury and indicates the importance that many editors, writers, and readers attached to it. The publications used for this purpose surfaced in my research somewhat serendipitously, and my examination of them is merely anecdotal. Though many of the newspapers and periodicals examined were national in scope, I made some effort to privilege those that either were published in the emerging Midwest or were readily available there. It was important to examine the language and imagery of the jury with which midwesterners would have been familiar. The midwestern publications studied

were: *Chicago American*; *Chicago Daily Times*; *Chicago Daily Tribune*; *Chicago Democrat*; *Chicago Press and Tribune*; *Christian Advocate and Journal* (Chicago); *Cincinnati Weekly Herald and Philanthropist*; *Democrat* (St. Louis); *Illinois Register* (Springfield); *Illinois State Gazette & Jacksonville News*; *Illinois State Journal* (Springfield); *Sangamo Journal* (Springfield, Ill.); *Telegraph* (Alton, Ill.); *Vandalia (Ill.) Free Press*. The publications with a national scope that were studied were: *American Masonic Register and Literary Companion* (Albany, N.Y.); *Anglo American: A Journal of Literature, News, Politics, the Drama, Fine Arts, Etc.*; *Anti-slavery Record*; *Atkinson's Casket*; *Atkinson's Saturday Evening Post* (Philadelphia); *Banner of the Constitution*; *Campbell's Foreign Semi-monthly Magazine*; *DeBow's Review*; *Friends' Review: A Religious, Literary and Miscellaneous Journal* (Philadelphia); *Harper's Weekly*; *Journal of Prison Discipline and Philanthropy*; *Law Reporter*; *Liberator* (Boston); *Literary World*; *Littell's Living Age*; *North American Magazine*; *North American Review*; *Oliver's Magazine*; *United States Intelligencer and Review*; *United States Magazine and Democratic Review*; *United States Review*; *Western Christian Advocate* (Cincinnati); *Western Law Journal*; *Workingman's Advocate*. Other publications consulted were: *Albion* (New York); *Boston Cultivator*; *Christian Register* (Boston); *Christian Watchman* (Boston); *Circular* (Brooklyn, N.Y.); *Family Magazine: Monthly Abstract of General Knowledge*; *Flag of Our Union* (Boston); *Knickerbocker: New York Monthly Magazine*; *National Era* (Washington, D.C.); *New York Daily Times*; *New York Evangelist*; *New-York Mirror: Weekly Gazette of Literature and the Fine Arts*; *New York Observer and Chronicle*; *New York Times*; *New-Yorker*; *Pennsylvania Law Journal*; *Philanthropist* (Cincinnati); *Princeton Review*; *Southern Literary Messenger*; *Southern Quarterly Review*; *Western Recorder* (Utica, N.Y.); *Zion's Herald* (Boston).

18. "The Trial by Jury," *Knickerbocker* 15 (June 1840); "Judicial Reform," *Cincinnati Weekly Herald and Philanthropist*, March 13, 1844; B. S. P, "Trial by Jury," *New-Yorker* 8 (February 1840): 304; St. George Tucker, ed., *Blackstone's Commentaries, with Notes and References to the Constitution and Laws of the Federal Government of the United States and of the Commonwealth of Virginia*, 5 vols. (Philadelphia: W. Y. Birchand A. Small, 1803; repr., Chicago: University of Chicago Press, 1979); J. Kendall Few, *Trial by Jury* (n.p.: American Jury Trial Foundation, 1993), 2, 75, 77; Christopher L. Tomlins, *Law, Labor, and Ideology in the Early American Republic* (Cambridge: Cambridge University Press, 1993), 69–70; Mark DeWolf Howe, "Juries as Judges of Criminal Law," *Harvard Law Review* 52 (February 1939): 582; Tucker, *Blackstone's Commentaries*, 4:349; Abraham Lincoln to James T. Thornton, December 2, 1858, in *The Collected Works of Abraham Lincoln*, ed. Roy B. Basler Jr., 8 vols. (New Brunswick, N.J.: Rutgers University Press, 1953), 3:344; Abraham Lincoln to John M. Brockman, September 25, 1860, Abraham Lincoln Presidential Library and Museum, Springfield, Ill.; Donald, *Lincoln*, 53. U.S. Supreme Court Chief Justice Roger Taney said: "Among the most cherished principles of the common law was trial by jury in civil and criminal cases. It was regarded as

a right of inestimable value, and the best and only security for life, liberty, and property." Few, *Trial by Jury,* 75.

19. "Lecture to Law Students by Professor B. Tucker," *Southern Literary Messenger* 4 (December 1834): 150; "John P. Hale's Lecture," *Chicago Daily Times,* January 19, 1856; Richard H. Sewell, *John P. Hale and the Politics of Abolition* (Cambridge, Mass.: Harvard University Press, 1965); "Value of Trial by Jury," *Philanthropist* (Cincinnati), November 7, 1837.

20. Speech of Abraham Lincoln, *Sangamo Journal* (Springfield, Ill.), February 3, 1838, p. 2, col. 4; "Trial by Jury: Remarks of Mr. DeFord of Fayette," *Pennsylvania Law Review* 1 (April 1842): 104; "Value of Trial by Jury"; Peter A. Brown, "Trial by Jury: A Speech on the Liberty of the Press," *North American Magazine* 3 (November 1833): 17; "The State of Louisiana," *DeBow's Review, Agricultural, Commercial, Industrial Progress and Resources* 1 (May 1846): 414.

21. "Southern Slavery and Its Assailants," *DeBow's Review, Agricultural, Commercial, Industrial Progress and Resources* 16 (January 1854).

22. "Trial by Jury," *Philanthropist,* April 14, 1837; Fugitive Slave Act (1850), 9 U.S. Statutes 462, September 18, 1850; Kermit L. Hall, ed., *The Oxford Companion to the Supreme Court* (New York: Oxford University Press, 1992), 320; Harriet Beecher Stowe, *Uncle Tom's Cabin, or Life among the Lowly* (Boston: J. P. Jewett, 1852); Linck C. Johnson, "'Liberty Is Never Cheap': Emerson, 'The Fugitive Slave Law,' and the Antislavery Lecture Series at the Broadway Tabernacle," *New England Quarterly* 76 (December 2003): 550–92; Ella Forbes, "'By My Own Right Arm': Redemptive Violence and the 1851 Christiana, Pennsylvania, Resistance," *Journal of Negro History* 83 (Summer 1998): 159–67.

23. Thomas Matijasic, "The Reaction of the Ohio General Assembly to the Fugitive Slave Law of 1850," *Northwest Ohio Quarterly* 55 (Spring 1983): 40–60; Paula J. Priebe, "Central and Western New York and the Fugitive Slave Law of 1850," *Afro-Americans in New York Life and History* 16, no. 1 (1992): 19–29; Jane H. Pease and William H. Pease, *The Fugitive Slave Law and Anthony Burns: A Problem in Law Enforcement* (Philadelphia: Lippincott, 1975); "Trial by Jury," April 7, 1837, "Trial by Jury," June 9, 1837, "Unconstitutional Laws of Ohio," 1, and "The Empire State Bowing the Knee to Slavery," April 21, 1843, all in *Liberator* (Boston); "Chase's Argument: Right of Trial by Jury," *Philanthropist* (Cincinnati), June 23, 1837, July 21, 1837, December 19, 1837, February 20, 1838; "Right of Trial by Jury," *New York Evangelist,* March 30, 1843; "Law for Slaves," *National Era* (Washington, D.C.), December 19, 1850; Fugitive Slave Act (1850), 9 U.S. Statutes 462; "News of the Week: A Personal Liberty Bill," *Circular* (Brooklyn, N.Y.), March 3, 1859; "New Jersey Right of Trial by Jury," *Philanthropist,* April 7, 1837; John Evans to W. B. Plano, September 4, 1854, printed in the *Chicago Daily Tribune,* September 11, 1854. An abolitionist writing to President-Elect Abraham Lincoln made a similar argument about the denial of jury rights to fugitive slaves and the dangers of such blatant disregard for the institution of the jury. Elias H. Derby

to Abraham Lincoln, November 29, 1860, Abraham Lincoln Papers, Library of Congress, Washington, D.C.

24. R. H., "Selection: Essay on the Trial by Jury," *Liberator,* December 17, 1852; *New York Evangelist,* March 31, 1853; *National Era,* March 31, 1853; *Literary World,* January 8, 1853; *North American Review,* January 1853; *United States Magazine and Democratic Review,* February 1851; David Wellman Jr. to Abraham Lincoln, July 28, 1860, Abraham Lincoln Papers, Library of Congress, Washington, D.C. The *National Era* of March 31, 1853, carried a notice about the availability of *Uncle Tom's Cabin* on the same page.

25. Forsyth, *History of Trial by Jury*; Worthington, *Inquiry into the Power of Juries*; Jeremy Bentham, *On the Art of Packing Special Juries* (London: Effingham Wilson, Royal Exchange, 1821); L., "Miscellany: Origins of Trial by Jury," *American Masonic Register and Literary Companion* (Albany, N.Y.), March 14, 1840, 281; "Trial by Jury," *Western Christian Advocate* (Cincinnati), July 10, 1835; "Independence of Jurors," *Atkinson's Saturday Evening Post* (Philadelphia), May 28, 1836.

26. Thomas A. Ford, *A History of Illinois from Its Commencement as a State in 1818 to 1847* (1854; repr., Ann Arbor, Mich.: University Microfilms, 1968), 84.

27. "The First Integrated Jury Impaneled in the United States, May, 1867," *Negro History Bulletin* 33 (October 1970): 134. This article also stated that from 1820 to the 1860s, "some Americans found themselves facing glaring inconsistencies between their professed principles of citizenship and their deep-seated desire to exclude certain groups permanently from the privileges of membership." However, this does not appear to have given rise to national or statewide efforts to extend citizenship rights or responsibilities. There would not be a racially integrated jury until 1867. Mark Allen Cyr, "'I Would Not Be a Master': Democracy and Political Culture of Mastering in Illinois, 1837–1858" (Ph.D. diss., Washington University, 2003); Glenn C. Altschuler and Stuart M. Blumin, "Limits of Political Engagement in Antebellum America: A New Look at the Golden Age of Participatory Democracy," *Journal of American History* 84 (December 1997): 85–85.

28. "Juries and Majorities," *Circular,* July 13, 1854; An Act Prescribing the Mode of Summoning Grand Jurors (March 23, 1819), *Laws Passed by the First General Assembly of the State of Illinois* (1819), 256; Act Relating to Juries, February 9, 1831 (Ohio), 490; Act Prescribing the Manner of Impanneling Petit Jurors, May 20, 1852 (Indiana), 24. There was an interesting situation in Hawaii. In 1842, a jury law there provided for impaneling foreign jurors. A section of the statute read: "If the accuser and the accused be both foreigners, then the jury shall be made up of foreigners only. If there be no foreigner on either side, then there shall be no foreigner on the jury. If there be a foreigner on one side and a native on the other, then in forming the jury, half shall be foreigners and half natives." This unusual practice was not in use in the United States. First Jury Statute in Kingdom of Hawaii (1842).

29. E. L., "Trial by Jury," *Friends' Review* (Philadelphia), August 24, 1850, 771.

30. H. Fowler, *Report of the Debates and Proceedings of the Convention for the Revision of the Constitution of the State of Indiana* (Indianapolis: Constitutional Convention of the State of Indiana, 1850), 147; R. David Edmunds, "Justice on a Changing Frontier: Deer Lick Creek, 1824–1825," *Indiana Magazine of History* 93 (March 1997): 48–52; N. Z. H, "The Murder Trial at Freehold," *New York Daily Times,* September 25, 1852. In 1760s Virginia, "justices and grand jurors adroitly used their positions to consolidate power and to build wealth." Blinka, "Trial by Jury on the Eve of the Revolution," 535.

31. *Illinois State Journal* (Springfield), December 9, 1856, April 21, 1857, April 30, 1857, May 11, 1860; *Daily Pantagraph* (Bloomington, Ill.), April 8, 1857; "Some of Old Knick's Jokes: Juries," *New York Daily Times,* October 4, 1851.

32. "Trial by Jury," *New York Daily Times,* May 13, 1857; "Judicial Reform," *Cincinnati Weekly Herald and Philanthropist,* March 13, 1844; "The Trial: From the Note-Book of a Deceased Lawyer," *Albion* (New York), April 16, 1859; E. L., "Trial by Jury"; "Trial by Jury, What Is It Worth? A Story of Former Times," *Journal of Discipline and Philanthropy* 13 (April 1858): 89; "Another Disgrace," *Chicago Press and Tribune,* December 13, 1859.

33. "Another Disgrace."

34. "Municipal Court," *Boston Cultivator,* November 20, 1841.

35. "Juries and Majorities," *Circular,* July 13, 1843; "Trial by Jury," *New York Evangelist,* August 8, 1850; "Another Disgrace"; T. Walker, "Rights and Duties of Grand Jurors," *Western Law Journal* 1 (May 1844): 388; David J. Bodenhamer, "Criminal Justice and Democratic Theory in Antebellum America: The Grand Jury Debate in Indiana," *Journal of the Early Republic* 5 (Winter 1985): 481–502; "Grand Juries," *United States Monthly Law Magazine* 1 (February 1850); New York Committee on Practice and Pleading, *Fourth Report of the Commissioners on Practice and Pleading, Code of Criminal Procedure* (Albany, N.Y., 1849), 118; Fowler, *Report for Revision of Constitution of Indiana,* 147; Brown, "Trial by Jury," 18; "Trial by Jury, What Is It Worth?"; B. S. P, "Trial by Jury," *New-Yorker* 8 (February 1840). "He who spares the guilty, punishes the innocent"; *Jenkin's Centuries of Reports,* 126, quoted in Charles Edwards, *The Juryman's Guide throughout the State of New York, and Containing General Matter for the Lawyer and Law Officer* (New York: Halstead Law Bookseller, 1831), xv.

36. "Judicial Reform," *Cincinnati Weekly Herald and Philanthropist,* March 13, 1844.

37. Fowler, *Report of the Debates and Proceedings of the Convention,* 146.

38. Henry A. Bullard, "A Discourse Delivered before the Historical Society of Louisiana, January 13, 1836," published as "Louisiana Historical Researches," *DeBow's Review, Agricultural, Commercial, Industrial Progress and Resources* 3 (January 1847): 33–34, quoted here from *Historical Collections of Louisiana,* vol. 1, comp. B. F. French (New York: Wiley and Putnam, 1846), 18; Thomas D. Clark, *The Rampaging Frontier: Manners and Humors of Pioneer Days in the*

South and Middle West (New York: Bobbs-Merrill, 1939), 164–67; Dell Upton, *Holy Things and Profane: Anglican Parish Churches in Colonial Virginia* (New Haven, Conn.: Yale University Press, 1986), 205–6; James R. Perry, *The Formation of a Society on Virginia's Eastern Shore, 1615–1655* (Chapel Hill: University of North Carolina Press, 1990), 230. Alexis de Tocqueville had noted that jury service itself served to enlighten the public. "On the Jury in the United States Considered as a Political Institution," in de Tocqueville, *Democracy in America,* 258–63; Edelberg, "Justice Here," 67–97.

39. Edwards, *Juryman's Guide.*

40. Fowler, *Report of the Debates and Proceedings of the Convention,* 147; Bodenhamer, "Criminal Justice and Democratic Theory," 481–502; Brown, "Trial by Jury," 18; "Trial by Jury, What Is It Worth?" 89; "Municipal Court," *Boston Cultivator,* November 20, 1841; "Trial by Jury: Should a Majority Convict?" *New York Times,* October 28, 1858.

41. "Supreme Court," *Boston Cultivator,* May 18, 1839; George Fitzhugh, "Popular Institutions," *DeBow's Review* 28 (November 1860).

42. "Trial by Jury," *Knickerbocker.*

43. "Trial by Jury," *Philanthropist*; David M. Gold, "Reforming the Civil Jury in the Nineteenth-Century West: Jury Size and Unanimity of Verdicts," *Western Legal History* 15 (Winter–Spring 2002): 137–64.

44. "Trial by Jury," *New York Evangelist,* August 8, 1850, 126.

45. "Russia and New York," *New York Times,* November 27, 1858; "Greece," *Littell's Living Age* (Boston), May 25, 1844; "Leiber's Civil Liberty and Self Government," *Southern Literary Messenger* 19 (December 1853): 714; "Trial by Jury," *Campbell's Foreign Semi-monthly Magazine* 5 (February 1844): 188; "Jury Trial and the Federal Court," *Southern Quarterly Review* 1 (July 1850); E. L., "Trial by Jury." The American jury system took its shape from the system in common-law England, but the jury was rooted in medieval civil and religious institutions as well. Neil Vidmar, ed., *World Jury Systems* (New York: Oxford University Press, 2000); Levy, *Palladium of Justice*; Moore, *Jury*; Harold C. Warner, "Development of Trial by Jury," *Tennessee Law Review* 26 (Summer 1959): 459–67; Lesser, *Historical Development of the Jury System*; von Moschzisker, *Trial by Jury,* 9–19.

46. "Independence of Jurors," *Atkinson's Saturday Evening Post,* May 28, 1836; "Trial by Jury in Ireland," *Littell's Living Age,* October 7, 1848; "Law Reform in England," *New York Daily Times,* November 23, 1854; "Law Reform in England," *Christian Advocate and Journal* (Cincinnati), February 1, 1855; H. Yoakum, "The Republics of Mexico and the United States," *DeBow's Review, Agricultural, Commercial, Industrial Progress and Resources* 21 (October 1856); "Trial by Jury in Ireland," *Littell's Living Age.*

47. Yoakum, "Republics of Mexico and the United States."

48. "Southern Convention at Vicksburg, Part 2," *DeBow's Review, Agricultural, Commercial, Industrial Progress and Resources* 27 (August 1859).

49. "The Difference: Despotism at Home," *Chicago Press and Tribune,* January 27, 1860, 2.

50. Fitzhugh, "Popular Institutions," 531; Alexander Gordon and M. J. Mercer, "Butcher, Edmund (1757–1822)," in H. C. G. Matthew and Brian Harrison, eds., *Oxford Dictionary of National Biography* (Oxford: Oxford University Press, 2004), available at http://www.oxforddnb.com/view/article/4174 (accessed August 13, 2010); Edmund Butcher, *An Excursion from Sidmouth to Chester in the Summer of 1803,* 2 vols. (1805).

51. "The Intrepid Juryman," *Anglo American,* May 23, 1846.

52. *Christian Watchman* (Boston), December 18, 1824; *Zion's Herald* (Boston), December 29, 1824; *Christian Register* (Boston), January 8, 1825; *Western Recorder* (Utica, N.Y.), January 11, 1825; *New York Telescope,* April 15, 1826; *Western Luminary* (Lexington, Ky.); *Man,* November 28, 1834; *Workingman's Advocate,* November 29, 1834; *Liberator,* May 23, 1835; *Boston Morning Post,* c. July 1845; *Christian Advocate and Journal,* June 19, 1835; *Western Christian Advocate,* July 10, 1835; *Family Magazine: Monthly Abstract of General Knowledge* 3 (May 1836): 364–65; *Catholic Telegraph,* March 22, 1838; *Southern Planter* 1 (April 1841): 55–56; *Subterranean, United with the Workingman's Advocate,* October 26, 1844; *Anglo American: A Journal of Literature, News, Politics, the Drama, Fine Arts, Etc.,* May 23, 1846.

53. "Trial by Jury," reprinted from *Boston Morning Post,* in *Western Christian Advocate,* July 10, 1835.

54. *Southern Planter* 3 (April 1841): 55.

Chapter 1: Jury Law and Tradition in the Antebellum Midwest

1. Josiah H. Blackmore II, "Not from Zeus's Head Full-Blown: The Story of Civil Procedure in Ohio," in *The History of Ohio Law,* ed. Michael Les Benedict and John F. Winkler, 2 vols. (Athens: Ohio University Press, 2004), 1:441.

2. Benjamin F. Wright Jr., "Political Institutions and the Frontier," in *Sources of Culture in the Middle West: Backgrounds versus Frontier,* ed. Dixon Ryan Fox (New York: D. Appleton–Century, 1934), 25–32. See also Horst Dippel, "Representation, Representatives and the Right to Vote, or the Arduous Path Towards Democratic Representative Representation in the United States, 1776–1849," *Parliaments, Estates & Representation* (2003): 25–42; Peter T. Harstad, "Indiana and the Art of Adjustment," in *Heart Land: Comparative Histories of the Midwestern States,* ed. James H. Madison (Bloomington: Indiana University Press, 1988), 167. In some ways, Wisconsin became a "maverick" state, but in terms of the development of its legal system, it was similar to the rest of the antebellum Midwest. John D. Buenker, "Wisconsin: As Maverick, Model, and Microcosm," in *Heartland: Comparative Histories of the Midwestern States,* ed. James H. Madison (Bloomington: Indiana University Press, 1988), 59–85; Ann Walsh Bradley and Joseph A. Ramney, "A Tradition of Independence: The Wisconsin Supreme Court's First 150 Years,"

Wisconsin Magazine of History 86 (Winter 2002–3): 42–49. This source describes the long tradition of innovation and reform-mindedness in Wisconsin.

3. Lawrence M. Friedman, *A History of American Law* (New York: Simon and Schuster, 1973), 108–9. One scholar has argued that southern influences on the development of the states carved out of the Old Northwest were at least as important as eastern influences. John D. Barnhart, "The Southern Influence in the Formation of Illinois," *Journal of the Illinois State Historical Society* 32 (September 1939): 358–78; Barnhart, "Southern Contributions to the Social Order of the Old Northwest," *North Carolina Historical Review* 17 (July 1940): 237–48; Barnhart, "The Southern Influence in the Formation of Indiana," *Indiana Magazine of History* 33 (September 1937): 261–76; Barnhart, "The Southern Influence in the Formation of Ohio," *Journal of Southern History* 3 (February 1937): 28–42.

4. Ohio const. of 1803, art. VIII, § 8; Indiana const. of 1816, art. I, §§ 5, 10, 13; Illinois const. of 1818, art. VIII, §§ 6, 8, 23; Michael Les Benedict, "Civil Liberty in Ohio," in *The History of Ohio Law,* ed. Michael Les Benedict and John F. Winkler, 2 vols. (Athens: Ohio University Press, 2004), 2:679; Ohio const. of 1803, art. VIII, § 6; Peter A. Brown, "The Trial by Jury: A Speech on the Liberty of the Press," *North American Magazine* 3 (November 1833): 15–21. Appellate case law backed up legislative guarantees of jury determination of law and fact: Crocker v. Goodsell, 2 Ill. 107 (1833); Wickersham v. People, 2 Ill. 127 (1834); Archer v. Spillman, 2 Ill. 552 (1839); Cook v. Scott, 6 Ill. 333 (1844); Pate v. People, 8 Ill. 644 (1846); Forshee v. Abrams, 2 Iowa 571 (1856); Fisher v. People, 23 Ill. 218 (1859); and Schnier v. People, 23 Ill. 17 (1859).

5. Michael H. Harris, "The Frontier Lawyer's Library: Southern Indiana, 1800–1850, as a Test Case," *American Journal of Legal History* 16 (July 1972): 239–40. Indiana laws respecting juries include An Act Regulating the Mode of Summoning and Empannelling Grand and Petit Jurors (January 31, 1824), *Revised Laws of Indiana* (1824), 234–36; An Act to Regulate the Mode of Summoning and Empannelling Grand and Petit Jurors (January 29, 1831), *Revised Laws of Indiana* (1831), 291–92; An Act Relative to Crime and Punishment (February 10, 1831), *Revised Statutes of the State of Indiana* (1831), 220; An Act Regulating Fees and Salaries of the Several Officers and Persons therein Named (February 7, 1831), *Revised Statutes of the State of Indiana* (1831), 252; An Act to Regulate the Mode of Summoning and Empannelling Grand and Petit Jurors (February 17, 1838), *Revised Statutes of the State of Indiana* (1838), 358–59. Indiana laws respecting juries up to 1850 include Of the Mode of Summoning and Empannelling Grand and Petit Jurors (1843), *Revised Statutes of the State of Indiana* (1843), 951–53. Indiana laws respecting juries up to 1860 include An Act Prescribing the Manner of Impanneling Petit Jurors, the Number and Compensation Thereof (May 20, 1852), *Revised Statutes of the State of Indiana* (1852), 2:24–25; An Act Regulating the Fees of Officers (June 16, 1852), *Revised Statutes of the State of Indiana* (1852), 2:289–90. Illinois laws respecting juries include An Act Prescribing the Mode of Summoning Grand Jurors (March

23, 1819), *Laws Passed by the First General Assembly of the State of Illinois* (1819), 201–3; An Act Concerning Petit Jurors (March 23, 1819), *Laws Passed by the First General Assembly of the State of Illinois* (1819), 186; An Act Defining the Powers and Duties of Justices of the Peace (March 25, 1819), *Laws Passed by the First General Assembly of the State of Illinois* (1819), 255–57; An Act Regulating the Fees of the Several Officers and Persons therein Named (March 29, 1819), *Laws Passed by the First General Assembly of the State of Illinois* (1819), 321; An Act Concerning Jails and Jailers (January 26, 1827), *Revised Code of Laws, of Illinois* (1827), 248; An Act Concerning Practice in Courts of Law (January 29, 1827), *Revised Code of Laws, of Illinois* (1827), 315; Criminal Code (January 30, 1827), *Revised Code of Laws, of Illinois* (1827), 162–63; An Act to Amend the Act Relative to Criminal Jurisprudence (January 30, 1827), *Public and General Laws of the State of Illinois* (1839), 242; An Act Concerning Justices of the Peace and Constables (February 3, 1827), *Public and General Laws of the State of Illinois* (1839), 407–8; An Act Concerning Salaries, Fees, and Compensation of the Several Officers and Persons therein Mentioned (February 19, 1827), *Public and General Laws of the State of Illinois* (1827), 407–8; An Act Relative to Criminal Jurisprudence (February 26, 1833), *Public and General Statute Laws of the State of Illinois* (1833), 218–33; An Act Regulating the Times and Holding of the Supreme and Circuit Courts, and Fixing the Salary of the Circuit Judge (February 13, 1835), *Public and General Statutes of the State of Illinois* (1835), 184–85; An Act to Amend "An Act Prescribing the Mode of Summoning Grand and Petit Jurors, and Defining Their Qualifications, Approved February 7, 1827" (February 13, 1835), *Public and General Statute Laws of the State of Illinois* (1835), 398–99. Illinois laws respecting juries up to 1850 include "Jurors," March 3, 1845, *Revised Statutes of the State of Illinois* (1845), 308–11. Illinois laws respecting juries up to 1860 include An Act to Increase the Compensation of Grand and Petit Jurors (February 12, 1853), *Laws of the State of Illinois* (1853), 657; An Act to Amend Chapter 83, of the Revised Statutes, Entitled "Practice" (February 11, 1859), *Public Laws of the State of Illinois* (1859), 150. Ohio laws respecting juries include An Act Relating to Juries (February 9, 1831), *Statutes of the State of Ohio* (1831), 489–96; An Act for the Relief of Jurors in Certain Cases (March 16, 1839), *Statutes of the State of Ohio* (1839), 497. Iowa laws respecting juries include An Act on Grand and Petit Jurors (January 4, 1839), *Iowa Territory Laws,* 1st sess. (1839), 277; "Jurors," "Compensation of Officers," "Offenses against Public Justice," "Impanneling Grand Jury," "Powers and Duty of Grand Jury," and "Challenging the Jury," all in *An Act for Revising and Consolidating the General Statutes of the State of Iowa* (1851), 241–43, 346, 364, 400–403, 411–13. Iowa law provided much more detail regarding the jury and trial procedure than did other midwestern states. Wisconsin laws respecting juries include "Of Grand and Petit Jurors," January 13, 1858, *Revised Statutes of the State of Wisconsin* (1858), 655–61.

6. Albert W. Alschuler and Andrew G. Deiss, "A Brief History of the Criminal Jury in the United States," *University of Chicago Law Review* 61 (Summer 1994):

878–79; Act Relating to Juries, February 9, 1831 (Ohio), 489–96; Act to Regulate the Mode of Summoning and Empannelling Grand and Petit Jurors, January 29, 1831 (Indiana), 291–92.

7. Act Prescribing the Manner of Impanneling Petit Jurors, May 20, 1852 (Indiana), 2:24–25; Act Relating to Juries, February 9, 1831 (Ohio), 489–96.

8. "Jurors," 1851 (Iowa), 241; "Of Grand and Petit Jurors," January 13, 1858 (Wisconsin), 655; "Jurors," December 5, 1855, *Revised Statutes of the State of Missouri* (1856), 2:910; Act Relating to Juries, February 9, 1831 (Ohio), 489–96.

9. Act Prescribing the Mode of Summoning Grand and Petit Jurors, February 7, 1827 (Illinois), 251; R. Carlyle Buley, *Old Northwest: Pioneer Period, 1815–1840*, 2 vols. (Bloomington: Indiana University Press, 1951), 2:108; Harstad, "Indiana and the Art of Adjustment," 167; Act Relating to Juries, February 9, 1831 (Ohio), 492–93.

10. *Revised Code of Laws, of the State of Illinois* (1827); *Revised Code of Laws of Illinois* (1829); *Revised Laws of Illinois* (1833); *Revised Statutes of the State of Illinois* (1845).

11. Act Prescribing the Mode of Summoning Grand Jurors, March 23, 1819 (Illinois), 201–2; Act Concerning Petit Jurors, March 23, 1819 (Illinois), 186. The origin of the number twelve is unknown, but it might have reflected the twelve prophets, the twelve disciples, or the twelve tables (customary law of Rome). Robert von Moschzisker, *Trial by Jury: A Brief Review of Its Origin, Development and Merits and Practical Discussions on Actual Conduct of Jury Trials, Together with a Consideration of Constitutional Provisions and Other Cognate Subjects of Importance* (Philadelphia: George T. Bisel, 1922), 290. For emerging middle-class values in the first half of the nineteenth century, see Timothy R. Mahoney, *Provincial Lives: Middle-Class Experience in the Antebellum Midwest* (Cambridge: Cambridge University Press, 1999); Stuart M. Blumin, *The Emergence of the Middle Class: Social Experiences in the American City, 1760–1900* (New York: Cambridge University Press, 1989); Karen Halttunen, *Confidence Men and Painted Women: A Study of Middle-Class Culture in America, 1830–1870* (New Haven, Conn.: Yale University Press, 1982); Thomas L. Purvis, "The Making of a Myth: Abraham Lincoln's Family Background in the Perspective of Jacksonian Politics," *Journal of the Illinois State Historical Society* 75 (Summer 1982): 148–60.

12. Act Prescribing the Mode of Summoning Grand Jurors, March 23, 1819 (Illinois), 201–2; Act Concerning Petit Jurors, March 23, 1819 (Illinois), 255–57; R. Blake Brown, "Challenges for Cause, Stand Asides, and Peremptory Challenges in the Nineteenth Century," *Osgoode Hall Law Journal* 38 (Fall 2000): 453–94; Act to Amend Chapter 83, February 11, 1859 (Illinois), 150.

13. Act Prescribing the Mode of Summoning Grand Jurors, March 23, 1819 (Illinois), 201.

14. Act Relating to Juries, February 9, 1831 (Ohio), 492; Of Grand and Petit Jurors, January 13, 1858 (Wisconsin), 658.

15. Act Prescribing the Mode of Summoning Grand Jurors, March 23, 1819 (Illinois), 201; Act Prescribing the Mode of Summoning Grand and Petit Jurors, February 7, 1827 (Illinois), 251.

16. Martha L. Benner and Cullom Davis, eds., *The Law Practice of Abraham Lincoln: Complete Documentary Edition,* 2d ed. (Springfield: Illinois Historic Preservation Agency, 2009), available at www.lawpracticeofabrahamlincoln.org (hereafter cited as *LPAL*). Also see Order, September 6, 1852, Record L, 546, Judge's Docket 1849–1853, and Order, August 29, 1850, Record K, 426, Luckett v. Garvey; Execution Docket D, 64, all in Sangamon County Circuit Court, Illinois Regional Archives Depository, University of Illinois, Springfield.

17. No evidence exists to suggest that blacks served on any juries in the emerging Midwest. There was no integrated jury in the United States until 1867. "The First Integrated Jury Impaneled in the United States, May, 1867," *Negro History Bulletin* 33 (October 1970): 134.

18. Act Relating to Juries, February 9, 1831 (Ohio), 489–96; Act for the Relief of Jurors in Certain Cases, March 16, 1839 (Ohio), 497; "Jurors," 1851 (Iowa), 241; "Of Grand and Petit Jurors," January 13, 1858 (Wisconsin), 655–6l; Richard P. Howard, *Illinois: A History of the Prairie State* (Grand Rapids, Mich.: William B. Eardman's Publishing, 1972), 134–37; James E. Davis, *Frontier Illinois* (Bloomington: Indiana University Press, 1998), 66–68. For a detailed discussion of the events of 1823 and 1824 related to the debate over Illinois' status as a "free" state, see James Simeone, *Democracy and Slavery in Frontier Illinois: The Bottomland Republic* (DeKalb: Northern Illinois University Press, 2000).

19. Act Regulating the Fees of the Several Officers, March 29, 1819 (Illinois), 321; Act to Amend "An Act Prescribing the Mode," February 13, 1835 (Illinois), 399; Act to Increase the Compensation, February 12, 1853 (Illinois), 657; Act Regulating Fees and Salaries of the Several Officers, February 7, 1831 (Indiana), 252; Act Regulating the Fees of Officers," June 16, 1852 (Indiana), 2:289–90; "Compensation of Officers," 1851 (Iowa), 346.

20. Act Prescribing the Mode of Summoning Grand Jurors, March 23, 1819 (Illinois), 201; Act Prescribing the Mode of Summoning Grand and Petit Jurors, February 7, 1827 (Illinois), 253; Act Regulating the Mode of Summoning and Empannelling Grand and Petit Jurors, January 31, 1824 (Indiana), 235; "Jurors," 1851 (Iowa), 243; "Of Grand and Petit Jurors," January 13, 1858 (Wisconsin), 657.

21. Act Regulating the Times and Holding of the Supreme and Circuit Courts, February 13, 1835 (Illinois), 184; Act to Regulate the Mode of Summoning and Empannelling Grand and Petit Jurors, January 29, 1831 (Indiana), 291; Act Relating to Juries, February 9, 1831 (Ohio), 489; "Jurors," 1851 (Iowa), 242; "Of Grand and Petit Jurors," January 13, 1858 (Wisconsin), 656.

22. Act Relative to Criminal Jurisprudence, February 26, 1833 (Illinois), 218; "Offenses against Public Justice," 1851 (Iowa), 364.

23. Act Concerning Jails and Jailers, January 26, 1827 (Illinois), 248; Act Prescribing the Mode of Summoning Grand Jurors, March 23, 1819 (Illinois), 202.

24. Samuel Howe, *Practice in Civil Actions and Proceedings at Law in Massachusetts* (Boston: Hilliard, Gray, 1834), 240; "Jurors," March 3, 1845 (Illinois), 311.

25. Reed v. State, 15 Ohio 217 (1846); Martin v. State, 16 Ohio 364 (1847); Shaw v. Wood, 8 Ind. 467 (1857); Ulmer v. Indiana, 14 Ind. 41 (1859); Settle v. Batie, 1 Iowa 141 (1855); Aetna Insurance Company v. Phelps, 27 Ill. 70 (1862); David J. Bodenhamer, "The Democratic Impulse and Legal Change in the Age of Jackson: The Example of Criminal Juries in Antebellum Indiana," *Historian* 45 (February 1983): 216–18. One legal historian has noted that bystander juries were common in Indianapolis, Indiana, for example, and that the use of bystanders was probably linked to the failure of citizens to show up for duty when called: see Bodenhamer, "Democratic Impulse," 217.

26. "Jury and Jurors," *Statutes of the State of Ohio* (1840), 1075–76; "Empanneling Jurors," May 20, 1852, *Revised Statutes of the State of Indiana* (1852), 2:106; "Jurors," March 3, 1845 (Illinois), 310; "Jurors," 1851 (Iowa), 258; "Of Grand and Petit Jurors," January 13, 1858 (Wisconsin), 659; Reed v. State; Martin v. State; Sovereign v. State, 4 Ohio St. 489 (1855).

27. Aetna Insurance Company v. Phelps; Settle v. Batie.

28. Sovereign v. State; Bodenhamer, "Democratic Impulse," 215–16; *Indiana Journal,* 6, January 1843, quoted in Bodenhamer, "Democratic Impulse," 215.

29. Shaw v. Wood; Ulmer v. State. In his extensive research of the Indiana juries, David Bodenhamer found some limited evidence to suggest that bystanders were younger members of their communities and thus had less wealth then their counterparts. His research in Marion County, Indiana, revealed that a small pool of bystanders owned, on average, $4,000 less than regular jurors. Their financial standing may well have made them vulnerable to accusations that they were not representative of the community. Bodenhamer, "Democratic Impulse," 218. See also Bodenhamer, *The Pursuit of Justice: Crime and Law in Antebellum Indiana* (New York: Garland Publishing, 1986).

30. Even though few legal historians have given the Midwest its due, much of their legal scholarship has utilized midwestern case law to some degree. Lawrence M. Friedman, *Crime and Punishment in American History* (New York: Basic Books, 1993); Friedman, *History of American Law*; James Willard Hurst, *Law and the Conditions of Freedom in the Nineteenth Century United States* (Chicago: Northwestern University Press, 1956; repr., Madison: University of Wisconsin Press, 1967); Peter Karsten, *Heart versus Head: Judge-Made Law in Nineteenth-Century America* (Chapel Hill: University of North Carolina Press, 1997); William G. Thomas, *Lawyering for the Railroad: Business, Law, and Power in the American South* (Baton Rouge: Louisiana State University Press, 1999); William J. Novak, *The People's Welfare: Law and Regulation in Nineteenth-Century America* (Chapel Hill: University of North Carolina Press, 1996).

31. I examined the reported summaries and opinions in 175 appellate cases in Indiana, Illinois, Iowa, Michigan, and Wisconsin (the bulk came from Indiana and Illinois). See the appendix for a complete annotated list.

32. Armstrong v. Jackson, 1 Blackf. 374 (Ind.) (1825); Archer v. Spillman, 2 Ill. 552 (1839); Jackson v. State, 6 Blackf. 461 (Ind.) (1843); Campbell v. Head, 13 Ill. 122 (1851); Ross v. Irving, 14 Ill. 170 (1852); Pryor v. Irving, 14 Ill. 170 (1852); Norval v. Rice, 2 Wis. 22 (1853); May v. Milwaukee & Mississippi Railway Company, 3 Wis. 218 (1854).

33. Robert T. Roper, "Jury Size: Impact on Verdicts' Correctness," *American Politics Quarterly* 7 (October 1979): 439; David M. Gold, "Reforming the Civil Jury in the Nineteenth-Century West: Jury Size and Unanimity of Verdicts," *Western Legal History* 15 (Winter/Spring 2002): 137–64; Jackson v. State; Norval v. Rice, 27; Terence P. Kemp, "Evidence in Ohio: A Two-Hundred-Year Work in Progress," in *The History of Ohio Law,* ed. Michael Les Benedict and John F. Winkler (Athens: Ohio University Press, 2004), 1:469.

34. Benedict, "Civil Liberty in Ohio," 698; Work v. State, 2 Ohio St. 296 (1853); May v. Milwaukee & Mississippi Railway Company, 220; Norris' House v. State, 3 Greene (Iowa) 513 (1852).

35. Act Defining the Powers and Duties of Justices of the Peace, March 23, 1819 (Illinois); Act to Amend the Act Relative to Criminal Jurisprudence, January 30, 1827 (Illinois); *LPAL;* Order, March 22, 1847, Record I and J, 385, Alexander v. Brown, and Order, April 1, 1841, Record G, 8, Baker v. VanBergen, both in Sangamon County Circuit Court, Illinois Regional Archives Depository, University of Illinois, Springfield; Order, June 8, 1840, General Record A, 39, Casey v. Bowles, Menard County Circuit Court, Menard County Courthouse, Petersburg, Ill.; Order, September 21, 1852, General Record F, Haines v. Jones and Gaither, Tazewell County Circuit Court, Tazewell County Courthouse, Pekin, Ill.; Jury Verdict [May 1861], case file 209, People v. Alsop, DeWitt County Circuit Court, DeWitt County Courthouse, Clinton, Ill.

36. The opinion went on to argue that "the legislature may altogether withhold a remedy, after a certain time, but if they give one it must be a constitutional one. Were it otherwise, this constitutional right of trial by our peers might soon be destroyed . . . the right of trial by jury, in all cases within this clause of the constitution must remain inviolate. We therefore conclude, that that part of the act authorizing the appointment of three commissioners to assess the value of improvements, or of the land without the improvements, is unconstitutional and void." Armstrong v. Jackson. The section of the law that allowed for the use of court-appointed commissioners to assess damages was repealed in 1829; *Revised Indiana Statutes* (1829), 101.

37. 27 U.S. 492 (1829).

38. Examples of such cases in Illinois include Chicago & Mississippi Railroad v. Loehr, McLean County Court, October 1852; Allen v. Chicago & Mississippi Railroad, Sangamon County Circuit Court, March 1853; Barger v. Illinois Central Railroad, DeWitt County Court, May 1853; Frazier v. Great Western Railroad, Vermilion County Circuit Court, May 1855. There were hundreds of these cases

during the 1850s, when railroad construction was in full swing. However, there were also earlier cases related to the building of the Illinois & Michigan Canal in northern Illinois. Every time a public road of any sort was chartered, litigation resulted from disputes regarding rights of way. *LPAL.*

39. Campbell v. Head; Ross v. Irving and Pryor v. Irving, argued together.

40. Ross v. Irving and Pryor v. Irving, argued together.

41. Henry v. Dubuque & Pacific Railroad, 2 Iowa 288 (1855); Dubuque & Pacific Railroad v. Crittenden, 5 Iowa 514 (1857); Milwaukee & Mississippi Railroad v. Elbe, 2 Pin. (Wis.) 334 (1851); Lafayette and Indianapolis Railroad v. Smith, 6 Ind. 200 (1855); Martinsville and Franklin Railroad Company v. Bridges, 6 Ind. 321 (1855); New Albany & Salem Railroad, 7 Ind. 26 (1855); Cemetery of Spring Grove v. Cincinnati, Hamilton & Dayton Railroad, 10 Ohio 251 (1849); Steubenville & Indiana Railroad v. Patrick, 7 Ohio St. 170 (1857); In the matter of the Wells County Road, 7 Ohio St. 16 (1857); Piper v. Connersville and Liberty Turnpike Road Company, 12 Ind. 345 (1859). Juries assessed damages in Ohio cases involving the development of public infrastructures.

42. The opinion in an appeal of a murder case in Indiana clarified the householder requirement in that state, arguing that under Revised Statutes, §§ 1 and 2, "a freeholder, merely, is not competent to sit upon a petit jury. He must be a householder . . . that a man may be a freeholder and not a householder, or a householder and not a freeholder, is a proposition so plain as to need no argument . . . a freeholder is such as hold a freehold estate, that is, land or tenement, in fee simple, fee tail, or for term of life . . . the Legislature has designated the class of citizens from which petit jurors shall be drawn, to wit: householders, and also the classes from which grand jurors shall be selected, to wit: freeholders or householders . . . courts have no more power to say that other classes than householders shall be received upon petit juries, than to excluded householders, because they are such, from grand juries." Bradford v. State, 15 Ind. 347 (1860); Lindley v. Kindall, 4 Blackf. 189 (Ind.) (1836). See also State v. Herndon, 5 Blackf. 75 (Ind.) (1839).

43. Davis v. People, 19 Ill. 73 (1857).

44. State v. Miller, 2 Blackf. 35 (Ind.) (1826); Byrne v. State, 12 Wis. 519 (1860); Barlow v. State, 2 Blackf. 114 (Ind.) (1827). Chief Justice Mason of the Iowa Supreme Court wrote: "The statute renders him a good grand juror if he was a qualified elector." Harless and Adams v. United States, 1 Morris 169 (Iowa) (1843).

45. State v. Groome, 10 Iowa 308 (1860).

46. Owners of the Ship "Milwaukie" v. Hale, 1 Doug. 306 (Mich.) (1844).

47. Trimble v. State, 2 Greene 404 (Iowa) (1850).

48. Spear v. Spencer, 1 Greene 534 (Iowa) (1848). See the appendix for an annotated case list.

49. "An Act Relating to Juries," February 9, 1831 (Ohio), 490; Act Prescribing the Manner of Impanneling Petit Jurors, May 20, 1852 (Indiana), 24; Act Concerning Petit Jurors, March 23, 1819 (Illinois), 256; "Jurors," 1851 (Iowa), 24.

50. Lafayette Plankroad Company v. New Albany & Salem Railroad, 13 Ind. 81 (1859); Barlow v. State; Sawyer v. Stephenson, 1 Ill. 24 (1820); State v. Gillick, 7 Iowa 287 (1858).

51. Office of the U.S. Census, Seventh Census of the United States (1850), Clinton County, Ill., 351.

52. Thomas J. McCormack, ed., *Memoirs of Gustave Koerner,* 2 vols. (Cedar Rapids, Iowa: Torch Press, 1909), 1:432; Guykowski v. People, 2 Ill. 476 (1838). Other appellate cases regarding alienage in the antebellum Midwest included State v. Taylor, 8 Blackf. 178 (Ind.) (1846); State v. Shoemaker, 5 Wis. 327 (1856); Keenan v. State, 8 Wis. 132 (1858). In the *Keenan* case, the juror in question had been born in Ireland and emigrated to the United States when he was three years old. Although he had been in the United States most of his life and was enjoying the benefits of citizenship, he had never been naturalized.

53. Greenup v. Stoker, 8 Ill. 202 (1846).

54. The Wisconsin Supreme Court also upheld its state statute respecting citizenship qualifications for jurors. Schumacker v. State, 5 Wis. 324 (1856).

55. Lafayette Plank Road Company v. New Albany & Salem Railroad Company.

56. Many appellate cases dealt with multiple errors, and the opinions in these cases frequently clarified more than one legal issue. Therefore, most of the cases examined for the purposes of this study are included in multiple categories described within this paragraph. See the appendix for a complete annotated case list.

57. Interestingly, all but one of these cases was in the Illinois Supreme Court. Crocker v. Goodsell; Wickersham v. People; Archer v. Spillman; Cook v. Scott; Pate v. People; Fisher v. People; Schnier v. People; and Forshee v. Abrams.

58. United States v. Cropper, 1 Morris (Iowa) 190 (1843); Wau-kon-chaw-neek-kaw v. United States, 1 Morris (Iowa) 332 (1843); Dutell v. State, 4 Greene (Iowa) 125 (1853); Harrison v. Singleton, 3 Ill. 21 (1839); Mitchell v. Likens, 3 Blackf. (Ind.) (1833); Mitchell v. Denbo, 3 Blackf. (Ind.) (1833); Lindley v. Kindall; State v. Conner, 5 Blackf. (Ind.) (1840); Adams v. State, 11 Ind. 249 (1858); Lloyd v. McClure, 2 Greene (Iowa) 139 (1849); Cook, Sargent and Cook v. Sypher, 3 Iowa 484 (1856); State v. Grady, 4 Iowa 461 (1857); Minter v. Hite, 4 Iowa 583 (1857); Stewart v. Burlington & Mississippi Railroad, 11 Iowa 62 (1860); Grable v. State, 2 Greene (Iowa) 559 (1850); Cole v. Swan, 4 Green (Iowa) 32 (1853); Tifield v. Adams, 3 Iowa 487 (1856); Cook and Owsley v. Watters, 4 Iowa 72 (1856); State v. Gillick, 10 Iowa 98 (1859); Territory of Wisconsin v. Doty, 1 Pin. (Wis.) 396 (1844); Keenan v. State; McKinney v. People, 7 Ill. 540 (1845); Pate v. People; McClintock v. Crick, 4 Iowa 453 (1857); Oshoga v. State, 3 Pin. (Wis.) 56 (1850); Johnson v. Howe, 7 Ill. 342 (1845); Webster v. McKinster, 1 Pin. 644 (Wis.) (1846); Rigg v. Cook 9 Ill. 336 (1847); Joy v. State, 14 Ind. 113 (1860).

59. Act on Grand and Petit Jurors, January 4, 1839; "Jurors," "Compensation of Officers," "Offenses against Public Justice," "Impanneling Grand Jury," "Powers

and Duty of Grand Jury," and "Challenging the Jury," all in *An Act for Revising and Consolidating the General Statutes of the State of Iowa* (1851).

60. Birchard v. Booth, 4 Wis. 85 (1855); Jones v. State, 3 Blackf. (Ind.) 37 (1832); Barger v. State, 6 Blackf. 188 (Ind.) (1842); Bissell v. Ryan, 23 Ill. 517 (1860).

61. Act Concerning Petit Jurors, March 23, 1819 (Illinois), 255; Act Regulating the Mode of Summoning and Empanelling Grand and Petit Jurors, January 31, 1824, 234; Act to Regulate the Mode of Summoning and Empanelling Grand and Petit Jurors, February 17, 1838 (Indiana), 358; Act Relating to Juries, February 9, 1831 (Ohio), 489; "Jurors," 1851 (Iowa), 241.

62. Illinois const. of 1818, art. VIII, § 6; Act Concerning Petit Jurors, March 23, 1819 (Illinois), 255–57; Act Prescribing the Mode of Summoning Grand and Petit Jurors, February 7, 1827 (Illinois), 251–54.

63. U.S. Bureau of the Census, *Historical Statistics of the United States, Colonial Times to 1970* (Washington, D.C.: U.S. Bureau of the Census, 1975), 27.

64. "Jurors," March 3, 1845 (Illinois), 308–9.

65. "Practice," *Revised Statutes of the State of Illinois* (1845), 416; "Criminal Jurisprudence," *Revised Statutes of the State of Illinois* (1845), 184.

66. Richard D. Younger, *The People's Panel: The Grand Jury in the United States, 1634–1941* (Providence, R.I.: Brown University Press, 1963), 83; "Jurors," March 3, 1845 (Illinois), 309.

Chapter 2: The Composition of Juries in Sangamon County, Illinois, 1830–60

1. Order, April 17, 1833, Record B, 121, State Bank of Illinois v. Bowling, Order, April 17, 1833, Record B, 122–23, State Bank of Illinois v. Parkinson, and Order, April 18, 1833, Record B, 126, People v. Millrose, all in Sangamon County Circuit Court, Illinois Regional Archives Depository, University of Illinois, Springfield; Benjamin P. Thomas, *Lincoln's New Salem* (Springfield, Ill.: Abraham Lincoln Association, 1934), 49–51, 54, 75–76; Kenneth J. Winkle, *The Young Eagle: The Rise of Abraham Lincoln* (Dallas, Tex.: Taylor Trade Publishing), 90, 95, 112–13.

2. Order, April 17, 1833, Record B, 121, State Bank of Illinois v. Bowling; Order, April 17, 1833, Record B, 122–23, State Bank of Illinois v. Parkinson; Order, April 18, 1833, Record B, 126, People v. Millrose; Office of the U.S. Census, Seventh Census of the United States (1850), Sangamon County, Ill.; Office of the U.S. Census, Eighth Census of the United States (1860), Sangamon County, Ill.; John Carroll Power, *History of the Early Settlers of Sangamon County, Illinois* (Springfield, Ill.: H. W. Rokker, 1876; repr., Springfield, Ill.: Phillips Brothers, 1970), 86, 267, 547, 579, 684–85, 758. Samuel Berry lost a bid for the Illinois House of Representatives in 1828, and William Kirkpatrick failed to win a seat in the same body in 1832. Theodore Calvin Pease, ed., *Illinois Election Returns, 1818–1848* (Springfield: Illinois State Historical Library, 1923), 239, 262.

3. Richard Yates's Charge to the Scott County Grand Jury, October 14, 1839, Winfred Harbison Collection of Richard Yates Papers, Wabash College, Crawfordsville, Ind.

4. Joseph Wallace, *Past and Present of the City of Springfield and Sangamon County, Illinois,* 2 vols. (Chicago: S. J. Clarke Publishing, 1904), 1:10, 13; Christopher Elliott Wallace, "The Opportunity to Grow: Springfield, Illinois, during the 1850s" (Ph.D. diss., Purdue University, 1983), 33, 35, 41; Joanne Towers Wheeler, "Springfield, 1850: The City, Its Places, Its People," manuscript, 1978, 2–9; J. Van Fenstermaker, "A Description of Sangamon County, Illinois, in 1830," *Agricultural History* 39 (July 1965): 136–40; Wheeler, "Springfield," 9; Don Harrison Doyle, *The Social Order of a Frontier Community: Jacksonville, Illinois, 1825–70* (Urbana: University of Illinois Press, 1978), 197; Paul M. Angle, *"Here I Have Lived": A History of Lincoln's Springfield, 1821–1865* (New Brunswick, N.J.: Rutgers University Press, 1935), 14–16; James A. Schellenberg, *Conflict between Communities: American County Seat Wars* (New York: Paragon House, 1987); Thomas J. Wood, "'Blood in the Moon': The War for the Seat of Edwards County, 1821–1824," *Illinois Historical Journal* 85 (Autumn 1992): 142–60; Roger L. Rosentreter, "Michigan's Eighty-three Counties: Wexford County," *Michigan History* 76 (July–August 1992): 9–12; Rosentreter, "Michigan's Eighty-three Counties: Tuscola County," *Michigan History* 75 (May–June 1991): 8–10; Stephen J. Buck, "To Hold the Prize: The County Seat War in Du Page County, 1867–1872," *Illinois Historical Journal* 85 (Winter 1992): 194–208.

5. *Sangamo Journal* (Springfield, Ill.), May 18, July 6, and October 19, 1833; R. Carlyle Buley, *The Old Northwest: Pioneer Period, 1815–1840,* 2 vols. (Bloomington: Indiana University Press, 1951), 2:107; *Daily Illinois State Journal* (Springfield), May 28, 1859; Wheeler, "Springfield," 37, 42.

6. In 1833, one visitor from the eastern United States exclaimed "What a country!" as he traveled throughout Sangamon County. This same visitor remarked that Springfield, as the site of the new state capitol, was not handicapped by false modesty. Buley, *Old Northwest,* 2:107; *Sangamo Journal,* May 18, July 6, and October 19, 1833.

7. Pease, *Illinois Election Returns,* 381, 392; Wallace, *Past and Present of the City of Springfield,* 1:11; Joseph C. G. Kennedy, comp., *Population of the United States in 1860* (Washington, D.C.: Government Printing Office, 1864), 81–83, 87, 103–5. See also Angle, *"Here I Have Lived"*; Helen van Cleave Blankmeyer, *The Sangamon Country* (Springfield, Ill.: Board of Education, 1935; repr., Springfield, Ill.: Phillips Brothers, 1965); Wallace, "Opportunity to Grow," 1.

8. Angle, *"Here I Have Lived,"* 63–65; Wheeler, "Springfield," 33–34; Franklin William Scott, *Newspapers and Periodicals of Illinois, 1814–1879* (Springfield: Illinois State Historical Library, 1910), 321–25; *Sangamo Journal,* May 18, July 6, and October 19, 1833.

9. Wallace, "Opportunity to Grow," 47–49; Angle, *"Here I Have Lived,"* 52, 184–85, 101–2.

10. Wallace, "Opportunity to Grow," 47–49; Angle, *"Here I Have Lived,"* 52, 184–88, 101–2; Thomas J. McCormack, ed., *Memoirs of Gustave Koerner, 1809–1896,* 2 vols. (Cedar Rapids, Iowa: Torch Press, 1909), 1:626.

11. Angle, *"Here I Have Lived,"* 201.

12. The 1860 population statistics were gleaned from the following sources: Office of the U.S. Census, Eighth Census of the United States (1860), Sangamon County, Ill.; Kennedy, *Population of the United States in 1860*; Richard K. Vedder and Lowell E. Gallaway, "Migration and the Old Northwest," in *Essays in Nineteenth Century Economic History: The Old Northwest,* ed. David C. Klingaman and Richard K. Vedder (Athens: Ohio University Press, 1975), 159–76; Wallace, "Opportunity to Grow."

13. "Jurors," March 3, 1845, *Revised Statutes of the State of Illinois* (1845), 308–9; Kennedy, *Population of the United States in 1860,* 80–81, 85.

14. Property requirements were typical in antebellum America. John A. Proffatt, *A Treatise on Trial by Jury, Including Questions of Law and Fact* (San Francisco: Sumner Whitney, 1877; repr., Littleton, Colo.: Fred B. Rothman, 1986), 171.

15. An Act Prescribing the Mode of Summoning Grand Jurors, March 23, 1819, and An Act Concerning Petit Jurors, March 23, 1819, both in *Laws Passed by the First General Assembly of the State of Illinois* (1819), 201–2, 255–57.

16. "Jurors," March 3, 1845 (Illinois), 308–9; Act Prescribing the Mode of Summoning Grand Jurors, March 23, 1819 (Illinois), 201–2; Act Concerning Petit Jurors," March 23, 1819 (Illinois), 255–57; Martha L. Benner and Cullom Davis, eds., *The Law Practice of Abraham Lincoln: Complete Documentary Edition,* 2d ed. (Springfield: Illinois Historic Preservation Agency, 2009), available at www.lawpracticeofabrahamlincoln.org (hereafter cited as *LPAL*). Many potential jurors would never serve because they would not be randomly selected from the entire pool. Albert W. Alschuler and Andrew G. Deiss, "A Brief History of the Criminal Jury in the United States," *University of Chicago Law Review* 61 (Summer 1994): 879. Sometimes, sheriffs were even lax in serving writs to collect judgments in competed legal cases. Anson L. Brewer to Abraham Lincoln, November 17, 1852, Lincoln Collection, Brown University, Providence, R.I.

17. Kennedy, *Population of the United States in 1860,* 80–83; Wallace, "Opportunity to Grow," 44–45.

18. "Practice," *Revised Statutes of the State of Illinois* (1845), 416; "Criminal Jurisprudence," *Revised Statutes of the State of Illinois* (1845), 184; Act Prescribing the Mode of Summoning Grand Jurors, March 23, 1819 (Illinois), 201–2; Act Concerning Petit Jurors, March 23, 1819 (Illinois), 255–57; *Revised Code of Laws, of the State of Illinois* (1827); *Revised Code of Laws of Illinois* (1829); *Revised Laws of Illinois* (1833); *Revised Statutes of the State of Illinois* (1845); *LPAL.* Jury service was not nearly as widespread as voting. Though most propertied men voted, very few served on juries. James A. Henretta and James D. Rice, "Law as Litigation: An Agenda for Research," *William and Mary Quarterly,* 3d serv. 50 (January 1993): 177.

19. *LPAL.*

20. Frederick Cople Jaher, ed., *The Rich, the Well Born, and the Powerful: Elites and Upper Classes in History* (Urbana: University of Illinois Press, 1973), 3. Some excellent historical studies have investigated the economic, social, political, and professional status of elites in antebellum America. Edward Pessen's 1973 book, which overturned earlier myths regarding the egalitarian nature of antebellum society, analyzed tax records and census data from four financially important cities (New York, Boston, Philadelphia, and Brooklyn, New York), looking for wealthy individuals and then connecting them to the economic, political, professional, and social structures of the communities in which they lived. Not only did Pessen find significant numbers of wealthy Americans and a skewed distribution of community wealth, he also found that these elites commanded a great deal of power and influence in economic activities, social structures, politics, and law. Pessen, *Riches, Class, and Power before the Civil War* (Lexington, Mass.: D. C. Heath, 1973). See also Pessen, "Philip Hone's Set: The Social World of the New York Elite in the 'Age of Egalitarianism,'" *New-York Historical Society Quarterly* 56 (July 1972): 285–308; Pessen, "The Wealthiest New Yorkers of the Jacksonian Era: A New List," *New York Historical Society Quarterly* 54 (April 1970): 145–72; Pessen, "The Egalitarian Myth and the American Social Reality: Wealth, Mobility, and Equality in the 'Era of the Common Man,'" *American Historical Review* 76 (October 1971): 989–1034. Other historians have offered evidence supporting Pessen's argument that antebellum America did have many elites who dominated culture. The scholarship that has contributed to our understanding of the role of elites in nineteenth-century history includes Sven Beckert, *The Monied Metropolis: New York City and the Consolidation of the American Bourgeoisie, 1850–1896* (New York: Cambridge University Press, 2001); Lee Benson, "Philadelphia Elites and Economic Development: Quasi-public Innovation during the First American Organizational Revolution, 1825–1861," *Working Papers from the Regional Economic History Research Center* 2 (1978): 25–54; Shearer Davis Bowman, *Masters and Lords: Mid-nineteenth Century U.S. Planters and Prussian Junkers* (New York: Oxford University Press, 1993); R. A. Burchell, "Character and Function of a Pioneer Elite: Rural California, 1848–1880," *Journal of American Studies* (Great Britain) 15 (1981): 377–89; Donald DeBats, *Elites and Masses: Political Structure, Communication, and Behavior in Antebellum Georgia* (New York: Garland Press, 1990); Paul D. Escott, *Many Excellent People: Power and Privilege in North Carolina, 1850–1900* (Chapel Hill: University of North Carolina Press, 1985); Burton W. Folsom II, "The Politics of Elites: Prominence and Party in Davidson County, Tennessee, 1835–1861," *Journal of Southern History* (August 1973): 359–78; Jaher, *The Rich, the Well Born*; Jaher, *The Urban Establishment: Upper Strata in Boston, New York, Charleston, Chicago, and Los Angeles* (Urbana: University of Illinois Press, 1982); Robert Rich, "'A Wilderness of Whigs': The Wealthy Men of Boston," *Journal of Social History* (Great Britain) 4 (Spring 1971): 263–76; Lee C. Soltow, *Men and*

Wealth in the United States, 1850–1870 (New Haven, Conn.: Yale University Press, 1975); William Banks Taylor, "Southern Yankees: Wealth, High Society, and Political Economy in the Late Antebellum Natchez Region," *Journal of Mississippi History* 59 (Summer 1997): 79–121; Stephen Thernstrom, *Poverty and Progress: Social Mobility in a Nineteenth-Century City* (New York: Atheneum, 1969); Christopher Waldrep, "Egalitarianism in the Oligarchy: The Grand Jury and Criminal Justice in Livingston County, 1799–1808," *Filson Club Historical Quarterly* 55 (July 1981): 253–67; Julie Winch, ed., *The Elite of Our People: Joseph Willson's Sketches of Black Upper-Class Life in Antebellum Philadelphia* (University Park: Penn. State University Press, 2000). Although there is more scholarship on elites in the northeastern United States, some work on elites has focused on the antebellum Midwest: Jeffrey F. Adler, *Yankee Merchants and the Making of the Urban West: The Rise and Fall of Antebellum St. Louis* (New York: Cambridge University Press, 1991); Jeffrey P. Brown, "Chillicothe's Elite: Leadership in a Frontier Community," *Ohio History* 96 (Summer–Autumn 1987): 140–56; Harry N. Scheiber, "Alfred Kelley and the Ohio Business Elite, 1822–1859," *Ohio History* 87 (Autumn 1978): 365–92; Lee C. Soltow, *Patterns of Wealthholding in Wisconsin since 1850* (Madison: University of Wisconsin Press, 1971); Wallace, "Opportunity to Grow."

21. Springfield residents who persisted in the community, the same elites who served on juries, owned an average of $9,195 in real property by 1860. Wallace, "Opportunity to Grow," 68, 164. One historian found that the average wealth of adult northern men in the mid-1800s was $2,040. Soltow, *Men and Wealth*, 65. As a reference point, a six-room frame house "of good stone work" foundation cost $1,200 to construct, and a simpler frame dwelling cost between $300 and $800. Wallace, "Opportunity to Grow," 69–70. The average wealth of men over the age of twenty in 1860 was $1,177 in Akron, Ohio; $1,019 in Youngstown, Ohio; and $3,011 in Warren, Ohio. David C. Klingaman, "Individual Wealth in Ohio in 1860," in *Essays in Nineteenth Century Economic History: The Old Northwest*, ed. David C. Klingaman and Richard K. Vedder (Athens: Ohio University Press, 1975), 180.

22. Wallace, "Opportunity to Grow"; 1850 census.

23. Adler, *Yankee Merchants*, 92.

24. Benson, "Philadelphia Elites," 25–54; Timothy R. Mahoney, *Provincial Lives: Middle-Class Experience in the Antebellum Midwest* (Cambridge: Cambridge University Press, 1999); David L. Westby, "The Civic Sphere in the American City," *Social Forces* 45 (December 1966): 161–69; Nicole Etcheson, *The Emerging Midwest: Upland Southerners and the Political Culture of the Old Northwest, 1787–1861* (Bloomington: Indiana University Press, 1996), 71–73; Burchell, "Character and Function of a Pioneer Elite," 377–89.

25. Wallace, "Opportunity to Grow"; Doyle, *Social Order of a Frontier Community*, 13–14; John Mack Faragher, *Sugar Creek: Life on the Illinois Prairie* (New Haven, Conn.: Yale University Press, 1988), 137–39; Mary P. Ryan, "Civil Society

as Democratic Practice: North American Cities during the Nineteenth Century," *Journal of Interdisciplinary History* 29 (Spring 1999): 559–84.

26. Richard S. Alcorn, "Leadership and Stability in Mid-Nineteenth-Century America: A Case Study of an Illinois Town," *Journal of American History* 61 (December 1974): 686. John Mack Faragher has argued that in Sangamon County, there "was considerably more social continuity among families than is indicated by the persistence statistics." He also has discussed how "original settler families strengthened their influence within the community by marrying locally and building family alliances." Intermarriage among elites further strengthened elite influence within the community. Faragher, *Sugar Creek,* 144. See also Doyle, *Social Order of a Frontier Community,* 106.

27. Richard Alcorn's study of Paris, Illinois, examined the complex relationship between community leadership and a stable, "flexible elite" who persisted within a community over time. Alcorn, "Leadership and Stability," 685–702. One scholar has noted that this type of social control was a mutual process in which elite domination of nonelites was never really complete. Lawrence Frederick Kohl, "The Concept of Social Control and the History of Jacksonian America," *Journal of the Early Republic* 5 (Spring 1985): 21–34.

28. In analyzing political elites, I made no distinction between those who held public office and those who were engaged only in local or state party organization. Individuals who served in public office and were involved in civic, volunteer organizations were "growing members of the community." Wallace, "Opportunity to Grow," 26.

29. Pease, *Illinois Election Returns*; Arthur Charles Cole, ed., *The Constitutional Debates of 1847* (Springfield, Ill., 1919), 949–83.

30. Robert Edward Colebert Jr., "John Williams: A Merchant Banker in Springfield, Illinois, 1824–1864." (Ph.D. diss., University of Illinois, 1963), 33, 45; Doyle, *Social Order of a Frontier Community,* 103. Conclusions about demographics here are drawn from biographical data collected from the 1860 Sangamon County census and from Power, *Early Settlers of Sangamon County*; Angle, *"Here I Have Lived"*; Faragher, *Sugar Creek*; Mahoney, *Provincial Lives*; Doyle, *Social Order of a Frontier Community*; Alcorn, "Leadership and Stability."

31. Digital images of all the extant legal documents of Lincoln's law practice are available in *LPAL.*

32. "Sangamon County Cases of the Lincoln Period," database, n.d., Papers of Abraham Lincoln, Springfield, Ill. This database is constructed from information extrapolated from the complete run of Sangamon County judge's dockets and Sangamon County Court Records between 1836 and 1861, Illinois Regional Archives Depository, University of Illinois, Springfield.

33. A sampling of heads of households in the 1860 census in Ohio revealed that 45 percent were farmers. Klingaman, "Individual Wealth in Ohio," 187. Pennsylvania in the 1840s is far from a perfect comparison for Illinois in the 1850s, but

in order to offer some such assessment, it is interesting to note that the greatest majority of jurors (49 percent) in Philadelphia during the 1840s made their living as skilled "artisans," such as carpenters, bricklayers, and plumbers. Retailers and wholesalers comprised 25 percent of jurors and farmers just 10 percent. The most significant characteristic of Pennsylvania and Illinois jurors in this regard was the large difference between the number of farmers who served on juries—63 percent in Springfield in the 1850s and just 10 percent in Philadelphia in the 1840s. Of course, Philadelphia was a much more urban location than Springfield, so it is important to remember the midwestern historical context here and resist the urge to use eastern sources to explain it. Tony A. Freyer, *Producers versus Capitalists: Constitutional Conflict in Antebellum America* (Charlottesville: University Press of Virginia, 1994), 26.

34. Demographic data on wealth come from the 1850 census, Sangamon County, Ill..

35. 1850 census, Sangamon County, Ill.; Power, *Early Settlers of Sangamon County,* 196–97. The federal census is not a perfect source for determining wealth. However, it does offer a relatively accurate way to measure wealth across households in a uniform manner. Because tax records for Sangamon County are scant, the census provides the most information on the most households in Sangamon County.

36. 1850 census, Sangamon County, Ill.

37. "Jurors," March 3, 1845 (Illinois); Mullen v. O'Connor, March 1846, Mullen v. O'Connor and Boyd, November 1848, Ex parte Crow, March 1851, and H. W. Derby & Co. v. Cary, August 1852, all in Sangamon County Circuit Court, Springfield, Ill.; People v. Cheek, December 1845, and People v. McHatton, December 1845, both in Illinois Supreme Court, Springfield, Ill.; *LPAL*; Eugene L. Gross, *A Digest of the Criminal Laws of Illinois* (Springfield: Illinois Journal, 1868), 90, 99–100.

38. Alcorn, "Leadership and Stability"; Jaher, *The Rich, the Well Born*; Stephen Richard Higley, *Privilege, Power, and Place: The Geography of the American Upper Class* (Lanham, Md.: Rowman and Littlefield, 1995); Pessen, *Riches, Class, and Power*; Rich, "Wilderness of Whigs"; Adler, *Yankee Merchants.* Research on the composition of juries in England has revealed that jurors there were older, with as many as two-thirds of those who served being in their forties and fifties. P. J. R. King, "'Illiterate Plebians, Easily Misled': Jury Composition, Experience, and Behavior in Essex, 1735–1815," in *Twelve Good Men and True: The Criminal Trial Jury in England, 1200–1800,* ed. J. S. Cockburn and Thomas A. Green (Princeton, N.J.: Princeton University Press, 1988), 261.

39. Although Illinois law did not allow licensed attorneys, clerks of the circuit court, and sheriffs to serve on grand or petit jurors, no appeals of judgments from trials on which any of them served appeared before the Illinois Supreme Court. "Jurors," March 3, 1845 (Illinois), 308; Gross, *Criminal Laws of Illinois*; Power, *Early Settlers of Sangamon County*; *LPAL.*

40. Waldrep, "Egalitarianism in the Oligarchy," 253.

41. Leonard W. Levy, *The Law of the Commonwealth and Chief Justice Shaw* (New York: Oxford University Press, 1957), 290; 1850 census, Sangamon County, Ill.; Henretta and Rice, "Law as Litigation," 177. The statistical analysis of Sangamon County residents, like that of petit and grand jurors, is extrapolated from 1850 U.S. census data.

42. Sangamon County Judge's Docket, Sangamon County Court Record, 1850, Illinois Regional Archives Depository, University of Illinois, Springfield; *LPAL.* Perlina Field is not listed in the federal census, in the local newspapers, or in any known county histories. I was unable to find definitive information on three of the grand jurors, so the total of real property does not exactly reflect the wealth of the entire panel.

43. Judge's Docket Entry, October 1860, Judge's Docket 1860, 245, and Order, October 25, 1860, Record U, 47, both in Sangamon County Circuit Court, Illinois Regional Archives Depository, University of Illinois, Springfield; *Daily Illinois State Register* (Springfield), November 9, 1860, p. 3, col. 2; 1860 census, Sangamon County, Ill., 132, 522.

44. Pease, *Illinois Election Returns,* 365; 1860 census, Sangamon County, Ill.

45. 1860 census, Sangamon County, Ill., 10–316.

46. *Daily Illinois State Register,* November 9, 1860; 1850 census, Sangamon County, Ill.; 1860 census, Sangamon County, Ill.; Power, *Early Settlers of Sangamon County,* 397, 459, 550, 709; Order, October 31, 1860, Record U, 134, and Order, November 8, 1860, Record U, 156, both in Sangamon County Circuit Court, Illinois Regional Archives Depository, University of Illinois, Springfield.

47. *LPAL*; Sangamon County Circuit Court Judge's Docket database, 1836–1860, Papers of Abraham Lincoln, Springfield, Ill.; An Act to Prevent the Immigration of Free Negroes into This State, February 12, 1853, *General Laws of the State of Illinois, Passed by the Eighteenth General Assembly, Convened January 3, 1853* (Springfield, Ill.: Lanphier and Walker, 1853), 57–60; Stacy Pratt McDermott, "'Black Bill' and the Privileges of Whiteness in Antebellum Illinois," *Journal of Illinois History* 12 (Spring 2009): 2–26.

48. Kennedy, *Population of the United States in 1860,* 80–83. For Springfield, see Angle, *"Here I Have Lived"*; *History of Sangamon County, Illinois* (Chicago: Inter-state Publishing, 1881); Blankmeyer, *Sangamon Country*; *LPAL.* For the status of African Americans in Illinois, see "Negroes and Mulattoes," March 3, 1845, *Statutes of the State of Illinois* (1856), 776–80; An Act to Prevent the Immigration of Free Negroes into This State," February 12, 1853, *Statutes of the State of Illinois* (1856), 780–84; Robert P. Howard, *Illinois: A History of the Prairie State* (Grand Rapids, Mich.: William B. Eardman's Publishing, 1972), 129–43. For the legal status of women in antebellum America and in Illinois, see Norma Basch, "Invisible Women: The Legal Fiction of Marital Unity in Nineteenth-Century America," *Feminist Studies* 5 (Summer 1979), reprinted in Nancy F. Cott, ed., *Domestic*

Relations and Law, History of Women in the United States 3 (Munich, Germany: K. G. Suar, 1992), 132–52; Basch, "The Emerging Legal History of Women in the United States: Property, Divorce, and the Constitution," *Signs: Journal of Women in Culture and Society* 12 (Autumn 1986), 100; Stacy Pratt McDermott, "The Law in an Illinois Corner: The Impact of the Law on an Antebellum Family," and "Dissolving the Bonds of Matrimony: Women and Divorce in Sangamon County, Illinois, 1835–1860," both in *In Tender Consideration: Women, Families and the Law in Abraham Lincoln's Illinois,* ed. Daniel W. Stowell (Urbana: University of Illinois Press, 2002), 71–103, 161–81.

49. Pease, *Illinois Election Returns,* 459; 1860 census, Sangamon County, Ill., 14, 209; Power, *Early Settlers of Sangamon County,* 376, 427; *LPAL.*

50. Ibid.

51. 1860 census, Sangamon County, Ill.; C. S. Williams, comp., *Williams' Springfield Directory: City Guide and Business Mirror, for 1860–61* (Springfield, Ill.: Johnson and Bradford, Booksellers, 1860); Power, *Early Settlers of Sangamon County*; *LPAL.*

52. Alcorn, "Leadership and Stability," 697.

53. Power, *Early Settlers of Sangamon County,* 78, 191, 401; Wallace, "Opportunity to Grow," 54–60.

54. Alcorn, "Leadership and Stability," 697; Act Prescribing the Mode of Summoning Grand Jurors, March 23, 1819 (Illinois), 201; Act Prescribing the Mode of Summoning Grand and Petit Jurors, and Defining Their Qualifications, Approved February 7, 1827 (February 13, 1835), *Public and General Statute Laws of the State of Illinois* (1835), 398–99.

55. David J. Bodenhamer, "The Democratic Impulse and Legal Change in the Age of Jackson: The Example of Criminal Juries in Antebellum Indiana," *Historian* 45 (February 1983): 215.

56. Power, *Early Settlers of Illinois,* 364; *Pease, Illinois Election Returns,* 229, 262, 459; 1850 census, Sangamon County, Ill., 118.

57. Cormac O'Grada and Eugene N. White, "The Panics of 1854 and 1857: A View from the Emigrant Industrial Savings Bank," *Journal of Economic History* 63 (March 2003): 213–40; Peter L. Rousseau, "Jacksonian Monetary Policy, Specie Flows, and the Panic of 1837," *Journal of Economic History* 62 (June 2002): 457–88; Peter v. Ball (1841), Peter v. Elkin (1840), Peter v. Hackett (1838), Peter v. Lasswell (1843), Peter v. Martin (1838), Peter v. Smith (1841), Peter v. Smith (1844), Peter v. Smith et al. (1841), Peter v. Tackett (1838), and People v. Peter (1838), all in Sangamon County Circuit Court, Springfield, Ill.; *LPAL.* In People v. Peter, Zachariah Peter was indicted for assault with intent to commit bodily injury. Lincoln filed a motion to quash the indictment, and the court sustained the motion, dismissing the case. Order, March 7, 1838, Record C, 500, and Order, March 17, 1838, Record C, 617, both in Sangamon County Circuit Court, Illinois Regional Archives Depository, University of Illinois, Springfield.

58. Allen v. Maxey (1840), Anderson, Bell & Co. v. Gambrel (1838), Johnson v. Wickham (1854), Neale v. Blankenship (1838), Payne v. Bryan (1838), People v. McCoy (1843), Ransdell v. Calhoun (1840), Roberts v. Radford (1840), Suddith v. Thatcher (1843), Brother v. Frink, Walker & Company (1843), Edmunds v. Simpson (1841), Hay v. Bryan (1841), Isaac R. Braucher & Company v. Repscher (1841), James Bell & Company v. Nesbit (1841), Mallory v. Elkin (1841), Norris v. Simpson (1841), and S. M. Tinsley & Company v. Bridges (1843), all in Sangamon County Circuit Court, Springfield, Ill.; Moore v. Nelson (1844), Beaver v. Taylor (1859), and Butler, Cecil and Rawson v. H. Bell & Company (1859), all in U.S. Circuit Court, Springfield, Ill.; *LPAL.*

59. 1860 census, Sangamon County, Ill.; Power, *Early Settlers of Sangamon County,* 304; Marriage of William C. Foley and Elizabeth E. Hutchinson, June 16, 1840, entry in Jordan Dodd, comp., *Illinois Marriages, 1790–1860* (Provo, Utah: Family History Library, 2004), online database.

60. Bruce Alexander Campbell, *The Sangamon Saga: 200 Years—An Illustrated Bicentennial History of Sangamon County* (Springfield, Ill.: Phillips Brothers, 1976), 88; *History of Sangamon County,* 519; Faragher, *Sugar Creek,* 140; Power, *Early Settlers of Sangamon County,* 372–73, 707–8; *Sangamo Journal* (Springfield, Ill.), June 7, 1834, 3:3, February 28, 1835, 3:6, and May 23, 1835, p. 3, col. 5; 1860 census, Sangamon County, Ill., 30; Order, August 28, 1849, Record K, 126, Sangamon County Commissioners v. Funderburk, Sangamon County Circuit Court, Illinois Regional Archives Depository, University of Illinois, Springfield; *LPAL.*

61. Judge's Docket Entry, March 1850, Judge's Docket, and Order, August 29, 1850, Record K, 426, both in Sangamon County Circuit Court, Illinois Regional Archives Depository, University of Illinois, Springfield; 1850 census, Sangamon County, Ill., 292, 297; Wallace, "Opportunity to Grow," 90.

62. Fee Book Entry, January 11, 1851, Fee Book M, 436, and Judge's Docket Entry, March 1850, both in Sangamon County Circuit Court, Illinois Regional Archives Depository, University of Illinois, Springfield; 1850 census, Sangamon County, Ill.; 1860 census, Sangamon County, Ill.; Power, *Early Settlers of Illinois,* 87, 113, 317, 325, 394, 539, 564, 625, 679, 729.

Chapter 3: The Work of Jurors in the Antebellum Illinois Courtroom

1. Order, June 15, 1854, Record N, 54, Sangamon County Circuit Court, Illinois Regional Archives Depository, University of Illinois, Springfield; Joanne Towers Wheeler, "Springfield, 1850: The City, Its Places, Its People," manuscript, 1978, 44, map 2; Christopher Elliott Wallace, "The Opportunity to Grow: Springfield, Illinois, during the 1850s" (Ph.D. diss., Purdue University, 1983), 168–69; Office of the U.S. Census, Seventh Census of the United States (1850), Sangamon County,

Ill., 109, 119; Wheeler, "Springfield," map 2. The monthly mean temperature for March 1851 was 38 degrees. *The American Almanac and Repository of Useful Knowledge, for the Year 1853* (Boston: Little, Brown, 1853), 97.

2. Order, March 26, 1844, Record H, 293, Polk v. Herndon (trespass), Order, November 23, 1844, Record H, 493–94, Merryman v. Newsom (debt), Order, November 19, 1844, Record H, 475, Taylor v. Dormody (assumpsit), Order, November 20, 1844, Record H, 481, Shepherd v. Lyons (mechanics' lien), and Order, September 6, 1849, Record K, 199, Russell v. Penny (debt), all in Sangamon County Circuit Court, Illinois Regional Archives Depository, University of Illinois, Springfield.

3. Judge's Docket Entry, July 1842, Docket Book C, Gardner v. Watson (assumpsit), Judge's Docket Entry, November 1843, Docket Book C, Gardner v. Johnson (petition and summons), Judge's Docket Entry, November 1843, Docket Book C, Gardner v. Johnson et al. (foreclosure of mortgage), Judge's Docket Entry, March 1844, Docket Book C, Gardner v. Corneau (petition and summons), and Judge's Docket Entry, March 1844, Docket Book C, Gardner v. Francis (foreclosure of mortgage), all in Sangamon County Circuit Court, Illinois Regional Archives Depository, University of Illinois, Springfield; Bill of Complaint, September 12, 1843, Mitchell v. Corneau (foreclosure of mortgage), Lincoln Collection, Lilly Library, Indiana University, Bloomington.

4. Roswell P. Abel, H. J. Armstrong, John S. Ball, Joseph Beam, Henry Bird, James A. Brundage, David Crouch, John J. Elliot, William P. Grimsley, James L. Hill, Hamilton A. Hough, Caleb Jackson, James W. Langston, Alexander Lindsay, John L. Peake, Moses Pierson, Charles W. Price, Jonathan R. Saunders, George W. Turley, and Bela C. Webster were just a few of the jurors who served in Sangamon County Circuit Court and who were also plaintiffs or defendants in civil actions. Martha L. Benner and Cullom Davis, eds., *The Law Practice of Abraham Lincoln: Complete Documentary Edition,* 2d ed. (Springfield: Illinois Historic Preservation Agency, 2009), available at www.lawpracticeofabrahamlincoln.org (hereafter cited as *LPAL*); James E. Davis, *Frontier Illinois* (Bloomington: Indiana University Press, 1998), 268–76; Edward J. Balleisen, *Navigating Failure: Bankruptcy and Commercial Society in Antebellum America* (Chapel Hill: University of North Carolina Press, 2001); Daniel W. Stowell, "Webs of Credit: S. C. Davis & Company and the Collection of Interstate Debts," paper presented at the Missouri Valley History Conference, Omaha, Neb., March 2002; *LPAL*; Cormac O'Grada and Eugene N. White, "The Panics of 1854 and 1857: A View from the Emigrant Industrial Savings Bank," *Journal of Economic History* 63 (March 2003): 213–40; Peter L. Rousseau, "Jacksonian Monetary Policy, Specie Flows, and the Panic of 1837," *Journal of Economic History* 62 (June 2002): 457–88.

5. Decree, March 26, 1851, Record L, 54, Ex parte Crow (appointment of conservator), Sangamon County Circuit Court, Illinois Regional Archives Depository, University of Illinois, Springfield; John A. Garraty and Mark C. Carnes, eds.,

American National Biography, 24 vols. (New York: Oxford University Press, 1999), 13:845–47; John Carroll Power, *History of the Early Settlers of Sangamon County, Illinois* (Springfield, Ill.: H. W. Rokker, 1970; repr., Springfield, Ill.: Phillips Brothers, 1970), 788–89; *History of Sangamon County* (Chicago: Inter-state Publishing, 1881), 78, 106–7; John M. Palmer, ed., *The Bench and Bar of Illinois: Historical and Reminiscent,* 2 vols. (Chicago: Lewis Publishing, 1899), 1:180, 184–85; 1850 census, Sangamon County, Ill., 73, 107, 131. No information on the last three jurors is available.

6. "Jurors," March 3, 1845, *Revised Statutes of the State of Illinois* (1845), 308; Order, April 17, 1833, Record B, 122–23, State Bank of Illinois v. Parkinson (assumpsit), Order, December 11, 1845, Opinion Record, Supreme Court, Central Grand Division, 225, People v. Cheek (debt), and Judgment, December 24, 1845, Opinion Record Supreme Court, Central Grand Division, 291–94, People v. McHatton (debt), all in Illinois Supreme Court, Illinois State Archives, Springfield; Order, December 4, 1850, Record K, 512, Mullen v. O'Conner (debt), Order, December 6, 1850, Record K, 521, Mullen v. O'Conner and Boyd (debt), Order, March 26, 1851, Record 11, 54, Ex parte Crow (appointment of conservator), and Order, September 6, 1852, Record L, 546, H. W. Derby & Company v. Cary (assumpsit), all in Sangamon County Circuit Court, Illinois Regional Archives Depository, University of Illinois, Springfield. Daniel W. Stowell et al., eds., *The Papers of Abraham Lincoln: Legal Documents and Cases,* 4 vols. (Charlottesville: University of Virginia Press, 2008), 4:273.

7. Order, September 6, 1852, H. W. Derby & Company v. Cary; Stowell, *Papers of Abraham Lincoln,* 4:273–74.

8. Judge's Docket Entry, November 1843, Gardner v. Watson and Moffett (Gardner v. Johnson) (petition and summons), Judge's Docket Entry, November 1843, Docket Book C, Gardner v. Johnson et al. (foreclosure of mortgage), Judge's Docket Entry, March 1844, Docket Book C, Gardner v. Corneau (petition and summons), Judge's Docket Entry, March 1844, Docket Book C, Gardner v. Francis (foreclosure of mortgage), Order, July 28, 1842, Record G, 437, Gardner v. Watson and Moffett (assumpsit), Judge's Docket Entry, November 1844, Docket Book C, Shepherd v. Lyons (mechanics' lien), Order, November 20, 1844, Record H, 481, Subpoena in Chancery, July 11, 1843, case file, Gardner v. Johnson et al. (foreclosure of mortgage), and Witness Affidavit, March 1851, case file, Gardner v. Watson (injunction), all in Sangamon County Circuit Court, Illinois Regional Archives Depository, University of Illinois, Springfield.

9. Harry E. Pratt, "'Judge' Abraham Lincoln," *Journal of the Illinois State Historical Society* 48 (Spring 1955): 33; 1850 census, Sangamon County, Ill., 137; John Mack Faragher, *Sugar Creek: Life on the Illinois Prairie* (New Haven, Conn.: Yale University Press, 1988), 68–69, 200; Power, *History of the Early Settlers,* 234; Decree, March 26, 1851, Ex parte Crow.

10. An Act Regulating the Estates of Idiots, Lunatics, and Persons Distracted, and for Other Purposes (February 12, 1823), *Public and General Statute Laws of the State of Illinois* (1839), 330; Decree, March 26, 1851, Ex parte Crow.

11. 1850 census, Sangamon County, Ill., 143; Power, *History of the Early Settlers,* 234; Lawrence M. Friedman, *Crime and Punishment in American History* (New York: Basic Books, 1993), 248.

12. *LPAL*; Jury Warrant, September 17, 1841, case file, Archer v. Clark (debt), Christian County Justice of the Peace Court, Christian County Circuit Court, Christian County Courthouse, Taylorville, Ill.; Order, June 4, 1846, Clerk's Docket, 74, Rawlings v. Field (debt), Gallatin County Circuit Court, Gallatin County Courthouse, Shawneetown, Ill.; Order, November 12, 1842, Court Record G, 269–70, State Bank of Illinois v. Corwith (trespass on the case), Jo Daviess County Circuit, Jo Daviess County Courthouse, Galena, Ill.; Jury Verdict, filed March 19, 1856, Taylor v. Humphries (ejectment), case file 25, Record Group 21, U.S. Circuit Court, Southern District of Illinois, National Archives, Great Lakes Region, Chicago.

13. Order, March 21, 1838, Law Record D, 39, Sugg v. Morris (assumpsit), Morgan County Circuit Court, Morgan County Courthouse, Jacksonville, Ill.; Order, April 25, 1855, Common Law Record A, 367, Hart v. Phlasterer (trespass), Woodford County Circuit Court, Woodford County Courthouse, Eureka, Ill.; Verdict, October 1842, case file, boxes 43–45, Scott v. Cox (slander), Vermilion County Circuit Court, Vermilion County Courthouse, Danville, Ill.; Order, June 15, 1854, Record N, 56, Rorax v. Arnold (replevin), Sangamon County Circuit Court, Illinois Regional Archives Depository, University of Illinois, Springfield; Order, September 2, 1852, Record L, 531, Alton & Sangamon Railroad v. Carpenter (appeal of assessment of damages), Sangamon County Circuit Court, Illinois Regional Archives Depository, University of Illinois, Springfield; Order, May 2, 1851, Circuit Court Record A, 60, Dunn v. Carle (seduction), Champaign County Circuit Court, Champaign County Historical Archives, Urbana Free Library, Urbana, Ill.; Jury Verdict, November 1, 1852, case file, Stewardson v. Stewardson (divorce), Shelby County Circuit Court, Shelby County Courthouse, Shelbyville, Ill.; Jury Verdict, October Term 1857, case file, T. F. Hamblin & Co. v. Lisenbey (mechanics' lien), DeWitt County Circuit Court, DeWitt County Courthouse, Clinton, Ill.; Jury Verdict, filed November 5, 1857, case file, People v. Norris (murder), Cass County Circuit Court, Cass County Courthouse, Virginia, Ill.; Verdict, May Term 1847, case file, box 16, People v. Lane (larceny), Menard County Circuit Court, Menard County Courthouse, Petersburg, Ill.; *LPAL.*

14. An Act Prescribing the Mode of Summoning Grand Jurors (March 23, 1819), *Passed by the First General Assembly of the State of Illinois* (1819), 201; An Act Relating to Juries (February 9, 1831), *Statutes of the State of Ohio* (1831), 492.

15. Richard D. Younger, *The People's Panel: The Grand Jury in the United States, 1634–1941* (Providence, R.I.: Brown University Press, 1963), 83.

16. David J. Bodenhamer, "Criminal Justice and Democratic Theory in Antebellum America: The Grand Jury Debate in Indiana," *Journal of the Early Republic* 5 (Winter 1985): 482–83.

17. David Davis, Charge to the Grand Jury, n.d., David Davis Family Papers, folder E-3, Abraham Lincoln Presidential Library and Museum, Springfield, Ill.

18. David Mark to Abraham Lincoln, May 2, 1849, Abraham Lincoln Papers, Library of Congress, Washington, D.C.; David Mark to Abraham Lincoln, May 7, 1849, box 252, Record Group 48, Entry 1: Records of the Office of the Secretary of the Interior, 1833–1864, Divisional Records, 1843–1943, Records of the Appointments Division, 1817–1922, Field Office Appointment Papers, National Archives, College Park, Md.

19. People v. Rountree (larceny); People v. Wiley Signey (larceny); People v. Wells (larceny); People v. Neal (larceny); People v. Wilson Cloyd (assault with intent to injure); People v. Webster Signey (assault with intent to injure); People v. Matthew Cloyd (assault with intent to injure); People v. Ross (bigamy); People v. McHenry (adultery); People v. Brown (selling liquor); People v. Hubbard (selling liquor); People v. Baker (obstructing road); People v. Ross (assault with intent to murder); People v. Davis (murder). Orders, March 22–27, 1850, Court Record K, 313–36, Sangamon County Circuit Court, Illinois Regional Archives Depository, University of Illinois, Springfield.

20. Order, March 25, 1850, Record Book K, 329, People v. Brown, Sangamon County Circuit Court, Illinois Regional Archives Depository, University of Illinois, Springfield; 1850 census, Sangamon County, Ill., 92–143; Power, *History of the Early Settlers,* 226, 341, 697, 700. The Sangamon County Circuit Court grand jurors in March 1850 were: John M. Allen, George Brunk, Caleb Burchall, Oramel Clark, John Cooper, Josiah Green, A. G. Henry, Lemuel Higby, William McDaniel, George H. Miller, Zachariah Peter, J. R. Saunders, William Shutt, Levi H. St. Clair, David Talbott, D. M. Vanderin, Jacob Willis, Nathan Yeamans.

21. 1850 census, Sangamon County, Ill., 89–289; 1850 census, Menard County, Ill., 267.

22. Order, September 8, 1851, Circuit Court Record M, 121, People v. Gutzweller (selling liquor), Madison County Circuit Court, Madison County Courthouse, Edwardsville, Ill.; Order, March 31, 1859, Circuit Court Record 2, 677, People v. Grosberrit (selling liquor), Logan County Circuit Court, Logan County Courthouse, Lincoln, Ill.; Order, April 1, 1853, Record M, 153, People v. Salzenstein (selling liquor), Sangamon County Circuit Court, Illinois Regional Archives Depository, University of Illinois, Springfield; Indictment, May 1853, file 45, box 1, People v. Sullivan, Macon County Circuit Court, Illinois Regional Archives Depository, University of Illinois, Springfield; Indictment, filed May 15, 1855, case file 9, People v. Kane (selling liquor), and Indictment, October 1855, case file 38, People v. Maloney (keeping tippling house open on Sunday), both in DeWitt County Circuit Court, DeWitt County Courthouse, Clinton, Ill.; 1850 census, Madison County, Ill., 370, Logan County, Ill., 179, Macon County, Ill., 669, DeWitt County, Ill., 569, and Sangamon County, Ill., 73; Office of the U.S. Census, Eighth Census of the United States (1860), Sangamon County, Ill., 367;

City Charter of Alton, Illinois, 1837; An Act to Prevent the Selling of Spirituous Liquors in This State, and for Other Purposes (February 14, 1823), *Public and General Statute Laws of the State of Illinois* (1839), 672; An Act to Prohibit the Retailing of Intoxicating Drinks (February 1, 1851), *Compilation of the Statutes of the State of Illinois* (1856), 389.

23. Ian R. Tyrell, *Sobering Up: From Temperance to Prohibition in Antebellum America, 1800–1860* (Westport, Conn.: Greenwood Press, 1979); James R. Rohrer, "The Origins of the Temperance Movement: A Reinterpretation," *Journal of American Studies* (Great Britain) 24 (August 1990): 228–35; Suzanne Thurman, "Cultural Politics on the Indiana Frontier: The American Home Missionary Society and Temperance Reform," *Indiana Magazine of History* 94 (December 1998): 285–302; David M. Fahey, *Temperance and Racism: John Bull, Johnny Reb, and the Good Templars* (Lexington: University Press of Kentucky, 1996); Thomas R. Pegram, *Battling Demon Rum: The Struggle for a Dry America, 1800–1933* (Chicago: Ivan R. Dee, 1998); Declaration, filed March 14, 1853, Bryan v. Bates (assault and battery during arrest for public drunkenness), Herndon-Weik Collection, Library of Congress, Washington, D.C.; Indictment, March 1852, case file, box 27, People v. Metzger (selling liquor in illegal quantities), Menard County Circuit Court, Menard County Courthouse, Petersburg, Ill.; Indictment, October 1851, case file, box 10, People v. Bailey (selling liquor in illegal quantities), Vermilion County Circuit Court, Vermilion County Courthouse, Danville, Ill.; Indictment, April 1850, case file, People v. Miller (keeping a tippling house open on Sunday), Woodford County Circuit Court, Woodford County Courthouse, Eureka, Ill.; Arrest Warrant, January 18, 1858, case file 697–98, Urbana, Illinois v. Ryan (selling liquor without a license), Urbana Police Magistrates Court, Champaign County Courthouse, Champaign, Ill.; Order, March 17, 1837, Record C, 358, People v. Salish (selling liquor without a license), and Order, October 6, 1836, Record C, 275, People v. Capps (keeping a tippling house open on Sunday), both in Sangamon County Circuit Court, Illinois Regional Archives Depository, University of Illinois, Springfield.

24. Bill for Divorce, filed November 20, 1836, case file, Ethridge v. Ethridge, Sangamon County Circuit Court, Illinois Regional Archives Depository, University of Illinois, Springfield; Bill for Divorce, filed January 9, 1849, Noyes v. Noyes, SC689, Abraham Lincoln Presidential Library, Springfield, Ill.; Bill for Divorce, filed May 3, 1854, case file, box 30, Foster v. Foster, Menard County Circuit Court, Menard County Courthouse, Petersburg, Ill.; Amended Declaration, filed May 5, 1854, Pearl v. Graham (trespass), Illinois State Archives, Springfield, Ill.; newspaper report on Reynolds v. Steele (trespass), *Pantagraph* (Bloomington, Ill.), September 17, 1856; newspaper report on People v. Shurtliff (riot), *Illinois State Register* (Springfield), May 27, 1854; Indictment, filed May 3, 1854, case file, box 282, People v. Sickler, Tazewell County Circuit Court, Tazewell County Courthouse, Pekin, Ill.

25. *LPAL*; Order, March 10, 1838, Record C, 603, People v. Salish, Sangamon County Circuit Court, Illinois Regional Archives Depository, University of Illinois,

Springfield; Order, June Term 1856, Circuit Court Record A, 493, People v. Yount, Champaign County Circuit Court, Urbana Free Library, Champaign County Historical Archives, Urbana, Ill.; Order, April 28, 1857, Circuit Court Record F, 184, People v. Sandusky, Vermilion County Circuit Court, Vermilion County Courthouse, Danville, Ill.

26. Indictment, May 1853, case file 45, box 1, People v. Sullivan, and Order, October 24, 1853, Circuit Court Record C, 203, People v. Sullivan, both in Macon County Circuit Court, Macon County Courthouse, Decatur, Ill.; Sullivan v. People, 15 Ill. 233 (1853).

27. Newspaper report on People v. Shurtliff; "A Reminiscence of the Whiskey Excitement of 1855 in Bloomington," *Pantagraph* (Bloomington, Ill.), March 25, 1874; "The Whiskey Mania of '54–55," *Pantagraph,* March 30, 1874; "The Whiskey Riot of '55," *Pantagraph,* March 31, 1874; Pearl v. Pearl, People v. Sickler, and Pearl v. Graham, in Stowell, *Papers of Abraham Lincoln,* 2:460–79; *Illinois Daily Journal* (Springfield), April 1, 1854, p. 3, col. 1; *Liquor Laws of Massachusetts, Maine, New York, South Carolina, Missouri, and Kansas with Extracts from Laws of New Jersey, Iowa, Illinois and Maryland* (Rutland, Vt.: Tuttle, 1902), x; Tyrell, *Sobering Up,* 260–62.

28. Bond, March 28, 1849, case file, box 19, Petersburg, Illinois v. Pillsbury, Bill of Exceptions [November 1844], case file, box 19, Petersburg, Illinois v. Moon, and Declaration, filed October 26, 1849, case file, box 19, Petersburg, Illinois v. Mappin, all in Menard County Circuit Court, Menard County Courthouse, Petersburg, Ill.

29. Justice of the Peace Transcript, October 14, 1844, case file, box 9, Petersburg, Illinois v. Moon (appeal of debt), Jury Verdict [November 1844], case file, box 9, Petersburg, Illinois v. Moon, and Settlement, January 1, 1845, case file, box 9, Petersburg, Illinois v. Moon, all in Menard County Circuit Court, Menard County Courthouse, Petersburg, Ill.; Jury Verdict [October 1844], Menard County Justice of the Peace Court, case file of the appeal, box 9, Petersburg, Illinois v. Moon (debt), Menard County Circuit Court, Menard County Courthouse, Petersburg, Ill.

30. 1850 census, Menard County, Ill.

31. Judge's Docket Entry, November 1844, Docket Book 1, Menard County Circuit Court, Menard County Courthouse, Petersburg, Ill.; 1850 census, Menard County, Ill., 274; Palmer, *Bench and Bar of Illinois,* 1:180. At least six of the jurors were from long-established Menard County families, possessed some wealth in real estate, or were skilled tradesmen in Petersburg. Jury Verdict [October 1844]; 1850 census, Menard County, Ill., 275–335.

32. Justice of the Peace Court Transcript, October 13, 1848, filed as evidence in Menard County Circuit Court, case file, box 19, and Order, November 7, 1849, General Record A, Menard County Circuit Court, both in Menard County Courthouse, Petersburg, Ill.; 1850 census, Menard County, Ill., 287–634.

33. Order, April 3, 1850, General Record A, 462, Petersburg, Illinois v. Pillsbury, and Order, April 4, 1850, General Record A, Petersburg, Illinois v. Mappin, both in Menard County Circuit Court, Menard County Courthouse, Petersburg, Ill.

34. Jury Instructions, April 1850, case file, box 19, Petersburg, Illinois v. Pillsbury, and Motion to Arrest Judgment, filed April 5, 1850, case file, box 19, Petersburg, Illinois v. Mappin, both in Menard County Circuit Court, Menard County Courthouse, Petersburg, Ill.; Petersburg, Illinois v. Mappin, 14 Ill. 193 (1852). In Lincoln's practice, Menard County Circuit Court juries convicted two defendants for the illegal sale of alcohol and acquitted two defendants for illegal gaming. In the latter two cases, the defendants were not proprietors of groceries but simply individuals caught playing cards for money. Apparently, jurors were less tolerant of gaming and liquor establishments than they were of private individuals playing cards. Order, May 4, 1847, General Record A, 327, People v. Phillips (gaming), Order, October 25, 1847, General Record A, 343, People v. Hinesly (gaming), Order, April 3, 1849, Circuit Court Record B, People v. Boyd (selling liquor), and Order, November 9, 1852, Circuit Court Record B, 41–42, People v. Metzger (selling liquor), all in Menard County Circuit Court, Menard County Courthouse, Petersburg, Ill. The gaming cases involved members of the prominent Trent family of Menard County. It is at least possible that the juries acquitted in the Trent cases because of the family's social status. Benjamin P. Thomas, *Lincoln's New Salem* (New Salem, Ill.: Lincoln's New Salem Enterprises, 1973; repr., Carbondale: Southern Illinois University Press, 1987), 21, 79.

35. *LPAL*; Indictment, filed June 6, 1848, case file, People v. Clark (gaming), Christian County Circuit Court, Christian County Courthouse, Taylorville, Ill.; Indictment, April Term 1850, case file, People v. Miller (keeping a gaming house), Woodford County Circuit Court, Woodford County Courthouse, Eureka, Ill.

36. Order, October 9, 1837, Record C, 453–54, People v. Camp, and Order, March 24, 1855, Record N, 384, Bridge & Brother v. Perce and Elder, both in Sangamon County Circuit Court, Illinois Regional Archives Depository, University of Illinois, Springfield.

37. Order, April 10, 1851, Common Law Record A, 207, People v. Clifton, and Indictment, filed April 1850, case file, People v. Clifton, both in Woodford County Circuit Court, Woodford County Courthouse, Eureka, Ill.; Order, June 6, 1848, General Record 1, 232, People v. Clark, Christian County Circuit Court, Christian County Courthouse, Taylorville, Ill.; Order, October 17, 1837, Record C, 497–98, People v. Capps, Sangamon County Circuit Court, Illinois Regional Archives Depository, University of Illinois, Springfield; Order, April 10, 1851, Common Law Record A, 206, People v. Miller (keeping a gaming house), Woodford County Circuit Court, Woodford County Courthouse, Eureka, Ill.; *LPAL.*

38. *DeKalb County Sentinel* (Sycamore, Ill.), June 25, 1859, 1:7. In this article, Charles Chase, who had served as a juror in one of Lincoln's cases, reflected on his courtroom experience and his opinions regarding Lincoln's humor.

39. An Act Concerning Practice in Courts of Law (January 29, 1827), *Revised Code of Laws, of Illinois* (1827), 315; Criminal Code (January 30, 1827), *Revised Code of Laws, of Illinois* (1827), 162; An Act Relative to Crime and Punishment (February 10, 1831), *Revised Statutes of the State of Indiana* (1831), 220; Act Relating to Juries, 492–93.

40. 1 Burr's Trial 418; Noble v. People, 1 Ill. 54 (1822); Smith v. Eames, 4 Ill. 76 (1841).

41. "The Circuit Court," *Illinois State Journal* (Springfield), November 20, 1856; Judge's Docket Entry, November 1856, Judge's Docket June Term 1856–June Term 1857, People v. Anderson, Sangamon County Circuit Court, Illinois Regional Archives Depository, University of Illinois, Springfield. Newspaper reports on People v. House provided details about this Sangamon circuit court murder case; see, for example, "Wednesday Afternoon April 29," *Illinois Daily Journal* (Springfield), April 30, 1857.

42. Noble v. People, 1 Ill. 54 (1822).

43. Ibid.. See the appendix for an annotated list of appellate cases used for this study.

44. Act Prescribing the Mode of Summoning Grand Jurors, March 23, 1819 (Illinois), 201; Act Relating to Juries, February 9, 1831 (Ohio), 492; "Of Grand and Petit Jurors," January 13, 1858, *Revised Statutes of the State of Wisconsin* (1858), 658; Pratt, "'Judge' Abraham Lincoln," 33; Christopher A. Schnell, *Stovepipe Hat and Quill Pen: The Artifacts of Abraham Lincoln's Law Practice* (Springfield: Illinois Historic Preservation Agency, 2002), 62–63; "The Opening of the Burdell Murder Trial—The Jury," lithograph, *Harper's Weekly,* May 9, 1857, 301; "The Trial of the Breach of Promise Case, Carstang vs. Shaw, at St. Louis, Missouri, March 1860," lithograph, *Harper's Weekly,* March 31, 1860, 201; "Federal Courtroom," photograph, in Susan Krause, *From Log Cabins to Temples of Justice: Courthouses in Lincoln's Illinois* (Springfield: Illinois Historic Preservation Agency, 2000), 43; Schnell, *Stovepipe Hat and Quill Pen,* 58. As de Tocqueville wrote: "Juries invest each citizen with a sort of magisterial office; they make all . . . feel that they have duties toward society and that they take a share in its government. By making men pay attention to things other than their own affairs, they combat that individual selfishness which is like rust in society"; Alexis de Tocqueville, *Democracy in America,* trans. Harvey C. Mansfield and Delba Winthrop (Chicago: University of Chicago Press, 2000), 262.

45. Charles Beneulyn Johnson, *Illinois in the Fifties or a Decade of Development: 1851–1860* (Champaign, Ill.: Flanigan-Pearson, 1918), 26; Schnell, *Stovepipe Hat and Quill Pen,* 17, 28–29, 63, 74, 76–77; "The Harrison Case," *Illinois State Journal* (Springfield), August 4, 1859. Periodically, the sheriff would hire someone for "scowering courthouse and juror rooms." Account, June 1845, People v. Dorman, Menard County Commissioner's Court, Illinois Regional Archives Depository, University of Illinois, Springfield.

46. Criminal Code, 163; "Jurors," *An Act for Revising and Consolidating the General Statutes of the State of Iowa* (1851), 258; William Faux, *Memorable Days in America: Being a Journal of a Tour to the United States* (1823; repr., New York: AMS Press, 1969), 81–82, 175; "The Trial of Wyant Continued," *Daily Pantagraph* (Bloomington, Ill.), April 14, 1857; Johnson, *Illinois in the Fifties,* 83; Parker v. Hoyt (trespass on the case), U.S. Circuit Court, District of Illinois (1855), *LPAL*; "An Important Suit Decided," *Chicago Daily Journal,* July 25, 1850; *Illinois State Register,* November 16, 1860; "Acquitted," *Illinois State Journal,* December 1, 1856; "U.S. District Court," *Daily Illinois State Journal,* January 18, 1858.

47. "Wednesday Afternoon April 29"; "Harrison Acquitted," *Illinois State Register,* September 4, 1859; "The Great Sand Bar Case," *Chicago Press & Tribune,* April 5, 1860, p. 1, col. 3; Newspaper Clipping, April 15, 1857, Fleming v. Rogers, McLean County Historical Society, Bloomington, Ill.; An Act Concerning Salaries, Fees, and Compensation of the Several Officers and Persons therein Mentioned (February 19, 1827), *Public and General Laws of the State of Illinois* (1827), 407–8; An Act Regulating Fees and Salaries of the Several Officers and Persons therein Named (February 7, 1831), *Revised Statutes of the State of Indiana* (1831), 252; An Act Prescribing the Manner of Impanneling Petit Jurors, the Number and Compensation Thereof (May 20, 1852), *Revised Statutes of the State of Indiana* (1852), 2:24–25; "Compensation of Officers," *An Act for Revising and Consolidating the General Statutes of the State of Iowa* (1851), 346.

48. Judge Aedanus Burke to Governor A. Vander Horst, December 8, 1796, General Assembly Papers, South Carolina Archives, quoted in John A. Hall, "That Onerous Task: Jury Service in South Carolina during the Early 1790s," *South Carolina Historical Magazine* 87 (January 1986): 5; Nancy King, "Juror Delinquincy in Criminal Trials in America, 1796–1996," *Michigan Law Review* 94 (August 1996): 2679–80; Friedman, *Crime and Punishment,* 243, 396.

49. Fee Book Entry, January 25, 1856, Fee Book O, 143, People v. Clary (disturbing a worshipping congregation), Sangamon County Circuit Court, Illinois Regional Archives Depository, University of Illinois, Springfield.

50. 1850 census, Sangamon County, Ill., 176; "Important Decision of the Illinois Supreme Court," *Illinois State Register,* February 26, 1853; Order, March 24, 1841, Record F, 593, People v. Johnson (obstructing watercourse), Order, March 27, 1841, Record F, 618, Davis v. Ekel (petition and summons), Order, November 22, 1842, Record G, 498, Taylor v. Wash (debt), Order, November 23, 1842, Record G, 511, Bryan v. Prentiss (appeal), Order, August 28, 1849, Record K, 137, Mauzy v. Brown (appeal of right of property), Order, September 3, 1849, Record K, 173, Baker v. Brown (covenant), Order, September 3, 1849, Record K, 176, Wilbourne v. Crenshaw (trespass), Order, September 6, 1849, Record K, 199, Russell v. Penny (debt), Order, March 25, 1850, Record K, 331, Penny v. McHenry (trespass), Order, September 6, 1852, Record L, 546, H. W. Derby & Co. v. Cary (assumpsit), Order, November 26, 1853, Record M, 390, People v. Clark (obstructing road), Order, June

18, 1855, Record N, 566, Johnson v. Richardson and Hopkins (assumpsit), and Jury Verdict [June 22, 1855], case file, Reed. v. Mickey (partition and dower), all in Sangamon County Circuit Court, Illinois Regional Archives Depository, University of Illinois, Springfield; Order, October 8, 1855, General Records, 1:14, Clark v. Stigleman (trespass on the case), Order, March 19, 1856, Complete Record Chancery, 3:45, Taylor v. Humphries (ejectment), and Complete Record Entry, June 27, 1857, Complete Law Record, 1c:320, Coffin v. Palmer (ejectment), all in Record Group 21, U.S. Circuit Court, Southern District of Illinois, National Archives and Records Administration, Great Lakes Region, Chicago.

51. Barret v. Saunders had six. Jury Verdict, filed July 17, 1848, case file, box17, Center v. Hutchinson (debt), Menard County Justice of the Peace Court, Menard County Courthouse, Petersburg, Ill.; Order, May 13, 1845, Court Record 2, 65, and Order, October 9, 1845, Court Record 2, 108, Eccles v. True (trespass quare clausum friget), both in Coles County Circuit Court, Coles County Courthouse, Charleston, Ill.; Order, July 10, 1839, Record D, 431, Williams v. Cabiness, and Order, April 9, 1842, Record G, 366, Barret v. Saunders, both in Sangamon County Circuit Court, Illinois Regional Archives Depository, University of Illinois, Springfield.

52. Order, July 10, 1839, Williams v. Cabiness; Declaration, filed October 1838, Huntington Library, San Marino, Calif.; Garraty and Carnes, *American National Biography,* 21:78–79; *LPAL.*

53. Act Prescribing the Mode of Summoning Grand Jurors, March 23, 1819 (Illinois), 201–2; An Act Concerning Petit Jurors (March 23, 1819), *Laws Passed by the First General Assembly of the State of Illinois* (1819), 255–57; Act Relating to Juries, February 9, 1831 (Ohio), 492; "Of Grand and Petit Jurors," January 13, 1858 (Wisconsin), 658.

54. Jumpertz v. People, 21 Ill. 374 (1859). Another example of the court housing jurors was in *People v. Wyant,* a murder trial in DeWitt County Circuit Court. The court put up those jurors at the Pike House, a hotel in Pekin, Illinois. "The Trial of Wyant," *Daily Pantagraph* (Bloomington, Ill.), April 6, 1857.

55. "Complimentary," *Daily Illinois State Journal,* December 2, 1856.

56. 1860 census, Sangamon County, Ill., 10, 15, 70.

57. Some of the midwestern cases that touch upon the issue of illegal interaction between jurors and others not on the jury include *Barlow v. State,* 2 Blackf. 114 (Ind.) (1827); Alexander v. Dunn, 5 Ind. 139 (1854); Fisher v. People, 23 Ill. 218 (1859); Rowland v. State, 14 Ind. 478 (1860); and Cole v. Swan, 4 Greene 32 (Iowa) (1853). See the appendix for an annotated list of appellate cases used for this study.

58. "A Statistical Portrait," in *LPAL*; Terry Wilson, "The Business of a Midwestern Trial Court: Knox County, Illinois, 1841–1850," *Illinois Historical Journal* 84 (Winter 1991): 249–67.

59. *LPAL*; "Sangamon County Cases of the Lincoln Period," database, n.d., Papers of Abraham Lincoln, Springfield, Ill. This database is constructed from

information extrapolated from the complete run of Sangamon County judge's dockets and Sangamon County Court Records between1836 and 1861, located in the Illinois Regional Archives Depository, University of Illinois, Springfield. The database includes the names of attorneys who practiced in Springfield as well as the docketing information of the cases they handled. These data offer some documentary evidence to compare the nature of Lincoln's law practice with that of his fellow lawyers at the bar.

60. *LPAL.* Jury verdicts in the Midwest were not predictable. Jurors weighed evidence and delivered verdicts in the context of that evidence and the circumstances of the crime. David J. Bodenhamer, "Criminal Sentencing in Antebellum America: A North-South Comparison," *Historical Social Research* (West Germany) 15 (1990): 77–94.

61. People v. Bosley, Vermilion County Circuit Court, May 1855; People v. Crockett, Moultie County Circuit Court, November 1852; People v. Davis, Clark County Circuit Court, July 1850; People v. Loe, DeWitt County Circuit Court, May 1853; People v. McNeely, Menard County Circuit Court, April 1859; People v. Rogers, Menard County Circuit Court, November 1857; People v. Thompson, Woodford County Circuit Court, April 1856. *LPAL.* Before 1845, the penalty for manslaughter was a sentence of up to three years in the penitentiary. Criminal Code (February 26, 1833), § 29, *Pubic and General Statute Laws of the State of Illinois* (1839), 203; Criminal Code (March 3, 1845), § 29, *Compilation of the Statutes of the State of Illinois* (1856), 363.

62. People v. Fraim, Hancock County Circuit Court, April 1839; People v. Weaver, Champaign County Circuit Court, May 1845; People v. Pulliam, Sangamon County Circuit Court, April 1860; Elizabeth Dale, "Not Simply Black and White: Jury Power and the Law in Late Nineteenth-Century Chicago," *Social Science History* 25 (Spring 2001): 10; Alan Rogers, "Murders and Madness: Law in Medicine in Nineteenth-Century Massachusetts," *Proceedings of the Massachusetts Historical Society* 106 (1994): 53–81; "Murder Trial," *Illinois Daily Journal,* May 2, 1857; "Trial of Wyant" ; People v. House, Sangamon County Circuit Court, April 1857; People v. Wyant, McLean County Circuit Court, April 1857; *Law Journal on the Law of Insanity,* c. 1857, David Davis Family Papers, Abraham Lincoln Presidential Library, Springfield, Ill.

63. Petition of Halsey O. Merriman and others to Augustus C. French [September 27, 1850], Illinois State Archives, Springfield.

64. Petition for Pardon of Moses Loe, August 18, 1857, People v. Loe, DeWitt County Circuit Court, Illinois State Archives, Springfield; *LPAL*; Anthony Thornton to Illinois Governor August C. French (an appeal for the pardon of a mentally disabled man convicted of manslaughter), November 22, 1852, Illinois State Archives, Springfield; James B. McKinley to Abraham Lincoln (regarding a list of signers on a petition for pardon, which included the names of several jurors), May 28, 1858, Abraham Lincoln Papers, Library of Congress, Washington,

D.C. For a southern comparison on this phenomenon, see Robert M. Ireland, "The Nineteenth-Century Criminal Jury: Kentucky in the Context of the American Experience," *Kentucky Review* 4 (Spring 1983): 52–70.

65. Order, October 31, 1860, Record U, 134, People v. Jones, Sangamon County Circuit Court, Illinois Regional Archives Depository, University of Illinois, Springfield; *Daily Illinois State Register,* November 9, 1860, p. 3, col. 2; *LPAL*; "Sangamon County Cases of the Lincoln Period," database.

66. Black Laws in Illinois, for example, barred free blacks from settling in the state, restricted their mobility within the state, barred them from jury service, and constrained them in other ways as well. An Act Respecting Free Negroes, Mulattoes, Servants and Slaves (March 30, 1819), An Act Respecting Free Negroes and Mulattoes, Servants, and Slaves (January 17, 1829), and An Act to Amend an Act Entitled "An Act Respecting Free Negroes, Mulattoes, Servants, and Slaves," approved March 230, 1819, all in *Statute Laws of the State of Illinois* (1839), 501–8; An Act to Prevent the Immigration of Free Negroes into This State (February 12, 1853), *Statutes of the State of Illinois* (1856), 780–83; Stephen Middleton, *The Black Laws in the Old Northwest: A Documentary History* (Westport, Conn.: Greenwood Press, 1993). Laws directed at American Indians denied them the right to testify against white people in criminal or civil court and prohibited them from purchasing alcohol, firearms and other weapons, blankets, and horses. "Who May Be Witnesses in Criminal Cases," Criminal Code, Third Division, January 19, 1829, An Act Concerning Practice (February 2, 1827), and An Act to Prevent the Selling of Spirituous Liquors in This State, and for Other Purposes (February 14, 1823), all in *Public and General Statute Laws of the State of Illinois* (1839), 201, 536, 627, respectively.

67. Richard F. Nation, "Violence and the Rights of African Americans in Civil War–Era Indiana: The Case of James Hayes," *Indiana Magazine of History* 100 (September 2004): 215–30. Although their legal status in antebellum Illinois was precarious, some blacks settled in the state, established communities, and lived successful lives. Roger D. Bridges, "Dark Faces on the Antebellum West Central Illinois Landscape," *Western Illinois Regional Studies* 6 (Fall 1983): 67–80.

68. An Act Prescribing the Mode of Summoning Grand and Petit Jurors, and Defining Their Duties and Qualifications, February 7, 1827, *Public and General Statute Laws of the State of Illinois* (1839), 396; Nomaqua v. People, 1 Ill. 145 (1825). One scholar has noted that "juries selected through prejudice deliberated with prejudice." Jeffrey Abramson, *We, the Jury: The Jury System and the Ideal of Democracy* (New York: Basic Books, 1994), 110.

69. Nomaqua v. People.

70. A writ of *Supersedeas* was an order to an inferior court to suspend legal proceedings in a particular case.

71. Nomaqua v. People.

72. P.J.R. King found that jurors "weighed mitigating circumstances" and that their decisions reflected different levels of evaluation "despite the hurried nature

of the decision-making process." King, "'Illiterate Plebians, Easily Misled': Jury Composition, Experience, and Behavior in Essex, 1735–1815," in *Twelve Good Men and True: The Criminal Trial Jury in England, 1200–1800,* ed. J. S. Cockburn and Thomas A. Green (Princeton, N.J.: Princeton University Press, 1988), 255. See the appendix for an annotated list of appellate cases used for this study.

73. Langworthy v. Myers, 4 Iowa 18 (1856); Norris' House v. State, 3 Greene 513 (Iowa) (1852); King, "Juror Delinquency," 2714; Affidavit of John Furrow and John Rice, [October] 24, 1852, case file, box 6, People v. Furrow, Vermilion County Circuit Court, Vermilion County Courthouse, Vandalia, Ill.; Abel v. Kennedy, 3 Greene 47 (Iowa) (1851).

74. Farrer v. Ohio, 2 Ohio St. 54 (1853); King, "Juror Delinquency," 2709; Birchard v. Booth, 4 Wis. 85 (1855); Forshee v. Abraham, 2 Iowa 571 (1856); Manix v. Malony, 7 Iowa 81 (1858); Schanler v. Porter, 7 Iowa 482 (1859); Forester v. Guard, 1 Ill. 74 (1823); Langworthy v. Myers, 4 Iowa 18 (1856).

75. "News Items and Varieties," *Chicago Daily Tribune,* March 29, 1856, 2.

76. Affidavit, April 17, 1852, Ramsey v. Wolf, Woodford County Circuit Court, Henry Horner Lincoln Collection, Abraham Lincoln Presidential Library and Museum, Springfield, Ill.; Order, September 24, 1852, Common Law Record A, 253, Ramsey v. Wolf, Woodford County Circuit Court, Woodford County Courthouse, Eureka, Ill.

77. Manix v. Malony; Ruble v. McDonald, 7 Iowa 90 (1858).

78. Criminal Code, January 30, 1827, § 172, 162; Act Relating to Juries, February 9, 1931, § 14 (Ohio), 492–93; Act Prescribing the Mode of Summoning Grand Jurors, March 23, 1819 (Illinois), 201–2; Act Concerning Petit Jurors, March 23, 1819 (Illinois), 255–57.

79. Sellers v. People, 4 Ill. 412 (1842).

80. Alexander v. Dunn, 5 Ind. 139 (1854); Baxter v. People, 8 Ill. 368 (1846); Bradford v. State, 15 Ind. 347 (1860); Crippen v. People, 8 Mich. 117 (1860); Davis v. People, 19 Ill. 73 (1857); Driskill v. State, 7 Ind. 338 (1855); Gardner v. People, 4 Ill. 83 (1841); Gates v. People, 14 Ill. 433 (1853); Goodwin v. Blachley, 4 Ind. 438 (1853); Hudson v. State, 1 Blackf. 317 (Ind.) (1824); Jones v. State, 2 Blackf. 475 (Ind.) (1831); Joy v. State, 14 Ind. 113 (1860); King v. Dale, 2 Ill. 512 (1838); M'Gregg v. State, 4 Blackf. 101 (Ind.) (1835); Maize v. Sewell, 4 Blackf. 447 (Ind.) (1837); Mississippi & Missouri Railroad Company v. Rousseau, 8 Iowa 373 (1859); Morgan v. Stevenson, 6 Ind. 136 (1855); Neely v. People, 13 Ill. 685 (1852); Noble v. People, 1 Ill. 54 (1822); Rice v. State, 7 Ind. 264 (1855); Romaine v. State, 7 Ind. 51 (1855); Schoeffler v. State of Wisconsin, 3 Wis. 823 (1854); Sellers v. People, 4 Ill. 412 (1842); Smith v. Eames, 4 Ill. 76 (1841); State of Iowa v. Gillick, 10 Iowa 98 (1859); State of Iowa v. Gillick, 7 Iowa 287 (1858); State of Iowa v. Sater, 8 Iowa 420 (1859); State of Iowa v. Shelledy, 8 Iowa 477 (1859); State of Iowa v. Thompson, 9 Iowa 188 (1859); State of Iowa v. Wilson, 8 Iowa 407 (1859); Stewart v. Ewbank, 3 Iowa 191 (1856); Thomas v. Leonard, 5 Ill. 556 (1843); Thompson v. People, 24 Ill.

61 (1860); Trimble v. State, 2 Greene 404 (Iowa) (1850); Van Blaricum v. People, 16 Ill. 364 (1855); Van Vacter v. M'Killip, 7 Blackf. (Ind.) 578 (1845); Vennum v. Harwood, 6 Ill. 659 (1844); Wau-kon-chaw-neek-kaw v. United States, 1 Morris 332 (Iowa) (1844).

81. *LPAL.*

82. Johnson, *Illinois in the Fifties,* 62; *LPAL;* Rousseau, "Jacksonian Monetary Policy," 457–88; Balleisen, *Navigating Failure;* Henry Clyde Hubbart, *The Older Middle West, 1840–1880: Its Social, Economic, and Political Life and Sectional Tendencies before, during, and after the Civil War* (New York: D. Appleton–Century, 1936; repr., New York: Russell and Russell, 1963); Raymond A. Mohl, "Poverty, Pauperism, and Social Order in the Pre-industrial American City, 1740–1840," *Social Science Quarterly* 52 (March 1972): 934–48.

83. Contract, January 30, 1844, and Agreement, February 23, 1844, both in case file, box 13, Center v. Hall, Menard County Circuit Court, Menard County Courthouse, Petersburg, Ill.; David Anthony, "Banking on Emotion: Financial Panic and the Logic of Male Submission in the Jacksonian Gothic," *American Literature* 76 (December 2004): 719–47; Account, filed January 14, 1856, case file, box 473, Beath v. Hainline, Tazewell County Circuit Court, Tazewell County Courthouse, Pekin, Ill.; Declaration, filed August 18, 1841, Maines v. Braucher, Herndon-Weik Collection, Library of Congress, Washington, D.C.; 1850 census, Logan County, Ill., 396.

84. For example, the large St. Louis wholesale firm of Black & Evers sued a small Menard County, Illinois, merchant in 1856 for failing to pay $200 in merchandise purchased on credit. The jury found for the plaintiff, ordering the defendant to pay. Order, October 6, 1856, Circuit Court Record B, 211, Black & Evers v. Trent and McHenry, Menard County Circuit Court, Menard County Courthouse, Petersburg, Ill.

85. Order, March 24, 1855, Record N, 384, Bridge & Brother v. Perce and Elder, Sangamon County Circuit Court, Illinois Regional Archives Depository, University of Illinois, Springfield; *LPAL.*

86. Declaration, filed February 2, 1838, and Plea, filed July 12, 1838, both in Anderson, Bell & Co. v. Gambrel, Herndon-Weik Collection, Library of Congress, Washington, D.C.; Order, July 13, 1838, Record D, 121, Anderson, Bell & Co. v. Gambrel, Sangamon County Circuit Court, Illinois Regional Archives Depository, University of Illinois, Springfield.

87. 1860 census, Sangamon County, Ill., 97, 124; Order, October 24, 1857, Record Q, 281, Priest v. Hoyt, Sangamon County Circuit Court, Illinois Regional Archives Depository, University of Illinois, Springfield; Promissory Note, January 19, 1854, Declaration, filed May 8 1854, and Jury Verdict, May 23, 1854, all in case file 677, Myers v. Brown, Champaign County Circuit Court, Champaign County Courthouse, Champaign, Ill.

88. 1850 census, Sangamon County, Ill., 109; Judge's Docket Entry, March 1841, Judge's Docket 1853–1856, Order, March 24, 1841, Record F, 627, and Writ of *Fieri*

Facias, April 18, 1841, all in Hay v. Hickox, Sangamon County Circuit Court, Illinois Regional Archives Depository, University of Illinois, Springfield.

89. 1860 census, Sangamon County, Ill., 302; Order, November 11, 1857, Record Q, 423, Writ of *Fieri Facias,* November 12, 1857, Alias Writ of *Fieri Facias,* October 7, 1864, and Judgment Docket Entry, November 18, 1865, Judgment Docket E, 257, all in Broadwell v. Strode, Sangamon County Circuit Court, Illinois Regional Archives Depository, University of Illinois, Springfield.

90. *LPAL*; Andrew J. King, "Constructing Gender: Sexual Slander in Nineteenth-Century America," *Law and History Review* 13 (Spring 1995): 63–110; Stacy Pratt McDermott, "Dissolving the Bonds of Matrimony: Women and Divorce in Sangamon County, Illinois, 1835–1860," in *In Tender Consideration: Women, Families and the Law in Abraham Lincoln's Illinois,* ed. Daniel W. Stowell (Urbana: University of Illinois Press, 2002), 82–83; An Act Concerning Divorces (January 31, 1827), *Revised Code of Laws of Illinois* (1827), 181–82; Decree, May 23, 1853, Circuit Court Record A, 139, Beard v. Beard (divorce and child custody), Champaign County Circuit Court, Champaign County Courthouse, Champaign, Ill.; Williams v. Williams (child custody), 13 Ind. 447 (1859); Decree, September 8, 1852, Record L, 561, Jones v. Jones (divorce and alimony), Sangamon County Circuit Court, Illinois Regional Archives Depository, University of Illinois, Springfield; Rourke v. Rourke (divorce and alimony), 8 Ind. 389 (1857); Rice v. Rice (divorce and division of property), 6 Ind. 81 (1855); Jane H. Pease and William H. Pease, *Ladies, Women, and Wenches: Choice and Constraint in Antebellum Charleston and Boston* (Chapel Hill: University of North Carolina Press, 1990), 31; Jane Turner Censor, "Smiling through Her Tears: Antebellum Southern Women and Divorce," *American Journal of Legal History* 25 (January 1981): 24–47; Norma Basch, "Relief in the Premises: Divorce as a Woman's Remedy in New York and Indiana, 1815–1870," *Law and History Review* 8 (Spring 1990): 1–24.

91. Illinois Statewide Marriage Index, vol. B, 256, Illinois State Archives, Springfield; 1850 census, McLean County, Ill., 15; Bill for Divorce, filed October 7, 1852, and Answer of Martin Beard, filed October 7, 1852, both in case file 104, Beard v. Beard, Champaign County Circuit Court, Champaign County Historical Archives, Urbana Free Library, Urbana, Ill.

92. Decree, October 2, 1852, Chancery Record 11, 175, Beard v. Beard, McLean County Circuit Court, McLean County Courthouse, Bloomington, Ill.; Witness List, filed May 25, 1853, case file 104, Beard v. Beard, Champaign County Circuit Court, Champaign County Historical Archives, Urbana Free Library, Urbana, Ill.; Decree, May 23, 1853, Beard v. Beard; Illinois Statewide Marriage Index, vol. C, 70, Illinois State Archives, Springfield.

93. Decree, November 14, 1851, Circuit Court Record C, 86, Ogden v. Ogden, Macon County Circuit Court, Macon County Courthouse, Decatur, Ill.; Bill for Divorce, filed May 9, 1851, case file A1037, Ogden v. Ogden, Macon County Circuit Court, Illinois Regional Archives Depository, University of Illinois, Springfield.

94. Declaration, filed May 13, 1852, Mitchell v. Mitchell, case file, Shelby County Circuit Court, Illinois State Archives, Springfield; 1850 census, Shelby County, Ill., 165; Illinois Statewide Marriage Index, vol. 1, 30, Illinois State Archives, Springfield.

95. Declaration, filed May 13, 1852, Mitchell v. Mitchell.

96. Ibid.; Witness Affidavit of Andrew Wakefield, May 27, 1852, Witness Affidavit of Thomas D. Hall, May 27, 1852, Witness Affidavit of James W. Rhodes, May 27, 1852, Witness Affidavit of William Sullivan, May 27, 1852, Witness Affidavit of Allen Wakefield, May 27, 1852, Witness Affidavit of Charles B. Williams, May 27, 1852, and Witness Affidavit of John Mitchell, May 27, 1852, all in case file, Mitchell v. Mitchell, Shelby County Circuit Court, Illinois State Archives, Springfield; Order, May 24, 1852, Circuit Court Record D, 351–52, Mitchell v. Mitchell, Shelby County Circuit Court, Shelby County Courthouse, Shelbyville, Ill.

97. Order, May 24, 1852, and Assignment of Judgment, May 27, 1852, case file, Mitchell v. Mitchell, Shelby County Circuit Court, Illinois State Archives, Springfield; Mark E. Steiner, "The Lawyer as Peacemaker: Law and Community in Abraham Lincoln's Slander Cases," *Journal of Abraham Lincoln Association* 16 (Summer 1995): 1. See King, "Constructing Gender," 63–110; Steiner, *An Honest Calling: The Law Practice of Abraham Lincoln* (DeKalb: Northern Illinois University Press, 2006).

98. An Act Declaring What Laws Are in Force in This State (February 4, 1819), *Laws of the State of Illinois* (1819), 3; St. George Tucker, ed., *Blackstone's Commentaries, with Notes and References to the Constitution and Laws of the Federal Government of the United States and of the Commonwealth of Virginia,* 5 vols. (Philadelphia: W. Y. Birch and A. Small, 1803; repr., New York: Augustus M. Kelley, 1969), 2:442; William Blackstone, *Commentaries on the Laws of England,* 4 vols. (1765–1769; repr., Chicago: University of Chicago Press, 1979), 1:430; Norma Basch, "Invisible Women: The Legal Fiction of Marital Unity in Nineteenth-Century America," *Feminist Studies* 5 (Summer 1979): 346–66. In only one of the slander suits that Abraham Lincoln handled did a jury fail to find in favor of the plaintiff. *LPAL.*

99. Gerda Lerner, *The Creation of Patriarchy* (New York: Oxford University Press, 1986); Morton Horwitz, *The Transformation of American Law, 1780–1860* (New York: Oxford University Press, 1992); Michael Grossberg, *Governing the Hearth: Law and the Family in Nineteenth-Century America* (Chapel Hill: University of North Carolina Press, 1985); Peter W. Bardaglio, *Reconstructing the Household: Families, Sex, and the Law in the Nineteenth-Century South* (Chapel Hill: University of North Carolina Press, 1995); Laura F. Edwards, "Law, Domestic Violence, and the Limits of Patriarchal Authority in the Antebellum South," *Journal of Southern History* 65 (November 1999): 733–70; Mary Beth Sievens, "Divorce, Patriarchal Authority, and Masculinity: A Case from Early National Vermont," *Journal of Social History* 37 (Summer 2004): 651–62; Daniel W. Stowell, ed., *In Tender Consideration: Women, Families and the Law in Abraham Lincoln's Illinois* (Urbana: University of Illinois Press, 2002), 5–6.

100. *LPAL;* Stowell, *In Tender Consideration.* Although Michael Grossberg previously argued that patriarchy explains the nineteenth-century legal situation, a recent article he coauthored provided much evidence to the contrary. Grossberg and Amy Elson, "Family Law in Indiana: A Domestic Relations Crossroads," in *The History of Indiana Law,* ed. David J. Bodenhamer and Randall T. Shepard (Athens: Ohio University Press, 2006), 60–70.

Chapter 4: The Struggle for Legal Power in Lincoln's America

1. Declaration, filed August 27, 1856, Fleming v. Rogers, McLean County (Ill.) Circuit Court, Lincoln Collection, Abraham Lincoln Library and Museum, Lincoln Memorial University, Harrogate, Tenn.; Richey v. West, 23 Ill. 329 (1860); Declaration, filed April 17, 1858, Macready v. Alton, Illinois, case file 335, Record Group 21, U.S. Circuit Court, Southern District of Illinois, National Archives, College Park, Md.; Narratio, filed March 14, 1855, case file, boxes 64–66, Bailey v. Western State Co., Vermilion County Circuit Court, Danville, Ill.; Browning v. Springfield, Illinois, 17 Ill. 143 (1855); Martha L. Benner and Cullom Davis, eds., *The Law Practice of Abraham Lincoln: Complete Documentary Edition,* 2d ed. (Springfield: Illinois Historic Preservation Agency, 2009), available at www.lawpracticeofabrahamlincoln.org (hereafter cited as *LPAL*); Edward Pessen, *Riches, Class, and Power before the Civil War* (Lexington, Mass.: D. C. Heath, 1973); Timothy R. Mahoney, *Provincial Lives: Middle-Class Experience in the Antebellum Midwest* (Cambridge: Cambridge University Press, 1999).

2. Jennifer L. Goloboy and Christopher Clark, "The Early American Middle Class," *Journal of the Early Republic* 24, no. 4 (Winter 2005): 537–45; T. H. Breen, *The Marketplace of Revolution: How Consumer Politics Shaped American Independence* (New York: Oxford University Press, 2004), 79–80; Susan Sessions Rugh, "Civilizing the Countryside: Class, Gender, and Crime in Nineteenth-Century Rural Illinois," *Agricultural History* 76 (Winter 2002): 58–81; C. Dallett Hemphill, "Middle Class Rising in Revolutionary America: The Evidence from Manners," *Journal of Social History* 30, no. 2 (Winter 1996): 317–44; Stuart M. Blumin, *The Emergence of the Middle Class: Social Experiences in the American City, 1760–1900* (New York: Cambridge University Press, 1989); Andrew R. L. Cayton, "The Failure of Michael Baldwin: A Case Study in the Origins of Middle-Class Culture on the Trans-Appalachian Frontier," *Ohio History* 95 (Winter–Spring 1986): 34–48; John B. Jentz, "Industrialization and Class Formation in Antebellum America: A Review of Recent Case Studies," *American Studies* (West Germany) 30 (1985): 303–35; Barbara A. Terzian, "Ohio's Constitutional Conventions and Constitutions," in *The History of Ohio Law,* ed. Michael Les Benedict and John F. Winkler, 2 vols. (Athens: University of Ohio Press, 2006), 1:58–59; Elizabeth R. Osborn, "Indiana Courts and Lawyers, 1816–2004," in *The History of Indiana Law,* ed. David J. Bodenhamer and Randall T. Shepard (Athens: Ohio University Press,

2006), 265–70; Joel Fishman, "An Early Pennsylvania Legal Periodical: *The Pennsylvania Law Journal,* 1842–1848," *American Journal of Legal History* 45 (January 2001): 22–50; Isabelle Lehuu, *Carnival on the Page: Popular Print Media in Antebellum America* (Chapel Hill: University of North Carolina Press, 2000); James Augst, "The Business of Reading in Nineteenth-Century America: The New York Mercantile Library," *American Quarterly* 50 (June 1998): 267–305; Michael H. Hoeflich, "John Livingston and the Business of Law in Nineteenth-Century America," *American Journal of Legal History* 44 (October 2000): 347–68; James W. Gordon, *Lawyers in Politics: Mid-nineteenth Century Kentucky as a Case Study* (New York: Garland Publishing, 1990); Mahoney, *Provincial Lives*; Maxwell Bloomfield, *American Lawyers in a Changing Society, 1776–1876* (Cambridge, Mass.: Harvard University Press, 1976).

3. John M. Palmer, *The Bench and Bar of Illinois: Historical and Reminiscent,* 2 vols. (Chicago: Lewis Publishing, 1899); Mark E. Steiner, "Lawyers and Legal Change in Antebellum America: Learning from Lincoln," *University of Detroit Mercy Law Review* 74 (Spring 1997): 427–64; Bloomfield, *American Lawyers*; Mahoney, *Provincial Lives.*

4. Phillip S. Paludan, "The American Civil War Considered as a Crisis in Law and Order," *American Historical Review* 77 (October 1972): 1013–34; Charles Cook, *The American Codification Movement: A Study of Antebellum Legal Reform* (Westport, Conn.: Greenwood Press, 1981); John Phillip Reid, *Law for the Elephant: Property and Social Behavior on the Overland Trail* (San Marino, Calif.: Huntington Library, 1980; repr., San Marino, Calif: Huntington Library, 1997); Herman Melville, "Bartleby the Scrivener: A Story of Wall Street" (1853; repr., New York: Simon and Schuster, 1997); Thomas H. Shreve, *Drayton: A Story of an American Life* (New York: Harper, 1851); Joseph S. Jones, *The People's Lawyer: A Comedy in Two Acts* (Boston: W. V. Spencer, 1856); Collin McCoy, "Democracy in Print: The Literature of Persuasion in Jacksonian America, 1815–1840" (Ph.D. diss., University of Illinois, 2001); Terence A. Tanner, "Newspapers and Printing Presses in Early Illinois," *American Periodicals* (1993): 100–113; Michael H. Harris, "Books for Sale on the Illinois Frontier: DeKalb County, 1855–1865," *American Book Collector* 21 (January 1971): 15–17; Franklin W. Scott, *Newspapers and Periodicals of Illinois, 1814–1879* (Springfield: Illinois Historical Collections, 1910). The publications listed here are just a sampling of the types of publications that published such commentary: *Sangamo Journal* (Springfield, Ill.), *Illinois State Journal* (Springfield), *Illinois State Register* (Springfield), *Chicago Press and Tribune, Harper's Weekly, Atkinson's Saturday Evening Post,* and *Cincinnati Weekly Herald and Philanthropist.*

5. Morton Horwitz, *The Transformation of American Law, 1780–1860* (New York: Oxford University Press, 1992); Renee B. Lettow, "New Trial for Verdict against Law: Judge-Jury Relations in Early Nineteenth Century America," *Notre Dame Law Review* 71, no. 3 (1996): 555; Albert W. Alschuler and Andrew G. Deiss,

"A Brief History of the Criminal Jury in the United States," *University of Chicago Law Review* 61 (Summer 1994): 868; "The Changing Role of the Jury in the Nineteenth Century," *Yale Law Review* 74 (November 1964): 170–92; Charles Sellers, *The Market Revolution: Jacksonian America, 1815–1846* (New York: Oxford University Press, 1991), 47.

6. Richard D. Younger, *The People's Panel: The Grand Jury in the United States, 1634–1941* (Providence, R.I.: Brown University Press, 1963); Renee Lettow Lerner, "The Transformation of the American Civil Trial: The Silent Judge," *William and Mary Law Review* 42 (October 2000): 195–264; Jon M. VanDyke, "The Jury as a Political Institution," *Center Magazine* 3 (March 1970): 17–26.

7. Paul Selby, *History of Sangamon County,* 2 vols. (Chicago: Munsell Publishing, 1912), 1:635.

8. Susan Krause, *From Log Cabins to Temples of Justice: Courthouses in Lincoln's Illinois* (Springfield: Illinois Historic Preservation Agency, 2000), 5; Mark Allen Cyr, "'I Would Not Be a Master': Democracy and Political Culture of Mastering in Illinois, 1837–1858" (Ph.D. diss., Washington University, 2003), 179–80; Thomas D. Clark, *The Rampaging Frontier: Manners and Humors of Pioneer Days in the South and Middle West* (New York: Bobbs-Merrill, 1939), 165.

9. Daniel David Blinka, "Trial by Jury on the Eve of the Revolution: The Virginia Experience," *University of Missouri Kansas City Law Review* 71 (Spring 2003): 533; Rhys Isaac, *The Transformation of Virginia, 1740–1790* (Chapel Hill: University of North Carolina Press, 1982), 88; Krause, *From Log Cabins to Temples of Justice,* 68; Selby, *History of Sangamon County,* 1:637.

10. Charles Beneulyn Johnson, *Illinois in the Fifties or a Decade of Development: 1851–1860* (Champaign, Ill.: Flanigan-Pearson, 1918), 87.

11. Peter Karsten, *Heart versus Head: Judge-Made Law in Nineteenth-Century America* (Chapel Hill: University of North Carolina Press, 1997); John G. Baker, "Indiana Judges: A Portrait of Judicial Evolution," in *The History of Indiana Law,* ed. David J. Bodenhamer and Randall T. Shepard (Athens: Ohio University Press, 2006), 303–24; Kermit L. Hall, "Social Backgrounds and Judicial Recruitment: A Nineteenth Century Perspective on the Lower Federal Judiciary," *Western Political Quarterly* 29 (June 1976): 243–57; John W. McNulty, "Sidney Breese, the Illinois Circuit Judge, 1835–1841," *Journal of the Illinois State Historical Society* 62 (Summer 1969): 170–86. The following sources provide much evidence for the economic, political, and social status that midwestern judges enjoyed throughout the nineteenth century: Susan Krause, *Judging Lincoln: The Bench in Lincoln's Illinois* (Springfield: Illinois Historic Preservation Agency, 2002); Palmer, *Bench and Bar of Illinois*; John Dean Caton, *Early Bench and Bar of Illinois* (Chicago: Legal News, 1893); Robert J. Maley and John R. Maley, "More Than Arbiters of Cases and Controversies: The Growing Impact of the Judiciary on Indiana's Legal Culture," in *The History of Indiana Law,* ed. David J. Bodenhamer and Randall T. Shepard (Athens: Ohio University Press, 2006), 278–302; Baker, "Indiana Judges," 303–24.

12. Maley and Maley, "More Than Arbiters of Cases and Controversies," 278–79; John F. Winkler, "The Legal Literature of Ohio," in *The History of Ohio Law,* ed. Michael Les Benedict and John F. Winkler, 2 vols. (Athens: University of Ohio Press, 2006), 2:501–52; John Phillip Reid, *Controlling the Law: Legal Politics in Early National New Hampshire* (DeKalb: Northern Illinois University Press, 2004); Lerner, "Transformation of the American Civil Trial," 208; *Jenkin's Centuries of Reports,* 139, as quoted in Charles Edwards, *The Juryman's Guide throughout the State of New York, and Containing General Matters for the Lawyer and Law Officer* (New York: Halsted Law Bookseller, 1831), xvi; Authorities written by Abraham Lincoln, n.d., Enos v. Capps, Herndon-Weik Collection, Library of Congress, Washington, D.C.; Lincoln and Herndon Commonplace Book, c. 1849, SC689, Abraham Lincoln Presidential Library and Museum, Springfield, Ill.; Authorities written by William H. Herndon, January 1860, Illinois Supreme Court, case file 2763, Brown v. Baker, Illinois State Archives, Springfield; Authorities written by Oliver L. Davis, May 1854, case file, boxes 67–69, Wilson v. Kingsbury, Vermilion County Circuit Court, Vermilion County Courthouse, Danville, Ill. Some compendiums from the period included Salmon P. Chase, ed., *The Statutes of Ohio and of the Northwest Territory Adopted or Enacted from 1788 to 1833 Inclusive* (Cincinnati, 1833); Thomas F. Gordon, *A Digest of the Laws of the United States, Including an Abstract of the Judicial Decision Relating to the Constitutional and Statutory Law* (Philadelphia: Thomas F. Gordon, 1837); Norman L. Freeman, *The Illinois Digest: Being a Full and Complete Digest and Compilation of All the Decisions of the Supreme Court of Illinois* (Chicago: S. C. Griggs, 1856).

13. Deirdre A. Harris, "Jury Nullification in Historical Perspective: Massachusetts as a Case Study," *Suffolk University Law Review* 12 (1978): 1002.

14. Richard Yates's Charge to the Scott County Grand Jury, October 14, 1839, Winfred Harbison Collection of Richard Yates Papers, Wabash College, Crawfordsville, Ind.

15. David Davis's Charge to the Grand Jury, c. 1848, and David Davis's Charge to the Grand Jury, c. 1849, both in folder E-3, David Davis Family Papers, Abraham Lincoln Presidential Library, Springfield, Ill.

16. Gilmore v. Ballard, 2 Ill. 251 (1836); Cowen v. People, 14 Ill. 348 (1853); Winkler, "Legal Literature of Ohio," 508. *Gilmore v. Ballard* determined that in the event litigants waived a jury trial, "the office of the judge is then completely merged into that of a jury." The judge was required to reach a verdict upon the applicable evidence, just as a jury was required to do.

17. Cook v. Scott, 6 Ill. 333 (1844).

18. Greenup v. Stoker, 8 Ill. 202 (1846). The court supported its decision on this point with the following authorities: Leigh v. Hodges, 4 Ill. 18 (1842); Gillet v. Sweat, 6 Ill. 475 (1844); Hill v. Ward, 7 Ill. 285 (1845); Edmunds v. Mitchell, 2 Term R. 4 and 5 Term R. 425; Seare v. Prentice, 8 East 348; Fleming v. Gilbert, 3 Johns. 528; Clark v. Dutcher, 9 Cowen 680.

19. Thomas Ford, *A History of Illinois from Its Commencement as a State in 1818 to 1847* (Chicago: S. C. Griggs, 1854; repr.; Ann Arbor, Mich.: University Microfilms, 1968), 85.

20. Harry E. Pratt, "'Judge' Abraham Lincoln," *Journal of the Illinois State Historical Society* 48 (Spring 1955): 29, 31; "Courts," March 3, 1845, *Revised Statutes of the State of Illinois* (1845), 146; "Lincoln as a Court Official," in *The Papers of Abraham Lincoln: Legal Documents and Cases,* ed. Daniel W. Stowell et al., 4 vols. (Charlottesville: University of Virginia Press, 2008): 4:279–80; *LPAL.*

21. Pratt, "'Judge' Abraham Lincoln," 30; Abraham Lincoln, Notes for a Law Lecture, c. 1859, Abraham Lincoln Papers, Library of Congress, Washington, D.C.; Mark E. Steiner, "The Lawyer as Peacemaker: Law and Community in Abraham Lincoln's Slander Cases," *Journal of the Abraham Lincoln Association* 16 (Summer 1995): 1–22.

22. Osborn, "Indiana Courts and Lawyers," 258–59; Hall, "Social Backgrounds and Judicial Recruitment"; McNulty, "Sidney Breese"; An Act Establishing County Courts, and Providing for the Election of Justices of the Peace and Constables, and for Other Purposes (February 12, 1849), and An Act to Provide for the Mode of Voting by Ballot, and for the Manner of Returning, Canvassing and Certifying Votes (February 12, 1849), both in *Laws of the State of Illinois* (1849), 62, 71; An Act to Establish a Uniform Mode of Holding Circuit Courts (January 7, 1835), *Public and General Statute Laws of the State of Illinois* (1839), 182; Michael E. Solimine and Richard B. Saphire, "The Selection of Judges in Ohio," in *The History of Ohio Law,* ed. Michael Les Benedict and John F. Winkler, 2 vols. (Athens: Ohio University Press, 2004): 1:211–37; David J. Bodenhamer and Randall T. Shepard, "The Narratives and Counternarratives of Indiana Legal History, in *The History of Indiana Law,* ed. David J. Bodenhamer and Randall T. Shepard (Athens: Ohio University Press, 2006), 13; Bloomfield, *American Lawyers,* 85. Some of this was the distrust that many midwesterners had of elected officials. Benjamin F. Wright Jr., "Political Institutions and the Frontier," in *Sources of Culture in the Middle West: Backgrounds versus Frontier,* ed. Dixon Ryan Fox (New York: D. Appleton–Century, 1934), 24.

23. Rodney O. Davis, "Lobbying and the Third House in the Early Illinois General Assembly," *Old Northwest* 14 (Winter 1988): 267–84. Sidney Breese served as a circuit judge and justice of the Illinois Supreme Court in the 1830s and 1840s and was in the U.S. Senate from 1843 to 1848; he was elected to the Illinois General Assembly in the 1850s, where he became Speaker of the House. His service as a state supreme court justice and as a U.S. senator overlapped. John A. Garraty and Mark C. Carnes, eds., *American National Biography,* 24 vols. (New York: Oxford University Press, 1999), 3:472–73; Palmer, *Bench and Bar of Illinois,* 1:33–34; *LPAL.* David Davis served as a member of the 1848 Illinois State Constitutional Convention and was elected as a circuit court judge the same year. Garraty and Carnes, *American National Biography,* 6:181–82; *LPAL.* Illinois Supreme Court justice

Samuel D. Lockwood was another judge who was a member of the 1848 constitutional convention at the same time he was serving on the bench. Allen Johnson, ed., *Dictionary of American Biography* (New York: Charles Scribner's and Sons, 1964), 6:1:344–45; Usher F. Linder, *Reminiscences of the Early Bench and Bar of Illinois* (Chicago: Chicago Legal News, 1879), 264–65. Thomas C. Browne served in Illinois' second and third territorial legislatures, and shortly after Illinois became a state, he gained an appointment to the Illinois Supreme Court. Frederick B. Crossley, *Courts and Lawyers of Illinois* (Chicago: American Historical Society, 1916), 1:84; John M. Scott, *Supreme Court of Illinois 1818: Its First Judges and Lawyers* (Bloomington, Ill., 1896), 75–99; *LPAL.*

24. Thomas J. McCormack, ed., *Memoirs of Gustave Koerner, 1809–1896,* 2 vols. (Cedar Rapids, Iowa: Torch Press, 1909),1:334.

25. People v. Field, 3 Ill. (2 Scam.) 79 (1839); Robert W. Johannsen, *Stephen A. Douglas* (Urbana: University of Illinois Press, 1973), 84–86; Arnold Shankman, "Partisan Conflicts, 1839–1841, and the Illinois Constitution," *Journal of the Illinois State Historical Society* 63 (Winter 1970): 337–48; Spragins v. Houghton, 3 Ill. 377 (2 Scam.) (1840) 377; Shankman, "Partisan Conflicts," 352–58; "Courts," approved March 2, 1845, in Norman H. Purple, comp., *A Compilation of the Statutes of the State of Illinois* (1845), 308; "Court Structure," in *LPAL.* As with U.S. Supreme Court justices at the federal level, it was typical during the early years of the nineteenth century for state supreme court justices to be responsible for circuit court districts within their states; a justice traveled designated circuits, presiding over the trial courts between sessions of his state's appellate court. Kermit L. Hall, ed., *The Oxford Companion to the Supreme Court of the United States* (New York: Oxford University Press, 1992), 145; Allen Sharp, "The U.S. Supreme Court on Circuit in Indiana, 1837–1891," in *The History of Indiana Law,* ed. David J. Bodenhamer and Randall T. Shepard (Athens: Ohio University Press, 2006), 344.

26. Cowen v. People, 14 Ill. 348 (1853).

27. James Sullivan, *The History of Land Titles in Massachusetts* (Boston, 1801), 342–45; William E. Nelson, *The Americanization of the Common Law: The Impact of Legal Change on Massachusetts Society, 1760–1830* (Athens: University of Georgia Press, 1975), 171–72; James Willard Hurst, *The Growth of American Law: The Law Maker* (Boston: Little, Brown, 1950), 185; Palmer, *Bench and Bar of Illinois,* 1:39–41; Johnson, *Dictionary of American Biography,* 2:2:575–76, 3:1:290–91; *United States Biographical Dictionary: Illinois Dictionary* (Chicago: American Biographical Dictionary, 1876), 674–75; *LPAL.*

28. Penny v. Graves, 12 Ill. 287 (1850); Lerner, "Transformation of the American Civil Trial," 203.

29. *LPAL*; John J. Duff, *A. Lincoln: Prairie Lawyer* (New York: Bramhall House, 1960); Christopher A. Schnell, *Stovepipe Hat and Quill Pen: The Artifacts of Abraham Lincoln's Law Practice* (Springfield: Illinois Preservation Agency, 2002), 32–33; Henry C. Whitney, *Life on the Circuit with Lincoln* (Boston: Estes and Lauriat, 1892; repr.,

Caldwell, Ohio: Caxton Printers, 1940); David Herbert Donald, *"We Are Lincoln Men": Abraham Lincoln and His Friends* (New York: Simon and Schuster, 2003), 67, 127; David M. Silver, *Lincoln's Supreme Court* (Urbana: University of Illinois Press, 1856; repr., Urbana: University of Illinois Press, 1998), 74; Willard L. King, *Lincoln's Manager: David Davis* (Cambridge, Mass.: Harvard University Press, 1960).

30. Sellers, *Market Revolution,* 49–50.

31. Alexis de Tocqueville, *Democracy in America,* trans. Harvey C. Mansfield and Delba Winthrop (Chicago: University of Chicago Press, 2000), 251. For Tocqueville, the American bar was as close to an aristocracy as any other group, and its members wielded a great deal of power and influence as a direct result of their aristocratic status.

32. Four books detail the rise of lawyers and the professionalization of their craft: Hurst, *Growth of American Law*; Bloomfield, *American Lawyers*; Gordon, *Lawyers in Politics*; Mahoney, *Provincial Lives.*

33. Richard Wade, *The Urban Frontier: The Rise of Western Cities, 1790–1830* (Cambridge, Mass.: Harvard University Press, 1959; repr., Cambridge, Mass.: Harvard University Press, 1967), 106–7; Mahoney, *Provincial Lives,* 170, 198; Bloomfield, *American Lawyers,* 85; Hurst, *Growth of American Law,* 254–55; David Herbert Donald, *Lincoln* (New York: Simon and Schuster, 1995), 20–27; Kenneth J. Winkle, *The Young Eagle: The Rise of Abraham Lincoln* (Dallas, Tex.: Taylor Trade Publishing, 2001), 76, 121–31; Cullom Davis, "Abraham Lincoln, Esq.: The Symbiosis of Law and Politics," in *Abraham Lincoln and the Political Process: Papers from the Seventh Annual Lincoln Colloquium,* ed. George L. Painter and Linda Norbut Suits (Springfield, Ill., 1992); Cullom Davis, "Law and Politics: The Two Careers of Abraham Lincoln," *Quarterly Journal of Ideology* 17 (June 1994): 61–75.

34. Cayton, "Failure of Michael Baldwin," 34–48; Jentz, "Industrialization and Class Formation," 303–35; Bloomfield, *American Lawyers,* 136; Gordon, *Lawyers in Politics,* xvii, 103, 226; William Faux, *Memorable Days in America: Being a Journal of a Tour to the United States* (1823; repr., New York: AMS Press, 1969), 81; Robert Stevens, *Law School Education in America from the 1850s to the 1980s* (Chapel Hill: University of North Carolina Press, 1983).

35. Stephen Thernstrom, *Poverty and Progress: Social Mobility in a Nineteenth-Century City* (Cambridge, Mass.: Harvard University Press, 1964; repr., New York: Atheneum, 1969), 80–114; Pessen, *Riches, Class, and Power,* 52–58; Davis, "Lobbying and the Third House," 267–84; Gordon, *Lawyers in Politics,* 231; Christopher Elliott Wallace, "The Opportunity to Grow: Springfield, Illinois, during the 1850s" (Ph.D. diss., Purdue University, 1983), 168–69. The "West" offered a spatial dimension for upward mobility and democratic achievements. Lacy K. Ford Jr., "Frontier Democracy: The Turner Thesis Revisited," *Journal of the Early Republic* 13 (Summer 1993): 144–63.

36. A. G. Roeber, *Faithful Magistrates and Republican Lawyers: Creators of Virginia Legal Culture, 1680–1810* (Chapel Hill: University of North Carolina Press, 1981); Gerard Gawalt, *The Promise of Power: The Emergence of the Legal Profession in*

Massachusetts, 1760–1840 (Westport, Conn.: Greenwood Press, 1979); Bloomfield, *American Lawyers,* 136–90; Maxwell Bloomfield, "Law v. Politics: The Self-Image of the American Bar, 1830–1860," *American Journal of Legal History* 12 (October 1968): 306–23; Anton-Hermann Chroust, *The Rise of the Legal Profession in America,* 2 vols. (Norman: University of Oklahoma Press, 1965); Gordon, *Lawyers in Politics,* 235–36; Charles Arthur Cole, ed., *The Constitutional Debates of 1847* (Springfield, Ill., 1919); Pessen, *Riches, Class, and Power,* 284–85; Sellers, *Market Revolution,* 48. Lawyers Norman B. Judd, Joseph Gillespie, Thomas L. Harris, Silas Noble, Jacob C. Davis, Josiah McRoberts, John Dougherty, and Thomas G. C. Davis served in the Illinois legislature. Theodore Calvin Pease, *Illinois Election Returns, 1818–1848* (Springfield: Illinois State Historical Library, 1923), 407–34; *United States Biographical Dictionary: Illinois Dictionary,* 257–59, 779–81; Office of the U.S. Census, Seventh Census of the United States (1850), Lee County, Ill., 88, Hancock County, Ill., 317, Vermilion County, Ill., 300, Union County, Ill., 231, and Massac County, Ill., 217.

37. David G. McCullough, *John Adams* (New York: Simon and Schuster, 2001); Noble E. Cunningham Jr., *In Pursuit of Reason: The Life of Thomas Jefferson* (Baton Rouge: Louisiana State University Press, 1987); William P. Cresson, *James Monroe* (Hamden, Conn.: Archon Books, 1971); Paul C. Nagel, *John Quincy Adams: A Public Life, a Private Life* (New York: Alfred A. Knopf, 1997); Robert Remini, *Andrew Jackson and the Course of American Empire* (New York: Harper and Row, 1977); Norman Gross, ed., *America's Lawyer-Presidents: From Law Office to Oval Office* (Evanston, Ill.: Northwestern University Press, 2004); in Garraty and Carnes, *American National Biography,* see: Forrest McDonald, "George Washington," 22:758–66; William Pencak, "John Adams," 1:100–107; Merrill D. Peterson, "Thomas Jefferson," 11:909–18; Lance Banning, "James Madison," 14:306–12; Harry Ammon, "James Monroe," 15:681–84; Mary W. M. Hargreaves, "John Quincy Adams," 1:107–11; Robert V. Remini, "Andrew Jackson," 11:732–37; Donald B. Cole, "Martin Van Buren," 22:159–62; K. R. Constantine Gutzman, "William Henry Harrison," 10:223–26; William G. Shade, "John Tyler," 22:77–79; James A. Rawley, "James Knox Polk," 17:622–27; Elbert B. Smith, "Zachary Taylor," 21:410–12; Tyler Anbinder, "Millard Fillmore," 7:910–12; Larry Gara, "Franklin Pierce," 17:495–97; and William E. Gienapp, "James Buchanan," 3:835–39.

38. Bloomfield, *American Lawyers,* 142; Hoeflich, "John Livingston and the Business of Law," 347–68; Perry Miller, *The Life of the Mind in America: From the Revolution to the Civil War* (New York: Harcourt, Brace and World, 1965), 99–266.

39. Shreve, *Drayton*; Jones, *People's Lawyer*; Melville, "Bartleby the Scrivener"; William Wirt, *Life of Patrick Henry,* 4th ed. (New York: M'Elrath and Bangs, 1831); Bloomfield, *American Lawyers,* 174; "Hotch-pot," *Monthly Law Reporter* 9 (1847): 476.

40. "'Justice' v. 'Law': Judge John Dudley's Charge to the Jury" (c. 1805), in *Law in Antebellum Society: Legal Change and Economic Expansion,* ed. Jamil Zainaldin (New York: Alfred A. Knopf, 1983), 83.

41. "The Sand Bar Case," *Chicago Press and Tribune,* March 26, 1860; *Illinois Daily Journal* (Springfield), August 21, 1851, p. 3, col. 1.

42. Abraham Lincoln, "Speech on the Practice of Law," [1859], Abraham Lincoln Papers, Library of Congress, Washington, D.C.

43. Lerner, "Transformation of the American Civil Trial," 202–3.

44. Sellers, *Market Revolution,* 49; Horwitz, *Transformation of American Law,* 28; Nelson, *Americanization of the Common Law,* 165–71; Cook, *American Codification Movement.*

45. Reminiscence of William H. Herndon, c. 1887, in William H. Herndon and Jesse W. Weik, *Herndon's Lincoln: The History and Personal Recollections of Abraham Lincoln,* 3 vols. (Chicago: Belford, Clark, 1889), 2:326.

46. Duff, *A. Lincoln,* 101; Donald, *Lincoln,* 151; John Frank, *Lincoln as a Lawyer* (Urbana: University of Illinois Press, 1961), 23–25; William Lewis Burke Jr., "A History of the Opening Statement from Barristers to Corporate Lawyers: A Case Study of South Carolina," *American Journal of Legal History* 37 (January 1993): 25–64; Abraham Lincoln's Arguments to the Jury in Hurd v. Rock Island Bridge Company, as reported in the *Chicago Daily Democratic Press,* September 24, 1857; Transcript of Testimony, Johnston v. Jones, U.S. Circuit Court, Northern District of Illinois, December 1861, Transcripts of Records 1861, vol. 4, December Term 1861, folder 3352–3586, U.S. Supreme Court, Washington, D.C.

47. Lawyers were establishing a profession at the same time that judges were the leading lawmakers in American society, so there is little surprise that the two groups would clash. Hurst, *Growth of American Law,* 85. One way lawyers gained power was through the introduction of equity proceedings in some states. These proceedings were held without a jury, and special judges, called chancellors, used special rules (created by lawyer-legislators). Sellers, *Market Revolution,* 49–50.

48. Ford, *History of Illinois,* 83.

49. Baxter v. People, 8 Ill. 368 (1846); Cowen v. People, 14 Ill. 248 (1853).

50. Lloyd E. Moore, *The Jury: Tool of Kings, Palladium of Liberty* (Cincinnati: W. H. Anderson, 1973), 152.

51. Baxter v. People, 8 Ill. 368 (1846).

52. Luman v. Kerr's administrator, 4 Greene 159 (Iowa) (1853).

53. De Tocqueville, *Democracy in America,* 262.

54. Leonard W. Levy, *The Law of the Commonwealth and Chief Justice Shaw* (New York: Oxford University Press, 1957), 290; Jeffrey Abramson, *We, the Jury: The Jury System and the Ideal of Democracy* (New York: Basic Books, 1994), 25; Godfrey D. Lehman, *We, the Jury: The Impact of Jurors on Our Basic Freedoms* (Amherst, N.Y.: Prometheus Books, 1997), 210.

55. *LPAL*; Horwitz, *Transformation of American Law,* 84. Jurors were characterized as being drawn from the unsophisticated "masses"; as having the "ill taste" to junket at saloons; and as being "promiscuously" selected from the "stupid," "corrupt," and unprincipled." J. B. S., "The Trial by Jury," *Atkinson's Casket,* January

1832; "Another Disgrace," *Chicago Press and Tribune,* December 13, 1859; "Judicial Reform," *Cincinnati Weekly Herald and Philanthropist,* March 13, 1844; "Trial by Jury," *New York Daily Times,* May 13, 1857.

56. Horwitz, *Transformation of American Law,* 28.

57. Langworthy v. Myers, 4 Iowa 18 (1856).

58. Davis v. People, 19 Ill. 73 (1857).

59. David J. Bodenhamer, "Criminal Justice and Democratic Theory in Antebellum America: The Grand Jury Debate in Indiana," *Journal of the Early Republic* 5 (Winter 1985): 481–502.

60. H. Fowler, *Report of the Debates and Proceedings of the Convention for the Revision of the Constitution of the State of Indiana* (Indianapolis: 1850 Constitutional Convention of the State of Indiana, 1850), 141, 147.

61. Alschuler and Deiss, "Brief History of the Criminal Jury," 880–81; Edward L. Ayers, *Vengeance and Justice: Crime and Punishment in the Nineteenth-Century American South* (New York: Oxford University Press, 1984), 113; "Trial of Juries," *Harper's Weekly,* May 9, 1857, 1; "Tampering with Juries," *Harper's Weekly,* June 19, 1858, 386; "The Jury System," *Harper's Weekly,* December 25, 1858, 818; "The Jury System," *Harper's Weekly,* January 29, 1859, 66.

62. "The Jury Farce," October 10, 1857, 642.

63. Publications that printed legal content included (but were not limited to) the following: *Albion Journal of News, Anglo-American, Anti-slavery Record, American Masonic Register, Atkinson's Saturday Evening Post, Boston Cultivator, Catholic Telegraph, Chicago Daily Tribune, Christian Advocate and Journal, Cincinnati Weekly Herald and Philanthropist, Circular, Family Magazine, Friend's Review, Goudy's Lady Book, Harper's Weekly, Illinois State Register, Journal of Prison Discipline and Philanthropy, Liberator, Littell's Living Age, National Era, North American Magazine,* and *Sangamo Journal.*

64. Crocker v. Goodsell, 1 Scam. (2 Ill.) 107 (1833), upheld the judge's right to determine a question of contract; Wickersham v. People, 1 Scam. (2 Ill.) 127 (1834), reinforced a jury's right to find law in criminal cases and recognized the judge's right to find law in civil cases. Throughout the first half of the nineteenth century, the Illinois Supreme Court reiterated this distinction in numerous cases. Other cases that revolved around the issue of the power of the bench, the bar, and the jury in the courtroom were: Grant v. Raymond, 31 U.S. 218 (1832); Lightburn v. Cooper, 1 Dana (31 Ky.) 273 (1833); Hogg v. State, 3 Blackf. 326 (Ind.) (1833); Swafford v. Dovenor, 1 Scam. (2 Ill.) 164 (1834); Commissioners of Highways of Warrick v. Judges of Orange County, 13 Wend. 432 (N.Y.) (1835); Gilmore v. Ballard, 1 Scam. (2 Ill.) 251 (1836); Heaton v. Kemper, 2 Scam. (3 Ill.) 367 (1840); Cook v. Scott, 1 Gilm. (6 Ill.) 33 (1844); Kimball v. Cook, 1 Gilm. (6 Ill.) 423 (1844); Greenup v. Stoker, 3 Gilm. (8 Ill.) 202 (1846); Baxter v. People, 3 Gilm. (8 Ill.) 368 (1846); Pate v. People, 3 Gilm. (8 Ill.) 644 (1846); Bowler v. Eldredge, 18 Conn. 1 (1846); Rigg v. Cook, 4 Gilm. (9 Ill.) 336 (1847); Anderson v. State, 2 Ga.

370 (1847); Williams v. Moseley, 2 Fla. 304 (1848); Dearing v. Lightfoot, 16 Ala. 28 (1849); Magee v. Carmack, 13 Ill. 289 (1851); Cowen v. People, 14 Ill. 348 (1853); Luman v. Kerr's Administrator, 4 Greene 159 (Iowa) (1853); Forshee v. Abrams, 2 Iowa 571 (1856); Edwards v. Evans, 3 East 452; Edmunds v. Mitchell, 2 Term R. 4; Seare v. Prentice, 8 East 348, and Robards v. Wolfe, 1 Dana 156.

65. Commonwealth v. Porter, 10 Metc. 263 (Mass.) (1845); Levy, *Law of the Commonwealth,* 290.

66. Chap. 152, Massachusetts Statutes (1855).

67. Commonwealth v. Anthes, 71 Mass. (5 Gray) 185 (1855).

68. Horwitz, *Transformation of American Law,* 28.

69. Lawrence M. Friedman, *A History of American Law* (New York: Simon and Schuster, 1973), 251–53; Order, September 24, 1852, Common Law Record A, 253, Ramsey v. Wolf, Woodford County Circuit Court, Woodford County Courthouse, Eureka, Ill.; Ruble v. McDonald, 7 Iowa 90 (1858); Manix v. Malony, 7 Iowa 81 (1858); Ruble v. McDonald, 7 Iowa 90 (1858); Hurst, *Growth of American Law*; James J. Gobert, *The Jury on Trial: A Political, Philosophical, and Psychological Examination of the Jury* (n.p., 1993), 101. See also Kimball v. Cook, 6 Ill. 423 (1844).

70. Ford, *History of Illinois,* 84–85.

71. Garraty and Carnes, *American National Biography,* 8:249–50; Palmer, *Bench and Bar of Illinois,* 1:32–33; Commonwealth v. Child, 10 Pick. (27 Mass.) 252 (1830).

72. Criminal Code (January 30, 1827), *Revised Code of Laws, of Illinois* (1827), 162–63; Schnier v. People, 23 Ill. 17 (1859); Fisher v. People, 23 Ill. 215 (1859); Elizabeth Dale, "Not Simply Black and White: Jury Power and the Law in Late Nineteenth-Century Chicago," *Social Science History* 25 (Spring 2001): 13; Ohio const. of 1803, art. VIII, § 6; Indiana const. of 1816, art. I, §§ 10, 13; Illinois const. of 1818, art. VIII, §§ 8, 23; Michigan const. of 1835, art. I, § 7.

73. Wickersham v. People is illustrative of this point. The opinion read: "In a civil case the jury are the judges of the facts only, but in a criminal one, they are not only the judges of the facts, but of the law, under the direction of the court." The court recognized a higher power of jurors in criminal cases. Wickersham v. People, 2 Ill. 127 (1834). Other appellate cases supporting the power of criminal juries to determine issues of law were: Pate v. People, 3 Gilm. (8 Ill.) 644 (1846); Cowen v. People, 14 Ill. 348 (1853); Fisher v. People, 23 Ill. 218 (1859); and Magee v. Carmack, 13 Ill. 289 (1851). See also Crocker v. Goodsell, 2 Ill. 107 (1833).

74. Abramson, *We, the Jury,* 37.

75. U.S. Census Office, Seventh Census of the United States (1850), La Salle County, Ill., 406; U.S. Census Office, Eighth Census of the United States (1860), La Salle County, Ill., 556.

76. Wesley B. Fisher married Clarissa Randull on March 18, 1858. Illinois Marriage Index, 1851–1900, Illinois State Archives, Springfield.

77. Fisher v. People, 23 Ill. 218 (1859).

78. Ibid.

79. Ibid.

80. Hall, *Oxford Companion to the Supreme Court,* 633; Ohio const. of 1803, art. VIII, § 6; Indiana const. of 1816, art. I, §§ 10, 13; Illinois const. of 1818, art. VIII, §§ 8, 23; Michigan const. of 1835, art. I, § 7.

81. An Act Relative to Criminal Jurisprudence (January 30, 1827), § 176, *Public and General Statute Laws of the State of Illinois* (1827), 163.

82. Fisher v. People, 23 Ill. 218 (1859).

83. Ibid.

84. Ibid.

85. Ibid.

86. Schnier v. People, an appeal of a murder case from Clinton County Circuit Court, was similar.

87. Fisher v. People.

88. Dissent in Fisher v. People.

89. Morton Horwitz, William E. Nelson, and Michael Grossberg have all, for example, focused on the ways in which court judgments cooperated with established patriarchal structures and ideas or performed a service for industrial and commercial interests at the expense of less privileged Americans (i.e., farmers, laborers, and women). Peter Karsten has argued that antebellum judges and juries mediated between established and somewhat rigid common-law principles and the "heart," which allowed them to be "more solicitous to suffering" than their counterparts of the previous century. Horwitz, *Transformation of American Law*; Nelson, *Americanization of the Common Law*; Karsten, *Heart versus Head,* 258–80.

BIBLIOGRAPHY

Abramson, Jeffrey. *We, the Jury: The Jury System and the Ideal of Democracy.* New York: Basic Books, 1994.

Adler, Jeffrey F. *Yankee Merchants and the Making of the Urban West: The Rise and Fall of Antebellum St. Louis.* New York: Cambridge University Press, 1991.

Alcorn, Richard S. "Leadership and Stability in Mid-Nineteenth-Century America: A Case Study of an Illinois Town." *Journal of American History* 61 (December 1974): 685–702.

Alschuler, Albert W., and Andrew G. Deiss. "A Brief History of the Criminal Jury in the United States." *University of Chicago Law Review* 61 (Summer 1994): 867–928.

Altschuler, Glenn C., and Stuart M. Blumin. "Limits of Political Engagement in Antebellum America: A New Look at the Golden Age of Participatory Democracy." *Journal of American History* 84 (December 1997): 855–85.

Amar, Vikram David. "Jury Service as Political Participation Akin to Voting." *Cornell Law Review* 80 (January 1995): 203–59.

The American Almanac and Repository of Useful Knowledge, for the Year 1853. Boston: Little, Brown, 1853.

Angle, Paul M. *"Here I Have Lived": A History of Lincoln's Springfield, 1821–1865.* New Brunswick, N.J.: Rutgers University Press, 1935.

Anthony, David. "Banking on Emotion: Financial Panic and the Logic of Male Submission in the Jacksonian Gothic." *American Literature* 76 (December 2004): 719–47.

Augst, Thomas. "The Business of Reading in Nineteenth-Century America: The New York Mercantile Library." *American Quarterly* 50 (June 1998): 267–305.

Ayers, Edward L. *Vengeance and Justice: Crime and Punishment in the Nineteenth-Century American South.* New York: Oxford University Press, 1984.

Baker, John G. "Indiana Judges: A Portrait of Judicial Evolution." In *The History of Indiana Law,* edited by David J. Bodenhamer and Randall T. Shepard, 303–24. Athens: Ohio University Press, 2006.

Balleisen, Edward J. *Navigating Failure: Bankruptcy and Commercial Society in Antebellum America.* Chapel Hill: University of North Carolina Press, 2001.

Bardaglio, Peter W. *Reconstructing the Household: Families, Sex, and the Law in the Nineteenth-Century South.* Chapel Hill: University of North Carolina Press, 1995.

Barnhart, John D. "Southern Contributions to the Social Order of the Old Northwest." *North Carolina Historical Review* 17 (July 1940): 237–48.

———. "The Southern Influence in the Formation of Illinois." *Journal of the Illinois State Historical Society* 32 (September 1939): 358–78.

———. "The Southern Influence in the Formation of Indiana." *Indiana Magazine of History* 33 (September 1937): 261–76.

———. "The Southern Influence in the Formation of Ohio." *Journal of Southern History* 3 (February 1937): 28–42.

Basch, Norma. "The Emerging Legal History of Women in the United States: Property, Divorce, and the Constitution." *Signs: Journal of Women in Culture and Society* 12 (Autumn 1986): 97–117.

———. "Invisible Women: The Legal Fiction of Marital Unity in Nineteenth-Century America." *Feminist Studies* 5 (Summer 1979): 346–66.

———. "Relief in the Premises: Divorce as a Woman's Remedy in New York and Indiana, 1815–1870." *Law and History Review* 8 (Spring 1990): 1–24.

Basler, Roy P., Jr., ed. *The Collected Works of Abraham Lincoln.* 10 vols. New Brunswick, N.J.: Rutgers University Press, 1953.

Beckert, Sven. *The Monied Metropolis: New York City and the Consolidation of the American Bourgeoisie, 1850–1896.* New York: Cambridge University Press, 2001.

Benedict, Michael Les. "Civil Liberty in Ohio." In *The History of Ohio Law,* 2 vols., edited by Michael Les Benedict and John F. Winkler, 2:675–747. Athens: Ohio University Press, 2004.

Benedict, Michael Les, and John F. Winkler, eds. *The History of Ohio Law.* 2 vols. Athens: University of Ohio Press, 2004.

Benner, Martha L., and Cullom Davis, eds. *The Law Practice of Abraham Lincoln: Complete Documentary Edition.* 2d ed. Springfield: Illinois Historic Preservation Agency, 2009. Available at www.lawpracticeofabrahamlincoln.org.

Benson, Lee. "Philadelphia Elites and Economic Development: Quasi-public Innovation during the First American Organizational Revolution, 1825–1861." *Working Papers from the Regional Economic History Research Center* 2 (Spring 1978): 25–54.

Bentham, Jeremy. *On the Art of Packing Juries.* London: Effingham Wilson, Royal Exchange, 1821.

Bigelow, Martha Mitchell. "Michigan: A State in the Vanguard." In *Heartland: Comparative Histories of the Midwestern States,* edited by James H. Madison, 32–58. Bloomington: Indiana University Press, 1988.

Blackmore, Josiah H., II. "Not from Zeus's Head Full-Blown: The Story of Civil Procedure in Ohio." In *The History of Ohio Law,* 2 vols., edited by Michael Les Benedict and John F. Winkler, 1:441–65. Athens: Ohio University Press, 2004.

Blackstone, William. *Commentaries on the Laws of England.* 4 vols., 1765–69. Reprint, Chicago: University of Chicago Press, 1979.

Blankmeyer, Helen van Cleave. *The Sangamon Country.* Springfield, Ill.: Board of Education, 1935. Reprint, Springfield, Ill.: Phillips Brothers, 1965.

Blinka, Daniel David. "Trial by Jury on the Eve of the Revolution: The Virginia Experience." *University of Missouri Kansas City Law Review* 71 (Spring 2003): 529–82.

Bloomfield, Maxwell. *American Lawyers in a Changing Society, 1776–1876*. Cambridge, Mass.: Harvard University Press, 1976.

———. "Law v. Politics: The Self-Image of the American Bar, 1830–1860." *American Journal of Legal History* 12 (October 1968): 306–23.

Blumin, Stuart M. *The Emergence of the Middle Class: Social Experiences in the American City, 1760–1900*. New York: Cambridge University Press, 1989.

Bodenhamer, David J. "Criminal Justice and Democratic Theory in Antebellum America: The Grand Jury Debate in Indiana." *Journal of the Early Republic* 5 (Winter 1985): 481–502.

———. "Criminal Sentencing in Antebellum America: A North-South Comparison." *Historical Social Research* (West Germany) 15 (1990): 77–94.

———. "The Democratic Impulse and Legal Change in the Age of Jackson: The Example of Criminal Juries in Antebellum Indiana." *Historian* 45 (February 1983): 206–19.

———. *The Pursuit of Justice: Crime and Law in Antebellum Indiana*. New York: Garland Publishing, 1986.

Bodenhamer, David J., and James W. Ely Jr., eds. *Ambivalent Legacy: A Legal History of the South*. Jackson: University Press of Mississippi, 1984.

Bodenhamer, David J., and Randall T. Shepard, eds. *History of Indiana Law*. Athens: Ohio University Press, 2006.

———. "The Narratives and Counternarratives of Indiana Legal History." In *The History of Indiana Law*, edited by David J. Bodenhamer and Randall T. Shepard, 3–34. Athens: Ohio University Press, 2006.

Booth, Douglas E. "Transportation, City Building, and Financial Crisis: Milwaukee, 1852–1868." *Journal of Urban History* 9 (May 1983): 335–63.

Botein, Stephen. *Early American Law and Society*. New York: Alfred A. Knopf, 1982.

Bowman, Shearer Davis. *Masters and Lords: Mid-nineteenth Century U.S. Planters and Prussian Junkers*. New York: Oxford University Press, 1993.

Bradley, Ann Walsh, and Joseph A. Ramney. "A Tradition of Independence: The Wisconsin Supreme Court's First 150 Years." *Wisconsin Magazine of History* 86 (Winter 2002–2003): 42–49.

Breen, T. H. *The Marketplace of Revolution: How Consumer Politics Shaped American Independence*. New York: Oxford University Press, 2004.

Bridges, Roger D. "Dark Faces on the Antebellum West Central Illinois Landscape." *Western Illinois Regional Studies* 6 (Fall 1983): 67–80.

Brown, Jeffrey P. "Chillicothe's Elite: Leadership in a Frontier Community." *Ohio History* 96 (Summer–Autumn 1987): 140–56.

Brown, R. Blake. "Challenges for Cause, Stand Asides, and Peremptory Challenges in the Nineteenth Century." *Osgoode Hall Law Journal* 38 (Fall 2000): 453–94.

Buck, Stephen J. "'To Hold the Prize': The County Seat War in Du Page County, 1867–1872." *Illinois Historical Journal* 85 (Winter 1992): 194–208.

Buenker, John D. "Wisconsin: As Maverick, Model, and Microcosm." In *Heartland: Comparative Histories of the Midwestern States,* edited by James H. Madison, 59–85. Bloomington: Indiana University Press, 1988.

Buley, R. Carlyle. *The Old Northwest: Pioneer Period, 1815–1840.* 2 vols. Bloomington: Indiana University Press, 1951.

Burchell, R. A. "Character and Function of a Pioneer Elite: Rural California, 1848–1880." *Journal of American Studies* 15 (December 1981): 377–89.

Burke, William Lewis, Jr. "A History of the Opening Statement from Barristers to Corporate Lawyers: A Case Study of South Carolina." *American Journal of Legal History* 37 (January 1993): 25–64.

Butcher, Edmund. *An Excursion from Sidmouth to Chester in the Summer of 1803.* 2 vols. 1805.

Campbell, Bruce Alexander. *The Sangamon Saga, 200 Years: An Illustrated Bicentennial History of Sangamon County.* Springfield, Ill.: Phillips Brothers, 1976.

Caton, John Dean. *Early Bench and Bar of Illinois.* Chicago: Chicago Legal News, 1893.

Cayton, Andrew R. L. "The Failure of Michael Baldwin: A Case Study in the Origins of Middle-Class Culture on the Trans-Appalachian Frontier." *Ohio History* 95 (Winter–Spring 1986): 34–48.

Cayton, Andrew R. L., and Peter S. Onuf. *The Midwest and the Nation: Rethinking the History of an American Region.* Bloomington: Indiana University Press, 1990.

Censor, Jane Turner. "Smiling through Her Tears: Antebellum Southern Women and Divorce." *American Journal of Legal History* 25 (January 1981): 24–47.

"The Changing Role of the Jury in the Nineteenth Century." *Yale Law Review* 74 (November 1964): 170–92.

Chase, Salmon P., ed. *The Statutes of Ohio and of the Northwest Territory Adopted or Enacted from 1788 to 1833 Inclusive.* Cincinnati, 1833.

Christensen, Lawrence O. "Missouri: The Heart of the Nation." In *Heartland: Comparative Histories of the Midwestern States,* edited by James H. Madison, 86–106. Bloomington: Indiana University Press, 1988.

Chroust, Anton-Hermann. *The Rise of the Legal Profession in America.* 2 vols. Norman: University of Oklahoma Press, 1965.

Clark, Thomas D. *Frontier America: The Story of the Westward Movement.* 2d ed. New York: Charles Scribner and Son, 1969.

———. *The Rampaging Frontier: Manners and Humors of Pioneer Days in the South and Middle West.* New York: Bobbs-Merrill, 1939.

Cole, Arthur Charles, ed. *The Constitutional Debates of 1847.* Springfield, Ill., 1919.

Colebert, Robert Edward, Jr. "John Williams: A Merchant Banker in Springfield, Illinois, 1824–1864." Ph.D. diss., University of Illinois, 1963.

Conzen, Kathleen Neils. *Immigrant Milwaukee, 1836–1860: Accommodation and Community in a Frontier City.* Cambridge, Mass.: Harvard University Press, 1976.

Cook, Charles. *The American Codification Movement: A Study of Antebellum Legal Reform.* Westport, Conn.: Greenwood Press, 1981.

Cresson, William P. *James Monroe.* Hamden, Conn.: Archon Books, 1971.

Crossley, Frederick B. *Courts and Lawyers of Illinois.* Chicago: American Historical Society, 1916.

Cunningham, Noble E., Jr. *In Pursuit of Reason: The Life of Thomas Jefferson.* Baton Rouge: Louisiana State University Press, 1987.

Cyr, Mark Allen. "'I Would Not Be a Master': Democracy and Political Culture of Mastering in Illinois, 1837–1858." Ph.D. diss., Washington University, 2003.

Dale, Elizabeth. "Not Simply Black and White: Jury Power and the Law in Late Nineteenth-Century Chicago." *Social Science History* 25 (Spring 2001): 7–27.

Davis, Cullom. "Abraham Lincoln, Esq.: The Symbiosis of Law and Politics." In *Abraham Lincoln and the Political Process: Papers from the Seventh Annual Lincoln Colloquium,* edited by George L. Painter and Linda Norbut Suits, 25–33. Springfield, Ill.: Lincoln Home National Historic Site, 1992.

———. "Illinois: Crossroads and Cross Section." In *Heartland: Comparative Histories of the Midwestern States,* edited by James H. Madison, 127–57. Bloomington: Indiana University Press, 1988.

———. "Law and Politics: The Two Careers of Abraham Lincoln." *Quarterly Journal of Ideology* 17 (June 1994): 61–75.

Davis, James E. *Frontier Illinois.* Bloomington: Indiana University Press, 1998.

Davis, Rodney O. "Lobbying and the Third House in the Early Illinois General Assembly." *Old Northwest* 14 (Winter 1988): 267–84.

DeBats, Donald. *Elites and Masses: Political Structure, Communication, and Behavior in Antebellum Georgia.* New York: Garland Press, 1990.

de Tocqueville, Alexis. *Democracy in America.* Translated by Harvey C. Mansfield and Delba Winthrop. Chicago: University of Chicago Press, 2000.

Dippel, Horst. "Representation, Representatives and the Right to Vote, or the Arduous Path Towards Democratic Representative Representation in the United States, 1776–1849." *Parliaments, Estates & Representation* (December 2003): 25–42.

Donald, David Herbert. *Lincoln.* New York: Simon and Schuster, 1995.

———. *"We Are Lincoln Men": Abraham Lincoln and His Friends.* New York: Simon and Schuster, 2003.

Doyle, Don Harrison. *The Social Order of a Frontier Community: Jacksonville, Illinois, 1825–70.* Urbana: University of Illinois Press, 1978.

Duff, John J. *A. Lincoln: Prairie Lawyer.* New York: Bramhall House, 1960.

Duis, Perry R. *Challenging Chicago: Coping with Everyday Life, 1837–1920.* Urbana: University of Illinois Press, 1998.

Edelberg, Jacqueline. "Justice Here? Alexis de Tocqueville and the Role of the Jury in the American Judicial Process and Republican Democracy." *Tocqueville Review* 17, no. 2 (1996): 67–97.

Edmunds, R. David. "Justice on a Changing Frontier: Deer Lick Creek, 1824–1825." *Indiana Magazine of History* 93 (March 1997): 48–52.

Edwards, Charles. *The Juryman's Guide throughout the State of New York, and Containing General Matter for the Lawyer and Law Officer.* New York: Halsted Law Bookseller, 1831.

Edwards, Laura F. "Law, Domestic Violence, and the Limits of Patriarchal Authority in the Antebellum South." *Journal of Southern History* 65 (November 1999): 733–70.

Elazar, Daniel J. *Cities of the Prairie: The Metropolitan Frontier and American Politics.* New York, 1970.

Ely, James W., Jr., and David J. Bodenhamer. "Regionalism and American Legal History: The Southern Experience." *Vanderbilt Law Review* 39 (April 1986): 539–67.

Escott, Paul D. *Many Excellent People: Power and Privilege in North Carolina, 1850–1900.* Chapel Hill: University of North Carolina Press, 1985.

Etcheson, Nicole. *The Emerging Midwest: Upland Southerners and the Political Culture of the Old Northwest, 1787–1861.* Bloomington: Indiana University Press, 1996.

Fahey, David M. *Temperance and Racism: John Bull, Johnny Reb, and the Good Templars.* Lexington: University Press of Kentucky, 1996.

Faragher, John Mack. *Sugar Creek: Life on the Illinois Prairie.* New Haven, Conn.: Yale University Press, 1986.

Faux, William. *Memorable Days in America: Being a Journal of a Tour to the United States.* 1823. Reprint, New York: AMS Press, 1969.

Fenstermaker, J. Van. "A Description of Sangamon County, Illinois, in 1830." *Agricultural History* 39 (July 1965): 136–40.

Few, J. Kendall. *Trial by Jury.* N.p.: American Jury Trial Foundation, 1993.

Finkelman, Paul. "Exploring Southern Legal History." *North Carolina Law Review* 64 (November 1985): 77–116.

"The First Integrated Jury Impaneled in the United States, May, 1867." *Negro History Bulletin* 33 (October 1970): 134.

Fishman, Joel. "An Early Pennsylvania Legal Periodical: *The Pennsylvania Law Journal*, 1842–1848." *American Journal of Legal History* 45 (January 2001): 22–50.

Folsom, Burton W., II. "The Politics of Elites: Prominence and Party in Davidson County, Tennessee, 1835–1861." *Journal of Southern History* 39 (August 1973): 359–78.

Forbes, Ella. "'By My Own Right Arm': Redemptive Violence and the 1851 Christiana, Pennsylvania, Resistance." *Journal of Negro History* 83 (Summer 1998): 159–67.

Ford, Lacy K., Jr. "Frontier Democracy: The Turner Thesis Revisited." *Journal of the Early Republic* 13 (Summer 1993): 144–63.
Ford, Thomas. *A History of Illinois from Its Commencement as a State in 1818 to 1847*. Chicago: S. C. Griggs, 1854. Reprint, Ann Arbor, Mich.: University Microfilms, 1968.
Forsyth, William. *History of Trial by Jury*. London: John W. Parker, 1852. Reprint, New York: James Cockcroft, 1875.
Fowler, H. *Report of the Debates and Proceedings of the Convention for the Revision of the Constitution of the State of Indiana*. Indianapolis: 1850 Constitutional Convention of the State of Indiana, 1850.
Fox, Dixon Ryan, ed. *Sources of Culture in the Middle West: Backgrounds versus Frontier*. New York: D. Appleton–Century, 1934. Reprint, New York: Russell and Russell, 1964.
Frank, John. *Lincoln as a Lawyer*. Urbana: University of Illinois Press, 1961.
Freeman, Norman L. *The Illinois Digest: Being a Full and Complete Digest and Compilation of All the Decisions of the Supreme Court of Illinois*. Chicago: S. C. Griggs, 1856.
Freyer, Tony A. *Producers versus Capitalists: Constitutional Conflict in Antebellum America*. Charlottesville: University Press of Virginia, 1994.
Friedman, Lawrence M. *Crime and Punishment in American History*. New York: Basic Books, 1993.
———. *A History of American Law*. New York: Simon and Schuster, 1973.
Garraty, John A., and Mark C. Carnes, eds. *American National Biography*. 24 vols. New York: Oxford University Press, 1999.
Gawalt, Gerard. *The Promise of Power: The Emergence of the Legal Profession in Massachusetts, 1760–1840*. Westport, Conn.: Greenwood Press, 1979.
Gobert, James J. *The Jury on Trial: A Political, Philosphical, and Psychological Examination of the Jury*. N.p., 1993.
———. *Justice, Democracy, and the Jury*. Brookfield, UK: Alderson, 1997.
Gold, David M. "Reforming the Civil Jury in the Nineteenth-Century West: Jury Size and Unanimity of Verdicts." *Western Legal History* 15 (Winter/Spring 2002): 137–64.
Goloboy, Jennifer L., and Christopher Clark. "The Early American Middle Class." *Journal of the Early Republic* 25 (Winter 2005): 537–45.
Gordon, James W. *Lawyers in Politics: Mid-nineteenth Century Kentucky as a Case Study*. New York: Garland Publishing, 1990.
Gordon, Thomas F. *A Digest of the Laws of the United States, Including an Abstract of the Judicial Decision Relating to the Constitutional and Statutory Law*. Philadelphia: Thomas F. Gordon, 1837.
Grinnell, Josiah B. *Sketches of the West, or the Home of the Badgers*, 2d ed. Milwaukee, 1847.
Gross, Eugene L. *A Digest of the Criminal Laws of Illinois*. Springfield: Illinois Journal, 1868.

Gross, Norman, ed. *America's Lawyer-Presidents: From Law Office to Oval Office.* Evanston, Ill.: Northwestern University Press, 2004.

Grossberg, Michael. *Governing the Hearth: Law and the Family in Nineteenth-Century America.* Chapel Hill: University of North Carolina Press, 1985.

Grossberg, Michael, and Amy Elson. "Family Law in Indiana: A Domestic Relations Crossroads." In *The History of Indiana Law,* edited by David J. Bodenhamer and Randall T. Shepard, 60–70. Athens: Ohio University Press, 2006.

Hall, John A. "That Onerous Task: Jury Service in South Carolina during the Early 1790s." *South Carolina Historical Magazine* 87 (January 1986): 1–13.

Hall, Kermit L., ed. *The Oxford Companion to the Supreme Court of the United States.* New York: Oxford University Press, 1992.

———. "Social Backgrounds and Judicial Recruitment: A Nineteenth Century Perspective on the Lower Federal Judiciary." *Western Political Quarterly* 29 (June 1976): 243–57.

Halttunen, Karen. *Confidence Men and Painted Women: A Study of Middle-Class Culture in America, 1830–1870.* New Haven, Conn.: Yale University Press, 1982.

Harris, Deirdre A. "Jury Nullification in Historical Perspective: Massachusetts as a Case Study." *Suffolk University Law Review* 12 (1978): 968–1011.

Harris, Michael H. "Books for Sale on the Illinois Frontier: Dekalb County, 1855–1865." *American Book Collector* 21 (January 1971): 15–17.

———. "The Frontier Lawyer's Library: Southern Indiana, 1800–1850 as a Test Case." *American Journal of Legal History* 16 (July 1972): 239–51.

Harstad, Peter T. "Indiana and the Art of Adjustment." In *Heartland: Comparative Histories of the Midwestern States,* edited by James H. Madison, 158–86. Bloomington: Indiana University Press, 1988.

Havighorst, Walter. *The Heartland: Ohio, Indiana, Illinois.* New York: Harper and Row, 1956.

Hemphill, C. Dallett. "Middle Class Rising in Revolutionary America: The Evidence from Manners." *Journal of Social History* 30 (Winter 1996): 317–44.

Henretta, James A., and James D. Rice. "Law as Litigation: An Agenda for Research." *William and Mary Quarterly* 50 (January 1993): 176–80.

Herndon, William H., and Jesse W. Weik. *Herndon's Lincoln: The History and Personal Recollections of Abraham Lincoln.* 3 vols. Chicago: Belford, Clark, 1889.

Higley, Stephen Richard. *Privilege, Power, and Place: The Geography of the American Upper Class.* Lanham, Md.: Rowman and Littlefield, 1995.

History of Sangamon County Illinois. Chicago: Inter-state Publishing, 1881.

Hoeflich, Michael H. "John Livingston on the Business of Law in Nineteenth-Century America." *American Journal of Legal History* 44 (October 2000): 347–68.

Hoffer, Peter Charles. "Custom as Law: A Comment on J. R. Pole's 'Reflections.'" *William and Mary Quarterly* 50 (January 1993): 160–67.

Horwitz, Morton. *The Transformation of American Law, 1780–1860.* New York: Oxford University Press, 1992.
Howard, Robert P. *Illinois: A History of the Prairie State.* Grand Rapids, Mich.: William B. Eardman's Publishing, 1972.
Howe, Mark DeWolf. "Juries as Judges of Criminal Law." *Harvard Law Review* 52 (February 1939): 582–616.
Howe, Samuel. *The Practice in Civil Actions and Proceeding at Law in Massachusetts.* Boston: Hilliard, Gray, 1834.
Hubbart, Henry Clyde. *The Older Middle West, 1840–1880: Its Social, Economic, and Political Life and Sectional Tendencies before, during, and after the Civil War.* New York: D. Appleton–Century, 1936. Reprint, New York: Russell and Russell, 1963.
Hurst, James Willard. *The Growth of American Law: The Law Makers.* Boston: Little, Brown, 1950.
———. *Law and the Conditions of Freedom in the Nineteenth Century United States.* Chicago: Northwestern University Press. 1956. Reprint, Madison: University of Wisconsin Press, 1967.
———. *Law and Social Order in the United States.* Ithaca, N.Y.: Cornell University Press, 1977.
Ireland, Robert M. "The Nineteenth-Century Criminal Jury: Kentucky in the Context of the American Experience." *Kentucky Review* 4 (Spring 1983): 52–70.
Isaac, Rhys. *The Transformation of Virginia, 1740–1790.* Chapel Hill: University of North Carolina Press, 1982.
Jaher, Frederick Cople, ed. *The Rich, the Well Born, and the Powerful: Elites and Upper Classes in History.* Urbana: University of Illinois Press, 1973.
———. *The Urban Establishment: Upper Strata in Boston, New York, Charleston, Chicago, and Los Angeles.* Urbana: University of Illinois Press, 1982.
Jentz, John B. "Industrialization and Class Formation in Antebellum America: A Review of Recent Case Studies." *American Studies* (West Germany) 30 (1985): 303–35.
Johannsen, Robert W. *Stephen A. Douglas.* Urbana: University of Illinois Press, 1973.
Johnson, Allen, ed. *Dictionary of American Biography.* New York: Charles Scribner's and Sons, 1964.
Johnson, Charles Beneulyn. *Illinois in the Fifties or a Decade of Development: 1851–1860.* Champaign, Ill.: Flanigan-Pearson, 1918.
Johnson, Linck C. "'Liberty Is Never Cheap': Emerson, 'The Fugitive Slave Law,' and the Antislavery Lecture Series at the Broadway Tabernacle." *New England Quarterly* 76 (December 2003): 550–92.
Jones, Joseph S. *The People's Lawyer: A Comedy in Two Acts.* Boston: W. V. Spencer, 1856.

Karsten, Peter. *Heart versus Head: Judge-Made Law in Nineteenth-Century America.* Chapel Hill: University of North Carolina Press, 1997.

Katz, Stanley N., ed. *A Brief Narrative of the Case and Trial of John Peter Zenger by James Alexander.* Cambridge, Mass.: Harvard University Press, 1963.

Kemp, Terence P. "Evidence in Ohio: A Two-Hundred-Year Work in Progress." In *The History of Ohio Law,* 2 vols., edited by Michael Les Benedict and John F. Winkler, 1:466–98. Athens: University of Ohio Press, 2004.

Kennedy, Joseph C. G., comp. *Population of the United States in 1860.* Washington, D.C.: Government Printing Office, 1864.

King, Andrew J. "Constructing Gender: Sexual Slander in Nineteenth-Century America." *Law and History Review* 13 (Spring 1995): 63–110.

King, Nancy. "Juror Delinquincy in Criminal Trials in America, 1796–1996." *Michigan Law Review* 94 (August 1996): 2673–751.

King, P. J. R. "'Illiterate Plebians, Easily Misled': Jury Composition, Experience, and Behavior in Essex, 1735–1815." In *Twelve Good Men and True: The Criminal Trial Jury in England, 1200–1800,* edited by J. S. Cockburn and Thomas A. Green, 254–304. Princeton, N.J.: Princeton University Press, 1988.

King, Willard L. *Lincoln's Manager: David Davis.* Cambridge, Mass.: Harvard University Press, 1960.

Kleppner, Paul. *The Cross of Culture: A Social Analysis of Midwestern Politics, 1850–1900.* New York: Free Press, 1970.

Klingaman, David C. "Individual Wealth in Ohio in 1860." In *Essays in Nineteenth Century Economic History: The Old Northwest,* edited by David C. Klingaman and Richard K. Vedder, 177–207. Athens: Ohio University Press, 1975.

Klingaman, David C., and Richard K. Vedder, eds. *Essays in Nineteenth-Century Economic History: The Old Northwest.* Athens: Ohio University Press, 1975.

———, eds. *Essays on the Economy of the Old Northwest.* Athens: Ohio University Press, 1987.

Kohl, Lawrence Frederick. "The Concept of Social Control and the History of Jacksonian America." *Journal of the Early Republic* 5 (Spring 1985): 21–34.

Krause, Susan. *From Log Cabins to Temples of Justice: Courthouses in Lincoln's Illinois.* Springfield: Illinois Historic Preservation Agency, 2000.

———. *Judging Lincoln: The Bench in Lincoln's Illinois.* Springfield: Illinois Historic Preservation Agency, 2002.

Lehman, Godfrey D. *We, the Jury: The Impact of Jurors on Our Basic Freedoms.* Amherst, N.Y.: Prometheus Books, 1997.

Lehuu, Isabelle. *Carnival on the Page: Popular Print Media in Antebellum America.* Chapel Hill: University of North Carolina Press, 2000.

Lerner, Gerda. *The Creation of Patriarchy.* New York: Oxford University Press, 1986.

Lerner, Renee Lettow. "The Transformation of the American Civil Trial: The Silent Judge." *William and Mary Law Review* 42 (October 2000): 195–264.

Lesser, Maximus A. *The Historical Development of the Jury System.* Rochester, N.Y.: Lawyers' Co-operative Publishing, 1894. Reprint, Buffalo, N.Y.: W. S. Hein, 1992.

Lettow, Renee B. "New Trial for Verdict against Law: Judge-Jury Relations in Early Nineteenth Century America." *Notre Dame Law Review* 71, no. 3 (1996): 505–54.

Levy, Leonard W. *The Law of the Commonwealth and Chief Justice Shaw.* New York: Oxford University Press, 1957.

———. *The Palladium of Justice: Origins of Trial by Jury.* Chicago: Ivan R. Dee, 1999.

Linder, Usher F. *Reminiscences of the Early Bench and Bar of Illinois.* Chicago: Chicago Legal News, 1870.

Looney, Rebecca. "Migration and Separation: Divorce in Kane County, 1837–1869." *Illinois Historical Journal* 89 (Summer 1996): 70–84.

Madison, James H., ed. *Heartland: Comparative Histories of the Midwestern States.* Bloomington: Indiana University Press, 1988.

Mahoney, Timothy R. *Provincial Lives: Middle-Class Experience in the Antebellum Midwest.* Cambridge: Cambridge University Press, 1999.

———. *River Towns in the Great West: The Structure of Provincial Urbanization in the American Midwest, 1820–1870.* New York: Cambridge University Press, 1990.

Maley, Robert J., and John R. Maley. "More Than Arbiters of Cases and Controversies: The Growing Impact of the Judiciary on Indiana's Legal Culture." In *The History of Indiana Law,* edited by David J. Bodenhamer and Randall T. Shepard, 278–302. Athens: Ohio University Press, 2006.

Mann, Bruce H. "The Evolutionary Revolution in American Law: A Comment on J. R. Pole's 'Reflections.'" *William and Mary Quarterly* 50 (January 1993): 168–75.

Marshall, Lynn L., and Seymour Prescher. "American Historians and Tocqueville's Democracy." *Journal of American History* 55 (December 1968): 512–32.

Matijasic, Thomas. "The Reaction of the Ohio General Assembly to the Fugitive Slave Law of 1850." *Northwest Ohio Quarterly* 55 (Spring 1983): 40–60.

McCormack, Thomas J., ed. *Memoirs of Gustave Koerner, 1809–1896.* 2 vols. Cedar Rapids, Iowa: Torch Press, 1909.

McCoy, Collin. "Democracy in Print: The Literature of Persuasion in Jacksonian America, 1815–1840." Ph.D. diss., University of Illinois, 2001.

McCullough, David G. *John Adams.* New York: Simon and Schuster, 2001.

McDermott, Stacy Pratt. "'Black Bill' and the Privileges of Whiteness in Antebellum Illinois." *Journal of Illinois History* 12 (Spring 2009): 2–26.

———. "Dissolving the Bonds of Matrimony: Women and Divorce in Sangamon County, Illinois, 1835–1860." In *In Tender Consideration: Women, Families and the Law in Abraham Lincoln's Illinois,* edited by Daniel W. Stowell, 71–103. Urbana: University of Illinois Press, 2002.

———. "The Law in an Illinois Corner: The Impact of the Law on an Antebellum Family." In *In Tender Consideration: Women, Families and the Law in Abraham Lincoln's Illinois,* edited by Daniel W. Stowell, 161–81. Urbana: University of Illinois Press, 2002.

McLaren, John, Hamar Foster, and Chet Orloff, eds. *Law for the Elephant, Law for the Beaver: Essays in the Legal History of the North American West.* Pasadena, Calif.: Ninth Judicial Circuit Historical Society, 1992.

McNulty, John W. "Sidney Breese, the Illinois Circuit Judge, 1835–1841." *Journal of the Illinois State Historical Society* 62 (Summer 1969): 170–86.

Melville, Herman. "Bartleby the Scrivener: A Story of Wall Street." 1853. Reprint, New York: Simon and Schuster, 1997.

Meyer, Douglas K. *Making the Heartland Quilt: A Geographical History of Settlement and Migration in Early-Nineteenth-Century Illinois.* Carbondale: Southern Illinois University Press, 2000.

Middleton, Stephen. *The Black Laws in the Old Northwest: A Documentary History.* Westport, Conn.: Greenwood Press, 1993.

Miers, Earl Shenck, ed. *Lincoln Day by Day: A Chronology, 1809–1865.* 3 vols. Washington, D.C.: Lincoln Sesquicentennial Commission, 1960.

Miller, Perry. *The Life of the Mind in America: From Revolution to Civil War.* New York: Harcourt, Brace and World, 1965.

Mohl, Raymond A. "Poverty, Pauperism, and Social Order in the Preindustrial American City, 1740–1840." *Social Science Quarterly* 52 (March 1972): 934–48.

Moore, Lloyd E. *The Jury: Tool of Kings, Palladium of Liberty.* Cincinnati: W. H. Anderson, 1973.

Murphy, Lucy Eldersveld, and Wendy Hamand Venet, eds. *Midwestern Women: Work, Community, and Leadership at the Crossroads.* Bloomington: Indiana University Press, 1997.

Murray, John J., ed. *The Heritage of the Middle West.* Norman: University of Oklahoma Press, 1958.

Nagel, Paul C. *John Quincy Adams: A Public Life, a Private Life.* New York: Alfred A. Knopf, 1997.

Nation, Richard F. "Violence and the Rights of African Americans in Civil War–Era Indiana: The Case of James Hays." *Indiana Magazine of History* 100 (September 2004): 215–30.

Nelson, William E. *The Americanization of the Common Law: The Impact of Legal Change on Massachusetts Society, 1760–1830.* Athens: University of Georgia Press, 1975.

New York Committee on Practice and Pleading. *Fourth Report of the Commissioners on Practice and Pleading, Code of Criminal Procedure.* Albany, 1849.

Novak, William J. *The People's Welfare: Law and Regulation in Nineteenth-Century America.* Chapel Hill: University of North Carolina Press, 1996.

O'Grada, Cormac, and Eugene N. White. "The Panics of 1854 and 1857: A View from the Emigrant Industrial Savings Bank." *Journal of Economic History* 63 (March 2003): 213–40.
Osborn, Elizabeth R. "Indiana Courts and Lawyers, 1816–2004." In *The History of Indiana Law,* edited by David J. Bodenhamer and Randall T. Shepard, 257–77. Athens: Ohio University Press, 2006.
Palmer, John M., ed. *The Bench and Bar of Illinois: Historical and Reminiscent.* 2 vols. Chicago: Lewis Publishing, 1899.
Paludan, Phillip S. "The American Civil War Considered as a Crisis in Law and Order." *American Historical Review* 77 (October 1972): 1013–34.
———. "Lincoln, the Rule of Law, and the American Revolution." *Journal of the Illinois State Historical Society* 70 (February 1977): 10–17.
Parker, William N. "From Northwest to Midwest: Social Bases of a Regional History." In *Essays in Nineteenth Century Economic History: The Old Northwest,* edited by David C. Klingaman and Richard K. Vedder, 3–34. Athens: Ohio University Press, 1975.
Pease, Jane H., and William H. Pease. *The Fugitive Slave Law and Anthony Burns: A Problem in Law Enforcement.* Philadelphia: Lippincott, 1975.
———. *Ladies, Women, and Wenches: Choice and Constraint in Antebellum Charleston and Boston.* Chapel Hill: University of North Carolina Press, 1990.
Pease, Theodore Calvin. *The Centennial History of Illinois,* vol. 2, *The Frontier State: 1818–1848.* Springfield: Illinois Centennial Commission, 1918. Reprint, Urbana: University of Illinois Press, 1987.
———. *Illinois Election Returns, 1818–1848.* Springfield: Illinois State Historical Library, 1923.
———. "The Ordinance of 1787." *Mississippi Valley Historical Review* 25 (September 1938): 167–80.
Pegram, Thomas R. *Battling Demon Rum: The Struggle for a Dry America, 1800–1933.* Chicago: Ivan R. Dee, 1998.
Perry, James R. *The Formation of Society on Virginia's Eastern Shore, 1615–1655.* Chapel Hill: University of North Carolina Press, 1990.
Pessen, Edward. "The Egalitarian Myth and the American Social Reality: Wealth, Mobility, and Equality in the 'Era of the Common Man.'" *American Historical Review* 76 (October 1971): 989–1034.
———. "Philip Hone's Set: The Social World of the New York Elite in the 'Age of Egalitarianism.'" *New-York Historical Society Quarterly* 56 (July 1972): 285–308.
———. *Riches, Class, and Power before the Civil War.* Lexington, Mass.: D. C. Heath, 1973.
———. "The Wealthiest New Yorkers of the Jacksonian Era: A New List." *New-York Historical Society Quarterly* 54 (April 1970): 145–72.
Pole, J. R. "Refections on American Law and the Revolution." *William and Mary Quarterly* 50 (January 1993): 123–59.

Power, John Carroll. *History of the Early Settlers of Sangamon County, Illinois.* Springfield, Ill.: H. W. Rokker, 1970. Reprint, Springfield, Ill.: Phillips Brothers, 1970.

Pratt, Harry E. "'Judge' Abraham Lincoln." *Journal of the Illinois State Historical Society* 48 (Spring 1955): 33.

Priebe, Paula J. "Central and Western New York and the Fugitive Slave Law." *Afro-Americans in New York Life and History* 16 (January 1992): 19–29.

Proffatt, John A. *A Treatise on Trial by Jury, Including Questions of Law and Fact: With an Introductory Chapter on the Origin and History of Jury Trial.* San Francisco: Sumner Whitney, 1877. Reprint, Littleton, Colo.: Fred B. Rothman, 1986.

Purvis, Thomas L. "The Making of a Myth: Abraham Lincoln's Family Background in the Perspective of Jacksonian Politics." *Journal of the Illinois State Historical Society* 75 (Summer 1982): 148–60.

Reid, John Phillip. *Controlling the Law: Legal Politics in Early National New Hampshire.* DeKalb: Northern Illinois University Press, 2004.

———. *Law for the Elephant: Property and Social Behavior on the Overland Trail.* San Marino, Calif.: Huntington Library, 1980. Reprint, San Marino, Calif.: Huntington Library, 1997.

Remini, Robert. *Andrew Jackson and the Course of American Empire.* New York: Harper and Row, 1977.

Rich, Robert. "'A Wilderness of Whigs': The Wealthy Men of Boston." *Journal of Social History* (Great Britain) 4 (Spring 1971): 263–76.

Roeber, A. G. *Faithful Magistrates and Republican Lawyers: Creatures of Virginia Legal Culture, 1680–1810.* Chapel Hill: University of North Carolina Press, 1981.

Rogers, Alan. "Murders and Madness: Law in Medicine in Nineteenth-Century Massachusetts." *Proceedings of the Massachusetts Historical Society* 106 (1994): 53–81.

Rohrer, James R. "The Origins of the Temperance Movement: A Reinterpretation." *Journal of American Studies* 24 (August 1990): 228–35.

Roper, Robert T. "Jury Size: Impact on Verdict's Correctness." *American Politics Quarterly* 7 (October 1979): 438–52.

Rosentreter, Roger L. "Michigan's Eighty-three Counties: Tuscola County." *Michigan History* 75 (May–June 1991): 8–10.

———. "Michigan's Eighty-three Counties: Wexford County." *Michigan History* 76 (July–August 1992): 9–12.

Rousseau, Peter L. "Jacksonian Monetary Policy, Specie Flows, and the Panic of 1837." *Journal of Economic History* 62 (June 2002): 457–88.

Rugh, Susan Sessions. "Civilizing the Countryside: Class, Gender, and Crime in Nineteenth-Century Rural Illinois." *Agricultural History* 76 (Winter 2002): 58–81.

Ryan, Mary P. "Civil Society as Democratic Practice: North American Cities during the Nineteenth Century." *Journal of Interdisciplinary History* 29 (Spring 1999): 559–84.

Sangamon County Illinois 1850 Census and Mortality Schedule. Springfield, Ill.: Sangamon County Genealogicial Society, 1976.

Scheiber, Harry N. "Alfred Kelley and the Ohio Business Elite, 1822–1859." *Ohio History* 87 (Autumn 1978): 365–92.

Schellenberg, James A. *Conflict between Communities: American County Seat Wars.* New York: Paragon House, 1987.

Schnell, Christopher A. *Stovepipe Hat and Quill Pen: The Artifacts of Abraham Lincoln's Law Practice.* Springfield: Illinois Historic Preservation Agency, 2002.

Scott, Franklin W. *Newspapers and Periodicals of Illinois, 1814–1879.* Springfield: Illinois Historical Collections, 1910.

Scott, John M. *Supreme Court of Illinois, 1818: Its First Judges and Lawyers.* Bloomington, Ill., 1896.

Selby, Paul. *History of Sangamon County Illinois.* 2 vols. Chicago: Munsell Publishing, 1912.

Sellers, Charles. *The Market Revolution: Jacksonian America, 1815–1846.* New York: Oxford University Press, 1991.

Sewell, Richard H. *John P. Hale and the Politics of Abolition.* Cambridge, Mass.: Harvard University Press, 1965.

Shankman, Arnold. "Partisan Conflicts, 1839–1841, and the Illinois Constitution." *Journal of the Illinois State Historical Society* 63 (Winter 1970): 336–67.

Sharp, Allen. "The U.S. Supreme Court on Circuit in Indiana, 1837–1891." In *The History of Indiana Law,* edited by David J. Bodenhamer and Randall T. Shepard, 342–62. Athens: Ohio University Press, 2006.

Shortridge, James R. *The Middle West: Its Meaning in American Culture.* Lawrence: University of Kansas Press, 1989.

Shreve, Thomas H. *Drayton: A Story of an American Life.* New York: Harper, 1851.

Sievens, Mary Beth. "Divorce, Patriarchal Authority, and Masculinity: A Case from Early National Vermont." *Journal of Social History* 37 (Spring 2004): 651–62.

Silver, David M. *Lincoln's Supreme Court.* Urbana: University of Illinois Press, 1956. Reprint, Urbana: University of Illinois Press, 1998.

Simeone, James. *Democracy and Slavery in Frontier Illinois: The Bottomland Republic.* DeKalb: Northern Illinois University Press, 2000.

Solimine, Michael E., and Richard B. Saphire. "The Selection of Judges in Ohio." In *The History of Ohio Law,* 2 vols., edited by Michael Les Benedict and John F. Winkler, 1:211–37. Athens: Ohio University Press, 2004.

Soltow, Lee C. *Men and Wealth in the United States, 1850–1870.* New Haven, Conn.: Yale University Press, 1975.

———. *Patterns of Wealthholding in Wisconsin since 1850.* Madison: University of Wisconsin Press, 1971.

———. "Tocqueville's View of the Northwest in 1835: Ohio a Generation after Settlement." In *Essays on the Economy of the Old Northwest,* edited by David C. Klingaman and Richard K. Vedder, 131–55. Athens: Ohio University Press, 1987.

Spooner, Lysander. *An Essay on the Trial by Jury.* Boston: John P. Jewett, 1852. Reprint, New York: Da Capo Press, 1971.

Steiner, Mark E. *An Honest Calling: The Law Practice of Abraham Lincoln.* DeKalb: Northern Illinois University Press, 2006.

———. "The Lawyer as Peacemaker: Law and Community in Abraham Lincoln's Slander Cases." *Journal of the Abraham Lincoln Association* 16 (Summer 1995): 1–22.

———. "Lawyers and Legal Change in Antebellum America: Learning from Lincoln." *University of Detroit Mercy Law Review* 74 (Spring 1997): 427–64.

Stevens, Edward W., Jr. "Structural and Ideological Dimensions of Literacy and Education in the Old Northwest." In *Essays on the Economy of the Old Northwest,* edited by David C. Klingaman and Richard K. Vedder, 157–85. Athens: Ohio University Press, 1987.

Stevens, Robert. *Law School Education in America from the 1850s to the 1980s.* Chapel Hill: University of North Carolina Press, 1983.

Stimson, Shannon C. *The American Revolution in the Law: Anglo-American Jurisprudence before John Marshall.* Princeton, N.J.: Princeton University Press, 1990.

Stowe, Harriet Beecher. *Uncle Tom's Cabin, or Life among the Lowly.* Boston: J. P. Jewett, 1852.

Stowell, Daniel W., ed. *In Tender Consideration: Women, Families, and the Law in Abraham Lincoln's Illinois.* Urbana: University of Illinois Press, 2002.

——— et al., eds. *The Papers of Abraham Lincoln: Legal Documents and Cases.* 4 vols. Charlottesville: University of Virginia Press, 2008.

———. "Webs of Credit: S. C. Davis & Company and the Collection of Interstate Debts." Paper presented at the Missouri Valley History Conference, Omaha, Neb., March 2002.

Sullivan, James. *The History of Land Titles in Massachusetts.* Boston: I. Thomas and E. T. Andrews, 1801.

Tanner, Terence A. "Newspapers and Printing Presses in Early Illinois." *American Periodicals* 3 (1993): 100–113.

Taylor, William Banks. "Southern Yankees: Wealth, High Society, and Political Economy in the Late Antebellum Natchez Region." *Journal of Mississippi History* 59 (Summer 1997): 79–121.

Terzian, Barbara A. "Ohio's Constitutional Conventions and Constitutions." In *The History of Ohio Law,* 2 vols., edited by Michael Les Benedict and John F. Winkler, 1:40–87. Athens: Ohio University Press, 2006.

Thernstrom, Stephen. *Poverty and Progress: Social Mobility in a Nineteenth-Century City.* Cambridge, Mass.: Harvard University Press, 1964. Reprint, New York: Atheneum, 1969.

Thomas, Benjamin P. *Lincoln's New Salem.* New Salem, Ill.: Lincoln's New Salem Enterprises, 1973. Reprint, Carbondale: Southern Illinois University Press, 1987.

Thomas, William G. *Lawyering for the Railroad: Business, Law, and Power in the American South.* Baton Rouge: Louisiana State University Press, 1999.

Thurman, Suzanne. "Cultural Politics on the Indiana Frontier: The American Home Missionary Society and Temperance Reform." *Indiana Magazine of History* 94 (December 1998): 285–302.

Tomlins, Christopher. *Law, Labor, and Ideology in the Early American Republic.* Cambridge: Cambridge University Press, 1993.

Tucker, St. George, ed. *Blackstone's Commentaries, with Notes and References to the Constitution and Laws of the Federal Government of the United States and of the Commonwealth of Virginia.* 5 vols. Philadelphia: W. Y. Birch and A. Small, 1803. Reprint, Chicago: University of Chicago Press, 1979.

Turner, Frederick Jackson. *The United States, 1830–1850: The Nation and Its Sections.* New York: Henry Holt, 1935. Reprint, Gloucester, Mass.: Peter Smith, 1958.

Tyrell, Ian R. *Sobering Up: From Temperance to Prohibition in Antebellum America, 1800–1860.* Westport, Conn.: Greenwood Press, 1979.

Upton, Dell. *Holy Things and Profane: Anglican Parish Churches in Colonial Virginia.* New Haven, Conn.: Yale University Press, 1986.

United States Biographical Dictionary: Illinois Dictionary. Chicago: American Biographical Dictionary, 1876.

U.S. Census Office. *Historical Statistics of the United States, Colonial Times to 1970.* Washington, D.C.: U.S. Bureau of the Census, 1975.

VanDyke, Jon M. "The Jury as a Political Institution." *Center Magazine* 3 (March 1970): 17–26.

Vedder, Richard K., and Lowell E. Gallaway. "Migration and the Old Northwest." In *Essays in Nineteenth Century Economic History: The Old Northwest,* edited by David C. Klingaman and Richard K. Vedder, 159–76. Athens: Ohio University Press, 1975.

Vidmar, Neil, ed. *World Jury Systems.* New York: Oxford University Press, 2000.

von Moschzisker, Robert. *Trial by Jury: A Brief Review of Its Origin, Development and Merits and Practical Discussions on Actual Conduct of Jury Trials, Together with a Consideration of Constitutional Provisions and Other Cognate Subjects of Importance.* Philadelphia: George T. Bisel, 1922.

Wade, Richard. *The Urban Frontier: The Rise of Western Cities, 1790–1830.* Cambridge, Mass.: Harvard University Press, 1959. Reprint, Cambridge, Mass.: Harvard University Press, 1967.

Waldrep, Christopher. "Egalitarianism in the Oligarchy: The Grand Jury and Criminal Justice in Livingston County, 1799–1808." *Filson Club Historical Quarterly* 55 (July 1981): 253–67.

Wallace, Christopher Elliott. "The Opportunity to Grow: Springfield, Illinois, during the 1850s." Ph.D. diss., Purdue University, 1983.
Wallace, Joseph. *Past and Present of the City of Springfield and Sangamon County, Illinois.* 2 vols. Chicago: S. J. Clarke Publishing, 1904.
Warner, Harold C. "Development of Trial by Jury." *Tennessee Law Review* 26 (Summer 1959): 459–67.
Westby, David L. "The Civic Sphere in the American City." *Social Forces* 45 (December 1966): 161–69.
Wheeler, Joanne Towers. "Springfield, 1850: The City, Its Places, Its People." N.p., 1985.
Whitney, Henry C. *Life on the Circuit with Lincoln.* Boston: Estes and Lauriat, 1892.
Williams, C. S., comp. *Springfield Directory: City Guide and Business Mirror for 1860–1861.* Springfield, Ill.: Johnson and Bradford, Booksellers, 1860.
Wilson, Terry. "The Business of a Midwestern Trial Court: Knox County, Illinois, 1841–1850." *Illinois Historical Journal* 84 (Winter 1991): 249–67.
Winch, Julie, ed. *The Elite of Our People: Joseph Willson's Sketches of Black Upper-Class Life in Antebellum Philadelphia.* University Park: Penn State University Press, 2000.
Winkle, Kenneth J. *The Young Eagle: The Rise of Abraham Lincoln.* Dallas, Tex.: Taylor Trade Publishing, 2001.
Winkler, John F. "The Legal Literature of Ohio." In *The History of Ohio Law,* 2 vols., edited by Michael Les Benedict and John F. Winkler, 2:501–52. Athens: Ohio University Press, 2006.
Wirt, William. *Life of Patrick Henry.* 4th ed. New York: M'Elrath and Bangs, 1831.
Wood, Thomas J. "'Blood in the Moon': The War for the Seat of Edwards County, 1821–1824." *Illinois Historical Journal* 85 (Autumn 1992): 143–60.
Wood, W. Kirk. "Alexis de Tocqueville and the Myth of Democracy in America." *Southern Studies* 5 (Fall–Winter 1994): 1–17.
Worthington, George. *An Inquiry into the Power of Juries to Decide Incidentally on Questions of Law.* London: S. Sweet, 1825. Reprint, Littleton, Colo.: Fred B. Rothman, 1995.
Wright, Benjamin F., Jr. "Political Institutions and the Frontier." In *Sources of Culture in the Middle West: Backgrounds versus Frontier,* edited by Dixon Ryan Fox. New York: D. Appleton–Century, 1934.
Younger, Richard D. *The People's Panel: The Grand Jury in the United States, 1634–1941.* Providence, R.I.: Brown University Press, 1963.
Zainaldin, Jamil. *Law in Antebellum Society: Legal Change and Economic Expansion.* New York: Alfred A. Knopf, 1983.

INDEX

Lightning Source UK Ltd.
Milton Keynes UK
UKOW02n0934280116

267295UK00014B/229/P

9 780821 419564